DATE DUE

The
CONSUMING
INSTINCT

PRAISE FOR *THE CONSUMING INSTINCT*

"Gad Saad has cleverly applied the insights of evolutionary psychology to our behavior as consumers. He is able to explain a huge amount of behavior using these insights. As consumers, we will profit from understanding the sources of our own behavior. Marketers will also benefit from understanding the deep evolutionary basis of the behavior of their customers. Moreover, the book is entertaining and readable. I recommend it strongly."

> —Paul H. Rubin,
> Samuel Candler Dobbs Professor of Economics,
> Emory University

"Gad Saad clearly and strongly shows how our evolved preferences and strategies influence our modern consumption decisions, and he doesn't pull any punches. Evolution matters—and those who understand its impact on human behavior, whether corporations or consumers, will reap the financial benefits."

> —Peter Todd, professor of cognitive science,
> informatics, and psychology, Indiana University;
> coauthor of *Simple Heuristics That Make Us Smart*

"Eventually, marketing will be informed by evolutionary analyses, as people who sell things strive to understand the design of the minds they're selling to. Saad is among the first to shine a Darwinian light on our consumerist proclivities. From advertising to zoophilia, in this well-written book, packed with research findings and interesting examples, *The Consuming Instinct* elegantly explains patterns of human consumption . . . and much more. . . ."

> —Robert Kurzban, author of
> *Why Everyone (Else) Is a Hypocrite*

"A wonderfully engaging and wide-ranging tour of human tastes, aversions, and desires, conducted with verve and wit, all soundly grounded in the sound principles of modern Darwinism."

> —Nigel Nicholson, professor of Organizational Behavior
> at London Business School; author of
> *Managing the Human Animal*

The CONSUMING INSTINCT

WHAT JUICY BURGERS, FERRARIS, PORNOGRAPHY, AND GIFT GIVING

Reveal about Human Nature

GAD SAAD

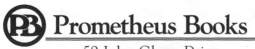

Prometheus Books

59 John Glenn Drive
Amherst, New York 14228–2119

Published 2011 by Prometheus Books

Cover image © Media Bakery
Cover design by Nicole Sommer-Licht

Inquiries should be addressed to
Prometheus Books
59 John Glenn Drive
Amherst, New York 14228–2119
VOICE: 716–691–0133
FAX: 716–691–0137
WWW.PROMETHEUSBOOKS.COM

15 14 13 12 11   5 4 3 2 1

Library of Congress Cataloging-in-Publication Data

Saad, Gad.
    The consuming instinct : what juicy burgers, Ferraris, pornography, and gift giving reveal about human nature / by Gad Saad.
        p. cm.
    Includes bibliographical references and index.
    ISBN 978–1–61614–429–6 (alk. paper)
    ISBN 978–1–61614–430–2 (e-book)
    1. Consumer behavior. 2. Consumption (Economics)—Psychological aspects.
3. Consumers—Psychology. 4. Evolutionary psychology. I. Title.

HF5415.32.S18 2011
339.4'7—dc22

                                                                      2010052000

Printed in the United States of America on acid-free paper

To Luna, bahebek

CONTENTS

Acknowledgments   7

Foreword   9

Chapter 1   Consumers: Born and Made   11

Chapter 2   I Will Survive   41

Chapter 3   Let's Get It On   67

Chapter 4   We Are Family   95

Chapter 5   That's What Friends Are For   121

Chapter 6   Cultural Products: Fossils of the Human Mind   149

Chapter 7   Local versus Global Advertising   177

Chapter 8   Marketing Hope by Selling Lies   203

Chapter 9   Darwinian Rationale for Consumer Irrationality   231

Chapter 10   Darwin in the Halls of the Business School   257

Chapter 11   Concluding Remarks   287

Notes   295

Index   341

ACKNOWLEDGMENTS

First and foremost I wish to thank Linda Greenspan Regan, my editor at Prometheus Books, for her support throughout the process but most importantly for believing in my book. She read the first draft of my book with great care and always responded to my queries in a timely and professional manner. In their able capacities as copyeditor, proofreader, production manager, and jacket designer, respectively, Dee Stiffler, Julia DeGraf, Catherine E. Roberts-Abel, and Nicole Lecht were a pleasure to interact with. Barbara Oakley and Steven Kotler provided me with valuable advice about many aspects of the trade book market, whereas Eva Samartzidis and Albert Saad Jr. offered their legal opinions regarding contractual matters. My graduate students Eric Stenstrom and Zack Mendenhall assisted me in procuring the photos along with the corresponding signed permissions forms. Eric's organizational skills were instrumental in managing the photo acquisitions process. I am thankful to all the photographers, and especially to the DeVore family, for their generosity in allowing me to use their photos for minimal fees (and in a few instances for free). The parental leave that was granted to me by both the Quebec government and by my university, coupled with the course remissions afforded by my Concordia University Research Chair, were instrumental in freeing up my time to write this book. My soul mate of more than ten years, Annie Ortchanian; my daughter, Luna; and our majestic Belgian shepherds, Amar and Samra; offered an endless stream of love and affection throughout my journey. I am deeply honored that one of my intellectual heroes, David M. Buss, agreed to write the foreword to this book. Finally, as I explained in the preface to my 2007 book, *The Evolutionary Bases of Consumption*, I was first exposed to the explanatory power of evolutionary psychology in 1990, when I read the book *Homicide* by Martin Daly and Margo Wilson. Earlier this year, Dr. Wilson, who served as one of the endorsers of my 2007 book, passed away. Her intellectual legacy will continue to influence many future generations of evolutionary behavioral scientists.

FOREWORD

David M. Buss

Evolutionary psychology is beginning to penetrate all disciplines that deal with human behavior. This progression is logical. All human behavior owes its existence to psychological mechanisms in conjunction with environmental inputs to those mechanisms. Psychological mechanisms, at some fundamental level, owe their existence to evolution by natural and sexual selection. Consequently, all fields that deal with human behavior will become more deeply illuminated by understanding underlying evolved psychological adaptations.

For a number of years, I envisioned marketing specifically and business more generally to be ideal disciplines for evolutionary psychological analysis. This integrative synthesis requires a scholar thoroughly knowledgeable about both fields. Dr. Gad Saad is that scholar. He brings a profound understanding of evolutionary psychology together with deep knowledge of marketing and business to illuminate the many and differing forms of consumer behavior. And he does so with a lively and engaging writing style that keeps the reader fascinated from start to finish.

In the process, *The Consuming Instinct* provides a profound understanding of many otherwise perplexing phenomena: Why are women so much more susceptible to eating disorders than men? Why do men "discount the future" (i.e., value immediate rewards more intensely) after seeing pictures of attractive women? Which underlying psychological adaptations are responsible for successful ad campaigns for men's products such as Axe? Why do women go to tanning salons, even with the knowledge that they cause skin damage, and why do they continue to wear high heels, despite the fact that they are so uncomfortable? Why is online pornography consumed primarily by men, yet women mainly fuel the multibillion-dollar romance novels industry?

I predict that *The Consuming Instinct* will become required reading at business schools; indeed, it should be required reading for everyone. The riches it offers are too great to ignore. Those who embrace the core evolutionary principles of this book—in their work and in their lives—will succeed. Those who don't will lose in the evolutionary marketplace of products and ideas.

CHAPTER 1

CONSUMERS: BORN AND MADE

Nature versus nurture is dead.
—*MATT RIDLEY*[1]

Expel nature with a pitchfork, she'll be back again.
—*HORACE*[2]

INTRODUCTION

Perhaps the most famous maxim in philosophy is René Descartes's "I think therefore I am." I suspect that a more telling adage that defines our daily existence is "I consume therefore I am." Humans possess a ravenous consummatory appetite. Most individuals will typically make hundreds of consumption-related decisions in any given day. Should I have breakfast or skip straight to lunch? What am I going to wear today? Will it be casual attire or a power suit? Should I put on my favorite perfume or try the new one that an old acquaintance recently gave me? For dinner, will I have a healthy and sensible tuna salad or head off to the deli for a thick pastrami sandwich? Valentine's Day is rapidly approaching. Will it be the customary flowers for my beloved, a day pass at a spa, or shall I finally take a principled stance against this marketer-made holiday? My nephew's birthday is coming up. What should I give him as a gift? I have been asked to be the best man for one of my closest friends. I need to organize a memorable bachelor party with all his friends to celebrate his imminent marriage. What should I do? Are we taking a vacation during spring break, and if so, where to and which book will I be bringing on the trip? I need to update the playlist in my iPod Nano for the long flight should we end up traveling. Should we postpone our vacation and instead place the money in our child's college fund? On the other hand, I just noticed that our glitzy neighbors recently bought a new Mercedes Coupe. Is it time for us to upgrade to a fancier car? My wife looks so beautiful tonight. I think I'll put on some Marvin Gaye and see where the night takes us.

I have chosen the aforementioned examples for two key reasons. First, they highlight my notion of all-encompassing consumption, which extends beyond the more restrictive definition of consumption as the purchase of goods and services. We consume traditional products (e.g., food and clothes) and services (e.g., massage at the spa); a wide range of relationships, including those with family members and friends (via gift giving) as well as mates (via an act of courtship); cultural products such as movies, song lyrics, religious narratives, literature, art, dance, celebrity gossip magazines, advertising, and television shows; and hedonic experiences (traveling), to name but a few. Second, the examples demonstrate how the great majority of consumption acts can be mapped onto one of four Darwinian overriding pursuits, namely, *survival* (preference for the fatty smoked meat), *reproduction* (offering flowers as part of an elaborate courtship ritual), *kin selection* (buying a gift for my nephew), and *reciprocity* (organizing the bachelor party).

The subtitle of my book—*What Juicy Burgers, Ferraris, Pornography, and Gift Giving Reveal about Human Nature*—recognizes the ubiquity of these four key Darwinian drives.[3] *Juicy burgers* refer to our penchant for fatty foods (chapter 2). *Ferraris* are used as a sexual signal in the mating arena (chapter 3). *Pornography* speaks to the evolutionary forces that have shaped human sexuality (chapters 3 and 9). Finally, I included *gift giving* within the subtitle because it is intimately linked to all four Darwinian overriding drives, and as such it carries great social and economic import. For example, for some retailers, 30 to 50 percent of their yearly sales are generated within the winter holiday season (wherein substantial expenditures are gift-related), and 10 percent of retail purchases in North America are gift expenditures.[4] In 2004, the American gift-giving market garnered sales revenues of $253 billion, with an average of $1,215 spent per capita on gifts in the United States (which corresponds to 2.7 percent of consumer expenditures per capita in 2004).[5] Gifts are central to the courtship ritual. In some instances, they are used as part of the wooing process (flowers, dinner invitations, promise rings, engagement rings), whereas in other cases they are meant to celebrate an existing relationship (Valentine's Day, wedding anniversaries) or even the termination of a relationship (divorce gifts). A defining feature of many wedding-related events is the offering of gifts to the bride and groom. These include engagement parties, bachelor's parties (as per the 2009 movie *The Hangover*), bachelorette parties, and bridal showers. When a couple is expecting the arrival of a new child, a baby shower is held, at which time gifts are offered to the expectant mother. Once the child is born, family members and friends visit the newborn while bearing gifts.

Other family and kin-based gifting include marketer-inspired occasions such as Father's Day and Mother's Day. They also include religious occasions such as Christmas, Easter, Hanukkah, baptisms, confirmations, first communions, bar mitzvahs, and bat mitzvahs. In some instances, gift giving occurs as a means to celebrate secular rites of passage (sweet sixteen parties, prom nights). Birthday gifts are exchanged between family members as well as with friends and acquaintances. Other occasions wherein gifts are exchanged among friends or kin include housewarming visits, home dinner invitations (e.g., bottles of wine), convalescence visits (e.g., flowers), promotions or retirements, going away to college or graduation parties, and celebrations for specific accomplishments (e.g., obtaining a driver's license). Not satisfied with all the innumerable occasions wherein gifts are exchanged, marketers have devised a whole new set of gift-giving occasions centered on the celebration of self. An example of such self-gifts is the recent practice of women buying themselves rings (which they wear on their right ring finger) as a form of self-affirmation and autonomy. The bottom line is that gift giving is a universal ritual that is an inextricable part of our human nature, and accordingly it is a topic that I address in chapter 3 (reproduction), chapter 4 (kin selection), and chapter 5 (reciprocity).

E. O. Wilson, the world-renowned Harvard evolutionist and two-time Pulitzer Prize–winning author, and James Watson, the Nobel Laureate and co-discoverer of the double helix structure of DNA, appeared together a few years ago on the *Charlie Rose Show*. During their discussion, they proclaimed that the twenty-first century would be defined by the joining of psychology and biology. My book operates at this exact nexus in that it highlights the importance of recognizing the biological and evolutionary roots of consumption. Whereas culture is important in understanding consumer behavior, of equal importance are the biological and evolutionary forces that have shaped our consuming minds and bodies. I hope to illuminate the relevance of our biological heritage in our daily lives as consumers, from the foods that we eat, to the gifts that we offer, to the products that we use to make ourselves more attractive in the mating market, and to the cultural products that tickle our emotional fancy (e.g., religion). *Homo consumericus* is a species that has evolved via the dual forces of natural and sexual selection. Failure to recognize this fact will continue to yield at best, incomplete—and at worst, erroneous—explanations of consumption phenomena. Ultimately, nothing in consumption makes sense except in the light of evolution.[6]

I will at times demonstrate how consumers engage in behaviors that are either homologous or analogous to those displayed by other animals. A homology refers to similarities between species that are indicative of a common ancestry. Homologies include DNA sequences, anatomical structures, morphological traits, physiological systems, and behavioral patterns. For example, several primate species display homologous facial grimaces when expressing fear, whereas humans and cats possess homologous forelimbs. Behavioral homologies refer to similarities between species along behavioral patterns. Alternatively, an analogous trait between two species is an example of convergent evolution; namely, the fact that two species evolved the same adaptation as a result of having faced similar selection pressures. In other words, in such instances, the biological analogy does not imply shared ancestry. Rather, it connotes the fact that natural selection, the Darwinian process by which organisms evolve adaptations, can yield the same solution when animals originating from different lineages share a common selection environment. Regardless of whether a given comparison with an animal is based on a homology or an analogy, my goal is to ultimately demonstrate that similar biological forces drive the behaviors of human consumers and animals alike. I recently gave a talk at an elite American business school where I received a very hostile reception from the members of the marketing department. One of the questions (paraphrased) posed by an audience member was as follows: "Sure, these evolutionary processes apply to animals. But consumers are humans. They are not animals. Are you suggesting that consumers are animals?" Yes, I am.

In this chapter, I provide an overview of evolutionary psychology and contrast it with the socialization perspective. I tackle some of the fallacies that persist with regard to evolutionary theory. I address the infamous nature-versus-nurture debate, as it helps in understanding which elements of consumption are learned, which are innate, and which are shaped by an inextricable mélange of both forces. Whereas many consumption phenomena fall under the rubric of evolutionary psychology (as in the use of status symbols as sexual signals), others lie outside it (for example, why a given consumer prefers bowling and another enjoys scuba diving). Ultimately the power of evolutionary theory rests in its ability to delineate the common features inherent to the consumer instinct from the idiosyncratic consumer preferences that define our unique individualities. Still, the bottom line is that not all consumption can be explained by evolutionary theory. The challenge for marketers is to know which phenomena fall under its universal rubric.

Key Doctrines of Evolutionary Psychology

Evolutionary psychology (EP) is a relatively new scientific discipline, roughly two decades old.[7] I was initially exposed to EP as a first-year doctoral student at Cornell University in fall 1990, when I read *Homicide*, the brilliant book coauthored by Martin Daly and the late Margo Wilson, two early pioneers of EP. The book provides a parsimonious account of universal patterns of criminality, using elegant and powerful explanations. For example, Daly and Wilson demonstrate that most killings of adult women occur at the hand of their male partners, with the overwhelming reason being suspected or realized infidelity.[8] Given the evolutionary costs associated with paternity uncertainty—there is no such thing as maternity uncertainty in nature—men have evolved a wide range of emotional (e.g., experiencing intense sexual jealousy), cognitive ("chastity is a good trait for a prospective wife to possess"), and behavioral (e.g., mate guarding) adaptations to thwart the threats of being cuckolded. Providing an adaptive explanation for such a heinous and violent act in no way justifies it, any more than explaining the metastasis of pancreatic cancer is meant to justify the disease! Providing scientific explanations for morally reprehensible acts (if not illegal ones) has nothing to do with the condoning of the acts in question.

Evolutionary psychology is the latest of a long list of Darwinian-based disciplines that have sought to understand the evolutionary and biological roots of human behavior. Some of its predecessors include human ethology, human behavioral ecology, human sociobiology, and Darwinian anthropology,[9] all of which remain thriving and exciting disciplines in their own right. Other Darwinian approaches for understanding human behavior include gene-culture coevolution (biological as well as cultural processes have shaped the evolution of humans) and memetic theory (applying Darwinian theory in understanding the spread of cultural content such as ideas and beliefs).[10] Evolutionary psychology construes the human mind as having evolved via the dual Darwinian forces of natural and sexual selection, namely the processes that confer onto organisms survival and reproductive advantage respectively. More specifically, EP proposes that the mind is made up of domain-specific algorithms, each having evolved as an adaptive solution to a specific problem of evolutionary import. Some of these domains include food foraging, avoiding environmental threats (e.g., predators or hostile strangers), mating, and investing in both one's kin (e.g., sibling-to-sibling, parenting) and in one's friends (reciprocity). Note that each of the listed domains corresponds to the four Darwinian drives that I mentioned earlier. My contention throughout this book is that many consumption phenomena are manifestations of innate needs, preferences, and drives that cater to one or more of these basic Darwinian overriding goals. Ultimately, to fully comprehend our consuming instinct requires that we recognize the evolutionary forces that have forged our human nature.

Evolutionary theory recognizes that phenomena can be investigated at two distinct levels. *Proximate* explanations deal with mechanistic descriptions of how something operates and which factors affect its inner workings. *Ultimate* explanations tackle the *why* question, namely, why has a given behavior, emotion, thought, preference, choice, or morphological trait evolved to be of a particular form (i.e., identifying its Darwinian genesis).[11] Whereas both levels of analyses are needed for a full understanding of the human condition, marketers along with many social scientists have largely focused on proximate explanations.

Two tangible examples will clarify the distinction between proximate and ultimate explanations. Pregnancy sickness is a universal physiological phenomenon. Irrespective of cultural setting or epoch, women have experienced its unpleasant symptoms in similar ways. A proximate perspective

might explore how a given hormone (e.g., estrogen) affects the unpleas-
antness of the experienced nausea. An ultimate focus would seek to
understand why such a physiological mechanism would have evolved in
the first place. Evolutionists have concluded that pregnancy sickness is an
adaptive solution to a woman's possible exposure to food pathogens
during a crucial part of the gestational period known as organogenesis.[12]
Hence, whereas proximate-informed physicians happily prescribe drugs
to assuage the symptoms of pregnancy sickness, evolutionists recognize
that such symptoms are beneficial to women and their fetuses. The practical implications of evolutionary theory should be evident. As a second
example, let us ask a fundamental question regarding human sexuality:
Why is sex pleasurable (at least to most people)? A proximate cause
might identify the neural bases of the pleasurable experience, such as the
release of dopamine during orgasms. The ultimate cause is rather obvious.
Engaging in the ultimate of all possible gene-propagating behaviors
should be pleasurable lest sexually reproducing organisms become
extinct. Generally speaking, pleasurable experiences are meant to augment behaviors that encourage contact (e.g., seeking to have sex or to eat
a tasty, juicy steak), whereas nonpleasurable ones trigger avoidance (e.g.,
avoiding foul-smelling foods). In other words, one would expect that evolutionary forces have honed our pleasure instinct.[13]

Another defining tenet of EP is that it construes explanations that
strictly attribute causality to learning, culture, and socialization as being
at best incomplete and at worst erroneous. Specifically, to simply
attribute the causes of a phenomenon to the broad shoulders of the
socialization process—the learning of the expected behaviors, norms,
beliefs, and values of one's society—is in most instances a nonexplana-
tion. To the extent that many socialization patterns occur in extraordinarily similar ways across cultural settings and time periods, it becomes
incumbent on those offering this approach to provide an explanation for
these universalities. I next discuss various movements that have historically been hostile toward biological explanations of human behavior.

Movements United against Biology

Social constructivists are scholars who believe that much if not all human phenomena are due to socialization. Central to their worldview is the premise that the human mind is a blank slate. Accordingly, they propose that cultural learning and other socialization forces shape our minds. Why do most men have a penchant for young and beautiful women? They learned it via media images. Why do the majority of women prefer tall and socially powerful men (recall the "tall, dark, and handsome" archetype)? Hollywood movies are to blame. Why are young men around the world more likely to display violent tendencies than their female counterparts? Of course, it must be because they play video games laden with violent images and listen to misogynistic rap lyrics. Any phenomenon, irrespective of how universal it might be, is ultimately linked to some environmental cause.

Are individuals natural-born consumers, or are they products of their environments? This question has been posed concerning countless phenomena of relevance to the human condition. Is intelligence innate or acquired? Is an individual born with the proclivity to be a charismatic leader, or can this elusive talent be taught? Bill Gates (Microsoft), Richard Branson (Virgin Records), Jeff Bezos (Amazon), Brian Glazer (movie producer), and Howard Schultz (Starbucks) are legendary entrepreneurs in their respective fields. Were they born with the penchant to be revolutionary agents of change, or did their idiosyncratic environments shape them? What of our political bents? Are individuals born with conservative or liberal dispositions, or does cultural learning forge our political worldviews? Are preferences for junk foods learned, or is the exposure to endless commercials for fast-food restaurant chains to blame? Do we come into this world with a fixed personality, or are our unique personhoods strictly determined by situational contexts? Most social scientists have historically adhered to social constructivism, which purports that the relevant causative agents can be assigned to the socialization process. According to this worldview, it is unequivocally clear that consumers are made. They are singularly products of their environments.

In the educational system, social constructivism sells hope by proposing that students who might otherwise perform poorly in school must have been negatively influenced by their environments. Hence, apparently no child can be born with a weak penchant for learning. If the child fails, the environment is to blame. A similar logic has been applied to the penal system. In this worldview, there are no innately violent criminals or heinous psychopaths, only toxic environments that resulted in poor life choices. Prior to the recent focus on pharmacological interventions, psychiatrists had taken a very similar stance regarding the etiology of mental illness. Every conceivable disorder including lifelong battles with clinical depression, schizophrenia, and autism were assigned to environmental causes. Recently, actress and model Jenny McCarthy has been a staunch and leading advocate of the mantra that autism is caused by childhood vaccinations. Ultimately, such a position is comforting to desperate parents, as it reassigns the root of the problem to a human-made cause, which hopefully can be reversed. Some medical practitioners argue that to eradicate certain endemic health problems such as the greater incidence of high blood pressure among some populations requires the eradication of poverty, racism, and injustice. Hence, individual factors that might otherwise serve as the key drivers of high blood pressure are ignored. The genesis of all ills is to be found in toxic environments.

In the 1980s and 1990s, many nonmainstream therapists practiced recovered memory therapy wherein they utilized a wide range of techniques (e.g., hypnosis or age regression) to recover otherwise repressed memories of sexual abuse. These therapists firmly believed that the roots of many mental health problems were due to childhood sexual abuse. If patients denied ever having been abused, then they had simply repressed the memory; thus, the central ideological dogma was unfalsifiable. In this case, the "one-size-fits-all" environmental cause had been identified. Whether a patient were suffering from debilitating low self-esteem, experiencing the affective ebbs and flow of bipolar disorder, or engaging in frequent suicidal ideation, the root cause was always the same: sexual abuse. Notwithstanding its falsity, this premise is rooted in a hopeful outlook. If the cause is always the same, and if a therapeutic intervention can be devised to undo the harm of sexual abuse, then the prognosis looks good.

A common theme throughout a better part of various strands of feminism is that gender is a social construction. Hence, short of an individual's genitalia, most sex-specific phenomena are thought to be due to the differential socialization of the two sexes. Writer and utopian feminist Charlotte Perkins Gilman famously wrote, "There is no female mind. The brain is not an organ of sex. As well speak of a female liver."[14] Some feminists have maintained that even sex-specific hormones are nothing more than a social construction. The infamous John Money, the Johns Hopkins University professor who advised surgeons to surgically reassign male infants (due to, say, a botched circumcision or if born with a micropenis), did so under the tenet that one's gender was strictly learned. Hence, to the extent that a child who was born male was shortly thereafter raised as a girl (with all the expected sex-specific norms of socialization), Money believed that no deleterious consequences would occur. This utterly outlandish premise has had devastating effects on unsuspecting patients, as per the eventual suicide of David Reimer (who had been raised a girl after his penis had been damaged during a fumbled circumcision). Credit goes to Milton Diamond, a professor at the University of Hawaii, who brought the case to the public eye as a means of highlighting the disastrous consequences of quack theories of human nature.

Some theorists propose that heterosexuality is an imposed norm. In other words, it is argued that heterosexuality should not be construed as an innate orientation. Interestingly, when it comes to a homosexual orientation, many gay lobbyists posit that they were born with their same-sex preference. Hence, by amalgamating these two premises, one ends up with the "facts" that heterosexuality is not innate but homosexuality is. This is indeed quite an extraordinary worldview for a sexually reproducing species. Of course, individuals who hold an ideological or theo-logical position against homosexuality claim that it is a choice, and therefore it can be reversed (see, for example, JONAH, an acronym for Jews Offering New Alternatives to Homosexuality, or NARTH, the National Association for Research and Therapy on Homosexuality). Again, "inconvenient" facts rooted in human biology are ignored and even rejected in the pursuit of ideological dogma.

In subsequent chapters, I address other frameworks that are anti-thetical to universal claims about human nature, including antiscience movements such as postmodernism and deconstructionism. I also cover religion, which provides us with the granddaddy of environmental causes—or, to be more precise, nonnatural causes—for observed phe-nomena. Clearly, the queue of ideologies that are hostile to a biological understanding of human affairs is a long one. Interestingly, many of these movements are united in aping the same set of antiquated and false concerns regarding evolutionary theory.[15]

ERRONEOUS ANTIEVOLUTION CONCERNS

I tackle here nine of the most pernicious antievolution issues, some of which are particularly relevant to the consumer context.

Claim 1: Darwinian theory is ideologically dangerous, as evidenced by the number of cretins who have misused it to advance their criminal ide-ologies (e.g., the Nazis, eugenicists, and social-class elitists under the moniker of Social Darwinism). An evolutionist must possess some sin-ister political agenda or hold reprehensible attitudes and views. Many social scientists are under the impression that proponents of evolu-tionary theory must be sexist or right-wing zealots.

Rebuttal: It is important to avoid conflating the gross misapplication of evolutionary principles with the actual tenets of the theory. Evolutionary theory provides overarching mechanisms for explaining the extraordinary biological diversity that exists in the natural world. It explains what is and certainly does not delve into the territory of what ought to be. Accordingly, there is nothing inherently sexist or patriarchal about evolutionary psychology. A substantial number of editors of the leading scientific journals of the field are women. For example, two of the four editors-in-chief of *Evolution and Human Behavior* are women (Martie Haselton and Ruth Lace). The editor-in-chief of *Human Nature* is a woman (Jane Lancaster). Two of the founders of evolutionary psychology are women (Leda Cosmides and Margo Wilson). One of the most famous of all popularizers of EP is a woman (Helen Fisher). Therefore, the notion that EP is a patriarchal male-dominated vehicle for justifying sexist stereotypes is outlandish.

What about political leanings? Are those subscribing to evolution members of a political conspiracy, as is often argued by those who reject evolutionary theory on ideological grounds? Interestingly, the Left accuses evolutionary behavioral scientists of being members of an ultra-right-wing conspiracy. At the same time, the Right accuses evolutionists of promulgating a godless liberal ethos! A recent study published in *Human Nature* explored the political leanings of evolutionary psychologists and found that they tended to be very liberal and progressive.[16] Nonetheless, the scientific veracity of evolutionary theory holds independently of any political, social, or economic implications.

Claim 2: Evolutionary theory amounts to biological determinism; namely, evolutionists believe that our genes usurp our free will. As such, Darwinian theory ignores the importance of the environment, including cultural and social forces, in shaping human behaviors, preferences, desires, and needs. For marketers, this is a particularly worrisome point, as they are in the business of developing actionable solutions.

Hence, if something is inscribed in one's genes, how could the marketer's reach be relevant in shaping consumption patterns?

Rebuttal: Biological determinism is an utter canard that has been propagated by people who otherwise have no understanding of evolutionary theory. For most human phenomena, genes interact with environmental contingencies, idiosyncratic talents and abilities, and unique life experiences in generating a given behavior, preference, or choice. Take the universal Darwinian drive for males to seek social status. Men in Peru, Kenya, the United States, and Japan might all wish to seek social status. This is the biologically based adaptive drive, as it caters to women's preference for men of high social standing. However, there are many ways by which this overriding goal can be achieved, depending on an individual's environmental realities and distinctive life circumstances. One can become a successful academic, a neurosurgeon, a ballet dancer, an entrepreneur, an investment banker, a novelist, or a corporate lawyer, among endless other possibilities. Hence, biological determinism exists only in the minds of those who are ignorant about our biology.

Evolutionary scientists espouse "interactionism," namely, the notion that our genes *interact* with our environments in shaping our individuality. Accordingly, the nature-nurture dichotomy is a grossly misconstrued idea. For most phenomena, we are an inextricable mix of both nature and nurture. I am particularly found of the "cake metaphor" in explaining this idea. When you bake a cake, you start off with clearly delineated ingredients such as sugar, eggs, flour, baking soda, cocoa, and milk. Subsequently, these are mixed together into a cake. If I were to ask you at that point to identify the sugar versus the eggs, you would think that this is a silly request, as the cake would be an inextricable mix of the original ingredients. Accordingly, not only are we all products of both nature and nurture but also nurture exists in its particular forms because of nature. In other words, our biological heritage constrains the range of possible socialization forces that can shape us. This is why no culture has ever been found in which men are taught to be virginal, chaste, and judicious about their sexual choices while women are taught to be indiscriminate in their sexuality. Our common biological heritage dictates universal patterns of nurture (as per the first quotation that introduces this chapter).

Two other rebuttals should hopefully lay to rest the concern regarding biological determinism. Epigenetic mechanisms,[17] which affect how genes are expressed without changing their genetic codes, can either turn on or off particular genes as a function of specific environmental triggers. Our epigenome (not to be confused with our genome) is a blueprint by which genes are activated or silenced. This demonstrates how absurd the biological determinism argument is. Genes interact with the environment in part via our epigenome in yielding unique individuals who are products of both nature and nurture. This explains why identical twins, who otherwise share the same genes, can end up with such radically different health outcomes. Finally, it is important to remind the reader that evolutionary processes (e.g., natural selection) take place within a given environmental niche. Evolution is a mechanism that is defined by the fact that it operates within a given environment in shaping unique adaptations. Thus, evolution explicitly recognizes the importance of environmental realities.

That our genes are at the root of our consuming instinct in no way affects the central role that marketers occupy in the marketplace. Humans have evolved gustatory preferences for fatty foods. Accordingly, companies (e.g., McDonald's, Wendy's, and Burger King) create innumerable products that cater to this biological-based preference, subsequent to which marketers and advertisers seek ways to ensure that we'll choose their hamburger the next time we are hungry. That our genetic and biological heritage guides our consummatory nature in no way renders the existence of marketers as useless and their quest as futile. That said, it is undeniably true that marketers are unlikely to be successful in creating needs and wants for products that are grossly antithetical or incongruent with our human nature. Start a company that sells

Harlequin-type romance novels strictly to men, and see where that takes you. Alternatively, try to launch a chain of "grass juice" outlets, and let me know how it goes. An infinite advertising budget cannot counteract products that are disconnected from our biological heritage.

Claim 3: Biological instincts and drives might be applicable when explaining the behaviors of zebras, eagles, monitor lizards, and tarantulas. However, humans are first and foremost cultural beings. "Vulgar" biology is simply irrelevant in explaining the complexity of human phenomena.

Rebuttal: I have often encountered this claim even within the hallowed halls of highly prestigious universities. I think that its genesis derives from two distinctly different sources. On one hand, all Abrahamic religions possess a narrative that places man at the apex of living creatures while being distinctly unique from "animals." Hence, there is a general uneasiness among many people to accept that the same Darwinian processes can give rise to the evolution of bacteria, amoeba, invertebrates, our family dog, and us! Religious narratives might be compelling stories, but they do not falsify the unequivocal evidence in support of the evolutionary tree of life, of which we are an integral part. There is no biological reason to think that the evolutionary processes that have generated the billions of species that have existed on Earth are somehow nonoperative when it comes to humans. Similarly, there is no scientific argument that justifies why evolutionary theory can explain how our pancreas, opposable thumbs, and eyes have evolved, but our brains have not. Human narcissism (and ignorance) compels many people to think that our humanity falls outside the purview of the universal forces of evolutionary theory. However, it is time to accept that all living systems are interconnected in a grand tree of life.

A second source for this false concern stems from the Standard Social Science Model,[18] which postulates that humans are born with minds that are blank slates.[19] These slates are subsequently filled by a wide range of socialization forces including cultural learning. Under such a worldview, biology is completely abdicated as an explanatory force in shaping human behavior. Perhaps the most infamous group of academics that held steadfast to this position are cultural relativists, who argued for the near-infinite malleability of cultural forms, and in so doing rejected the idea that human universals could exist. The reality is that although endless cross-cultural differences exist, there are countless documented human universals[20] (many of which I will explore). If anything makes us unique in comparison to most animals, it is the fact that *Homo sapiens* is both a cultural and biological animal.

Claim 4: Evolutionary psychology is strictly concerned with the cataloging of human universals, while most social scientists are interested in understanding behavioral heterogeneity or variety (or, why do some consumers prefer Coke and others prefer Pepsi?). Accordingly, Darwinian theory and related biological formalisms may matter, but they are largely unimportant and irrelevant in elucidating consumer-related phenomena.

Rebuttal: It is indeed true that evolutionary psychologists seek to identify human universals. But they are equally interested in understanding the adaptive forces that give rise to individual differences. The study of personality is a perfect example of how one might investigate differences between individuals from an evolutionary perspective. Clearly, unlike fixed traits (e.g., we all have five fingers on each hand), there is great heterogeneity across people when it comes to their personality profiles. Why would this be the case? How might evolution explain the maintenance of such differences? The answer is elegantly simple: There is no unique optimal personality type for all possible social and environmental contexts. Let us assume that there were only three personality types (P1, P2, and P3) and only three possible social niches (S1, S2, and S3). Perhaps P1 is optimal in social niche S3, P2 is optimal in social niche S2, and P3 is optimal in social niche S1. There could not be a species-wide fixation of one optimal personality profile. To reiterate, understanding differences across individuals is very much within the purview of evolutionary theory.

Evolutionary theory is the only framework that can identify which types of consumer phenomena are universally valid (e.g., men are the overwhelming consumers of hardcore pornography in every known society; see chapter 9); which are culturally determined, albeit because of biological reasons (e.g., the use of spices in culinary customs varies across cultures as a function of the density of food pathogens within a particular environment; see chapter 2); and which are due to idiosyncratic individual differences (e.g., person A prefers to bowl, and person B prefers to read) or to idiosyncratic cultural traditions (e.g., the Swiss consume a greater amount of chocolate than Egyptians do).[21] I am not suggesting that evolutionary theory can explain every conceivable consumer choice. However, it provides an extraordinarily powerful framework for understanding the biological bases of our consummatory nature.

Claim 5: Darwinian theory largely consists of unfalsifiable, post-hoc, fanciful, and elaborate just-so stories.

Rebuttal: In my opinion, this is one of the most irksome claims, as it is often cast by otherwise sophisticated academics who regrettably know little about evolutionary theory. If one were to rank scientific theories in terms of how much supporting evidence they have accumulated thus far, evolutionary theory would be on top of any such ranking. Yet given the grand nature of evolutionary-based theories, the ability to refute evolutionary principles is actually much greater than other theories.[22] For example, the parental investment hypothesis[23] posits that for sexually reproducing species, the sex that bears the greater parental investment will typically be smaller, less aggressive, and more sexually restrained (e.g., more careful when making mating choices). For most species, females bear the greater investment and so are typically the smaller, more sexually coy, and less aggressive sex. In a much smaller number of species, males provide the greater parental investment (e.g., cassowaries), so the theory would predict that the sexual dimorphisms (i.e., the pattern of observable differences between the sexes) would be perfectly reversed.[24] This is exactly borne out by the data. The theory is about as falsifiable as can be. If a scientist were to find a single culture in the history of humankind in which women are more sexually aggressive than men, then the theory would be falsified. If a scientist were to find a single sexually reproducing species wherein the pattern of sexual dimorphism did not accord with the theory, it would be falsified. Yet despite millions of existing species, the theory still stands. Hence, it is not that evolutionary principles cannot be falsified. Rather, they have withstood all dogged and assiduous attempts at falsification because they are universally true.

Claim 6: Darwinian theory amounts to believing in a godless universe. As such, it is part and parcel of the growing atheist, secularist, and humanist movements. Richard Dawkins and public intellectual Christopher Hitchens, card-carrying members of the new atheism movement,[25] you shall rot in hell for your antitheist Darwinian views!

Rebuttal: Whereas it is indeed true that Darwinian theory provides a parsimonious, elegant, and complete explanation for the evolution of biological forms—and in so doing crowds out God from the relevant narrative—its raison d'être is not to lay any claims on matters of religion. It is clear that evolutionary theory is inconsistent with creation narratives along with their "scientific" offshoots (creationism and Intelligent Design). The late Harvard evolutionist and paleontologist Stephen Jay Gould proposed that religion and science (and hence evolution) cover Non-Overlapping Magisteria (NOMA principle). Specifically, he proposed that whereas science seeks to comprehend empirical truths about the natural world, religion addresses existential matters as well as morality.[26] In so doing, Gould was trying to placate religious believers by proposing a conciliatory worldview wherein everyone's outlook was welcomed. In this case, I am with Dawkins and other new atheists in being vehemently against such a pacification program. Morality is certainly within the purview of scientific scrutiny and is not the sole domain of religion.[27] As far as existential matters go, it is unclear that religion is superior in assuaging our fear of mortality. I address this point in greater detail in chapter 8. Evolutionary theory does indeed serve a fatal blow to a wide range of religious doctrines. That said, it is technically incorrect to conflate Darwinism with atheism, albeit the great majority of scientists in general, and certainly evolutionary scientists in particular, are nonbelievers.

Claim 7: Darwinian theory is morally dangerous in that it provides explanations for reprehensible actions such as adultery, rape, and child abuse. In so doing, it condones and justifies these behaviors as part of the natural order of things.

Rebuttal: As noted earlier, this argument is as logically sophisticated as arguing that an oncologist who studies pancreatic cancer must be justifying and condoning cancer. After all, cancer is part of our natural world and those who "waste their time" studying it must have sinister pro-cancer motives. Evolutionary psychologists do not conduct their research to justify, excuse, or condone any particular phenomenon. They are no different from all other scientists who apply the scientific method as a means of better understanding the world around us (the scientific method involves the empirical testing of hypotheses via the collection and subsequent analysis of relevant data). They do not commit the so-called naturalistic fallacy, namely, the conjuring of what ought to be from what is. As I explained in my rebuttal to the first claim, evolutionists do not comprise some monolithic supra-organism bent on justifying evil behaviors. Their sole focus is to explain behavior using the scientific method, as informed by an evolutionary lens.

Claim 8: Darwinian theory posits that humans are brutish and selfish creatures engaged in an endless "survival of the fittest" struggle. What about kindness, love, and compassion?

Rebuttal: Such a view is part of a broader outlook that nature is violent and cruel, as exemplified by British poet Lord Alfred Tennyson's famous line "Nature, red in tooth and claw."[28] From this perspective, it is thought that evolutionary theory proposes that humans are bestial creatures in pursuit of their lowly animal instincts. This is another concern that has been repeatedly explained away by countless proponents of evolutionary theory, apparently to no avail. Humans have the capacity to be both competitive and cooperative. They can engage in extraordinary acts of selfless altruism, kindness, and generosity. They are endowed with a deeply developed moral conscience. They experience profound love, be it as lovers, family members, or friends. All these capacities arose via the same evolutionary mechanisms that can also cause humans to be brutish, violent, competitive, and vengeful. In chapters 4 and 5, I specifically deal with the evolutionary roots of altruism toward kin and nonkin, and in so doing provide a detailed argument against claim 8.

Claim 9: Providing a datum at the individual level that is contrary to a fact that holds true at the population level is sufficient to falsify a given evolutionary principle. For example, the premise that men have a universal preference for young women is falsified by the existence of a single man who prefers older women.

Rebuttal: It is a biological fact that within the human species, males constitute the physically larger sex. This is not invalidated by the fact that a singular woman is taller or heavier than a singular man (e.g., Katie Holmes and Nicole Kidman are each taller than their respective husbands Tom Cruise and Keith Urban). As a matter of fact, most women in the Women's National Basketball Association are taller than many men. Oprah Winfrey weighs more than Tiger Woods, and former professional wrestler Chyna, a woman, is bulkier than comedian Chris Rock. One can provide ten thousand additional examples, and it would remain true that men are taller and heavier than women. If an evolutionist proclaims that men are more likely than women to be interested in uncommitted sexual liaisons, the provision of singular examples of women who might be more promiscuous than some specific men again does not invalidate the statement at the population level (e.g., "My uncle Joe has only been with one woman in his whole life, but my aunt Jennie has had a hundred lovers."). Women do prefer high-status men, even though your aunt Jennie might have married an unemployed plumber. All other things equal, men prefer to mate with younger women even though Ashton Kutcher is married to Demi Moore, who is more than fifteen years his senior. See figure 1 for one possible statistical manifestation of this fact using sex differences in height.

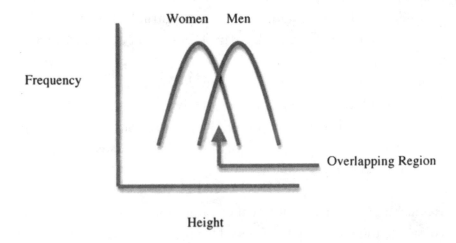

Figure 1. The left bell curve corresponds to the distribution of heights of women; the one on the right, the height of men. The mean of men's heights is greater than that of women, and yet there is an overlap in the two distributions. Specifically, there are some women who are taller than some men. This does not invalidate the fact that at the population level, men are taller than women.

THIS BOOK'S ROAD MAP, ALONG WITH ITS KEY TAKEAWAYS

Recognizing the myriad ways in which our biology affects our consumer behavior is ripe with important takeaways for consumers, marketers, and policy makers alike. Let's explore these takeaways.

Consumer Takeaways

Know Thyself. Possessing insightful and accurate self-knowledge about the biological forces that fuel our consummatory drives is a liberating and empowering objective. I will investigate the following:

- Why do men's testosterone levels rise when they drive a Porsche? Why do men constitute the majority of car collectors and 99 percent of Ferrari owners in North America?[29]
- Why do consumers engage in conspicuous consumption (e.g., luxury brands)?
- How does a woman's menstrual cycle affect her consumption, be it the clothes she wears, the types of foods she eats, and the activities she engages in?
- Why are high heels so alluring to men?
- Are women's fashion styles less conservative during economic crises?
- What do perfume preferences say about our immunogenetic profiles?
- Are all four grandparents equally invested in their grandchildren (e.g., via gift giving)?
- Why are men more likely to support compulsory DNA paternity testing in hospital nurseries?
- Do dogs resemble their owners?
- How does the fashion industry play on our instinctive need to belong?

- Are toys made to fit the innate play preferences of boys and girls, or do toys socialize children into their gender-specific play preferences?
- Why do men prefer hardcore pornography to erotica (and the reverse for women)?
- Why is religion the most successful product ever devised? More generally, why do consumers succumb to the marketing of hope by the selling of fables, whether peddled by religious narratives, cosmetic companies, or self-help gurus?

The answer to each of the latter questions and countless others is best tackled by recognizing that *Homo consumericus* is a Darwinian organism shaped by millions of years of evolution. Consumers do not hang their biological heritage at the door once engaged in an act of consumption. It is my hope that after reading this book, individuals will walk away with an appreciation of the multitude of means by which our consumer choices are manifestations of our common biological heritage.

Marketer Takeaways

The consumer resides at the center of any marketing system, and as such any insights that augment marketers' understanding of consumer behavior is advantageous. To the extent that much of marketing has operated outside of biology and evolutionary theory, marketers have had at best an incomplete comprehension of consumer behavior. At the most fundamental level, the key takeaway for marketers is the recognition that consumers display many human universals that transcend cultural and temporal settings. Consequently, individuals possess a common consumer instinct not because of the hegemony of American cultural imperialism (as espoused by many marketing luminaries) but rather because many of the commonalities that unite Indonesian, Brazilian, Japanese, and Egyptian consumers are rooted in our shared biological history.

A second broad takeaway for marketers deals with new product development, which is integral to the success of most consumer companies. Few marketers recognize that natural selection is the most prolific and successful of all product designers. The new field of biomimicry highlights the manner by which natural selection contributes to the design of new products or in the improvement of existing ones (see chapter 10). Interestingly, dogs' noses are more discriminating than existing human-made machines. A gecko's feet contain adhesive properties unrivaled by any human-made synthetic compound, and a spider's silk is tougher and stronger than any human-made material. In each instance, natural selection has had millions of years to tinker in arriving at the optimal "product." Marketers (and policy makers) would be well served to learn from the "product offerings" of natural selection.

Some of the practical questions of relevance to marketers that I shall tackle are:

- Can one identify products that are doomed for failure because they are incongruent with evolved preferences? For example, a publisher of romance novels recently offered new storylines in which male heroes were positioned as more "sensitive" than traditional ones typically portrayed within this literary genre. Eventually, this repositioning strategy failed, as women—who comprise the overwhelming majority of this market—were uninterested in the "gentle and sensitive" male archetype, as this is incongruent with their evolutionary-based mating preferences (as related to male heroes).
- Are there universal images of beauty that can be used in advertising? Does sexual imagery in advertising occur in similar manners across cultural settings?
- When should companies use a local versus global advertising strategy?
- Are there particular retail or urban environments that appeal to our evolved senses?

- Why do all successful global fast-food restaurants seem to do one thing well: offer tasty and highly caloric foods?
- How can marketers use innate sensorial preferences to create successful brands? For example, are there voice types that are perceived as universally appealing for telemarketing or radio endorsements?
- How is relationship marketing—namely, the strategies by which firms foster long-term associations with their clients—congruent with our evolved human nature?
- Can birth order be used to segment adopters of new product innovations?
- Can consumers be segmented along evolutionarily relevant morphological cues, such as their finger digit ratio or facial features?

Ultimately, an understanding of the biological forces that drive consumer behavior can only augment the marketer's ability to create products that better meet the consumer's needs and wants.

Policy Maker Takeaways

Numerous governmental agencies are mandated to protect consumers' interests (e.g., the Food and Drug Administration, the Federal Trade Commission). Policy makers have a very practical interest in possessing the most scientifically accurate and complete understanding of consumption. Any framework that does not recognize the biological roots of maladaptive consumption (see chapter 9) will yield suboptimal intervention strategies. Most social marketers operate from the perspective of humans possessing a tabula rasa mind. They assume that if consumers behave "irrationally," it must be because of incomplete information (i.e., the mind is not filled with the "correct" information) or exposure to negative socialization (the mind is filled with "wrong" information). I provide herewith a few illustrations of "negative socialization," noting that the evidence in support for a supposed socialization link to bad behavior is tenuous at best.

- Exposure to pornography leads to rape. We therefore must regulate pornography.
- Violent video games and movies lead to violence. We therefore must regulate the contents of these products.
- Car chases in cop movies lead to reckless driving. We therefore must regulate the contents of these films.
- Exposure to fast-food commercials causes childhood obesity. We therefore must regulate advertising content.
- Exposure to pretty and skinny women causes eating disorders. We therefore must regulate such images.
- Hip-hop and rap songs lead to misogynistic attitudes. We therefore must regulate lyrical content (recall former Second Lady Tipper Gore's crusade in the 1980s).
- Barbie dolls and GI Joe action figures promote gender stereotypes. We therefore must encourage toy manufacturers to come up with gender-neutral toys.

As a result, from a policy perspective, it boils down to either the provision of new information or the regulation of "bad" information. In both instances, such programs can be quite costly to implement while being minimally effective.

I do not wish to imply that governmental policies meant to educate consumers always fail. For example, the recycling initiative has been very successful in large part because of the systematic education of consumers regarding the environmental benefits. However, it is important to recognize which type of information is needed in a particular context. Reminding teenage males of the death-defying nature of reckless driving is a poor strategy, as young men engage in such acts precisely because it is a costly and hence an honest signal of their courage ("I faced death and came out unscathed, while some do not").[30] Showing young women the aesthetic consequences of sun exposure on their skin (as in wrinkles) will be more effective than telling them that they will risk contracting melanoma in thirty years (the discounting of future costs for immediate benefits is itself an evolutionary mechanism). Demonstrating to young male smokers the immediate risk of impotence is more powerful than educating them about the prospective risks of heart disease they'll face at the age of fifty. Other examples of practical takeaways for policy makers include:

- Pharmaceutical and biomedical firms have relied on evolutionary theory in developing numerous products and programs of incalculable societal benefits (e.g., vaccinations). Interestingly, natural selection has given rise to superbugs that are resistant to antibiotics. In this case, humans have provided the selection pressures for such superbugs to evolve via the overprescription of antibiotics coupled with patient error (e.g., not completing the prescribed treatment). The bottom line is that evolutionary theory is centrally important in the management of consumers' health.

- The recognition that particular demographic groups are universally more susceptible to specific forms of maladaptive consumption (see chapter 9). For example, men are much more likely to succumb to pathological gambling, pornographic addiction, and excessive risk taking, whereas women are the majority of sufferers when it comes to compulsive buying, eating disorders, and excessive suntanning. Understanding the reasons behind these universal epidemiological realities can yield more targeted intervention strategies.

- Understanding our biophilic nature (i.e., our love of nature) inspires our creation of work, commercial, urban, and hospital spaces that are aligned with our evolutionary-based landscape preferences (see chapter 2). For example, patients who are housed in rooms with windows recover more quickly than their counterparts in windowless spaces. Housing projects in US cities are a prime example of the consequences of seeking to optimize the wrong metric (e.g., minimize the cost of the building) rather than attempting to develop green settings that promote communal sociality.

Policy makers are entrusted with an onerous responsibility—they must enact intervention strategies that protect the consumer's well-being. Such an objective cannot be fully realized if the great majority of policy makers are unaware of how our evolved biology shapes our preferences, choices, and behaviors. Needless to say, an accurate understanding of the interplay between our genes and our unique life experiences is needed to advance the most effective social policies of relevance to consumer welfare. In the end, our happiness as consumers is driven by the intricate interplay of cultural and biological factors.

CONCLUSION

Consumers are cultural as well as biological beings. Although countless consumer-related preferences, needs, and desires vary across cultural settings, numerous others are universally similar because they are manifestations of a common consumer instinct. In some instances, cross-cultural consumer differences are themselves due to biological forces (i.e., nature shapes nurture). Our shared biological heritage, which has been forged by the dual Darwinian forces of natural and sexual selection, unites us within the proverbial global consumer village. Ultimately, to recognize the Darwinian roots of our consuming instinct is invaluable in order to understand our common human preferences, needs, and desires.

CHAPTER 2

I WILL SURVIVE

First we eat, then we do everything else.
—*MARY FRANCES KENNEDY FISHER,*
AMERICAN FOOD CRITIC
AND FOOD AUTHOR[1]

N atural selection selects for traits and behaviors that augment an organism's likelihood of surviving long enough to reproduce and pass on its genes. As such, the most fundamental goal of all organisms is the quest for survival. The single most important survival challenge faced by animals is to ensure that they obtain the caloric requirements needed to stay alive. Furthermore, if they are not apex predators—the top animal in the relevant food chain—a related problem is to avoid becoming someone else's dinner. Hence, many survival-related adaptations are linked to food foraging and predator avoidance. Let's examine the ways in which these two survival challenges manifest themselves in the consumer arena.

If the sloth is one of the laziest animals, then the hummingbird might take the crown for being the most energetic. Given its extraordinarily high basal metabolic rate, a hummingbird regularly consumes more than its body weight on a daily basis to thwart starvation. Grizzly bears face a desperate yearly race for survival; they must hoard, consume, and store a sufficient number of calories prior to the start of their seasonal hibernation. Failure to amass the necessary layers of fat could result in death. One food hoarding strategy that addresses this adaptive problem is gorging on salmon as these fish make their way up the river for their spawning runs. More generally, the act of gorging on highly caloric food sources is an adaptive strategy across countless species, as caloric uncertainty and caloric scarcity are two key survival problems faced by all animals. Humans are no different. For much of our evolutionary history, we did not have readily available food sources. Instead, we have faced recurring evolutionary pressures tied to caloric scarcity and caloric uncertainty. This has led to our developing a so-called thrifty genotype; we have the innate physiological capacity, along with the associated behaviors, for the swift storage of fat during times of plenty as an evolutionary adaptation for subsequent endemic bouts of severe food scarcity.[2]

How do food-related adaptations manifest themselves in the consumer realm? Humans around the world have a universal preference for fatty, highly caloric foods. In other words, our taste buds have evolved to prefer juicy burgers to raw broccoli. It is not surprising then that the most successful global fast-food restaurant chains share one commonality: they deliver tasty and fatty foods to insatiable mouths. Trade publication *Restaurants & Institutions* produces a yearly ranking of the four hundred top-selling restaurant chains.[3] The top ten in 2008 were (in decreasing order) McDonald's, KFC, Burger King, Starbucks, Subway, Pizza Hut, Wendy's, Taco Bell, Domino's Pizza, and Dunkin' Donuts. The rankings were the same for 2007. What do these restaurants have in common? What makes them so successful? They produce and sell highly caloric foods that appeal to our evolved gustatory preferences. No one contests the fact that McDonald's has produced a long list of memorable advertisements. However, such ads are not meant to create new needs or to provide any new or meaningful information. Rather, they remind you that the next time your blood sugar is low and your stomach begins to rumble from hunger, McDonald's golden arches should be at the top of your mind. The Atkins diet is a commercial success because it plays on individuals' evolved preferences for fatty foods. In the same manner that grizzly bears have an evolved penchant for fatty salmon, it is equally instinctual for humans to wish to consume copious quantities of eggs, steak, and bacon strips (all of which are permitted by the Atkins diet). In this instance, the success of a product is directly linked to its congruence with an evolved predisposition.

I EAT TO LIVE, AND I LIVE TO EAT

The human obsession with food manifests itself in innumerable ways. The existence of the Food Network television channel is a testament to that fact. Nearly all important rituals and rites of passage incorporate food within them, be it a first date, a bar mitzvah, a wedding, a family get-together (e.g., Thanksgiving dinner), friends inviting one another for dinner for their respective birthdays, and even funerals. Our most important life passages are indeed paved with succulent buffets. It is not surprising, then, that many cultural products contain food as a central theme. Food-related paintings include several famous renditions of the Last Supper, impressionist works such as Édouard Manet's *Le déjeuner sur l'herbe* and Pierre-Auguste Renoir's *Le déjeuner des canotiers*, and more recently pop artist Andy Warhol's *32 Campbell's Soup Cans*. Several highly successful sitcoms have taken place in a food-related setting or have had numerous food-related themes including *Alice*, *Three's Company*, *Cheers*, and the British comedy *Fawlty Towers*. Food-related movies come in many varieties—romantic comedies, dramas, and animated features. A partial list of such films include *Julie & Julia*, *Big Night*, *No Reservations*, *Chocolat*, *Ratatouille*, *La Grande Bouffe*, *The Mistress of Spices*, *Willy Wonka and the Chocolate Factory*, *Tampopo*, *Eat Drink Man Woman*, *Mostly Martha*, *Babette's Feast*, *Bottle Shock*, *Sideways*, *Woman on Top*, and *Like Water for Chocolate*. At times, a movie or television show is best known for a food-related iconic scene. Three that come to mind are the sensual exchange of food as a prelude to sex in *9½ Weeks*, the fake orgasm scene at the diner in *When Harry Met Sally*, and the restaurant scene that closed *The Sopranos* television series.

All said, perhaps no measure can capture the importance of food to the human experience quite as vividly as the number of food idioms that exist in the English language (and undoubtedly in other languages as well). Here is a fun sample: acquired taste, apple of my eye, as cool as a cucumber, as easy as apple pie, as sweet as honey, bad apple, bear fruit, big cheese, bite off more than one can chew, bite the hand that feeds you, born with a silver spoon in one's mouth, bring home the bacon, can't stomach it, chew the fat, couch potato, cream of the crop, cry over spilled milk, eat dirt, eat humble pie, eat like a bird, eat like a horse, eat one's words, eat out of your hands, eat someone for breakfast, food for thought, forbidden fruit, fruit of one's labor, go bananas, goose is cooked, greatest thing since sliced bread, half-baked idea, have a bigger fish to fry, have one's cake and it eat too, having a lot on one's plate, icing on the cake, in a nutshell, like taking candy from a baby, make a meal of it, meal ticket, meat-and-potatoes guy, no free lunch, not my cup of tea, out to lunch, packed in like sardines, pie in the sky, piece of cake, putting all of one's eggs in one basket, rub salt in one's wounds, selling like hotcakes, spill the beans, spoon-fed, take it with a grain of salt, that's the way the cookie crumbles, tub of lard, walk on eggshells, work for peanuts. It is clear that humans are obsessed with food.

DARWINIAN GASTRONOMY

Despite the fact that many food preferences are innate (e.g., our penchant for fatty foods), the environment also plays an important role in shaping our culinary tastes. Of note, it develops our tastes through biological-based transmission. For example, both prenatal and postnatal exposure to foods, via amniotic fluid and breastfeeding respectively, have been shown to influence a child's subsequent food preferences.[4] In my consumer behavior course, I often ask students to list consumer-related examples that are culture specific. Invariably, one or more students will mention food consumption to highlight the importance of culture in shaping our consumer habits. The Chinese eat more rice than the French do, while the latter consume more cheese than the former. Caribbean food is a lot spicier than British cuisine. The Germans drink a lot of beer, and Saudi Arabia prohibits alcohol. Countless cultures eat chicken; however, the manner in which it is prepared can be radically different (Lebanese shish taouk, Peruvian rotisserie, Tandoori chicken, and deep-fried chicken in the American South). In some Thai traditions, a host of insects and insect larva are considered delicious delicacies, a practice known as entomophagy. In my own Lebanese heritage, we consume delicacies from which most Westerners would recoil at their mere mention. These include cow's tongue, brains, and bone marrow; goat testicles; and raw meat with bulgur. Crustaceans (e.g., crabs, shrimps, lobsters) and swine meat are forbidden by kosher laws but are staple foods at Chinese buffets. The examples are nearly endless.

Cultural anthropologists revel in simply cataloging the panoply of culinary customs without necessarily providing any explanation as to what might have led to such cross-cultural differences. Whereas many culinary traditions are undoubtedly due to idiosyncratic cultural and historical factors, might it be the case that Darwinian forces shape some of these gastronomic differences? According to Paul W. Sherman, an evolutionary scientist at Cornell, many culinary traditions are adaptations to local conditions, an idea he called *Darwinian gastronomy*. His focus was to explore a specific element of culinary traditions, particularly the extent to which spices are used with meat versus vegetable dishes. Do you think that very spicy foods are more likely to be associated with hot or cold climates? We hear of spicy Mexican, Thai, and Caribbean foods but not in regard to Swedish, Canadian, or British cuisine. As a deduction, it would appear that people in warmer climates are more likely to use spices. The antimicrobial hypothesis provides a compelling explanation for the association between ambient temperature and spice use. Specifically, the use of spices is meant to combat food pathogens. Such a battle is more operative in hot versus cold climates because the prevalence and assortment of pathogens is greater, and their diffusion rates are more rapid, in warmer climates. Furthermore, Sherman and his colleagues highlight the fact that meat dishes are more likely to contain food pathogens than vegetable dishes. This theoretical framework permitted the researchers to predict cross-cultural differences in culinary traditions that would have otherwise been next to impossible to make were they not approaching the problem from an evolutionary perspective.[5]

In two separate papers,[6] Sherman and his associates conducted content analyses using cookbooks from thirty-six different countries, spanning six continents and covering sixteen of the nineteen linguistic families; the sample was exceptionally heterogeneous and provided global coverage. Many meat and vegetable dishes from each of the identified countries were coded in terms of the amount of spices that the particular recipe required for each given dish. Additionally, the average yearly temperature for each country was recorded. The key conclusions are quite revealing in demonstrating the adaptive nature of culinary traditions. First, the use of spices is indeed positively correlated with a country's ambient temperature, and this holds true for both meat and vegetable dishes. Second, the positive correlation is more pronounced for meat dishes. Incidentally, the findings were valid not only when making comparisons between countries but also when contrasting spice use across different regions of a single country (China and the United States). Additionally, the differential use of spices across countries was not related to the availability of spices in different regions, further lending support to the biological-based explanation. Sherman and Billing conclude: "Thus, cookbooks from different eras are more than just curiosities. Essentially, they represent written records of our coevolutionary races against food-borne diseases. By cleansing foods of pathogens before consumption, spice users contribute to the health, longevity, and fitness of themselves, their families, and their guests. A Darwinian view of gastronomy thus helps us understand why 'some like it hot' (spicy, that is!)."[7]

Yohsuke Ohtsubo recently applied the antimicrobial hypothesis to investigate the use of spices and vinegar in Japanese cuisine.[8] Specifically, he predicted that meat-based dishes, summer recipes, recipes from warmer regions, and unheated recipes (e.g., sushi) would require greater use of spices and of vinegar than vegetable dishes, winter recipes, recipes from cooler regions, and heated recipes, respectively. Across two data sets, the predictions were largely borne out. Interestingly, whereas the Japanese practice of food pickling might serve as an adaptive culinary practice, it has also been linked to the high rate of stomach cancers in Japanese society.[9]

Many religious dietary laws can be analyzed from such a Darwinian perspective. For example, in light of the differences in the likelihood of food pathogens for meat versus nonmeat sources, it is not surprising that all fruits and vegetables are considered kosher while many meat-based protein sources are not. Oysters and clams can contain dangerous biotoxins (with no known antidotes) that result in paralytic shellfish poisoning. An individual can die in as little as thirty minutes after having consumed a contaminated animal. Of note, one cannot visually identify which of two shellfish is infected, nor can one assume that the water's quality or clarity is an indicator of how likely it is for a shellfish to be contaminated. Seeing other animals (e.g., marine birds) consuming shellfish in a particular area does not serve as an accurate indicator of the likelihood of contamination either. Cooking contaminated animals does not remove the biotoxins. Finally, the spoilage of these creatures increases as a function of the ambient temperature (and ensuing lack of refrigeration).[10]

One might imagine that the lack of refrigeration during the Bronze Age coupled with the scorching heat of the Middle East provided suboptimal conditions for the consumption of such animals. Since ancient

Jews were unaware of biotoxins and could not rely on visual information to gauge sources of contamination (and therefore could not transmit these through cultural learning), they passed a "divine" edict that forbade the consumption of clams and shellfish. Which is the more likely explanation? Mine is based on a set of consistent and parsimonious scientific facts versus the religious one that is rooted in an invisible omnipotent and omniscient deity who happens to have a particular interest in our food choices. Occam's razor is in order here, as it postulates that when faced with alternative explanations for a given phenomenon, the simpler and more parsimonious one is preferable. As a side note, I should point out that when the Torah lists specific animals that may or may not be eaten, its human-made origins are quite telling. God seems to have a limited knowledge of the world's existing and extinct fauna, as all the animals listed in the Torah are restricted to the Middle East and to the specific period of the Bronze Age. There are no specific food edicts for or against the consumption of dinosaurs, mammoths, koalas, llamas, polar bears, Amazon River dolphins, cassowaries, and platypuses.

INSCRIBED IN OUR GENES: SALT AND MILK AS CASE STUDIES

African Americans are much more likely to be obese and to suffer from hypertension compared with their Caucasian counterparts.[11] Some people have proposed that culture-specific dietary habits are to blame (e.g., the penchant for fried foods in the Deep South). While it is certainly true that lifestyle choices affect health outcomes, some recent evidence regarding hypertension suggests that it might be linked to the forces of natural selection. Salt is a strong culprit when it comes to hypertension, which is why the first line of medical intervention for those who have high blood pressure is to decrease those patients' salt intake. However, it turns out that the human body's ability to metabolize salt is inscribed in our genes. In other words, two individuals who consume the same amount of salt will metabolize the mineral in radically different ways. Of particular interest, the distribution of specific gene polymorphisms (variant expressions of a given gene) connected with an individual's sensitivity to salt and his or her ability to retain water is associated with distance from the equator.[12] People who live closer to the equator possess the gene polymorphisms that accentuate water retention; these gene variants become less frequent as one moves away from warmer climates. This research is important in that it demonstrates how the body's ability to metabolize particular foods and condiments is in part shaped by selective pressures. From a medical perspective, knowing such information is very valuable. All other things equal, Lebanese individuals are more likely to need to watch their salt intake than Russians are.

Not only is our ability to metabolize salt inscribed in our genes but also cultural attitudes toward salt seem to be biologically derived. Anthropologist Susan Parman explored the link between the extent to which cultures are exposed to salt in their diets and their culturally prescribed attitudes toward salt (e.g., "not worth his salt").[13] She found that in cultures where the diets are largely animal-based (and hence have greater salt consumption), the attitudes toward salt were more negative than those where the diets were largely plant-based (and hence have less salt consumption). That is, a culture's attitude toward salt, a condiment that is very important for survival (e.g., salt intake can serve as a protective strategy against catastrophic fluid loss due to pathogenic infestation[14]), is intimately linked to the diets that the people of that culture have historically eaten. Parman's study reaffirms that many culture-specific practices and attitudes are shaped by biological realities.

One of the most compelling cases of gene-culture coevolution within the dietary realm is the geographical distribution of lactose tolerance across human populations. Characteristically, peoples who have historically led pastoral modes of subsistence (i.e., they herded cattle) and were more likely to consume dairy products underwent a genetic selection for a lactase-persistent allele of the human lactase gene. The frequency of this allele is much more common among European peoples whose history is rooted in pastoral living as compared with the nonpastoral Chinese; in China, 1 percent of the population possesses this genetic mutation.[15] This is a telling example of how the differential frequency of a cultural practice (pastoral subsistence) can yield genetic changes across human populations. Our genes affect our cultures, but our cultures can also impact our genes (the causal effect works in both directions). Incredibly, this gene-culture coevolution process has also affected cattle genes. For example, cattle genes for the quicker weaning of calves are more common in pastoral societies, as there is a premium for having earlier access to the cattle's milk for the herders' diet.[16] This yet again demonstrates the silliness of those who argue that evolutionary theory ignores the importance of culture and other environmental forces. Pastoralists' genes as well as their cattle's genes were both altered as a result of a cultural practice, namely, their mode of subsistence.

VARIETY IS THE SPICE OF LIFE

Recently, my family took a two-week all-inclusive vacation to the Riviera Maya in Mexico. While I was very much in need of a restful break, I was weary of one irresistible allure that might entrap me while frolicking in the sun: the all-you-can-eat buffets. Having spent the previous three months on a restrictive protein-based diet and achieving substantial weight loss, I worried that fourteen days of gluttonous debauchery might undo my efforts. I have been on several all-inclusive vacations (e.g., at Club Med and Sandals) and have spoken to individuals who work at these resorts. The general consensus is that it is quite common for people to put on three to five pounds per week. What makes the repeated call of the buffet so irresistible? First, buffets cater to our innate penchant for food hoarding. Recall that caloric scarcity and caloric uncertainty were endemic survival problems in our evolutionary past. It does not take much to convince our brain to engage in repeat "approach" behavior when faced with endless amounts of succulent foods. Second, buffets offer a great variety of foods, which most individuals find hard to ignore.

Several studies have demonstrated a *variety effect*, which holds that an increase in the offered food varieties yields a corresponding increase in the total amount eaten.[17] Variety can be captured in one of several ways. For example, one can offer foods A and B versus foods A, B, C, and D (while holding the total amount of calories constant across the two sets of offerings). For example, A, B, C, and D can refer to chicken wings, pizza slices, french fries, and M&M candies. The variety effect in this case might manifest itself in the greater amount of consumed calories when four food items are available. A second way to explore the variety effect is by holding the type of food constant but offer one flavor versus multiple flavors of the food item (e.g., yogurt). It has indeed been shown that when three yogurt flavors are available, individuals consume more yogurt than when a single flavor is available.[18] A third way by which the variety effect has been confirmed is the one that I consider most interesting. By simply varying a tasteless and odorless feature of a given food item (e.g., its shape or color), the eaten amount of food increases. For example, Barbara Kahn and Brian Wansink created different batches of M&M candies by altering the number of colors as well as the distribution of colors within a given batch.[19] They found that the amount of eaten candies increased by as much as 77 percent simply by manipulating these two features of the offered foods. Similar findings have been obtained using different shapes of pasta; a greater number of shapes led to a greater amount of eating.[20] Irrespective of whether there is an actual variety in the offered foods or a perceived one (i.e., by manipulating tasteless and odorless cues), variety results in increased food consumption. The marketing implications of the variety effect are substantial. For example, an increase in the number of displayed jams (six or twenty-four) at a tasting booth increased the number of customers who stopped at the booth by 20 percent.[21]

Why do consumers succumb to this variety effect? The evolutionary answer is quite simple. Our attraction to food variety stems from the fact that we are omnivores (i.e., generalist food foragers). Even lesser generalists such as herbivores can vary along their variety-seeking food intake; some limit themselves to relatively few plants as others incorporate a more varied diet (i.e., a greater number of plants). Generally speaking, the evolution of variety seeking in food foraging is linked to two distinct mechanisms: (1) maximizing the likelihood of obtaining the necessary amount of varied nutrients and (2) minimizing the likelihood of ingesting too great an amount of toxin from a singular food source.[22] The so-called dessert effect is due to our innate penchant to sample a variety of foods. Accordingly, even though we might be calorically satiated, we nonetheless cannot resist making extra room for that chocolate mousse.

The variety effect should not be confused with the standard view purported by classical economists that when all other things are equal, having more choices is better than having fewer, a position that has since been challenged by numerous behavioral scientists. For example, the greater the number of funds that are available to choose from for contributing to one's 401(k) retirement plans (ranging from a low of 2 up to 59), the *lower* the participation rate. With all other things being equal, each additional ten funds made available within the total set of choices yielded a 1.5 percent to 2 percent decrease in the participation rate.[23] In his excellent book *The Paradox of Choice: Why More Is Less*, Barry Schwartz highlights that having more choices is often detrimental across a wide range of decisions. As a prelude to demonstrating the diminishing returns of having an ever-increasing number of choices, Schwartz provides some startling figures about the variety of products in his average-sized supermarket, including (number of options in parentheses): crackers (85), cookies (285), iced teas and adult drinks (75), snacks such as chips and pretzels (95), soups (230), pasta sauces (120), salad dressings (175), cereals (275), barbecue sauce

(64), suntan oil and sunblock (61), toothpaste (40), lipstick (150), and shampoo (360).[24] He goes on to emphasize the explosion of choices in other areas, including electronic gadgets, university majors, television stations, utilities, health insurance, and retirement plans. Of particular relevance, Brian Wansink and Jeffery Sobal point out that individuals make over 225 daily food-related decisions (e.g., how much to eat, when to eat, where to eat), of which fifty-nine specifically deal with food choices.[25] When facing so many decisions, it is clear that the less-is-more adage is notably relevant here—or else consumers would spend hours doing nothing but making food choices.

Whereas humans in general seek food variety, the drive for such variety is different across individuals. How often do you try new restaurants or new kinds of cuisine? Are you the type of individual who has three or four favorite restaurants to which you always return? Do you order the same dish each time you visit a favorite eatery? Can you eat rotisserie chicken without side dishes, or must you have food variety at any given meal (e.g., chicken must be served with some salad, a baked potato, bread, etc.)? The answer to these questions captures the extent to which you are a variety seeker when it comes to food choices. Paul Rozin, one of the preeminent food psychologists over the past four decades, and Maureen Markwith have demonstrated that people's food variety seeking correlates across food categories.[26] For instance, if you are a variety seeker when it comes to fruits or vegetables, you are also likely to seek variety when it comes to soups. That food variety seeking is operative for multiple food categories does not necessarily imply that it translates into variety seeking across multiple product categories and contexts outside of the food setting. For example, I would venture to say that one might be a high food variety seeker but a low sex variety seeker (the Sociosexual Orientation Inventory captures one's preference for restrained versus unrestrained sexuality).

Proclivities for food variety seeking exist not only at the individual level but also have been documented cross-culturally. Rozin, along with several of his colleagues, asked consumers from France, Germany, Italy, Switzerland, the United Kingdom, and the United States two questions meant to capture their desire for food variety (using ice-cream parlors and restaurants as the choice stimuli).[27] Specifically, participants were asked whether they preferred an ice-cream parlor that offers ten or fifty flavors, and whether they expected that a restaurant should have many dish choices or a few chef suggestions. Although consumers in all six countries appreciated some variety, respondents from Britain and the United States held a substantially more pronounced preference for greater variety of ice-cream flavors and a greater number of dish choices. In my opinion, this is likely due to the mass customization movement that first came to prominence in the 1980s, when marketers created ever smaller microniches of consumer markets meant to cater to endless idiosyncratic tastes. Chef Gordon Ramsay stars in *Kitchen Nightmares*, a television show dedicated to revitalizing failing restaurants. A frequent problem identified by Ramsay is a menu that is too large and burdensome, which emphasizes owners' penchant to provide a wide variety of dish options to a broad clientele. His solution is always to suggest a smaller and more targeted menu, not only because it creates less confusion for the patrons but also because it permits the cooks and chefs to turn dishes around more quickly. To conclude, variety might indeed be the spice of life, but only if consumers do not end up experiencing information overload. The spoils go to those restaurateurs who strike the right balance.

SITUATIONAL INFLUENCES ON FOOD INTAKE

Food consumption is a phenomenon that is strongly influenced by a wide range of situational variables. The amount of calories ingested in any given seating is affected by one's mood, situational hunger, the extent of available food, and hormonal influences, to name but a few key driving factors.[28]

Mood

The relationship between our moods and our food intake is a complex one. I am referring to situational moods, and not to personality traits that might generate individual differences in dispositions toward being happy or sad. First, one has to differentiate between different temporal definitions of mood, as well as their valence (i.e., the strength of the mood state). Someone might be clinically depressed, with a severe and long-lasting negative mood. An individual might be slightly dysphoric, a milder and more transient state of blueness. Or one might be in a bad mood because he or she had a hard day at work. Similar distinctions can be drawn for states of good moods. Furthermore, it is important to distinguish between mood as a precursory factor prior to eating versus mood as a consequence of eating. A researcher might ask whether an individual is more likely to eat if in a positive versus in a negative mood. In this case, mood is an antecedent to eating. One might also investigate whether eating chocolate affects one's mood, in which case mood is an outcome of food consumption. Having provided a brief enumeration of the ways in which mood and food might be linked, I shall restrict my discussion to emotional eating; namely, how our situational mood affects how much, and to some extent, what we eat.

Anecdotally, it would seem that both good and bad moods could result in an increase in food intake. We have all heard of using comfort foods to curb the effects of sadness, loneliness, or boredom. Similarly, happy people often proclaim that their good moods induce appetite. Studies have indeed found that both positive and negative moods can augment one's cravings. For example, participants in one study reported that they were more likely to eat following happy life events (e.g., getting married or having a child) as opposed to sad ones (e.g., a romantic breakup).[29] On the other hand, people who were induced to be in a sad mood state (after watching *Love Story*) ate more buttered popcorn than those who were put in a happy mood (after watching *Sweet Home*

Alabama). More generally, sad moods increased the consumption of hedonic foods (buttered popcorn and M&M candies) but decreased for a healthier alternative (raisins).[30] Still, it would seem that we are doomed to eat more, regardless of what our situational moods are.

Not only do our moods potentially affect the amount of food we eat but also they have an impact on the types of foods we crave. Whereas both happy and sad people might seek comfort foods, the specific types of comfort foods vary. Individuals who are happy are more likely to seek healthier comfort foods than their sad counterparts (e.g., steak instead of chips). Interestingly, there exists a pronounced sex difference in the preferred comfort foods. Ice cream, chocolate, and cookies were women's favorite comfort foods; ice cream, soup, and pizza or pasta were the corresponding preferred comfort foods for men.[31]

It would appear that short of a debilitating depression wherein one's appetite can be severely curtailed, the full spectrum of mood states serve to augment one's proclivity to eat. This is perhaps not surprising from an evolutionary perspective, given our innate penchant for food hoarding. Our moods are indeed prisoners to our guts!

Food Availability

As a Canadian residing in Montreal but who travels regularly to the United States, I am continually amazed by the portion sizes that are considered normal in America. Of course, true to the cliché "When America sneezes, Canada catches a cold," the American supersizing phenomenon (see the 2004 documentary *Super Size Me*) has slowly filtered into the Canadian ethos. The reality is that the gradual increase of portion sizes is a phenomenon that can easily take hold in any culture, as it triggers our innate capacity for food hoarding. Supersizing manifests itself in numerous ways, including in the average increase in the portion sizes of vending machine snacks, the standard sizes of packaged foods in supermarkets, and the standard portion sizes of restaurant meals. The bottom line is that for most food choices, the average portion size is much larger today than it was several decades ago. Of course, if humans had an innate capacity to stop eating when they reached satiety, then an increase in portion size would carry little effect. Alas, most of us lack this mechanism. Instead, we have the diametrically opposed instinct—to gorge when presented with an amount of food that is greater than our threshold of satiety.

Numerous studies have shown that an increase in food availability, as captured by larger portion sizes, results in greater caloric intake at any given seating. This holds true across a wide range of foods, including pasta, popcorn, and sandwiches, and for adults as well as for children.[32] One wonders whether the parental practice of forcing children to finish everything on their plates might at times exacerbate our innate penchant to overeat when a plentiful amount of food is available. "Mom, there is a positive correlation between caloric intake and portion size, so please do not force me to clean my plate. The portion sizes are too big!" In all seriousness, the practical implications for weight management are quite clear. It is imperative to control our portion sizes, or else it is nearly guaranteed that we'll overeat. For example, if you are about to sit down to watch a movie at home and are craving potato chips, do not eat from the large "mother lode" bag, as this will ensure that you'll gorge. Instead, transfer a lesser amount of chips to a small bowl, which will serve as your satiety cue. Small behavioral changes of this sort can go a long way toward curtailing our food-hoarding instinct.

Situational Hunger

A central food-related edict is to avoid making food decisions when hungry, as this can often lead to poor nutritional and dietary outcomes. The accumulated evidence suggests that hunger clouds our judgment in detrimental ways. Decisions might include what to prepare for dinner, what to order at a restaurant, or what and how much to purchase at a grocery store. For example, nonobese consumers spend more in a super-market the longer they have been deprived of food.[33] Our attitude toward food is more positive when hungry, and more specifically our attitude toward high-fat foods increases when hungry.[34] Our situational hunger can also cause us to overeat. This is a reason that starvation diets can backfire because one can easily succumb to gorging if famished. Instead, diets that prescribe small caloric intake on several occasions throughout the day can potentially curb one's hunger, and in doing so reduce the likelihood of overeating at any given mealtime.

Situational hunger has an effect not only on our food-related behaviors but also on our mating preferences. Specifically, when hungry, men display a more pronounced preference for heavier women.[35] This puts a whole new twist to the adage that the way to a man's heart is through his stomach! Incredibly, being hungry makes us desire money more, and triggering an increased situational desire for money makes us hungrier.[36] It would seem that our innate capacity to hoard food when hungry (the ancestrally relevant measure for resources) is usurped for the purposes of hoarding a more recent culturally defined proxy measure of resources (money).

Menstrual Cycle

As I mentioned in chapter 1, pregnancy sickness is an adaptation meant to protect the growing fetus from potential ravages if exposed to food pathogens. Many food cravings and aversions during pregnancy can also be construed as a manifestation of situational preferences meant to protect the fetus during organogenesis (the process during the first trimester of a pregnancy when the organs are forming in utero). That said, there are many other food-related issues linked to a woman's reproductive status best explained via an evolutionary framework. How much a woman eats, and which types of foods she is most likely to crave, are highly predicted by her menstrual cycle.[37] Eric Stenstrom—one of my doctoral students—and I tracked women's food-related desires, preferences, and purchases across thirty-five contiguous days. We found that during the luteal phase (as compared with the fertile phase), women reported that they craved more highly caloric foods, felt hungrier, consumed more calories, and spent more money on food.[38] Many women are undoubtedly aware of these facts if only via their personal experiences. Nevertheless, it is helpful to remind women that their fluctuating appetites are in part shaped by their shifting hormones. Think of the weight management implications that such a simple nugget of information might carry.

Food Disgust

I have focused here mainly on the capacity of food to serve as an attractant. However, food can also serve as one of the strongest known repellants. Food-related disgust is an adaptation against possible exposure to harmful contagions, and as such possesses universal elements that hold true irrespective of cultural setting. For example, the facial features associated with disgust are universally the same. In cross-cultural studies of the triggers of disgust, bodily secretions and spoiled, decaying food constitute two of the most common triggers.[39] How might this information be applied in a marketing context? Company-related urban legends and rumors come in many varieties. A great majority of these are meant to elicit food disgust. A rumor that company X is owned by a satanic cult is not nearly as juicy as the one about company Y using sheep eyes in their meat products. In other words, the diffusion rate of company rumors is greatest when the meme in question (*meme* is the cultural analog of a gene, a term introduced by Richard Dawkins in 1976) is related to food disgust. Hence, a rumor about a fast-food restaurant where an employee was caught urinating on decaying hamburger meat is the ultimate of company rumors, as it combines the two greatest elicitors of disgust. Accordingly, understanding these principles can alert a multinational firm to the potentially globally devastating effect of disgust-related rumors.

Several years ago, one of the groups in my undergraduate course in consumer behavior studied the effect of product contagion and its associated links to disgust. They conducted an observational study at a supermarket in which they counted the number of times that consumers would refrain from taking the first item on a shelf and instead pick one from farther back on the shelf. In this particular case, the behavior was irrational in that the products were packaged, and hence the possibility of a hand-to-product contagion was nil (as might otherwise occur when handling produce at a fruit stand). Nonetheless, the students documented the behavior in question for many consumers. Consumers' instincts to avoid food contaminants had caused people to misapply it in a context in which it was otherwise "irrational" to do so. The pull to avoid food contaminants is such an ingrained element of our food psychology that most consumers subconsciously extend their vigilance to otherwise benign settings. This hypervigilance manifests itself not only behaviorally but also on a physiological level. Being exposed to photographs of individuals spreading their germs (e.g., via sneezing or coughing) is sufficient to elicit a boost in one's immunological defense system.[40]

LANDSCAPE PREFERENCES, LOVE OF NATURE, AND HUMAN-MADE ENVIRONMENTS

Since caloric hoarding is a central survival problem, I have dedicated much of my discussion here to food-related issues. However, there are many other survival challenges that all organisms—including humans—have had to face, perhaps none as terrifying as becoming someone else's dinner. Furthermore, in our evolutionary history, another environmental danger that we faced was the possibility of running into "conspecifics" (i.e., members of our species) who were not part of our in-group. For those reasons, we possess an evolved preference for landscapes that provide us simultaneously with a good *prospect* (to see possible dangers) and safe *refuge* (to be protected from such dangers). Such landscapes have also afforded us good vantage points when hunting game. Since our visual sense constitutes roughly 90 percent of our sensorial processing, it is not surprising that our preferred habitats are visually stimulating. Numerous studies have indeed uncovered that when people are shown a wide range of landscapes, they tend to prefer those that are most congruent with the topography implicit to prospect-refuge theory. We humans prefer savannalike habitats[41] precisely because they offer a wide visual prospect and opportunities for refuge. Many features found in residential homes, such as verandas and indoor balconies, are consistent with central tenets of prospect-refuge theory.[42] Being close to water sources is another element of the savannalike landscapes that served as the cradle of our species. Accordingly, many of our favorite vistas contain water as a central feature (e.g., waterfalls).[43] It is also a key reason that much of the world's population lives close to large bodies of water.

Habitat preferences have been shown to be species-specific adaptations. The ideal environment for polar bears is different from that of camels. Though this seems obvious when contrasting the habitats and landscapes of wildly different species, it might seem unclear at first whether humans should have an optimally preferred habitat or landscape. After all, one of the key advantages of *Homo sapiens* has been our ability to adapt to radically different ecological niches. Notwithstanding our adaptability as a species, studies conducted over the past thirty years across a wide range of cultural and geographic settings have established highly convergent landscape and habitat preferences. These innate penchants are best captured when eliciting preferences from children.[44] As individuals grow, they gain familiarity with their local habitats such that these become increasingly favored. Hence, the Maasai of Kenya, the Inuits of the Canadian North, the Australian aboriginals, and the Yanomamö of the Amazonian jungle would likely all exhibit an innate liking to savannalike landscapes, in addition to idiosyncratic preferences for their respective local niches. Our instinctual landscape preferences are manifested across a broad range of cultural products, including landscape paintings stemming from radically different cultural traditions, landscape calendars, cave paintings, landscape and garden designs (e.g., Richard Haag's work), landscape descriptions in literary narratives, natural parks, and architectural design (e.g., some of Frank Lloyd Wright's designs).

Nature is not unlike the proverbial femme fatale; it is both alluring and dangerous. We have an innate love for living systems (biophilia) as well as innate fears of particular aspects of nature (biophobia). For example, arachnophobia (fear of spiders) and ophidiophobia (fear of snakes) are adaptive in that throughout our human history, it would have been well advised to stay clear of potentially fatally venomous animals. I am utterly mortified by mosquitoes, a specific kind of entomophobia (fear of insects). I have often been teased that it would be manlier to have phobias of wolves, sharks, or bears. My response is that my fear is perfectly adaptive given that mosquitoes are probably responsible for the greatest number of deaths in human history. Despite our trepidation toward some aspects of nature, plants and animals have been an integral part of our own evolution as a species, and as such we have a biophilic instinct (i.e., an instinctual love of nature).[45] Zoos, safaris, and marine parks cater to our biophilic needs. Aquariums bring our love of nature to our homes. Individuals fortunate enough to swim with dolphins refer to it as a mystical and awe-inspiring experience. I have interacted with wolves at a New Mexican sanctuary, and I can unequivocally state that it was a deeply moving experience. Horticultural therapy has many physical and psychological benefits, so much so that it is frequently used in diverse rehabilitative settings including convalescence homes, hospitals, and prisons. Natural vistas trigger feelings of spiritual wonder akin to those typically associated with religious rapture. As a matter of fact, whereas the concept of God is a recent human-made phenomenon, nature's awe-inspiring capacity is a vestige of our evolutionary past. Each year, millions of visitors flock to national parks such as Yosemite, Zion, Bryce Canyon, Grand Canyon, and Yellowstone precisely because of our innate capacity to be moved by such grand vistas.

The health benefits that accrue to those who interact with nature are substantial.[46] Such interactions might include interacting with animals, watching natural vistas, or hiking in the wilderness or in city parks. Some restorative environments such as spas typically incorporate elements of nature within their design (e.g., well-manicured gardens, indoor waterfalls). On the other hand, perhaps the most important of all restorative spaces—hospitals—have been grossly lacking in catering to our biophilic needs. Hospitals tend to be antiseptic, dreary, and ominous places void of any aesthetic qualities that are appealing to humans. In one of the classic studies of the restorative effects of the outdoors, postoperative patients who were placed in hospital rooms with windows yielded better outcomes than their counterparts without windows to the outside world.[47] More generally, allowing daylight indoors has been shown to increase retail sales, employee productivity, and students' test scores.[48] Mental fatigue and stress are reduced, and life satisfaction, one's outlook on life, mental concentration, and productivity are all improved via a contact with nature. I see this firsthand every year in Montreal as the city wakes up from its long winter hibernation and proceeds to the hedonic outdoor debauchery that accompanies spring and summer. Montrealers' reactions to the arrival of spring reminds me of the 1990 movie *Awakenings*, in which Robert De Niro's character literally awakens from the catatonic state that he had been in for many years.

Our contemporary environments and fast-paced lifestyles have made it increasingly more difficult to meet the innate biophilic needs that we all crave. To use the poignant term of author and journalist Richard Louv, modern urban living has created individuals who suffer from Nature Deficit Disorder. Think about images of cities located behind the Iron Curtain, the urban projects in Chicago's South Side or in the Bronx, or the row houses in industrial towns in Britain. What are the first words or descriptors that come to mind? Often: *drab, gray, dull, depressing, intimidating, ominous,* and *colorless.* The minimization of construction costs was the operative architectural criterion that drove the design in each of the latter three examples. Innate aesthetic preferences along with our inborn biophilic needs were construed as being irrelevant to a building's functionality. Ultimately, such a cost-oriented outlook creates urban spaces that have a profoundly deleterious effect on the people who inhabit those areas. In the recent past, several organizations have recognized this issue and have accordingly sought to transform urban spaces in ways that are compatible with our biophilic needs.[49]

The need to create urban landscapes that conform to our biophilic desires extends well beyond instinctive aesthetic appreciation. Feeling safe in urban settings (e.g., campuses) is linked to prospect-refuge theory.[50] With the exception of a few cities (e.g., New York), the great majority of American cities are "unwalkable." Accordingly, not only do Americans take fewer steps in any given day, thus failing to meet the minimal daily requirement of walking ten thousand steps,[51] but also the amount of time spent in their cars could be better spent outdoors. In 2006, the *Journal of the American Planning Association* published a special issue on the links between well-planned built environments (e.g., neighborhoods) and a wide range of health outcomes. For example, the walkability of an urban neighborhood is correlated to the average weight of its inhabitants.[52] Neighborhoods that conform to our biophilic instincts are literally healthier for our bodies and our minds.

Eugene Tsui is perhaps the world's most renowned evolutionary-minded architect.[53] He has argued that we need to study nature's designs as a source for inspiration. Numerous animals have evolved architectural designs that constitute adaptive solutions to specific survival or reproductive challenges. These include spiderwebs, termite mounds, bird nests, bird bowers, beehives, beaver dams, and the King Cobra nest mound (composed of rotting leaves). The famed evolutionary biologist Richard Dawkins has proposed that such structures are extended phenotypes (observable characteristics that lie outside of the organism and within its environment that are affected by its genes).[54] In other words, evolutionary processes need not be restricted to an organism's phenotype but can also include species-specific architectural creations that are within the purview of genetic influence. If designed with our biophilic instinct in mind,[55] human-made environments can become integral elements of our extended phenotypes, the ultimate expression of green living!

Biophilic design need not be restricted to urban landscapes. The principles are applicable to the optimal design of commercial spaces including shopping malls, store layouts, and hotel lobbies as well as residential spaces (e.g., the television series *World's Greenest Homes*). Suzanne C. Scott, a researcher who studies interior design, has found that one important element of attractive interiors is their capacity to create opportunities for prospect and refuge.[56] For example, cafés do not typically have spatial arrangements meant to maximize the number of patrons who can fit into the space. Such a layout would create a "cafeteria feeling" that most café patrons would frown upon. Rather, attractive café interiors generate a feeling of intimacy, part of which is created by having delineated spaces (affording refuge) that otherwise permit the viewing of others (prospect). On a related note, biophilic store design refers to the greening of retail and commercial settings as a means of improving the experience of employees and consumers alike.[57] The television series *Restaurant Makeover* specializes in redesigning the menus as well as the atmospheres of otherwise failing restaurants. More often than not, the redesign of the interior spaces conforms to key tenets of prospect-refuge theory.

CONCLUSION

Two key survival challenges faced by most species is food foraging and predator avoidance. Within the consumer context, numerous phenomena are expressions of adaptive solutions to the latter survival challenges. Our universal preference for highly caloric foods is an adaptation to the environment of caloric scarcity and uncertainty in which we evolved. Our culinary traditions (e.g., the extent of spice use) are cultural adaptations to local environments (e.g., ambient temperature). At times, our cultural traditions shape our genes, as is the case with the relationship between pastoral subsistence and lactose tolerance. Our moods, situational hunger, food availability, and fluctuating hormones all have a profound effect on the amount and types of foods that we consume. Finally, countless urban settings, be they our neighborhoods, buildings, malls, and homes, can be designed in greener ways not only in terms of yielding a smaller ecological footprint but also in terms of their congruence with both our biophilic instinct (love of nature) and our innate aesthetic preferences for spaces that offer a wide visual prospect and opportunities for refuge.

CHAPTER 3
LET'S GET IT ON

What holds the world together, as I have learned from bitter experience, is sexual intercourse.
> —*HENRY MILLER,*
> *AMERICAN PLAYWRIGHT AND AUTHOR*[1]

All nature's creatures join to express nature's purpose. Somewhere in their mounting and mating, rutting and butting is the very secret of nature itself.
> —*GRAHAM SWIFT, BRITISH NOVELIST*[2]

Sex is a part of nature. I go along with nature.
> —*MARILYN MONROE, AMERICAN ACTRESS*[3]

We have seen how the forces of natural selection shape consumer phenomena that are linked to our survival instinct. In order to pass on their genes, though, organisms must not only survive but must also reproduce. Sexual selection is the process that results in the evolution of traits and behaviors that yield an advantage in the mating domain. For example, the peacock's large and colorful tail did not evolve because it confers a survival advantage; rather, it serves to attract prospective hens. Similarly, the horns of a ram are not linked to survival. They are used for intrasexual combats, the winner of which can lay sexual claim to the ewes. Not unlike other sexually reproducing species, sexual selection has had a profound effect on the evolution of our own species, as manifested by the fact that we are a sexually dimorphic species; particularly, men and women are different in their many physical, emotional, cognitive, and behavioral traits.[4] Of course, many of these differences manifest themselves in the consumer arena.

Much of what we do as consumers is ultimately related to sex. Choosing a mate itself can be construed as the ultimate consumption decision. Humans are products in the mating market. They advertise themselves to prospective suitors via products meant to serve as sexual signals (e.g., cosmetics, high heels, luxury cars, perfumes, haircuts, plastic surgery). Women shop for good genes, deciding when and with whom to have a sexual dalliance, or in the attributes that they seek via sperm banks or online dating services. Men consume pornography whereas women more than men prefer erotica and romance novels. Men offer engagement rings as part of an elaborate courtship ritual. They engage in runaway forms of conspicuous consumption to signal their social status ("keeping up with the Joneses"). They partake in various forms of risk taking including day trading, extreme sports, and gambling. All these consumption choices are shaped by sexual selection. Our hormones influence our consumption patterns in ways that are congruent with evolutionary theory. For instance, men's testosterone levels rise when they drive a Porsche (a form of sexual signaling), while women's consumption patterns are profoundly affected by their menstrual cycles (e.g., what they wear, what they eat, how much they eat).

Let's begin with a brief discussion of the proverbial birds and the bees via a comparison of elements of courtships that both birds and humans engage in, as a means of demonstrating how similar we are to our animal cousins.

BIRDS DO IT . . . AND SO DO WE

What does a male red-capped manakin (bird) have in common with the world-famous Russian dancer Mikhail Baryshnikov? Both utilize their dancing prowess to attract the admiring gaze of prospective female mates. Kimberley Bostwick, a Cornell University ornithologist, used a high-speed imaging camera (five hundred frames per second) to capture the manakin's extraordinary dance. She has dubbed the manakin the original moonwalker (in reference to the dance move made famous by pop star Michael Jackson in the 1980s). In a recent paper published in *Nature*, William M. Brown and his colleagues found that men's dance abilities were positively correlated to their bodily symmetry, a measure of phenotypic quality.[5] Anecdotally, one often hears that individuals' abilities on the dance floor are indicative of their corresponding talents in the bedroom. Such a link seems to make intuitive sense. In actuality, the finding obtained by Brown and his colleagues reinforces the connection between one's talents in implementing a behavior (dance) with one's genetic quality (body symmetry). Managers of boy bands such as New Kids on the Block in the late 1980s and Backstreet Boys and 'N Sync in the late 1990s vied for commercial success by choosing attractive young men who danced well. In some instances, members of a species engage in dance not as a means of attracting prospective mates but rather to solidify the devotion within a bonded pair, as is the case with the red-crowned crane. Not surprisingly, humans also engage in such a bonding ritual, perhaps none as memorable as the first dance at a wedding when the newlyweds engage in a public display of their devotion. Given the importance of dance as a courtship ritual, it is not surprising that television shows such as *Dancing with the Stars* and *So You Think You Can Dance* have been hugely successful.

One of the premier tourist destinations in Newport, Rhode Island, is the world-famous Cliff Walk, where admiring tourists can gaze in wonderment at the lavish mansions and castles of many enormously wealthy industrialists—such as the Vanderbilts and the Astors—of the Gilded Age. What do these ostentatious homes have in common with the Great Bowerbird of Australia or the Vogelkop Gardener Bowerbird of New Guinea? These birds have a somewhat unique form of sexual signaling. Rather than utilizing song repertoires, beautiful plumage, or dance ability, male bowerbirds impress the females with their artistic and architectural abilities. Specifically, they build and decorate structures known as bowers, which serve no functional purpose other than to display their architectural prowess. Whereas the Newport mansions were not meant to signal artistic ability, they did serve as honest signals of one's social standing. Both the bower and the Newport mansions can be construed as extended phenotypes in that they serve as species-specific artifacts rooted in a biological imperative.

To continue with avian species, we may ask what the peacock's tail has in common with an ostentatiously expensive luxury car such as an Aston Martin, a Bugatti, a Duesenberg, or a Maybach. The peacock's tail is very burdensome in its size, and as such it increases the risk of falling victim to predation. Accordingly, its evolution is due to sexual and not natural selection. Specifically, the tail is an honest phenotypic signal of the genetic quality of its carrier.[6] It effectively says, "Clearly, I am a peacock with high fitness, as otherwise I would not be able to 'pull off' this tail." The signal is honest because suboptimal males are incapable of faking it. I have argued elsewhere that many forms of conspicuous consumption in the human context are nothing but honest and costly advertisements, a perfect example of which is men's use of luxury cars as sexual signals.

CARS

Unlike many American cities where the downtown areas become ghost towns after-hours, Montreal is a city with an exciting and vibrant urban center. The city is particularly known for its bustling summertime nightlife, in part due to its long and punishing winters. As mentioned earlier, Montrealers feel the need to compensate for their winter hibernations by coming out to play in full force with the arrival of warmer weather. In this sense, downtown Montreal serves as the ultimate lekking ground (physical space where males of a species typically congregate to show off to the females), or—to use a more familiar term—meat market for hormonally charged men and women wishing to see and be seen. Not surprisingly, the two sexes engage in radically different forms of sexual signaling as a means of drawing attention to themselves. Innumerable women can be seen strolling the downtown streets in scantily clad attire as an equally impressive number of men appear to be driving aimlessly around the same downtown blocks in souped-up cars, with the windows rolled down and music blasting.

Why do men incessantly drive around the blocks for hours? Are they all having a hard time finding parking spots? Why does not a single culture exist in which men parade in ballet tights (to show off their bodies) while women drive around the downtown areas in Porsches, Ferraris, and Aston Martins? After all, if these consumption acts (beautifying one's self and signaling one's resources) were due to socialization, one would expect to identify at least one culture in which these forces happened to operate in the opposite manner. These signaling behaviors occur in exactly the same form in Tel Aviv, Kingston (Jamaica), Rio de Janeiro, Tokyo, Dakar (Senegal), Auckland (New Zealand), and Moscow because they are rooted in our common evolved biology. They were equally valid three thousand years ago in ancient Greece (although fancy cars would not have been the social status signal du jour), and in all likelihood will be equally true in three thousand years.

One of my former graduate students John Vongas and I investigated how men's testosterone (T) levels respond to the effects of conspicuous consumption.[7] Young men drove two cars, an expensive Porsche and a decrepit, old Toyota sedan, in one of two environments (downtown Montreal and on a somewhat deserted freeway). As a result, each male participant had four driving sessions (Porsche-downtown, Porsche-highway, Toyota-downtown, and Toyota-highway). We predicted that men's T levels (which were measured via salivary assays) would rise when driving the Porsche and more so when in the public setting (downtown). Furthermore, we hypothesized that T levels would decrease when driving the old sedan, and more so in the downtown area. In other words, "winner" and "loser" signals should particularly matter when there is a viewing audience. We assumed that driving a Porsche in a deserted area where no one would be watching would be ineffective, but having numerous beautiful women in downtown Montreal gaze admiringly at the Porsche they'd be driving would be intoxicating. We found that regardless of the environment, men's testosterone levels rose significantly when driving the luxury sports car. It appears that the Porsche revs up men's endocrinological engines, given its potency as a sexual signal.

A quick perusal of famous car collectors reveals that they are invariably men. These include Jay Leno, Jerry Seinfeld, the Sultan of Brunei, John McMullen (businessman), Art Astor (radio entrepreneur), Ralph Lauren, Jay Kay (lead singer of the group Jamiroquai), and many soccer players—most notably the marketing icon David Beckham, who currently applies his trade with the LA Galaxy. Clearly, there are many wealthy women who could just as easily start their own car collections. Yet somehow they do not feel that need, although it does happen on rare occasions (e.g., Oprah Winfrey recently offered three of her luxury cars to a charity auction). Women might collect high heels (more on this topic later), but seldom do they "waste" their money on an endless array of luxury vehicles. On a related note, I have occasionally watched televised Barrett-Jackson luxury car auctions and noted an overwhelming preponderance of male buyers.

The American political satirist and author P. J. O'Rourke famously quipped, "There are a number of mechanical devices that increase sexual arousal, particularly in women. Chief amongst these is the Mercedes-Benz 380L convertible."[8] Men use expensive cars to display their social status to women because women are attracted to high-status males. However, might men be judged to be more *physically* attractive if only by virtue of driving high-status cars? In other words, might the same man be judged as physically more or less attractive as a function of whether he is driving a Toyota Corolla or an Aston Martin DB7? This would be an incredible finding in that it would demonstrate a transfer from the prestige of the car to the perceived morphological features of a man. Michael J. Dunn and Robert Searle tested this intriguing proposition.[9] They took photographs of a man and a woman (of equal attractiveness) seated in one of two cars of varying prestige (a silver Bentley Continental GT or a red Ford Fiesta ST). They then asked men and women to rate the attractiveness of the opposite sex targets in either the high-status or low-status car. The hypothesis was that the attractiveness scores obtained from women would vary depending on the status of the car that the male was seated in. Specifically, women would assign a higher attractiveness score to the *same* man when he was seated in the Bentley as compared with when he was seated in the Ford Fiesta. Conversely, since men do not care about the social status of women when making mate choices (or care about it much less than women do), their elicited attractiveness ratings should not be different across the two conditions. This is exactly what the psychologists found. Drive a hot car and you'll be perceived as hot, but only if you are a man.

A similar experiment using the Hot or Not website[10] was recently conducted to test the premise that a man's physical attractiveness ratings would depend on the car that he is shown standing next to.[11] This particular website allows individuals to post photographs, which are then rated by others in terms of "hotness." It allows for the collection of a large sample of data with minimal effort. The researchers in question uploaded, at separate time periods, one of four photos of the same man, standing either by himself (i.e., without any car visible) or next to one of three cars of varying prestige. When the man was shown next to the most prestigious of the three cars (a Mercedes C Class C300), he was rated as more attractive than when standing alone or when standing next to the least prestigious of the three cars (a tired looking Dodge Neon). Again, hot cars translate into hot men.

We are a hierarchical species. Humans assort themselves on a dominance hierarchy, and accordingly the manner in which people interact with one another is in part determined by their actual (or perceived) social status. Are there social consequences to the car that one drives? Though it may seem incredible, how likely you are to be honked at or how likely you are to honk at someone is highly dependent on the car that you drive. In an elegant field experiment conducted more than four decades ago, researchers stopped one of two cars (high versus low status) at a red light.[12] They then measured how quickly the driver in the car immediately behind the "blocking car" would honk once the light turned green. Drivers were more likely to honk and to do so more quickly when blocked by a lower-status car. The patience that was afforded to the drivers of the high-status car appears to be a form of social deference commonly seen in various species that establish dominance hierarchies.

One could also investigate how the car status of the "blocked" drivers might affect the likelihood of an aggressive response. This is precisely what sociologist Andreas Diekmann and his colleagues investigated in a study conducted in Munich, Germany.[13] The blocking car was always a Volkswagen Jetta (apparently perceived as a lower-middle-class car), and the aggressive behaviors included honking and the flashing of headlights. A positive correlation was found between aggressive behavior and the status of the blocked cars. It would seem that not only are people deferential to those who drive fancy cars, but also that those who drive such cars are more likely to be bullies! I suppose that the French maxim *à tout seigneur, tout honneur* (honor to whom honor is due) is applicable here.

COURTSHIP GIFTS

For many species, the likelihood that mating will occur between prospective suitors is largely driven by the "appropriateness" of a nuptial gift. In many instances, the nuptial gifts are tantamount to offering, sharing, or providing access to food. For example, in many insect species, males will offer food packets to females, which the females will eat while being inseminated by the males. The most extreme form of this phenomenon is sexual cannibalism, a mating behavior found in several insect species including the black widow spider and the praying mantis. The benefit to the male is that as he is being eaten alive (and hence serving as nutrition for his mate), he is inseminating his partner. Talk about dying for love! In the majority of cases in which sexual cannibalism occurs, it is typically the females that eat the males. As predicted by sociobiologist Robert Trivers's parental investment theory, the females are much larger than the males. Girl power is in full effect when it comes to sexual cannibalism.

Other species also engage in food-for-sex exchanges, including some ungulates (hoofed mammals such as antelopes) that defend resource-rich territories and then allow females to graze within the territory in exchange for sexual access. Chimpanzees, our closest animal cousins, also engage in this exchange. Specifically, males who share their food with females increase their mating opportunities.[14] In the human context, there are indeed many courtship rituals that involve food. For example, first dates often take place at restaurants, as do Valentine's Day celebrations and wedding anniversaries. As a matter of fact, one telltale sign of growing intimacy between a newly bonded couple is the sharing of food at a restaurant (feeding one another or allowing the other to access one's plate). There are boundless types of courtship gifts within the human context, but I will restrict my discussion to engagements rings and the offering of flowers.

There are numerous social settings where the offering of flowers has become an expected norm. Immeasurable rites of passage from the most joyous of occasions (e.g., wedding ceremonies) to the most solemn ones (e.g., funerals) incorporate flowers as an integral artifact. Other occasions wherein flowers are offered include the *quinceañera* (the coming of age of fifteen-year-old Latina girls into womanhood), sweet sixteen parties, Valentine's Day, a first date, prom night, repeat offering of flowers in a marriage, and visits to someone convalescing at a hospital. The custom of presenting flowers appears to be universal and seems to transcend cultural periods. For example, flowers have been found at a Neanderthal burial site known as Shanidar (in modern-day Iraq) dating from sixty thousand to eighty thousand years ago. In some cultures, the giving of a particular type of flowers is laden with implicit meaning. In France, if a husband were to offer his wife yellow flowers, this suggests that he is apologizing for an extramarital affair. In contrast, yellow flowers are appropriate for funerals in some Latin American countries.

Globally, cut flowers constitute a $40 billion industry. Two-thirds of flowers sold in the United States are offered to women, and two-thirds of flowers are offered as gifts.[15] Given that the majority of cut flowers have a life expectancy of a few days to up to a week (although technically they die when they are cut), this is an extraordinary business. Forty billion dollars is spent on a product that has an extremely short life span. What motivates people to engage in such a practice? When presented with flowers, individuals experience an instinctual and genuinely positive feeling, as typically captured by a Duchenne (i.e., nonfake) smile.[16] One possibility is that this is a manifestation of the biophilia hypothesis, which was discussed earlier. This might explain why flowers are central features of the courtship ritual in varied cultural settings as well as for other species, such as the male bowerbird that uses flowers to beautify its bower as a means of attracting prospective mates. Incidentally, the amount of money spent by consumers at a flower shop increases if the store is playing ambient romantic music (as opposed to pop music or no music at all).[17] If you want your man to offer you a more expensive and intricate bouquet, convince your local florist to restrict the musical playlist to Barry White songs.

Contemporary human courtships typically culminate with a marriage proposal along with the requisite engagement ring offered by a man to his prospective bride. The accepted norm in terms of how much one should spend for a diamond ring is 25 percent of one's yearly salary. Why does such a norm exist? Is it nothing but an arbitrarily sexist standard promulgated by diamond companies? The short answer is no. In the same manner that nuptial gifts in other species are used to gauge the suitor's commitment and qualities, the same can be said of engagement rings. If the offering of a flower were all that it took to convince a woman that you had serious intent regarding your prospective union, the potential for male duplicity would be limitless. On the other hand, if an engagement ring has to be "financially painful," then it serves as a means of separating the real suitors from the pretenders. The importance of diamond rings as central elements of the courtship ritual is captured in numerous popular culture settings. For example, in 2000, *Advertising Age* named De Beers Consolidated Mines' advertising slogan "A diamond is forever" as the best advertising slogan of the twentieth century. Several iconic songs attest to the importance placed on diamond rings, including "Diamonds Are a Girl's Best Friend" sung by Marilyn Monroe in the classic 1953 movie *Gentlemen Prefer Blondes* (and mimicked in Madonna's 1985 music video of her hit song "Material Girl"), as well Dame Shirley Bassey's unforgettable "Diamonds Are Forever," the title song for the 1971 James Bond movie.

Lee Cronk and Bria Dunham investigated the amount that men spend on engagement rings as well as factors that might affect the amount spent.[18] The average yearly income of the surveyed men was $41,858.20, with the average amount spent on engagement rings $3,531.72. In other words, men spent 8.44 percent of their annual incomes on the rings, which is a far cry from the 25 percent norm. The total spent on rings was positively correlated to the annual incomes of both men and women but negatively correlated to women's ages. Cronk and Dunham suggest that the size of the expenditure is thus affected by the "quality" of the individuals comprising a couple, as gauged in this study by yearly income of both parties and a prospective bride's age. One wonders whether, all other things being equal, if more attractive women might receive larger diamond rings.

Courtship gifts, including engagement rings, need not necessarily be expensive in order to signal commitment; the thought often trumps the price of the gift.[19] In many instances, women prefer a gift that is more personal and demonstrative of a man's attentive nature. "You once said that your favorite color is mauve. I also remember that you told me that you've always wanted a gourmet espresso machine. Well, there is a Lithuanian company that manufactures mauve espresso machines. I had it flown from Vilnius, and then I had it engraved with the words *I love you* using your favorite font—which, if I remember correctly, is Book Antiqua." Most women would find such a gesture much more romantic and touching than if they were offered a check for twice the amount of the romantic gift. Whereas the cost of the gift can serve as a signal of commitment, it is certainly not the sole relevant metric. This is precisely the reason that gift giving is such a dangerous land mine, as it is laden with subtle subplots. On a related note, women place a high premium on whether a marriage proposal is unique and well thought out, as it demonstrates a suitor's likely commitment.

PERFUMES AND THE POWER OF OLFACTION

Napoleon Bonaparte famously sent a message to his concubine, Josephine, in preparation of his return from the battlefield: "Je reviens en trois jours; ne te laves pas!" (I return in three days. Don't wash!) This erotic communiqué was meant to capture the intoxicating allure of smelling the body odor of one's lover. Olfaction is one of the most powerful forms of sexual signaling, and accordingly it is used by innumerable species as a central element of their courtship ritual. We tend to think that olfactory signals are crucial to many species but play a negligible role in human mating. However, evolutionary behavioral scientists have uncovered several lines of evidence that suggest otherwise. In one of the classic studies of evolutionary psychology, Steve Gangestad and Randy Thornhill found that women had highly discriminating noses. Specifically, they were asked to evaluate the olfactory pleasantness of T-shirts that had been worn by men for two nights while sleeping. The researchers also provided the men a restrictive set of instructions meant to mitigate all sources of odors other than their natural body odors (e.g., no smoking, having sex, or eating particular foods). For women who were not taking the pill and who were at the maximally fertile stage of their menstrual cycle (or close to it), the favorite scents were those of the men possessing the least amount of fluctuating asymmetry (the extent of divergence from bilateral symmetry, an example of which is facial symmetry).[20] In other words, when conception was highly likely, women's noses were sufficiently discriminating in judging the phenotypic quality of prospective suitors' visible traits . . . the nose truly knows! This astonishing finding suggests that women exhibit sensorial convergence in identifying optimal males. Whether they use their eyes or noses, they arrive at the same final mate choice.

Generally speaking, we tend to prefer mates who are similar to us (i.e., "birds of a feather flock together"). However, there is a notable exception, and again our noses are responsible for this particular evaluative process. The major histocompatibility complex (MHC) corresponds to a group of genes involved in defining an individual's immunocompetence (capacity of one's immune system to battle infections and diseases). To the extent that it pays to have an immune system that can successfully respond against the greatest number of possible challenges, sexually reproducing organisms—including humans—should prefer to mate with individuals who are highly dissimilar to them in terms of their MHC. Such a mating preference ensures that offspring will likely be born with a more varied immunological profile. Several studies have indeed confirmed that humans prefer the smell of others who are maximally dissimilar from them along the MHC.[21] Can our understanding of MHC-related mating preferences be applied in a marketing context? The obvious candidate is in the design of perfumes.

Annual perfume sales in the United States hover around $25 to $30 billion per year,[22] so the commercial implications are quite clear. What are some factors that drive consumers to purchase a particular perfume (Drakkar Noir versus Old Spice; Chanel No. 5 versus Dolce & Gabbana's Pour Femme)? In some instances, individuals purchase perfumes as a function of the celebrities who endorse them. If you are a fan of Jennifer Lopez, you are undoubtedly more likely to purchase J. Lo's Blue Glow. The branding of a perfume is an important antecedent of its likely commercial success. However, there is one undeniable biological factor that affects self-preferences of perfumes: these are intimately linked to one's MHC.[23] Specifically, we tend to prefer perfumes that are most likely to advertise our unique odors and idiosyncratic immunogenetic profiles on the mating market. Additional evidence suggests that it is indeed possible to detect specific gene expressions of the MHC when describing individuals' natural body odors.[24] Once again, the nose knows.

The "Axe effect" refers to the highly successful advertising campaign in which a man, subsequent to having sprayed himself with the body fragrance, is aggressively accosted by hoards of beautiful women. The campaign has been successful because it recognizes a key Darwinian imperative for each sex. First, its key selling point is the promise of having multiple sexual partners, which is particularly appealing to men. Second, olfaction is an important element of human mate choice, particularly for women in choosing between prospective suitors.[25] Interestingly, the so-called Axe effect seems to actually exist. In a recent study, men were sprayed either with a deodorant imbued with an active concoction (flavor oil and an antimicrobial constituent) or with a nonactive version. Subsequently, they were asked to provide several self-evaluations (e.g., self-confidence and self-attractiveness). Then short videos were recorded of the male participants, which were subsequently viewed by female raters, who rated the men along several metrics (confidence and attractiveness). Incredibly, not only did the men who received the active deodorant provide higher ratings of self-confidence but also women rated these men as more attractive (based on viewing the short video clips).[26] Incidentally, if you wish to improve your olfactory signature without spending money on perfumes and deodorants, simply reduce your consumption of red meat.[27] In this case, our carnivorous instinct conflicts with our instinctual desire to emit a maximally pleasing body odor.

HIGH HEELS

Men collect cars. Women collect shoes. Imelda Marcos, former First Lady of the Philippines, was reputed to own one of the world's most extensive shoe collections. One of the products most bought by compulsive buyers—90 percent of whom are women (see chapter 9 for additional details)—are shoes; specifically, shoes that beautify the silhouette, as is the case with stilettos. The alluring Marilyn Monroe, known for her beguiling beauty and sensuality, apparently once stated "I don't know who invented the high heel, but all men owe a lot to him." Pornographic actresses, strippers, and female bikini contestants almost always wear stilettos as a means of flaunting their sexuality. In chapter 2 of her book *Stripping, Sex, and Popular Culture*, Catherine M. Roach reports on the use of high heels as part of the exotic dancer's trade. Even though strippers complain of the physical pain and possible injuries that can occur when wearing high heels, the women are quick to point out their importance. When asked if she might prefer to wear shoes with smaller heels, one stripper replied, "No, I don't think so, because I think they're sexy. I think high heels are very sexy." When another stripper was asked whether she missed working as a stripper, she retorted, "I miss the shoes!" She then added, "If bars allow less than three inches, they're stupid."[28] She further explained how high heels not only improve the appearance of a woman's body but they also alter the way that she sways (in a manner that is visually alluring to men).

In the 2005 British movie *Kinky Boots*, an owner of a floundering family-owned shoe factory decides, upon meeting a transvestite singer, to begin manufacturing high-heeled boots for the transvestite niche market. Thinking that comfort and functionality might be important attributes in such boots, the first trial product consists of a flat heel that lacks the requisite sexual oomph. Upon seeing the sexless prototype, his transvestite partner utters, "Look to the heel, young man. The sex is in the heel." This is followed by a rather astute comment by an elderly shoemaker: "Stilettos require constant balance from the upper leg causing the muscles of the backside to tense and appear pert and ready for mating." Is the old shoemaker on to something?

The wearing of high heels hoists the derriere by approximately 20 to 30 degrees as a function of the heel's size. The larger the heel is, the greater the lift. As we age, gravity becomes a growing nemesis to our figures, especially for women. Perky body parts are associated with youth, sagging parts with age. Accordingly, any product that can "reverse" the effects of gravity by yielding a more youthful-looking body is an easy seller, be it high heels or push-up bras. In addition to serving as a Gestalt cue for youth, a raised backside is attractive to men because it mimics lordosis, the sexually receptive position that mammalian females adopt prior to mating.[29] Also, high heels cater to men's preference for longer legs; a recent study found that both sexes preferred individuals whose legs were 5 percent longer than the average.[30]

In addition to the perceptual changes associated with women's figures when wearing high heels, might it be the case that a woman's gait is differentially attractive as a function of the shoes that she is wearing? Incredibly, this is precisely what two Japanese scientists found. Specifically, in judging women's gaits, men evaluated those wearing high heels to be more feminine and physically attractive than their counterparts walking in loafers.[31] Returning to exotic dancers, who make a living out of moving seductively in high heels: the amount of tips strippers generate is linked to their menstrual cycles. When maximally fertile, they received the largest tips. This effect can be due to the fact that the strippers engaged in more sexually enticing dances when maximally fertile (thus garnering larger tips). Or patrons might have picked up subtle cues in the dancers so that they were more likely to select ovulating strippers for lap dances. This was the first study to demonstrate a relationship between a woman's menstrual cycle and her income within a service industry.[32]

To some, this whole discussion is offensive, as it objectifies women as creatures of sexual enticement. Furthermore, given that the wearing of high heels leads to numerous types of podiatric and orthopedic injuries,[33] detractors of high heels argue that this cruel fashion accoutrement is yet another means by which men abuse women. It might surprise the makers of Manolo Blahnik, Jimmy Choo, and Christian Louboutin high-heeled shoes to know that they are part of a conspiracy to defeat women. Women wear high heels because they feel sexy and desirable when doing so, and it happens to arouse men's evolved visual preferences as well. The reality is that both sexes doggedly seek to impress one another in the mating arena, even when such efforts can be self-injurious. Men assume great physical risks (see chapter 9) as a means of signaling their value as a mate to women, be it in the extreme sports in which they participate, the occupational hazards that they are willing to assume, or the intrasexual violence in which they partake. No one proclaims that there is a conspiracy that imposes these dangerous behaviors on men as a means to get them killed. The innate need to be attractive on the mating market is a key driver of the human experience. Individuals are willing to assiduously pursue the optimal strategy that makes them stand out. The wearing of high heels is but one such strategy out of an endless repertoire of beautification rituals.

Notwithstanding the fact that the wearing of high heels does cause injuries, Maria Angela Cerruto, an Italian urologist and self-professed lover of heeled shoes, conducted a study with her colleagues and found that the wearing of heels improved women's pelvic floor muscle activity. Women might be interested to know that such an improved capacity can result in better sex, even though some might be dismayed to find out that high heels and good sex might be positively correlated! Cerruto and her colleagues proclaimed, "As paladin of all women who love heeled shoes, I tried to find something healthy in them, and at the end I reached my goal."[34]

Whereas the wearing of high heels is largely a win-win state of affairs (it titillates men's visual preferences and is a potential conduit to improved sex for women), there is a potential downside to wearing high heels, namely, the possibility of towering over one's male partner. Height is a trait that is highly desired by women. However, the most crucial element to this ubiquitous preference is that women abhor dating men who are shorter than they are. As a matter of fact, a study exploring this exact issue found that the woman was taller than her male partner in only 1 of 720 couples.[35] It is not so much that men should be taller than a particular threshold, but for most women, towering over a prospective suitor is a deal breaker. I am assuming that for celebrity couples such as Tom Cruise and Katie Holmes or Nicole Kidman and Keith Urban that the wearing of high heels is forbidden, as the ladies might otherwise dwarf their husbands!

CLOTHES MAKE THE MAN . . . AND THE WOMAN

Both men and women use clothes as a form of sexual signaling. Women are much more likely to use their attire to highlight physical attributes, and men are correspondingly more likely to use clothes as a status symbol. Is it true that the clothes make the man? There is a simple way to test this proposition. Take the same man and have him wear one of several attires, each of which signals a different level of socioeconomic status. For example, you could place a man in a McDonald's uniform or in medical scrubs. Alternatively, you could have him wear a sleeveless shirt and unfashionable jeans versus dressing him in a high-powered suit along with an expensive watch. Women are then asked to rate how physically attractive the man is across the various status conditions. Not surprisingly, the same man is construed as much more attractive when wearing high-status garb. Furthermore, the likelihood of women being willing to initiate any one of six types of relationships with the man in question, from the most casual to the most intimate, is positively correlated in all six instances with the status that is signaled by the man's apparel. When the same manipulation is administered to men using female models, men generally care less about the social status of women's attires.[36] For most men, whether a woman is wearing Prada or Wal-Mart knock-offs is utterly irrelevant. However, any garment that accentuates a woman's curves is noticed. This is not something that is specific to contemporary Western cultures. Take the corset, an accoutrement from the past. The average corset creates an hourglass figure,[37] which typically falls within the near-universal male preference for a waist-to-hip ratio of 0.68 to 0.72.[38]

Over the past nine decades, several scholars have noted a correlation between economic conditions and hemlines,[39] the so-called Hemline Index: as the economy strengthens, the miniskirts come out. On a related note, the Lipstick Index, as put forth in 2001 by Leonard Lauder, the former chief executive office of Estée Lauder, suggests that as the economy worsens, lipstick sales amplify.[40] Finally, Elizabeth Semmelhack, curator of the Bata Shoe Museum in Toronto and author of *Heights of Fashion: A History of the Elevated Shoe*, has noted that the height of heels increases during difficult economic times.[41] Several plausible arguments have been offered to explain these related phenomena, including women's desire to signal confidence or austerity (in the case of the Hemline Index), and to self-indulge or engage in escapism when facing challenging times. However, none recognizes the possibility that evolutionary-based biological forces might otherwise explain these intriguing relationships between fashion styles and economic conditions.

Several evolutionary-minded scholars have argued that the link between economic conditions and women's attire (e.g., as captured via the length of hemlines) is shaped by female intrasexual rivalry. In one study, women's fashions as represented in *UK Vogue* between 1916 and 1999 were examined.[42] Tougher economic climates, which typically engender greater intrasexual rivalry, yielded fashion trends that were less conservative (contrary to the Hemline Index). Physical attributes are most likely to be used by women as a form of intrasexual competition, including in the economic sphere. In a similar vein, Nigel Barber, a fellow *Psychology Today* blogger, uncovered a negative correlation between the length of skirts and the number of educated women in society (in any given period).[43]

COSMETICS

The use of cosmetics as a means of beautification has been documented for several millennia, dating as early as the Sumerian and ancient Egyptian civilizations, and more recently to the Roman Empire.[44] Men have at times applied cosmetics (e.g., prior to heading off to battle), but instances when men use cosmetics as a form of beautification are quite rare.[45] Generally, women are overwhelmingly more likely to use cosmetics, and this statement holds true irrespective of cultural setting or time period. Very powerful women including pharaohs, queens, heads of state, and senior diplomats have worn cosmetics (e.g., Cleopatra, Queen Elizabeth II, Benazir Bhutto, Angela Merkel, Madeleine Albright, Hillary Clinton, and Condoleezza Rice). I accessed *Fortune* magazine's 2009 list of women CEOs of Fortune 1000 companies.[46] Twenty-eight female CEOs are listed, twelve of whom had links to their photos. Every one of these exceptionally powerful and highly accomplished women was wearing makeup.

The banal truth is that women wear cosmetics because it increases their attractiveness.[47] Furthermore, women who wear cosmetics are judged by both sexes as possessing more positive personality traits[48] and are judged to be healthier. In a recent field experiment (i.e., conducted in the real world rather than in the lab), women wearing makeup were approached more often and more quickly when at a bar, as compared to alternate days when they showed up without any makeup.[49] On a related note, waitresses who wore makeup were more likely to receive tips as well as a greater tip amount as compared with when they did not wear makeup.[50] Several reasons have been proposed to explain the beautification effect of cosmetics. Some have argued that cosmetics mimic cues of sexual arousal and sexual interest (e.g., the reddening of the lips and cheeks, eye makeup to mimic dilated pupils). In some instances, cosmetics are used to create a more youthful looking face (e.g., to hide wrinkles or age spots), although younger women will at times wear makeup to look older and thus appear more nubile. Since clear and smooth skin is considered a universal metric of beauty, cosmetics serve to hide oily skin, blemishes, and acne. Cosmetics are also used to create greater facial symmetry, which is a proxy for beauty. As a matter of fact, symmetric facial and body decorations increase facial attractiveness, and perhaps more tellingly they also increase the perceived attractiveness of abstract artistic renditions.[51] Richard Russell has shown that women use cosmetics to accentuate the luminance contrast between their eyes and mouth, and the facial regions adjacent to these.[52] Specifically, the skin around the eyes and mouth is generally lighter, and this contrast is more pronounced in women. The application of cosmetics further accentuates this contrast in luminance, yielding a more feminine face.

Cosmetic companies around the world promote their skin care products using terms such as "age-defying," "wrinkle busting," "anti-aging," "age spot removal," "youthful smooth skin," and "blemish removal." Woodbury Soap's slogan "A skin you love to touch" reflects the importance of clear and smooth skin. I am unaware of a culture in which these key selling points are not operative. This is not due to arbitrary beauty standards; skin quality conveys a lot of valuable information about prospective female mates. For example, fewer blemishes, smoother skin, and less hairy skin signal lower androgen and higher estrogen levels. Eighty-three percent of women with acne had polycystic ovary syndrome. Interestingly, the quality of a woman's skin fluctuates across her menstrual cycle in a manner that highlights its crucial role within the mating arena.[53]

Not only are cosmetics a powerful means to beautify one's self, but also specific colors are particularly enticing. Of all lipstick colors, perhaps none is as alluring as red, as exemplified by the sultry actress Scarlett Johansson. It is instructive to note that *lipstick* translates to *rouge à lèvres* (red to lips) in French. More generally, red seems to be a color that is linked to romance (e.g., Valentine's Day) and sexuality (e.g., red lingerie). Beautiful and alluring women are often cloaked in red accoutrements, as poignantly captured in popular culture (e.g., in the 1984 movie *The Woman in Red* starring Gene Wilder, Gilda Radner, and Kelly LeBrock as well as in Chris de Burgh's 1986 worldwide hit song "Lady in Red"). Why might this be the case? The biological argument proposes that for many species—including our close primate cousins—red is a strong marker of estrus (e.g., engorged genitalia). In the human context, one visual marker of female sexual arousal involves the reddening of various erogenous regions of the body. Therefore, various cultural rituals of reddening might be derived from an original visual penchant that men hold for this particular color. Using this logic, psychologists Andrew J. Elliot and Daniela Niesta conducted five studies that demonstrated that men find women who are peripherally associated with the color red as more attractive than the same women void of this association (or associated with another color). This held true for measures of attractiveness, sexual desirability, dating intention, and amount of money willing to spend on a date, but it did not apply to their ratings of intelligence, kindness, and overall likeability. Hence, the effect does not generalize across measures;

it is restricted to mating-related variables. Incidentally, women did not exhibit the "red effect" when evaluating other women, suggesting that the penchant for red is a male-specific preference.[54]

HAIR

Why do many women past a certain age seem to have roughly the same short hairstyle? In many instances, elderly women who have long hair are viewed in a pejorative manner (e.g., the evil witch). The answer is frankly quite simple. As we age, the quality of our hair worsens. It loses its luster, shine, and thickness, and becomes more brittle. It is no coincidence that shampoo companies display young women who possess extraordinarily radiant, thick, and silky hair. Accordingly, it makes sense to reduce the amplitude of a signal that otherwise advertises a trait of deteriorating phenotypic quality. Of note, women who are single and who do not have any children have longer and better quality hair, and women in better health sport longer hair.[55] Not surprisingly, men are quite apt at making the link between a woman's long hair and good health.[56] Taken together, these findings explain why in many religions—most notably Islam—women are required to cover their hair with a hijab. Whereas this is supposedly a divine edict meant to ensure female modesty, the reality is that hair is a sexually enticing trait and, accordingly, strongly patriarchal societies find very "earthly" means of controlling women's ability to advertise their sexuality.

Role-playing is a common means by which consenting adults explore their sexual fantasies. Some of the most frequent archetypes include the vixen nurse and the heroic fireman. A central feature in such sexual games involves the wearing of wigs. However, these are much more likely to be worn by women than by men. Wigs come in all varieties, be they short or long, straight or curly, or blonde, brunette, or red. Not surprisingly, wigs are chosen in a manner that should drastically alter a woman's look. If she has long dark hair, she might wear a short blonde wig. The goal is to galvanize men's desires for sexual variety. Since the same proclivity is not as pronounced in women, dark-haired men do not typically wear blond wigs in the bedroom. The same principle applies to hair coloring. Women are much more likely to use hair colorants, not only to hide their graying hair but also for radical color departures. Again, this is a likely aesthetic response to men's desire for sexual variety, at least in the instances when coupled women engage in the practice.

SHOPPING FOR GOOD GENES: WHEN OVULATING, DRESS PROVOCATIVELY

Females in a large number of species are receptive to mating during short periods of estrus. When in heat, they will exhibit conspicuous advertisements of their sexual receptivity, be it via olfactory and visual signals or by increased sexual soliciting. Female baboons, for example, display their sexual receptivity via an engorgement of their genitalia. Males of some species have evolved the Flehmen response, which is a type of facial grimace meant to gauge where a female is in terms of her heat cycle (by sniffing the air for pheromones). It has generally been assumed that women experience cryptic ovulation, meaning that their ovulatory status is concealed to the outside world. It is thought that this phenomenon has evolved because it ensures that a woman's male partner will maintain his interest in her throughout the cycle, promoting the evolution of long-term bonding, which is needed for bi-parental species. Several studies have found that while a woman's ovulatory status is somewhat concealed, subtle morphological and physiological signals as well as not-so-subtle behavioral cues provide hints to a woman's menstrual status to prying eyes and noses. For example, when a woman is ovulating, her skin quality is at its most beautiful, her face and breasts are more symmetric, and she exudes a more pleasant smell.[57]

On the behavioral end, when maximally fertile, women advertise themselves with greater aplomb via various forms of beautification. Eric Stenstrom and I contrasted women's beautification practices across the luteal (nonfertile) and fertile phases of their menstrual cycles. Women reported much greater beautification-related behaviors (e.g., wearing sexy clothes) during the fertile phase of their menstrual cycles.[58] Several other studies have found equally compelling evidence of women's stronger desire to promote themselves on the mating market when maximally fertile.[59] It is important to point out that most women engage in these behaviors without any conscious awareness of the relevant evolutionary forces. Rather, women will speak of feeling "sexier," "less bloated," and "more self-confident" during their maximally fertile window. It is these positive feelings that translate into the subsequent pronounced desire to advertise one's self on the mating market. Incidentally, the importance of a woman's menstrual cycle to her daily behaviors has not gone unnoticed by enterprising software entrepreneurs, several of whom have developed iPhone applications to help men track the menstrual cycle of the women in their lives (see, for example, PMS Buddy and MyMate).

DECEPTIVE CONSUMER SIGNALING

Countless species engage in various forms of deceptive signaling (or false advertising). In some instances, the fake signal has evolved for the purposes of survival, be it as a means of obtaining food or in the hope of avoiding becoming someone's food. The alligator snapping turtle uses a lure that looks like a worm and protrudes from its mouth to attract unsuspecting fish. Some nonvenomous snakes have evolved coloration that seeks to mimic aposematic warnings (cautions to stay clear). Rhymes are used to allow people to differentiate between truly dangerous snakes and their mimics (e.g., "Red on yellow, kill a fellow; red on black, friend

of Jack."). In other instances, the deceptive signals are used for the purposes of gaining an advantage in the mating game. In this sense, males and
females in many sexually reproducing species are involved in an evolutionary arms race. One sex (typically males) evolves ways by which to
dupe the females of their quality, while females evolve counterstrategies
to differentiate between the cheats and the truly fit suitors.

This Machiavellian dance manifests itself in countless ways in the
consumer arena. Women wear push-up bras, breast padding, the booty-
pop "butt bra" (to elevate their buttocks), and high heels; they apply
makeup to enhance their perceived skin quality and constitute 90 percent of patients who seek plastic surgeries. All these elements work as a
means of altering (faking) key features of their bodies and faces. On the
other hand, men purchase all sorts of sham luxury items (e.g., counterfeit Rolex watches) to deceptively fake their social status, as well as lie
about their incomes and occupational achievements. An old friend of
mine who owned an Audi once visited a dealership to obtain the
insignia of a more luxurious model, with the expressed intention of
having it placed on his car. He might have owned "only" the A4 model,
but he was hoping to signal to the world that he drove the fancier A6. I
doubt that many women would engage in this form of deceptive signaling, as the use of luxury cars to signal one's social status is largely a
male strategy. I am willing to bet that men constitute the great majority
of individuals who seek fake diplomas from "correspondence universities." Fake wedding bands are at times worn by single men under the
assumption that married men are more desirable (although this folk
belief was refuted in a 2003 study[60]). The bottom line is that many men
and women are more than willing to engage in endless forms of consumer-related deception if it augments their standing in the mating
market. In this case, it seems that the end (reproductive success) justifies
the means (deceptive consumer signaling).

Canal Street in New York is the mecca of fake goods. Every imaginable "luxury" item from belts to wallets to purses to clothing items can

be purchased for a small fraction of the genuine brands' price. A recent 2007 OECD report estimated the global size of the counterfeit market in 2005 at $200 billion, a figure estimated to be larger than the Gross Domestic Product of 150 national economies.[61] The International AntiCounterfeiting Coalition estimates the annual value at a much higher $600 billion, with roughly 4 percent of this total reserved for luxury items.[62] The need to falsify one's standing on mating attributes of evolutionary import via the use of deceptive products is a human universal. Cultural traditions might at times alter the expression of the attribute to be faked. For example, male social status might be signaled via a Ferrari in Western countries and via the number of cattle owned by Maasai men. But the sex-specificity of the deceptive signaling is the same across all cultures; namely, men and women will be more likely to fake social status and appearance, respectively. Another instance in which these deceptions manifest themselves is in personal ads and online chats. Men lie about their height, income, occupation, and social status; women lie about their weight, age, and appearance.[63] Deceptive signaling is what causes people to drive with their car windows closed in the stifling summer heat even though they do not have air conditioning, chat on fake cell phones, and fill their grocery carts with extremely expensive food items and then abandon the cart quietly once they've finished parading through the aisles.[64]

CONCLUSION

Given that we are a sexually reproducing species, it is not surprising that many consumer purchases are related to sex. Men and women use a wide range of products to ameliorate their standing on the mating market. As we've seen, men are much more likely to purchase luxury sports cars (as a means of signaling their status), and women are much more likely to beautify themselves (via cosmetics and provocative attire). Many consumer purchases serve as central features of the courtship ritual, including the offering of flowers and engagement rings. Sex-specific hormones have a powerful effect in the consumer arena. Men's testosterone levels rise markedly when engaging in an act of conspicuous consumption (e.g., driving a Porsche), whereas women's menstrual cycles and associated fluctuating hormones shape their desire to advertise themselves. Our sexual nature leaves an indelible mark on our consumer choices and preferences.

CHAPTER 4

WE ARE FAMILY

Blood is thicker than water.

An ounce of blood is worth more than a pound of friendship. (Spanish proverb)

In time of test, family is best. (Burmese proverb)

Treat your family like friends and your friends like family.[1]

African wild dogs live in tight kin-based packs. They have been known to display extraordinary levels of devotion and investment toward old or injured members of their pack. Similar kin-based altruism has been documented in insects (e.g., social ants), birds (e.g., wild turkeys), fish (e.g., Atlantic salmon), and mammals (e.g., monkeys, apes, hyenas, lions, ground squirrels, and allomaternal elephants; this last example refers to the provision of maternal care to a calf by family members other than its biological mother). Of course, humans are social animals who develop tight family liaisons as well. Why would anyone risk her life to save a sibling, cousin, parent, or offspring? If the Darwinian imperative is for organisms to care solely for their own survival, then costly forms of altruism seem to run counter to this desire. However, once we recognize that evolution "cares" about the propagation of genes, it makes perfect sense for organisms to invest in those with whom they share genes.

As described in the above epigraphs, cross-cultural proverbs repeatedly hail the unique nature of familial bonds. That said, the importance of families could be seen in nearly all forms of cultural creations and products. Some of the most gripping literary narratives revolve around family dynamics, be it biblical stories (Cain and Abel), Greek tragedies (*Oedipus Rex*), or Shakespearean plays (*Hamlet*). The majority of popular sitcoms over the past four decades have taken place within the context of a family. Some of these family-based shows include *The Adventures of Ozzie and Harriet* (1952–1966), *Leave It to Beaver* (1957– 1963), *My Three Sons* (1960–1972), *The Beverly Hillbillies* (1962– 1971), *The Addams Family* (1964–1966), *The Munsters* (1964–1966), *The Brady Bunch* (1969–1974), *The Partridge Family* (1970–1974), *All in the Family* (1971–1979), *Sanford and Son* (1972–1977), *The Jeffersons* (1975–1985), *Family Ties* (1982–1989), *The Cosby Show* (1984–1992), *Growing Pains* (1985–1992), *Married . . . with Children* (1987–1997), *Roseanne* (1988–1997), *Family Matters* (1989–1998), *The Simpsons* (1989–today), *Home Improvement* (1991–1999), *Malcolm in the Middle* (2000–2006), *Arrested Development* (2003–2006), and *Modern Family* (2009–today). Family dynamics are also at the root of numerous movies (*Guess Who's Coming to Dinner*, *The Godfather*, *The Shining*, *Sophie's Choice*, *Hannah and Her Sisters*, *Moonstruck*, *Father of the Bride*, *Meet the Parents*, *It Runs in the Family*, *The Family Stone*, *Little Miss Sunshine*, *Dan in Real Life*, and *Four Christmases*).

Family relationships are central to numerous advertising slogans. These include "Shouldn't your baby be a Gerber baby?" (Gerber Foods), "Kid tested. Mother approved" (Kix breakfast cereal), and "Choosy moms choose Jif," which was subsequently changed to the more politically correct, "Choosy moms, and dads, choose Jif" (Jif Peanut Butter). In each case, the slogan targets parents' innate instinct to invest in their children. The importance of families to the human experience has not been lost on those who create religious narratives and religious institutions (as in Father; Sister; Mother Superior; Brother; and Father, Son, and the Holy Spirit). Members of the same college fraternity or sorority are referred to as fraternity brothers and sorority sisters. In fact, the Latin etymology of *fraternity* and *sorority* is *frater* and *soror* ("brother" and "sister," respectively). In the street vernacular, terms such as *brother*, *bro*, *cuz*, and *son* are commonly used between nonkin to reflect strong affiliational bonds. The expression "brothers in arms" refers to soldiers who fight on the same side (e.g., the HBO television series *Band of Brothers* chronicled the lives of a group of soldiers during World War II). Fellow soldiers are described in kin-based terms precisely because of the levels of altruism that they are each willing to provide to one another, which is otherwise typically expected to occur between family members.

KIN SELECTION: IT'S A FAMILY AFFAIR

Charles Darwin thought that natural selection operated at the level of the individual organism. As such, it was difficult for him to provide definitive explanations for the endless documented cases, spanning many species (including humans), of costly altruistic acts toward one's kin. He certainly knew that traits were heritable; however he was unfamiliar with Mendelian genetics or with the units of heredity, namely DNA. Accordingly, he did not possess the necessary knowledge to recognize the gene-centric view of natural selection. Bill Hamilton, an Oxford biologist who tragically died of Malaria in 2000 while on an expedition to Congo to test his theory about the origins of HIV, solved this cross-species puzzle. Hamilton did so by moving the level at which selection operates, from the organism (as per Darwin's theorizing) to a gene-centric perspective. In other words, if the gene is the most fundamental unit on which selection pressures operate, then kin-based altruism makes perfect sense. This mechanism known as *kin selection* was formally described in highly sophisticated mathematical detail in a paper Hamilton published in 1964.[2] Other evolutionary scientists had intuited this fundamental insight, albeit using less rigorous formalisms prior to Hamilton's seminal work. This was the case with the British geneticist J. B. S. Haldane, who had famously remarked when asked if he would save a brother who was drowning: "No, but I would to save two brothers or eight cousins."[3] Since brothers share on average half their genes, and first cousins share one-eighth of theirs, Haldane was providing the "genetic break-even" points that would justify his laying down his life (from a gene-centric perspective).

Kin selection is related to a broader mechanism known as *inclusive fitness*. In biological terms, fitness refers to the extension of one's genes. The most obvious way to increase one's fitness is to have children, and individuals can augment their direct fitness via reproduction (reproductive fitness). On the other hand, individuals can also boost the propagation of their genes by investing in those with whom they are related. If your daughter, your grandson, or your nephew were to have a child, this child would be indirectly increasing your own fitness. Hence, this form of indirect fitness is part and parcel of the more general term known as inclusive fitness.

One direct implication of kin selection is that organisms including humans will provide differential investments to kin versus nonkin, as well as providing greater investment to those who are closer kin.[4] Numerous studies have indeed established this fact, several of which are relevant to the consumer (spending) context. For example, support for higher education is greater for biological children as compared with stepchildren (when comparing between families in which both parents are biological with families in which one parent is a stepparent).[5] Not surprisingly, stepsiblings are less educated than biological children within a given family.[6] The distribution of hypothetical lottery earnings is correlated to genetic relatedness and is shaped by the extent (if any) of paternity uncertainty of a given relationship.[7] Genetic relatedness also predicts the pattern of bequeathing (in wills),[8] as well as the extent of bereavement that is felt by twins when one of them passes away.[9] Specifically, it is more painful to lose a monozygotic co-twin than it is to lose a dizygotic one. Full siblings are more likely than half-siblings or stepsiblings to know whether their siblings are alive or dead (this serves as a measure of closeness).[10] Genetic relatedness also predicts the likelihood of helpfulness, especially when the prospective recipient is facing a perilous situation.[11] Within a Mormon community, full siblings feel greater affiliation with one another than do half-siblings.[12] Furthermore, full siblings engage in greater social investment with one another than do half-siblings.[13] Across several studied cultures, the amount of physical pain that individuals are willing to incur (in order to provide a reward to a prospective recipient) is linked to genetic relatedness.[14] Finally, there is evidence that family-run firms generate superior performance,[15] perhaps in part due to the greater cooperative and intense efforts that are expended when the beneficiaries of the labor are one's kin.

My former doctoral student Tripat Gill and I applied kin selection theory to predict how gift expenditures would be allocated between givers and recipients.[16] We hypothesized that the amount spent on a gift would be distributed in line with the genetic relatedness (r) between givers and recipients (average percentage of genes shared between two individuals). Specifically, genetically closer recipients would receive a larger share of the budget than their more distant counterparts. For any individual, his/her r scores with kin are as follows: parent (r = 0.50), sibling (r = 0.50), grandparent (r = 0.25), uncle (r = 0.25), aunt (r = 0.25), half-sibling (r = 0.25), first cousin (r = 0.125), identical twin (r = 1.0), stepparent (r = 0), step-sibling (r = 0). As predicted, we obtained a positive correlation between genetic relatedness and the amount of money to be spent on the next gift. The means across the participants were $73.12, $19.03, and $18.56 for close (r = 0.50), moderate (r = 0.25), and distant (r = 0.125) kin, respectively. Ergo, people differentiated between close kin and other kin (i.e., moderate and distant kin received roughly the same projected gift expenditures).

I end this section with a brief discussion of organ donations, as these literally constitute the gift of life, and as such the differential favoritism displayed toward kin should be particularly evident in such a context. On season 5 of *Curb Your Enthusiasm* in the episode titled "Lewis Needs a Kidney," Larry David (co-creator of *Seinfeld*) and his friend Jeff Greene (played by Jeff Garlin) debate about who will have to step up and help their friend (Richard Lewis) who needs a live kidney donation. The comedic thread to the plot rests on the fact that neither man is particularly keen on being the altruist, and as such they use the "eeny, meeny, miny, moe" rhyme to decide who will donate a kidney. However, even this solution proves difficult to implement, as the two friends cannot agree whether the person who is "it" (in the riddle) is the one that must donate the organ or is the one who is safe from doing so. Of course, this plotline works well because it is rooted in the Darwinian fact that such a gift of life is extraordinarily more likely to occur between kin. From a kin selection perspective, it is expected that organ donations, especially those arising from living donors, are overwhelmingly most likely to be offered to one's family members. The data certainly supports this. Over a two-year period (2000–2002), of 11,672 living donations performed in the United States, only 31 were anonymous ones (i.e., to strangers).[17] In a more recent study of 362 individuals who had signed up to be living organ donors, 232 were family members of the recipient, 95 were spouses, and 35 were "other unrelated" (one would naturally assume most of these are close friends, not strangers).[18] In 1988, less than 1 percent of kidney transplants were from living unrelated donors. By 1997, this number had grown but still remained low at 5 percent.[19] It is clear that the costly gift of life is much more likely to be dispensed to one's family members, as fully predicted by kin selection.

WEDDINGS: THE JOINING OF TWO FAMILIES

Of the key rites of passage in an individual's life, a wedding is possibly the most important in bringing family members and friends together. The average number of guests at an American wedding is 164.[20] This figure is quite telling, as it comes very close to the upper limit of group sizes in which we've evolved in our ancestral environments. The biological anthropologist Robin Dunbar has argued that for much of our evolutionary history, we were unlikely to have interacted with more than 150 close individuals.[21] In other words, our social networks have always been very tight and cohesive units. Some of you might recall Robert De Niro's character announcing to his prospective son-in-law (played by Ben Stiller) in *Meet the Parents* that he was moving his son-in-law into his circle of trust. Well, Dunbar's number of 150 can be viewed as the outer layer of the concentric circles of trust. The people whom we invite to our weddings constitute a gathering of our band of close allies (kin and nonkin), and in this sense we are re-creating a social reality that stems from our evolutionary past.

Weddings are replete with numerous other indications of our evolved kin-based psychology. For example, the breakdown of the 164 guests is likely indicative of several Darwinian realities associated with how we've evolved to treat kin of varying levels of genetic relatedness, as well as friends of varying levels of intimacy. For both the bride and groom, a greater number of family members from the maternal side will typically attend (in light of paternal uncertainty). Moreover, the monetary value of gifts stemming from the maternal sides of the bride and groom will be greater than the corresponding one from the paternal side. Finally, I posit that genetically closer relatives will be seated closer to the host table; also, family members from the maternal sides will be on average seated closer to the host table than their paternal counterparts. Seating arrangements are powerful signals of intimacy, as they advertise the importance that a particular individual holds in relation to the bride or groom.[22] I am personally aware of at least one family member who had an acrimonious altercation with her sister because she felt slighted by where she was seated at her nephew's wedding.

This differential closeness felt more by the maternal side should manifest itself in uncountable familial settings. For example, I predict that maternal aunts are more likely to wet-nurse their nephews and nieces than are paternal aunts (again, because of paternity uncertainty), which supports research that has found that maternal aunts provide greater care.[23] I have some anecdotal evidence in support of my hypothesis. My parents both come from very large families. My father has nine sisters and one brother, and my mother has six sisters (I am unsure how many are currently alive as most do not live in Canada, and we are rarely in touch). Interestingly, several of my maternal aunts have proclaimed that my survival as a child somehow rested on the fact that they had nursed me, even if I am unsure of the veracity of these claims. No such proclamation has ever come from my paternal aunts. Incidentally, in Arabic, there are distinct terms for paternal and maternal aunts and uncles. Paternity uncertainty rears its ugly head yet again.

TOY GIFTS AND THE ADAPTIVE VALUE OF PLAY

Parental investment comes in many forms, although none generates as much excitement to a child as when offered a new toy. Your children are unlikely to show you much gratitude for the sleepless nights that you've endured, the innumerable diapers that you've changed, the breast-feeding, and the endless other ways by which you've provided parental care. However, give your child a new toy, and watch the love and appreciation flow in your direction. In 2005, retail sales of toys in the United States totaled $21.3 billion.[24] Many aspects of toys can be analyzed from an evolutionary perspective. Fundamentally, to the extent that such gifts constitute a symbol of parental investment, they fall within the purview of kin selection. This does not imply that we possess a gene to offer toys. Rather, it simply means that this form of parental gift giving constitutes another form of parental care.

A second way by which evolutionary theory is relevant to the study of toys is their supposed role in the gender socialization of children. Social constructivists have often argued that one of the earliest sources of such socialization occurs via the sex-specific types of toys that are offered to young boys and girls. Little Christopher is offered a dark-colored and menacing-looking male action figure hero (e.g., GI Joe), whereas little Christina receives a pink-colored and feminine-looking Barbie doll. Subsequently, the parents provide differential patterns of encouragement to their children in terms of the appropriate ways to interact with the toys. Christopher is encouraged to play rough with his new toy; Christina is invited to play nice with hers. This early form of gender socialization apparently continues in an unabated fashion throughout the child's developmental stages, resulting in the eventual gender roles. This is a nice storyline, albeit it is fully removed from reality as well as any semblance of common sense. Toys exist in their particular forms because they cater to universal sex-specific toy preferences. Toy companies are in the business of knowing such facts, and accordingly they have successfully marketed products around the world that are consistent with evolved play preferences.

Congenital adrenal hyperplasia (CAH) is an endocrinological disorder that can result in the masculinization of girls' morphological features (e.g., enlarged clitoris) and behavioral patterns (e.g., increased likelihood of engaging in rough-and-tumble play). Congenital adrenal hyperplasia provides an opportunity to explore whether toy preferences are socially constructed or are driven by innate sex differences. It turns out that little girls who suffer from CAH exhibit an increased preference for male-specific toys (e.g., cars and fire engines) and a decreased preference for female-specific toys (e.g., dolls and kitchen supplies).[25] What about boys? Might boys also display a differential level of sex-specific play behavior as a function of how masculinized they are? In this case, rather than using CAH as an agent of masculinization, one can study normal populations by exploring individuals' finger lengths. Specifically, the relative lengths of the index and ring fingers known as the 2D:4D ratio, is a sexually dimorphic trait such that men on average have smaller ratios than women. In other words, the difference in finger length between the index (2D) and ring (4D) fingers is more pronounced in men than it is in women. It is thought that this sex difference is due to the differential exposure in utero to sex-specific androgens (testosterone).[26] How one scores on a masculinization-feminization continuum is captured in part by his or her digit ratio. Returning to play behavior, the sex-typed play of preschool boys is negatively correlated to their digit ratios; the more masculinized their digit ratios (as captured by a smaller ratio), the more masculinized their play behaviors.[27] Two separate hormone-based studies, using both clinical and nonclinical samples, have arrived at the same conclusion: children's play preferences and play behaviors are rooted in physiological realities that have little if anything to do with socialization. The proverbial final nail in the coffin, of the premise that toys are powerful agents of gender socialization, stems from studies that found that several species of monkeys (vervet and rhesus) exhibit sex-specific toy preferences that are akin to those of human children.[28] Unless social constructivists wish to argue that parent monkeys display the same "arbitrary and sexist" stereotypes in socializing their offspring, this nurture premise is dead.

Why do children play? As a matter of fact, why do so many mammalian species, especially those with a long developmental period, seem to engage in incessant frolicking? Several theories have been proposed regarding the adaptive nature of play, the most compelling of which argues that play is a means of preparing for future unexpected contingencies and serves as a low-risk forum for trying out various novel behavioral and social strategies.[29] Whether playing chase games that mimic predator-prey interactions, engaging in roughhousing as a means of mimicking future intrasexual combats, or in the unique case of human infants engaging in pretend play by assuming adult social roles (e.g., playing house or playing doctor), juvenile play exposes offspring to environmental contingencies that are adaptively important. From childhood games such as Marco Polo and Hide and Go Seek to the adolescent thrills associated with viewing horror movies and riding roller coasters, these pursuits are in part thrilling because they involve having to navigate through situations fraught with unexpected twists. Children play, in part via the use of toys, because it is adaptive for them to do so.

A fourth and final way that toys can be analyzed from an evolutionary perspective is by exploring the morphological features of some of the most popular toys. Konrad Lorenz, a Nobel Laureate and founding father of ethology, argued that neotenous features (i.e., juvenile-looking traits such as large eyes and a small nose) evolved to trigger an instinctual positive affective response from human parents toward their children. Of course, one easily notices that the young of countless species appear to possess very exaggerated neotenous features. Think of a bear cub, a puppy, or a kitten. Most people are very drawn to the facial features of such seemingly helpless creatures. These facts have not gone unnoticed by toy marketers who are, after all, Darwinian beings. Take, for example, the infamous teddy bear. Several scholars have noted that the facial features of the teddy bear have evolved greatly over the past hundred years.[30] Whereas the earlier versions of the toy were more accurate representations of a bear in terms of its facial features, over the years these features have mutated into greater juvenility and "cuteness." Interestingly, the teddy bear "mutations" were driven by consumer preferences. Rather than having natural selection guiding the selection process, or breeders doing so in the case of artificial selection, in this case consumers' innate preferences served as the selective force. Stephen Jay Gould, the late Harvard evolutionist and paleontologist, made the same argument when describing the evolution of Mickey Mouse, the venerable Disney icon.[31]

It is conceivable that the gradual youthfulness of the features of teddy bears is in part owed to the famous experiments of Dmitri K. Belyaev, a Russian scientist who was interested in artificially selecting silver foxes that displayed docility and tameness toward humans. Of course, artificial selection is itself a Darwinian process in which the agent of selection is man rather than natural selection. Whereas natural and sexual selection select for traits that yield survival and reproductive advantage, respectively, the metric of artificial selection can be as whimsical as humans' aesthetic preferences for particular canine traits. For example, the Great Dane and the papillon have extraordinarily varied morphological traits, let alone size and weight differentials. These were generated via selective breeding, which is ultimately the means by which all purebred dogs develop. Returning to Belyaev's research, he was able to selectively breed for tameness in silver foxes in relatively few generations of selective breeding. Of relevance to our discussion on toys, he discovered that selecting for a behavioral trait led to morphological changes in the retained animals. The tame silver foxes developed neotenous features, including larger eyes, smaller teeth, and floppy ears. Incredibly, by selection for a particular behavior (tameness), a concomitant effect on morphological features developed that is typically associated with the behavior in question. This is an example of *pleiotropy*, namely, a given gene affects the expression of multiple traits (in this case, these consist of both behavioral as well as morphological characteristics).

Toy-related disputes are some of the earliest representations of sibling conflicts in a child's life. With that in mind, I turn to an evolutionary analysis of sibling rivalries, and demonstrate how such familial conflicts manifest themselves in the consumer setting.

BIRTH ORDER AS A FORM OF SIBLING RIVALRY

Sibling rivalry takes many forms in the animal kingdom, the most extreme being siblicide (the killing of one's sibling). In some avian species, being the second to hatch commits you to a brutal and cruel demise. Specifically, the older sibling's behavior might range from monopolizing the food (or more "charitably" in the monopolization of the highly nutritious food), resulting in the slow starvation of the younger chick, to throwing out the younger sibling from the nest or pecking it to death. Violent sibling combats occur very early among many mammals as well (e.g., hyenas). In some instances, the violent sibling rivalries start off in utero and take the form of cannibalistic siblicide (e.g., sand tiger sharks). Inferentially, the documented siblicide in the Bible—Cain kills his brother, Abel—is rooted in the natural history of numerous species. Fortunately, much of human sibling rivalry takes a much more benign form, regardless of the intense feelings of competition that such dynamics might engender.

According to historian of science Frank Sulloway, one's birth order triggers sibling rivalry via a process that he coined the *Darwinian Niche Partitioning Hypothesis*.[32] In the same way that products are often positioned to cater to an unfilled market niche, Sulloway argued that children seek to position themselves within an unoccupied offspring niche as a means of appearing unique in their parents' eyes. By definition, firstborns have all possible niches available to them. They can be the rebellious child or the good child. Each subsequent child that is born has one fewer niche to choose from than his immediately older sibling. Sulloway argued that this early challenge leads to lasting personality differences between children of different birth orders. Generally speaking, lastborns tend to score higher on openness to new experiences and ideas, given the fact that they've had to think outside the box in uniquely positioning themselves within a smaller set of available niches.

Sulloway tested his theory by investigating the birth order of individuals who had founded or supported 28 radical scientific innovations versus those who were the most vehement detractors of such novel ideas. In 23 of the 28 cases, laterborns were indeed the driving engines of the radically new scientific theories. When I lecture about this theory, I inform the audience that I am the lastborn of four children, which provides a partial explanation for my iconoclastic research. Risk taking need not be restricted to scientific revolutions, however. Younger siblings are more likely to partake in various forms of athletic risk taking (e.g., participating in perilous sports and base stealing in baseball).[33] How might Sulloway's theory be put to the test within the consumer setting? Consumer conformity is a strong driver across many product categories (e.g., when following fashion trends), whereas the early adoption of product innovations demonstrates a capacity to be open to new ideas and experiences. Tripat Gill, Rajan Nataraajan, and I demonstrated that laterborns scored higher on a product innovation scale and firstborns scored higher (marginally so) on a conformity scale.[34] In so doing, we validated the veracity of Sulloway's theory in the consumer realm.

The niche approach can be applied to many other contexts besides scientific revolutions, athletic risk taking, and product innovations. Life paths in general, and occupational choices in particular, might constitute another ripe area to test Sulloway's hypothesis. Siblings will generally travel radically different life paths partly as a means of maximally differentiating themselves within their family. I know of two brothers who could not be any more different in terms of their career paths. One is a hedge fund guru who operates within the freedoms afforded by unbridled capitalism; the other is an anticapitalist Che Guevara–type who organizes unions. With that in mind, I always find it surprising when siblings pursue the same path, especially when the older sibling has already established a strong reputation in the field in question. For example, Beyoncé Knowles's sister, Solange, is also a singer. How likely is Solange to outdo her exceptionally famous sibling? It seems that such a choice is fraught with potential for sibling jealousy and career disappointments.

THE DARK SIDE OF FAMILIES

Earlier I mentioned how *Homicide*, the book by Martin Daly and Margo Wilson, had served as my epiphany in understanding the explanatory power of evolutionary theory. Let's return to their work for a moment. They showed that the presence of a stepparent in a home is one of the greatest dangers that a child faces, a phenomenon that has since been coined the *Cinderella effect*.[35] There is a hundred-fold increase in the likelihood of various forms of child abuse when a stepfather is present in the home. This tragic occurrence was captured poignantly in the 2007 movie *An American Crime*, which depicted the torture and sadistic murder of the teenager Sylvia Likens by her caretaker, Gertrude Baniszewski, in Indiana in 1965. As dreadful as this reality is, humans are hardly the sole species to display such differential parental solicitude when it comes to investing in offspring who are not theirs. Male lions that have just taken over a new pride (by kicking out if not killing the resident male(s) outright) will systematically kill the very young cubs in the pride, as the newly crowned kings could not have sired them. In addition, they will drive off older cubs from the pride. Once the brutal killings are complete, the lionesses go into estrus. Forget about roses, some ambient soulful music, and a candlelight dinner. Killing a female's offspring to get her in the mood is a most gruesome form of foreplay.

The banishment of older cubs from the pride by the newly crowned dominant males has its equivalent practice among polygynous sects. For example, the so-called Lost Boys of the FLDS (Fundamentalist Church of Jesus Christ of Latter Day Saints) constitute a group of young men who are unceremoniously kicked out from the only world they have known under the pretext of having committed "fatal" transgressions or displayed rebelliousness. The reality is that the older male members of the sect cannot "implement" God's edict that they be granted sexual access to multiple women unless prospective young male competitors are removed from the group once they become sexually mature. It is quite a coincidence that young women are seldom kicked out of the group unless it is for their staunch refusal to accept "God's will" to mate with lecherous husbands who are at times forty years their senior. Incidentally, the banished men can return to the group if accompanied by new wives! This is yet further proof of how God's will seems to cater to the sexual desires of men in power.

PATERNAL UNCERTAINTY REARS ITS UGLY HEAD

Recall that individuals share on average one-fourth of their genes with their grandparents. Hence, from a kin selection perspective, each of the four grandparents should be equally likely to invest, and to the same extent, in their grandchildren. However, the data do not support this expectation. Rather, there appears to be a great difference in the investment patterns of the four grandparents, a phenomenon coined *differential grandparental solicitude*. Genetic relatedness is only one part of the story. One must also gauge the assuredness of a given genetic relationship. As mentioned earlier, paternity uncertainty is at the root of many sex-specific phenomena (e.g., the lesser ability of men to forgive sexual infidelities). The extent to which grandparents will invest in their grandchild is driven by the certainty of the genetic link. Of the four grandparents, maternal grandmothers face no parental uncertainty (as both generations are maternally assured since there is no such thing as maternity uncertainty), whereas paternal grandfathers face two sources of paternal uncertainty (one in each of two generations). As such, one should expect maternal grandmothers to invest the most in their grandchildren, paternal grandfathers to invest the least, and the two remaining grandparents to be somewhere in between. This is exactly what has been found in several studies.[36] On a related note, a review of cross-cultural studies found that grandmothers, and particularly maternal grandmothers, are quite important to the survival of children.[37]

My wife and I recently celebrated the one-year anniversary of the birth of our daughter, Luna. Today, most people proclaim that Luna looks like a representative mix of both my wife and me. However, this was not the case early in our childbearing adventure. When we underwent our first ultrasound around the two-month gestational mark, we received the customary photos from the technician. As occurs with most expecting parents, we proudly displayed the photos on our fridge. When my mother-in-law first saw the photos, she excitedly and unequivocally proclaimed: "Gad, the baby looks exactly like you. He has your profile!" This was quite an extraordinary proclamation, given that it is next-to-impossible to gauge which species is represented in the ultrasound photo, let alone to suggest that the photo of the fetus bears a striking resemblance to me! Although my mother-in-law would not wish to admit this, she was assuaging my potential concerns of paternity uncertainty, a phenomenon that has been found in several studies.[38]

From a child's perspective, paternal resemblance is crucially important, as fathers provide greater investment to children who look like them. Coren Apicella and Frank Marlowe collected data from men regarding the perceived similarity between them and their children. They also elicited three measures of investment from the men, none of which incidentally dealt with financial investment; paternal investment was captured by how much time and attention a given man dedicated to his child. As expected, the greater the perceived resemblance, the greater the paternal investment in the child.[39] A recent study conducted in polygynous Senegalese villages found that father-child resemblance, as captured via both visual and olfactory cues, predicted the extent of paternal investment. This differential solicitude ultimately had an effect on a child's health, as measured by the children's body mass index and mid-arm circumference.[40]

Paternity doubt manifests itself in numerous other commercial settings. Not surprisingly, when asked about their attitude toward the administering of paternity testing for newborns at hospitals, men favored the practice more than women did.[41] In this case, an attitude toward a new service (paternity exclusion testing) is largely driven by an evolutionary logic, namely, the male-specific threat of being cuckolded. Adoption decisions also seem to incorporate the calculus of paternity uncertainty. At first, this might seem unusual given that adoption decisions remove the issue of parental resemblance. Nonetheless, some anecdotal evidence suggests that interracial couples prefer to adopt a child of one of the parents' races, as this at the very least creates a "peripheral" semblance of resemblance. For example, if the prospective mother and father are black and white respectively, they are likely to prefer to adopt a baby of one of their two races rather than an Asian child. Needless to say, this is not due to any malignant racism. It is likely rooted in the desire to generate cues of parental resemblance and, more specifically, paternal resemblance.

ARE SONS AND DAUGHTERS TREATED EQUALLY?

If parents are asked if they love all their children equally, most will recoil at the possibility that they might have a favorite offspring. Instead, the standard parental answer is that they love all their children equally. From a kin selection perspective, and assuming that fathers are assured of their paternity, all children have a genetic relatedness of 0.50 to their parents, and we might be tempted to believe in the proclamations of equal parental love toward their offspring. However, parents do display patterns of biased investment toward their offspring under some circumstances. The Trivers-Willard (TW) hypothesis posits that a biased offspring sex ratio (e.g., producing more sons than daughters) can occur as a function of parental conditions. Maternal diet is one of the means by which offspring sex ratio can be affected.[42] A recent study uncovered that women who had consumed richer diets in the preconception period were more likely to produce sons, as Y-carrying chromosomes (male) are more likely to thrive in glucose-rich environments.[43] Whereas food and sex can each trigger complex sensorial pleasures, few could have imagined that food could affect the sex of the baby.

The TW hypothesis also predicts that varying parental conditions can yield differential parental investment toward one sex subsequent to a child's birth. All other things equal, if the parents are of high social status, the bias will be toward sons (as status is a stronger driver of reproductive variance for males); if the parents are of low status, the bias will be toward daughters.[44] In a recent study, Elissa Z. Cameron and Fredrik Dalerum found that male billionaires produce significantly more sons than is expected within the human population, providing compelling support for the TW hypothesis. Furthermore, sons of billionaires were generally richer than the daughters, suggesting that part of this difference stems from greater parental allocation of resources to male offspring.[45] On the other hand, Lee Cronk has documented several cultures in which parental favoritism is directed toward daughters.[46]

In the Lebanese-Jewish Arabic dialect, adolescence is referred to as the age of obnoxiousness (*Sin il ch'lout*). Teenagers can try the nerves of even the most patient of parents. This is the time period when young individuals are trying to forge their own identities while remaining under direct parental authority. This gives rise to endless parent-teenager conflicts, be it about what to wear, when to go out, curfew hours, whom to go out with, and so forth. This universal familial conflict is rooted in biological realities.[47] For example, the sitcom *8 Simple Rules for Dating My Teenage Daughter*, originally starring John Ritter, recognizes the universal fact that parents are much more territorial and vigilant about their daughters' romantic lives. This has nothing to do with sexist double standards and everything to do with the differential costs borne by sons and daughters were they to have a child (parental investment theory). No culture has ever been discovered where parents are singularly concerned about the prospects of their sons wearing "revealing" clothes (e.g., tight jeans), but myriad cultures exist wherein the dress code of daughters is closely monitored. "Oh, no—you are not wearing THAT!" is largely reserved for daughters, and this holds true across all cultural settings.

I wrap up this section with a discussion of the unique effects that father absence has on young girls while noting that such an absence affects young boys as well, albeit in different ways. Menarche, the onset of the menses, is a colossal event in a young girl's life, cross-culturally recognized as an important rite of passage. The age at which menarche occurs varies substantially across girls, as a result of a wide range of ecological factors. Several evolutionists have argued that environmental instability (e.g., father absence and the level of familial strife) contributes to the earlier onset of menarche.[48] Note again how this example demonstrates the importance of gene-culture interactions, and as such this should further dispel the notion that evolutionary theory is tantamount to genetic determinism. How might the differential timing of menarche be linked to consumer phenomena? In addition to the earlier onset of menarche, father absence accelerates pubertal sexual activity. Accordingly, it is quite conceivable that young girls who hail from unstable familial environments might sexualize themselves via the use of specific products at a much earlier age (e.g., the wearing of cosmetics, provocative attire, and high heels). I am unaware of any studies that have tested my proposition. If this were to be empirically verified, it would perhaps constitute the first demonstration of how environmental conditions (family instability) trigger the earlier onset of a physiological event (menarche) coupled with associated sexual behaviors (earlier sexual activity), these in turn driving the earlier demand of particular products (beautification).

PETS AS FAMILY MEMBERS

Many marketers are now rightfully recognizing that our beloved pets are integral elements of our families. In the United States, almost twice as many households have a pet as opposed to children.[49] This is an extraordinary statistic, which reminds me of the quip attributed to an anonymous author: "Children are for people who can't have dogs." Americans spend more than $40 billion per year on their pets. This includes pet food and veterinarian bills, but more recently it has grown to include more eclectic services such as pet hotels, pet acupuncture, and pet insurance. The human love for pets is certainly not restricted to the United States, as people from cultures spanning several millennia (e.g., the Egyptian pharaohs) have enjoyed deeply intimate relationships with their pets. On rare occasions, religious doctrines sublimate our innate penchant to love animals (e.g., Islamic teachings regarding dogs), but overwhelmingly pets are construed as integral members of family units. Our innate need for communion with pets is so engrained in our psyche that those who harm animals are typically the most dangerous members of society. Specifically, one of the key telltale signs of serial killers is a history of committing acts of animal cruelty as a child. All told, it is quite surprising that in light of the importance of animal companions in our daily lives—and given the commercial might of the pet industry—so few business and marketing scholars have tackled this topic.[50]

Is the deep bond between humans and animal companions a Darwinian anomaly? Are there evolutionary principles that might explain this interspecies relationship? The natural world is replete with symbiotic relationships that yield mutual benefits to the species involved. The oxpecker bird, for example, eats parasites (e.g., ticks) off a zebra's fur, as well as serves as an early warning system against prospective predators (to the zebra). A wide range of cleaner fish provide grooming services, including the removal of dead skin as well as a wide range of parasites from their hosts' bodies and at times from inside their ominous-looking mouths! As far as the cleaner fish is concerned, trust is de rigueur when swimming inside an otherwise dangerous predator. From the perspective of the predatory fish that is receiving the service, it does not pay to violate the trust, as the grooming is too beneficial to risk losing in the quest for an easy meal. In some instances, mutualism occurs between species from different kingdoms, such as that between bees and flowers. In this case, the exchange is one that is frequently found within a given species, namely food for sex. The bees consume nectar from one flower and in return they pollinate another flower (reproduction). In the human context, our guts serve as hosts to several hundred species of bacteria, which provide a wide range of helpful services. Might our relationship with our pets originate in similar coevolutionary symbiotic processes?

The benefits that we accrue from pets are endless, a topic that is typically studied by anthrozoologists. Pets offer unconditional companionship that yields psychological as well as physiological benefits (e.g., reduced blood pressure). Dogs are used as shepherds, guards, and bomb sniffers. They are integral parts of search and rescue operations. They guide the blind, sense epileptic seizures in their human companions prior to their onset, sniff cancer (when human technology might miss such early diagnoses), and provide therapeutic assistance to patients ranging from the elderly to autistic children. At times, unscrupulous men might even use dogs (e.g., cute puppies) to meet and impress women, as per the 2005 movie *Must Love Dogs* starring John Cusack and Diane Lane. As a matter of fact, men accompanied by a dog are more likely to obtain women's phone numbers.[51] In a sense, a man who shows tenderness and affection to an animal is signaling his emotional acuity, a desired trait in a long-term suitor. Notwithstanding these and many other benefits that pets provide, this is not what is meant when referring to Darwinian benefits. That dogs improve our cardiovascular fitness by promoting in us a more active lifestyle does not mean that this translates into *inclusive fitness* (in the Darwinian sense of the term).

John Archer has argued that these benefits are not what drove the deep reciprocal bonds that tie humans to pets. Instead, he proposed that pets usurp our parental instincts to their benefit.[52] In the same manner that the cuckoo bird drops off its eggs into the nest of another species, which then raises the chicks as though they were its own (a behavior known as brood parasitism), pets have always engaged in a similar form of "parasitism." They utilize our innate preferences for particular behaviors (e.g., playfulness) and specific morphological traits such as neotenous features (e.g., large eyes), which evolved to cater to our parental instincts, to "lure" us into loving them. This explanation applies more so to cats and dogs than it does for, say, a pet tarantula. Incidentally, there is an ongoing debate regarding the way in which wolves evolved into our domesticated dogs. The most popular theory has posited that we drove the process via artificial selection (e.g., adopting tame wolf pups, which were subsequently mated with other tame wolves). A more recent theory argues that the wolf "self-domesticated" by hanging around human encampments as scavengers. Wolves that were less timid in terms of the acceptable distance that they were willing to stand from humans were perhaps more successful in obtaining the necessary daily caloric requirements than those that might have otherwise been more flighty. Richard Dawkins has proposed that the evolution of the dog was likely a two-step process beginning with the wolf's self-domestication followed by our application of artificial selection for tameness.[53]

It is interesting to note that animals are used in endless products targeted to children, especially those that deal with language acquisition. Think of children's books or nursery rhymes. These are laden with animal themes not only because of our instinctual affection for animals but also because we have an equally innate capacity to anthropomorphize them (to endow human qualities to nonhuman entities). This can at times result in canine behavioral problems, as often depicted on the hugely successful television series *Dog Whisperer*, starring Cesar Millan. His success is due to his uncanny and innate ability to understand dog psychology. His show's tag line—"I rehabilitate dogs. I train people."—captures his approach to handling canine behavioral problems. In most instances, the problem lies squarely with the human handlers. One of the most common problems encountered on his show is the anthropomorphizing of dogs. Such a frequent occurrence speaks to our innate penchant to attribute humanlike qualities to our four-legged family members.

I end this section with a discussion of the popular belief that dogs and their owners look alike. To the extent that family members frequently bear a resemblance to one another—and in light of the fact that we view our pets as family members—could we be actually choosing pets that resemble us, and if so what might explain such a phenomenon? One undeniable fact about both dogs and humans is that members of both species display great variance in their looks. If you have ever watched the Westminster Kennel Club Dog Show, you are immediately struck by the extraordinary diversity of visible dog traits. Among many metrics of differentiation, dogs vary in size and weight (e.g., Chihuahua versus Great Dane), in the length of their coats (e.g., Mexican hairless versus Afghan hound) and whether the coat is curly or straight (e.g., poodle versus Irish setter), in the shape of their ears (floppy-eared Labrador versus the erect-eared German shepherd), in the size of their snout (e.g., British bulldog versus Irish wolfhound), and in the color of their coats (e.g., the black Groenendael versus the white Kuvasz). Some have playful neotenous facial expressions (e.g., Pomeranian), and others have a more ominous stern stare (e.g., Rottweiler). Some move with grace (e.g., Borzoi), as others lumber along (Giant Mastiff). It is also worthy to note that dogs vary greatly in terms of their temperaments and personalities. As a matter of fact, the more social a species is, the greater the amount of heterogeneity (i.e., variety) is found among individuals within that species. Consequently, one might expect cheetahs (solitary species) to display lesser heterogeneity in their personalities than lions (social species). Of course, humans vary on all these variables as well, so the original question is indeed fascinating: Do dogs and owners resemble one another?

To test this premise, studies have applied a "match-photo" methodology. Specifically, a set of shuffled photos of dogs and their owners are shown to participants. They are then asked to match each dog to its owner. If the actual number of matches exceeds that which is expected by chance, then this result serves as compelling proof in support of the original premise. In two separate studies, researchers have indeed found that we tend to choose pets that "look" like us.[54] The argument as to why this occurs is quite interesting if somewhat speculative. It is rooted in the fact that when it comes to human mate choice, the "birds of a feather flock together" adage is much more operative than the competing "opposites attract" theory, a fact evidenced by eHarmony's success as an online matching service based on its compatibility test, which has twenty-nine items. In other words, successful romantic unions are much more likely to occur when couples possess key similarities along important variables such as beliefs and values. It would seem that our penchant for similarity-based romantic matching is displayed when we choose our pets!

CONCLUSION

This chapter identified the Darwinian forces that compel consumers to partake in a wide range of investments (such as spending patterns) meant to solidify bonds of kinship. Although families can be the source for love and nurturance, they can also serve as springboards for conflict, rivalry, and favoritism, all of which are also rooted in biological processes. Given the importance of the family in catering to our innate need for sociality, it is not surprising that the kin-based investments that we make, be it the toys that we buy our children, the love that we provide our pets, and the gifts that we offer our family members, manifest themselves in innumerable ways within the consumer arena.

CHAPTER 5

THAT'S WHAT FRIENDS ARE FOR

A good friend is worth many relations. (global proverb)

One good friend is more than nine relatives / A good friend is my nearest relation. (Estonian proverb)

Kind friends are better than unkind brothers. (Chinese proverb)[1]

We have seen how kin selection drives altruistic acts between family members. However, there are innumerable documented cases of great acts of altruism between nonkin, in both the human context and across numerous other animal species. Why would anyone engage in such selfless behavior toward nonkin (e.g., strangers or friends)? Robert Trivers solved this Darwinian puzzle via his theory of reciprocal altruism.[2] Specifically, he described the conditions under which reciprocity would evolve between unrelated members of a given species (and at times members of different species). These include the need for repeat interactions (otherwise a debt cannot be repaid) and the capacity to recognize and remember the persons with whom such interactions have taken place. In the human context, reciprocal altruism is likely to have evolved as an insurance policy against possible starvation. Two unrelated families might have struck the following arrangement: "If my family brings down a large prey today, we'll share it with your family. In the future, when you successfully hunt down a large animal, you'll share it with us." The proverbial tit for tat—"I'll scratch your back if you'll scratch mine"—was likely operative on the ancestral plains of the African savanna.

There are many forms of reciprocal altruism found across species. For example, social grooming within primate species serves as the basis for forming new alliances and coalitions, and helps solidify bonds of friendship. In this sense, grooming is a social lubricant within primate society. Individual A grooms individual B (i.e., removal of ticks and other parasites) with the expectation that at some future date, the favor will be repaid either by returned grooming or via agonistic support (individual B intervenes in a fight in support of individual A). Alarm calling against a predator and predator mobbing are two other documented instances of reciprocal altruism. That said, perhaps the most common form of reciprocal altruism in the animal kingdom deals with food sharing. Vampire bats of Costa Rica exhibit one the classic examples of reciprocal altruism. They can often return to their caves after a night of predation empty-handed (or, rather, with empty stomachs). In such instances, other biologically unrelated bats come to the rescue by regurgitating their spoils (blood) into the mouths of the starving individuals. Ultimately, given that two of the key survival challenges faced by organisms are caloric scarcity/uncertainty coupled with predator avoidance (unless you are the apex predator), it is perhaps not surprising that many of the documented instances of reciprocal altruism deal with these evolutionary challenges.

As explicitly recognized in the cross-cultural proverbs listed in this chapter's epigraphs, friendships can often be more important than family ties. In the previous chapter, I discussed a gift giving study that I conducted with Tripat Gill to explore gift expenditures across a wide range of recipients, including one's mate, kin, and friends. We found that the largest gift expenditures were in decreasing order to one's mate, close kin (i.e., parents and siblings), close friends, and, lastly, more distant kin (e.g., uncles, aunts, grandparents, half-siblings, closest first cousin). The important point to note here is that close friends trumped more distant family members. Ultimately, gift-giving rituals between friends are a form of reciprocity that helps strengthen nonkin affiliational bonds. Several studies have contrasted the extent of altruism toward kin versus nonkin. In some instances, nonkin are shown greater altruism,[3] while in other cases and as expected by kin selection theory, kin are preferred.[4] Interestingly, men and women seem to possess somewhat different friendship styles. Specifically, women are much more likely to construe friends as kin, but men band with other nonkin males when facing inter-group conflict.[5] This male perspective on friendships supports the alliance hypothesis, which posits that the need for friendships has evolved in part to help in the establishing of nonkin coalitions.[6]

BONDS OF FRIENDSHIP: A PERSONAL STORY FROM THE ASHES OF WAR

In 1975, my family left Lebanon under the imminent threat of death. The Lebanese civil war had erupted earlier that year between dizzying numbers of warring militia (e.g., Maronite Phalanges known as the Kataeb in Arabic, Shi`ia Amal fighters, Sunni PLO fighters, and the Druze militia, to name four key factions). At its most elemental level, it was a war between Christians and Muslims. My being Jewish in Lebanon at that point in the country's history was not a good situation. Americans might be surprised and perhaps horrified to know that the Lebanese populace has, in addition to the standard passport for international travel, an internal ID card that states each individual's religion. This is hardly surprising in the context of the Middle East, as social life in that part of the world is always viewed via the prism of one's religion. The Lebanese political system was designed with religious affiliations at the forefront. What would be unconstitutional in the United States is woven into the fabric of Lebanon's political realities. Lebanon's constitution explicitly recognizes religion as a central element in the governance of the country.

Returning to the civil war: one early form of civilian massacres took place at roadblocks as erected by both Muslim and Christian militia (no one held a monopoly over brutal and sadistic behaviors). Car passengers would be asked to produce their ID cards, and if they had the misfortune of being of the "wrong" religion, the gravest consequence befell them. As Jews, we were in the unenviable position of knowing that there weren't too many roadblocks that we could clear, given that the majority of militia groups were hostile to Jews. This problem was exacerbated by the fact that we were referred to as "Israelis" on our ID cards and not as "Jews," triggering much more virulent animus toward us. In other words, we were stripped of our in-group status as Lebanese/Arab Jews by being lumped with the out-group mortal enemy (Israel).

Through my parents' established social networks, we were able to hire Palestinian militia to drive us to the Beirut International Airport to catch a flight out of Lebanon (after having witnessed several months of the most extraordinary violence that could ever be documented). Obtaining the protection from PLO militia was crucial, as they controlled the passage to the airport. Hence, there was no other way to escape the carnage without the help of Muslim militia. I do not wish to make it sound as though they protected us out of the kindness of their hearts; if memory serves, there was a substantial payment for rendering such a protective service. However, my point in recounting this very painful and traumatic period of my life is to highlight the power of social networks and long-lasting friendships in that part of the world. To the people who helped us, we were friends. This trumped the fact that we were Jews.

Over the next five years, my parents kept traveling between Montreal, Canada (our new home), and Beirut. In 1980, they were kidnapped by Fatah (a military and political faction of the Palestine Liberation Organization) and presumed dead. In Lebanon, kidnappings were quite common, and the outcome was almost always the same. Your life was not worth the price of the bullet used to execute you. During the week or so that they had disappeared, my three siblings—all of whom are much older than me—were working my parents' social connections to obtain information and, if by sheer miracle they were still alive, were seeking ways to free my mother and father. As these events were transpiring, the truth was withheld from me. I knew that everyone around me was stressed and highly agitated but I, fifteen years old at the time, was given a cover story to protect me from the ugly truth. I believe that the kidnapping was driven by one of the seven deadly sins: greed. My dad's commercial neighbor had his eye on my father's store. He hired a militia group to extract an admission from my parents that they were Israeli spies. This would entitle the militia to execute my parents "legally," and the store would revert to the landlord (given that we had no remaining kin in Lebanon). Of course, my parents were hardly spies, so they spent several extremely unpleasant days in brutal captivity.

My mother's best friend at the time, a Syrian Muslim woman with ties to the highest political echelon in Syria, engineered their eventual rescue. The networking wheels were set in motion, a number of infamous Middle Eastern dignitaries got personally involved in the ordeal, and a deal was finally struck for the discharge of my parents. As my mother and father were driven to the airport, their close friends advised them that as difficult as it was for them to say this, Lebanon was no longer a place for them. They could no longer guarantee their security. All the people who were instrumental in my parents' release risked their social standing, their reputations—if not their lives—to rescue my parents. They all shared two things in common: none were family members and none were Jewish. Strictly speaking, the bonds of friendship between my parents and these heroic individuals trumped all other realities. Close friendships are truly vestiges of our biological heritage.

On a lighter note, peoples from the Middle East are known for their extraordinary levels of hospitality. I propose that such cultural traditions are rooted in the Darwinian process of reciprocity. I turn to this topic next.

HOSPITALITY AS A FORM OF RECIPROCITY

Hospitality is a cultural norm that is found across highly disparate societies (e.g., Southern hospitality in the United States and Arab/Bedouin hospitality). Its virtues have been extolled for several millennia in the sacred texts of Judaism, Christianity, Islam, and Hinduism. It is captured by similar adages, such as *make yourself at home, mi casa es su casa* (my home is your home), and *fais comme chez toi* (act as though you were at your home). The Matti Kuusi International–type system of proverbs contains sayings from around the world. Here are some that relate to hospitality, along with their cultural origin:

> Small presents keep up friendship. (Western European, Islamic, and older Asiatic [Orient])

> The dish sent by a neighbor does not satisfy you, but increases good will. (Persian)

> Good accounts make good friends. (Greek)

> Hospitality asks for equal treatment in return. (Finnish/other Baltic sea cultures; European in general; sub-Saharan Africa; older Asiatic [Orient] cultures)

> Courtesy on one side can never last long. (global)

Note that countless disparate cultures recognize that gift giving, hospitality, and generosity are important forms of social behavior while also noting that reciprocity is expected. As a Lebanese Jew (but atheist by conviction), I am lucky to have been exposed to the exceptional norms of hospitality in both Jewish teachings as well as in Arabic culture. I recall the warmth with which Rabbi Eli Silberstein and his wife, Dr. Chana Silberstein (who at the time was a fellow graduate student at Cornell), hosted a barrage of undergraduate and graduate Cornellians at their home for Friday night Shabbat dinners. One might think that such hospitality is rooted in the desire to engage in in-group proselytizing (given that out-group proselytizing is extremely rare in Judaism). In reality, this practice has its origins in a Mitzvah known as *Hachnasat orchim*, which literally means "the welcoming of strangers."

Arab hospitality is equally legendary. There are numerous rules of etiquette regarding the manner by which one should receive guests within the home. For example, meals are typically extraordinarily lavish affairs coupled with repeated insistences that the guests eat well beyond their hearts' content. It can be quite insulting to a Middle Eastern host if a guest were to eat minimally. Consequently, if Westerners think they are behaving politely by not appearing gluttonous, this is actually interpreted as highly offensive to the host ("Does he not like the food that we've prepared?"). As a matter of fact, there is an ancient code within Arab culture that one's guest must be protected from all sources of harm—the ultimate act of hospitality, I suppose. What is it about Arab culture that has allowed it to evolve such a defining ethos of hospitality? Some have argued that its genesis lies in Bedouin societies. Imagine having to travel through the harsh desert terrain, with endless challenges that include excessive physical fatigue, hunger, and thirst. Knowing that you can count on the hospitality of strangers when traversing such formidable landscapes is a reassuring insurance policy. This underlines my earlier point regarding the likely evolutionary origins of reciprocal altruism, expressly that it served as an insurance policy against famine.

Whenever Middle Eastern friends go out together (whether to a movie or a restaurant), a ritual often ensues that is seldom seen among American/Western friends. Each friend will "fight" and "insist" on paying the bill for everyone. The interaction typically involves melodramatic ritualized posturing about being offended, insulted, and hurt (that others might not accept one's insistence to foot the bill). Eventually, one of the friends manages to "win" the right to be generous to the utter "dismay" of the accompanying friends. This is a ritualized social dance that is meant to signal one's willingness to be generous to one's friends; the reality is that all the friends are adept at keeping tabs of the number of times that each person has "won" or "lost" this ritual in relation to the other group members. If the same individual were to pay the collective bill on each of the last ten outings, this ritual would become unsustainable. Ultimately, this jibes with the notion that humans choose their friends in part on their perceived capacity to reciprocate,[7] which was captured by a few of the cross-cultural proverbs regarding hospitality I mentioned earlier.

FRIENDSHIPS IN POPULAR CULTURE, COMMERCE, AND INTERNATIONAL RELATIONS

Not surprisingly, friendships within the human context constitute some of the most important relationships in one's life. Whereas the lion's share of songs deal with mating (see chapter 6), friendships constitute a recurring theme (e.g., "Lean on Me" by Bill Withers; "You've Got a Friend" by James Taylor). Many of the most successful television sitcoms revolve around the deep friendships that take place between groups of nonkin individuals: *The Odd Couple*; *M*A*S*H*; *Welcome Back, Kotter*; *Laverne & Shirley*; *Three's Company*; *Taxi*; *Cheers*; *Friends*; *Seinfeld*; *Will and Grace*; and *My New BFF*, featuring the insufferable Paris Hilton hosting her own reality show in which contestants compete to become her latest *best friend forever*. In some instances, shows include both family relationships as well as close friendships: *I Love Lucy*, *The Honeymooners*, and *The King of Queens*.

The importance of friendships is also depicted on the big screen. There is a large litany of movies in which the key theme or driving subplot is about specific friendships. Sometimes the friendships are all-female: *Beaches, Steel Magnolias, Fried Green Tomatoes, Thelma & Louise, Waiting to Exhale, Circle of Friends, The First Wives Club*, and *Divine Secrets of the Ya-Ya Sisterhood*. In other instances, they depict all-male friendships (also known as "bromances" in today's urban vernacular): *The Odd Couple, Butch Cassidy and the Sundance Kid, Deliverance, American Graffiti, The Deer Hunter, Midnight Express, Stand by Me, Lethal Weapon, GoodFellas, Wayne's World, Unforgiven, Dumb and Dumber, The Shawshank Redemption, Good Will Hunting*, and *I Love You, Man*. Note that this list of all-male friendship movies spans the gamut of film genres, including coming-of-age, comedies, dramas, cop, buddy, prison, war, and crime movies. Of course, there are iconic movies that deal with mixed-sex friendships as a central theme (which at times turn into romances): *The Big Chill, St. Elmo's Fire, The Breakfast Club, Ferris Bueller's Day Off, When Harry Met Sally, Four Weddings and a Funeral, Clueless, My Best Friend's Wedding*, and *Just Friends*. Interspecies friendships are also depicted in movies, typically between dogs and humans (but not always as per the 1979 classic *Black Stallion*): *Lassie Come Home, The Return of Rin Tin Tin, Old Yeller, Benji, Mad Max 2: The Road Warrior, K-9, Turner & Hooch, White Fang, Beethoven, Dr. Dolittle, A Dog of Flanders, Scooby-Doo*, and *Eight Below*. And movies can at times capture intergalactic friendships, as memorably depicted in *ET: The Extra-Terrestrial*. Friendships are ubiquitous across all these cultural products because they serve as universal triggers of affective and cognitive engagement.

The innate importance of friendships is depicted in numerous marketing settings. Many company slogans specifically refer to friendship and the associated possibility of forging bonds of reciprocity. Prototypical examples include "Like a good neighbor, State Farm is there" (State Farm), "You have a friend at Chase Manhattan" (Chase Manhattan

Bank), "Your friend in the digital age" (COX Communications), "Fly the friendly skies" (United Airlines), and "Friends don't let friends drive drunk" (US Department of Transportation). At times, a company's name serves as a clear indication that it is to be trusted, as would be the case with a close friend (e.g., the insurance company The Co-operators). The State Farm slogan speaks to the business philosophy known as relationship marketing, whose central tenet is firmly rooted in the Darwinian process of reciprocity (and cooperation). Its foundational premise is that repeat interactions between customers and firms should be based on a long-term view rather than a one-shot interaction. A relationship is forged with the customer (akin to a friendship) in a manner that promotes customer loyalty.

Suppose that you own a store that sells air-conditioning units, and this summer has been scorchingly hot. Your store is the only one that has units in stock. Given the high demand, you can gouge consumers by charging a huge price for the remaining units (the basic law of supply and demand). However, recognizing that you engage in repeated interactions with many of the customers, you make the wise decision of pricing your products fairly. Hence, you've implemented the tit-for-tat strategy to perfection. You've acted honorably, and in return you've garnered the customer's loyalty (for future purchases). Generally speaking, relationship marketing has not been construed as a Darwinian process,[8] although it is clear that its whole premise is rooted in the principle of reciprocity. In the end, relationship marketing is predicated on the fact that reciprocity is a powerful social lubricant.

The innate desire to form friendships and coalitions need not be restricted to relationships between individuals or between firms and their customers. It can equally apply to larger groups, even nation-states. It is generally thought that democracies are less likely to go to war against one another if they have deep-rooted economic interconnectedness (i.e., trade). More generally, the greater the connectedness between two countries, be it economic ties or other cementing bonds (as in cul-

tural exchanges), the more likely peace will reign between them. Even
though some scholars have contested this viewpoint, it would nonetheless seem that friendship is a useful term to apply to entities as large as
nation-states.[9]

ARE AMERICANS FRIENDLY BUT SHALLOW?

As a graduate student at Cornell University, I was fortunate to meet
fellow students from highly disparate cultures. Although in many
instances we did not share a common language, common cultural rituals,
or a common religion, we all seemed to share one opinion: Our conception of friendship was radically different from that of many of our American cohorts. We all agreed that Americans seemed extremely friendly
and were very approachable. However, American friendships were much
easier to dissolve as well. The bonds of friendship appeared to be defined
in radically different ways between many non-Americans and their
American counterparts. Why? The obnoxious and incorrect response is
that Americans are somehow inherently shallow, and as such they hold a
rather cavalier attitude toward friendships. The reality is that Americans
are no different in their depth than individuals from any other society.
Instead, there are societal reasons that have caused the cementing bonds
of friendships to be somewhat different across cultural settings.

Imagine that you were born in the same small Sicilian village where
your family has lived for the past two hundred years. Furthermore,
assume that the likelihood of your leaving the village is remote (e.g., your
family owns vineyards, which you are expected to take over). Your social
roots in this village are likely to be extraordinarily deep. You've probably
grown up with the same set of friends since early childhood. Your respective families are likely to know one another. In all likelihood, you will
spend your whole life in this village. Such a reality is one that most
humans have faced throughout our evolutionary history; they would

have interacted only with a restricted group of individuals within a limited geographical region. Now contrast this to the reality of the modern world as exemplified by American society. Our lives are defined by our incessant mobility. A young man whose family belonged to the working class might obtain an Ivy League education, become an Internet multimillionaire, and in so doing move up the echelons of the social strata (socioeconomic mobility). The same young man might have grown up in Cleveland, Ohio, obtained his undergraduate degree at Brown University (Providence, Rhode Island), his MBA at Stanford University (Palo Alto, California), and set up his Internet venture in Ramat Gan, Israel. This geographical mobility is typical of today's professional. For example, the average MBA switches jobs on eight occasions during her career.[10] Therefore, while individuals from the "old country" are likely to originate from social niches defined by lesser mobility (e.g., one is born into an Indian caste with no possibility for movement between the castes), the American experience shatters all such boundaries. I strongly believe that this is at the root of the difference in attitudes that Americans and non-Americans hold toward friendships. All other things equal, tight-knit communities that involve minimal socioeconomic and geographical mobility engender deeper bonds of friendship. These in turn affect norms of hospitality, some of which manifest themselves in various consumer settings.

LEGAL CONTRACTS VERSUS MY WORD IS MY HONOR

I spent two years (2001–2003) as a visiting associate professor at the University of California-Irvine. While it was easy to acclimate to the beauty of the landscape and the sun's bright luminosity, to habituate to the endless legal contracts that seemed to regulate every social interaction was a much taller order. Our rental lease agreement must have been longer and more complex than the Camp David Accords signed by

Israel, and Egypt, and witnessed by the United States in 1978! We had to waive our rights to litigate against endless past contingencies as well as possible future ones. For example, the rental complex had used some insecticides in the past and might use other ones in the future. We had to waive our right to sue for any purpose that might be linked to such uses. We also had to sign that we were aware that air traffic noise might be heard from our townhouse. We also had to waive the right to sue were anything to happen while using the swimming pools, Jacuzzis, or athletic facilities. I also had to provide detailed financial information to prove that I had the necessary income to pay the rent. How ironic that renting an apartment in 2001 involved such Draconian measures, but a few years later the unemployed were strongly encouraged to take out $500,000 mortgages (subprime mortgage lending practices), leading to the debacle of the housing market.

I recall the first time that we took our car to the mechanic in Southern California. Our car, which we had brought with us from Montreal, had to pass the more stringent California smog tests. The mechanic walked around the car and marked every single minor scratch both inside and outside the car, and made me sign a form attesting to the existence of these scratches. This would protect him against a lawsuit if I were to claim that he had scratched the car while working on it. This litigious and contract-driven ethos manifested itself in nearly all other interactions, be it when deciding which medical insurance plan to choose (a rather strange exercise for me, given that, as a Canadian, I had always had universal health care) or when drafting my course outlines (I was reminded that the course outline is viewed as a contract between the professor and her students). Contrast these formalized contracts with the traditional manner of doing business in the Middle East—a handshake and your word sufficed. Asking that all expectations be laid down in a contract would have been historically construed as insulting to the Arab. The reaction would have been: "Why are you giving me all these papers to sign? Do you not trust my word?"

Are Arabs inherently more honorable than their American counterparts, and if so, do they not require legal contracts to formalize their business dealings? The short answer is no. The difference between the extensive legal contracts in Southern California and the "my word is my honor" ethos prevalent in the Arab world lies in the realities of the Dunbar number. Recall that this refers to the average group size within which humans have historically interacted in their day-to-day lives. In such an environment, your reputation is your most important social capital. You might be able to cheat on your social contract on any one occasion, but once word spreads that you are a cheat, you are cooked. Accordingly, in "old country" settings where individuals are likely to live out their entire lives within a constrained geographical area and tight social networks, legal contracts are not needed. Rather, the social setting, which more closely mimics the environment in which we've evolved ancestrally as compared to the unanimity afforded by the transient nature of Southern Californian society, serves as the means by which one's word is enforced.

Ultimately, social networks that are cohesive and nontransitory are more amenable to the building of trust between individuals. This is an important point to make, as one of the strongest predictors of a country's economic vitality is the level of trust that is present within its economic, social, and political environments. This insight led the neuroeconomist Paul Zak to explore the neurobiological drivers of trust across a wide range of economic contexts.[11] In doing so, his team has identified the crucial role that our brain's oxytocin plays in facilitating trust between individuals. In the same way that testosterone drives a man's desire to engage in various forms of sexual signaling, oxytocin has evolved to facilitate interactions between individuals. Hence, it is released in widely different settings of evolutionary import, including postcoitus (causing it to be coined the *cuddling hormone*), during breastfeeding (thus promoting maternal nurturance), and interactions between nonkin (a frequent occurrence for social species). The bottom line is that our capacity to trust other economic agents is rooted in neurobiological circuits that originally evolved to solve the adaptive challenges linked to interacting with strangers. Oxytocin is a vestige of our human sociality.

US VERSUS THEM

In 1999, I visited Israel to present my joint work (with Tripat Gill) on the Ultimatum Game, and then spent several days vacationing in Dahab (which means "gold" in Arabic), a resort area in the Sinai Desert (Egypt). As soon as the hotel staff, made up largely of Egyptians, found out I was an Arabic-speaking Jew, I rapidly became the star guest. There were the "others" (i.e., the Israeli Jews) but I was part of their in-group. Somehow, my Jewish heritage was trumped by my Arabic identity. Such innate tribalism is particularly operative in the context of the Middle East. Coalitional thinking is a prism through which we view the world, partly because throughout our evolutionary history we were much more likely to forge reciprocal alliances with in-group members. Muzafer Sherif and Henry Tajfel are perhaps the most famous social psychologists to have investigated our innate proclivity for the "us versus them" mindset. Tajfel's minimal group experiments assigned participants into groups using random and meaningless cues (e.g., blue versus red stickers placed on participants' shirts). Participants, who might otherwise be different on endless real parameters, utilized the categorization cue in triggering their innate coalitional psychology (e.g., they displayed favoritism toward their newly defined in-group).

At the 2009 Social & Affective Neuroscience Society Annual Meeting, Reem Yahya and her colleagues from the University of Haifa presented their intriguing work on the manner in which images of inflictions of pain are processed when these are linked to in-group versus outgroup individuals, as well as to a control group. As might be expected from an evolutionary perspective, pain ratings were highest when linked to in-group members. Human empathy is strategically allocated in ways that are consistent with our innate coalitional psychology. A group of Italian scientists recently conducted a similar study to gauge whether empathic brain responses are moderated by in-group and out-group distinctions. African (black) and Italian (white) participants were shown films of white, black, or purple (unnatural color) hands being pricked with a needle. Using transcranial magnetic stimulation, the scientists found that participants (who had exhibited implicit in-group favoritism) displayed empathy (at the physiological level) toward same-race hands as well as to the purple hands. In other words, people have the capacity to be empathetic to another's pain (as per the finding regarding the purple hand) but are particularly prone to feel or shut off empathy depending on whether the sufferer is of the same in-group.[12]

On a related note, Chaim Fershtman and Uri Gneezy, two Israeli economists, explored coalitional thinking in the context of several economic games. Examples of such games include the Ultimatum and Dictator Games. In the former, player A receives a fixed sum of money (say $10) and is told that he should offer a split of the money to player B. If player B accepts the offer, each of the two players receives his respective split. If player B rejects it, both players walk away with nothing. The Dictator Game functions in the same manner, with one crucial difference: player B does not have any veto power. Fershtman and Gneezy explored whether in the context of Israeli society behaviors in such economic games might depend on the ethnic origins of the players in question. Specifically, they were interested in exploring two groups in particular, namely Ashkenazi Jews (hailing originally from Eastern and Central Europe) and Sephardic Jews (African and Middle Eastern Jews). Would participants engage in a coalitional bias; that is, would they behave more altruistically toward those of their ethnic origins (as gauged via their prototypical ethnic names)? Interestingly, Fershtman and Gneezy found that men of both ethnicities seemed to have greater mistrust of Sephardic men, as well as providing more generous offers to Sephardic men. These differential behaviors were much more prevalent among men than they were among women. It is not difficult to see how coalitional thinking might lead to various forms of out-group stereotypes and prejudices, if not outright xenophobic attitudes. Perhaps most surprising are the self-prejudices displayed by Sephardic men toward their own ethnic group. As a Sephardic man, I am disappointed by these findings.

The "us versus them" mindset coupled with our social nature implies that we have an innate need to belong[13] to clearly defined in-groups. Perhaps no consumer setting caters to this universal desire of belongingness more so than the fashion industry. The world can be neatly divided into those who are fashionable (the desired in-group) and others.

FASHION AS GROUP IDENTITY

The economic, cultural, and social impact of fashion is undeniable. The global fashion market is one of the largest of all industries, generating conservatively several hundred billion dollars in economic activity. Fashion TV is a channel solely dedicated to fashion-related matters. Several television shows have roughly the same theme: namely, "rebranding" an individual via the use of a fashion makeover. These include *Queer Eye for the Straight Guy*, *What Not to Wear*, *Extreme Makeover*, and *10 Years Younger*. *Fashion Police* uses the wit of Joan Rivers to critique the fashion decisions of celebrities. An endless array of fashion magazines caters to consumers' voracious appetites for style; some of the better-known ones include *Cosmopolitan*, *Vogue*, *Elle*, *Allure*, *Glamour*, *InStyle*, *Marie Claire*, *Esquire*, and *GQ* (note the preponderance of magazines targeted to women). Several movies are particularly famous for their focus on fashion: the iconic *Breakfast at Tiffany's*, *Prêt-à-Porter*, *Clueless*, *The Devil Wears Prada*, *Confessions of a Shopaholic*, *Coco before Chanel* (French), and *Sex and the City* (both the television series and the two movies). The gist is that fashion is a ubiquitous element of popular culture.

In a most basic sense, clothing serves a survival function; it protects us from the elements. However, few people today think of clothing in such a restrictive manner. The predominant purpose of clothing in particular, and fashion more generally, caters to our need to express our individuality. After all, our clothes and related accoutrements signal who we are to the world. We communicate our individuality via an endless number of fashion decisions. Paradoxically, fashion also caters to our innate need to belong. In adopting a particular style, we wish to demonstrate our membership within one of an endless number of fashion subcultures, which include styles such as preppy, Goth, boho chic, eco-chic, emo, business casual, clubwear, street wear, hip-hop fashion, punk, rave, New Romantic, grunge, glam, and Skag trendy. Of course, many of these fashion trends are associated with youth movements, as these constitute the primary demographic group seeking to define their identities via their clothing decisions. The British writer Quentin Crisp famously wrote, "The young always have the same problem—how to rebel and conform at the same time. They have now solved this by defying their elders and copying one another."[14] The goal of most teenagers is to be as similar as possible to those within their group but as dissimilar as possible from those without.

From a fashion marketer's perspective, the brilliance of this industry rests on the fact that the metrics of belongingness change with every fashion season. Although the styles associated to particular fashion subcultures remain relatively the same throughout the years (e.g., Goth), most individuals do not belong to such "static" subcultures. Most persons construe the world as consisting of two fashion groups: fashion aficionados and the rest. Accordingly, if you wish to be a good-standing member of the fashionistas, it becomes incumbent on you to stay informed of the latest styles. If brown is the in-color this fall, it is time to "brown up" your closet. Next fall, brown might be out and gray may be in. At that point, you would not be caught dead with the formerly gorgeous brown sweater. As a professor in Montreal, I am on the frontline of fashion trends. Montreal is an extraordinarily fashion-conscious city. Unlike American campuses where students might get away with wearing sweatpants and flip flops, Montrealers are not nearly as forgiving. My classrooms serve as microcosms of fashion shows. A few years ago, I noticed a new trend being displayed by many of the young female undergraduate students. They would wear their pants snuggly tucked inside Ugg boots (or similar-looking knock-offs). At one point, this fad was so ubiquitous that I started to think that my university might have instituted a new standardized uniform akin to that in private high schools! The herd mentality was truly extraordinary.

Often, fashion styles become iconic representations of a particular time period (although earlier styles can become fashionable again). For example, beehives and miniskirts are relics from the sixties, bell-bottom pants and platform shoes are time travelers from the seventies, and shoulder pads and pastel colors (think *Miami Vice*) capture the essence of the eighties. Fashion styles also signal one's membership in a particular social class. Wearing a wife-beater shirt while sporting a mullet serves as a clear signal of one's social standing. Of course, clothing also serves to signal one's belongingness to a particular ethnic, cultural, or religious group (e.g., the hijab or the kippah). In some instances, body modifications such as tattoos have historically signaled one's membership as part of the antiestablishment. However, today more than 20 percent of Americans have a tattoo, and 10 percent of the populace in contemporary Western countries has some form of body modification.[15] The growing popularity of the tattoo culture has not gone unnoticed by television executives, as evidenced by the slew of recent tattoo-based reality shows such as *Inked*, *Miami Ink*, *LA Ink*, and *Rio Ink*.

In the 2007 movie *Eastern Promises*, Viggo Mortensen plays the role of a Russian enforcer seeking to become a member of the Russian mob (the Vory). During his induction ceremony, tattoos are shown to constitute a central element of the rite of passage. First, he displays his existing tattoos, which indicate his criminal past (e.g., which prison he served time in). Second, as a new inductee, he is tattoo-branded with the colors of the criminal organization in question. The use of tattoos in criminal organizations is not restricted to Russian criminals. Tattoos are indelible features of criminal and prison cultures in many countries. For example, the three-leaf clover symbolizes membership within the Aryan Brotherhood, and the teardrop tattoo often signals that its wearer is a murderer. Tattoos constitute tags of group membership in many noncriminal contexts including the military and rebellious nonconformists. Of note, getting a tattoo is forbidden by some groups (e.g., in Judaism), and hence serves to delineate the us-versus-them mentality.

Although one of the motives for getting a tattoo is rooted in the desire to signal group membership, paradoxically a tattoo is also meant to express one's individuality (as a fashion statement). Note that the act of getting a tattoo as an expression of nonconformity to societal norms ends up being a form of belongingness to the "rebellious others." The tension between these two universal forces of human identity (conformity and individuality) is well captured by optimal distinctiveness theory,[16] which posits that humans seek an optimal equilibrium between these two opposing pulls. Men's professional attire constitutes another example of this phenomenon. Within a given industry such as investment banking, the majority of men's suits look alike (conformity); individuality is signaled via the choice of ties to wear.

Beyond fashion, there are numerous other ways by which consumers demonstrate their allegiances to a group, perhaps none as emotionally consuming as that displayed by sports fans around the world.

SPORTS VIEWING AND MERCHANDISING AS GROUP IDENTITY

I have long been a supporter of the French national soccer team, so I was delighted when they reached the World Cup Final in 2006. I remember vividly the morning of the big match. My companion and I took our dog for a walk, and she noticed that I was visibly tense. "What's wrong?" she asked, to which I replied that I was nervous about the upcoming final. One might think that this is irrational. After all, I do not know any of the players personally. I am not a French citizen. I did not have a monetary bet riding on the game. Yet I was experiencing the physical symptoms of stress that should be reserved for the players who were about to partake in this historic event. The power of affiliation that I felt for the French players had resulted in a vicarious emotional and physiological reaction in me. This innate capacity to band with an in-group and disassociate from out-group members is at the root of sports viewing. Few individuals attend a match (regardless of the sport) as neutral and dispassionate spectators. The power of the experience, whether viewing an event live or on television, stems from the vicarious emotions that we experience in seeing "our" team come out victorious.

As a social species that forms dominance hierarchies, humans wish to affiliate with winners, and disassociate from losers (also known as *cutting off reflected failure*). In a classic set of studies published in 1976, psychology and marketing expert Bob Cialdini and his colleagues explored the phenomenon of *basking in reflected glory* as applied to a university football team's performance.[17] Specifically, the researchers kept track of the number of students who wore their university's apparel the Monday following a win or loss by their school's football team. Furthermore, they monitored students who wore another school's apparel. As predicted, students were more likely to wear their school's apparel following a victory than a defeat (the rate of wearing the attire of a school other than theirs was unaffected by their school's victory or defeat). Clearly, this particular clothing choice is intimately linked to the students' desire to affiliate with the winning camp and disassociate with "losers." Cialdini and his colleagues also found that students were more likely to use "we" when describing their team's victory, and more likely to use some "non-we" pronoun (e.g., "they") when describing a defeat. On a related note, researchers found that the likelihood that fans would visit the websites of Dutch and Belgian soccer teams was based on whether they had won or lost their previous game.[18] This is yet another example of individuals' desire to associate with winners and avoid losers (literally).

The sales of sports merchandising (e.g., NFL jerseys or soccer shirts) are highly correlated to the performance of the teams or players in question. For example, some of the currently highest-selling NFL players' jerseys are those of Super Bowl–winning quarterbacks (Eli Manning, Peyton Manning, and Tom Brady). The highest-selling soccer club jerseys correspond to teams that have performed exceptionally well throughout the years (Manchester United, Barcelona, Real Madrid, Liverpool, AC Milan). The same applies for the top-selling national team soccer jerseys (e.g., Italy, France, Brazil, Germany, Argentina, England, the Netherlands). There is little demand for soccer jerseys of the national teams of Estonia, Venezuela, or Vietnam. The reason for this association between merchandising sales and athletic performance is rooted in a clear Darwinian mechanism: *"We're* number 1. *They* (others) are losers."

The powers of coalitional thinking and the allure of banding together to defend the group (and its resources) manifest themselves in sports at the endocrinological level. Male soccer players have higher testosterone levels when playing at home than when playing away[19] (a form of territorial defense). This effect is also moderated by the rivalry of the match in question. Not only do players' testosterone levels fluctuate as a result of winning or losing, but also their fans experience similar changes in their own T levels;[20] such are the intense coalitional feelings that fans possess for their teams. *The Real Football Factories International* is a television series originally broadcast on the Bravo network that documents soccer hooliganism globally. The most shocking element to each episode is the deep-seated hatred that rival factions feel for one another, which can lead to extraordinary violence. You begin to see how the home field advantage can result in a cascading set of testosterone effects. In a manner similar to historical NFL rivalries between specific teams (typically if they play in the same division) or professional baseball's famed "subway" series between the Mets and the Yankees, such fierce rivalries in soccer are referred to as derby matches. They typically correspond to club teams who are geographically close to one another (e.g., in the same city), though this is not always the case. Famous examples of soccer derbies include Manchester United versus Manchester City (England), Rangers versus Celtic (Scotland), AC Milan versus Inter Milan (Italy), Barcelona versus Real Madrid (Spain), Ajax versus Feyenoord (The Netherlands), Galatasaray versus Fenerbahce (Turkey), Flamengo versus Fluminense (Brazil), and Boca Juniors versus River Plate (Argentina).

The elite professional soccer clubs are global brands that command the diehard allegiance of millions of fans. Historically, supporters could not readily connect with one another if they lived in different geographical regions. But the Internet has successfully turned our vast world into the proverbial global village, making it easy for fans to connect with one another via, say, the creation of a Facebook page. More generally though, in eradicating geographical barriers, online social networking platforms have allowed us to cater to our instinctual need for connectedness at the click of a mouse.

ONLINE SOCIAL NETWORKING AND HUMAN INTERCONNECTEDNESS

Over the past few years, social networking websites and associated tools have become an absolute craze. First, there was MySpace and Facebook, which allow individuals to form and maintain friendships online; Twitter is a more recent entrant into this niche that takes the online interconnectivity between people to new heights. The adoption rate of these Internet platforms has been nothing short of staggering. Why have these online platforms been so successful? I propose that they cater to our innate need to connect to others, as rooted in our instinctual desire to forge reciprocal alliances. We are a social species, and as such we need to connect with others. Human sociality is a defining feature of our species, and it has in part shaped the evolution of the human mind. George Vaillant, the Harvard psychiatrist who is the current head of the seven-decades-long Harvard Study of Adult Development, stated the following when asked to identify the key finding of the megaproject: "That the only thing that really matters in life are your relationships to other people."[21] The need for social contact is so strong that prisoners in violent maximum-security prisons often prefer to take their chances in general population rather than remaining within the guaranteed safety of solitary confinement. This need to affiliate manifests itself across countless social species. For instance, given their pack mentality, dogs fare very poorly when left alone, at times experiencing debilitating separation anxiety fears. Such fears are seldom if ever documented in cats, which are solitary animals.

The importance of human interconnectedness has generated a burgeoning interest in the study of human social networks. More generally, many phenomena, whether in nature or human-made, are manifestations of networks.[22] For example, the human brain is effectively a distributed network of neurons connected via synapses. The Internet is an extraordinarily large interlinked web of computer networks. Human diseases can be mapped along a network as a means of demonstrating the interconnectedness of the genetic roots of particular diseases.[23] Scientometrics is the study of academic citation networks (i.e., who cites whom). Sociometry is the quantitative analysis of networks of social relationships (e.g., identifying an opinion leader by mapping the informational flow between the members of a social clique).

Recent books that have demonstrated the power of human social networks include Duncan J. Watts's *Six Degrees: The Science of a Connected Age*; John T. Cacioppo and William Patrick's *Loneliness: Human*

Nature and the Need for Social Connection; and Nicholas A. Christakis and James H. Fowler's *Connected: The Surprising Power of Our Social Networks and How They Shape Our Lives*. Watts's book provides compelling demonstrations of how interconnected all humans are to one another (coined the Small World Phenomenon), which is akin to the Six Degrees of Kevin Bacon game (all actors are connected professionally to Bacon using six or fewer links). Cacioppo and Patrick highlight the wide range of psychological and medical benefits reaped by those who possess deep and meaningful networks of friendships (those not socially isolated). Christakis and Fowler show that many phenomena diffuse to three levels within a given social network. For example, whether you gain weight or whether you are happy may be linked to whether your friend's friend's friend has gained weight or is happy. In other words, whereas all individuals in the world (who do not live in closed societies) might be linked to one another via at most six degrees of separation, the diffusional power of social networks extends mainly to three degrees of separation. This finding is relevant to many consumer-related phenomena such as the diffusion of fads and marketing memes (catchy slogans or memorable ad jingles), through processes such as viral marketing and word of mouth. Ultimately, YouTube's societal and commercial impact lies in its ability to serve as the effortless viral propagator of countless types of messages to millions of people.

Cultural transmission via information sharing is an evolved capacity of the human mind. Accordingly, it is not surprising that online brand communities—an example of which would be a weblog of aficionados of the Harley-Davidson brand and lifestyle—have become powerful marketing tools, as they ultimately facilitate the innate desire to share information (in this case with like-minded individuals). Brand communities constitute a direct application of the human need to be connected, and to create coalitional groups. In this case, like-minded consumers connect not only to one another but also to the product or brand that they feel passionate about. The benefits of such connectivity are multifaceted. Brand communities serve as a supraorganism for new product ideas. Consumers who belong to brand communities display great loyalty to their preferred product, as such this forum triggers our innate proclivity to engage in coalitional thinking or, more colloquially, the us-versus-them mentality. A diehard Mac user typically construes the world into a clear dichotomy: Mac users (us) and others (them). Belonging to a brand community of Mac lovers only serves to accentuate that feeling of belonging, which is a central element of any social species. Marketers' recognition of the power of human sociality has spawned new marketing terms, such as tribal marketing[24] (establishing tribes or brand communities of individuals who possess a passion for a brand and wish to be connected to one another via their common passion) and herd marketing[25] (targeting consumers' instinct to influence and copy one another akin to the movement of a herd). These concepts are rooted in an understanding of our biological-based human nature.

Facebook, which has recently surpassed five hundred million users, is a fertile environment for exploring human universals. Recall Dunbar's number, the notion that humans have evolved to live in bands of no greater than 150 individuals. Several studies, some of which have used data sets consisting of several million users, have found that the average number of friends for Facebook users hovers around the expected 150.[26] Various facets of our innate human nature manifest themselves in a completely novel environment (the Internet), which is radically different from the environments faced by our ancestors.[27] The manner in which Facebook users present themselves in their profiles is another ripe area for an evolutionary analysis.[28] For example, women are undoubtedly more likely to use appearance-related cues in their profiles (e.g., a greater number of photos highlighting their looks), while men are more likely to incorporate cues regarding their social status (e.g., which prestigious schools they've attended; occupational status). The means by which the sexes present themselves to the world is replicated within the online medium, be it on social networking sites or personal web pages.

CONCLUSION

Humans are a social species with a deep need to connect with others. Human sociality is in part driven by the evolutionary imperative to form bonds of reciprocity. These human universals manifest themselves in numerous consumer settings, such as the gifts that we offer to our close friends, the traditions of hospitality found in otherwise disparate cultures, the trust that is inherent in economic transactions, and the innate need to signal in-group membership (e.g., wearing the latest fashions, sporting a tattoo, supporting a sports team). Finally, the recent explosion of online social networking sites (e.g., Facebook, Twitter, YouTube, brand communities) speaks to the evolutionary forces that drive our desire for human interconnectedness.

CHAPTER 6

CULTURAL PRODUCTS: FOSSILS OF THE HUMAN MIND

The genes hold culture on a leash.
—E. O. WILSON, AMERICAN BIOLOGIST[1]

Paleontologists utilize skeletal and fossil remains when seeking to understand the evolutionary history of a species. In the October 2, 2009, issue of *Science*, a group of scientists led by Tim D. White reported their paleontological finds of a remarkable set of hominid fossils predating the infamous Lucy partial skeleton by more than one million years. In doing so, they added one missing link to the phylogenetic history of humankind. Generally, skeletal and fossil remains have been at the forefront of the efforts to reconstruct the evolutionary tree of life. Other techniques such as molecular phylogenetics use mitochondrial DNA and proteins as the key substrate in mapping the similarity of species within the grand tree of life. Species that are more closely related (in terms of their evolutionary history) will typically have more similar molecular structures. The famous dictum that 98 percent of our DNA is identical to that of chimpanzees is a testament to their being our close evolutionary cousins.

For the evolutionary psychologist, these approaches are difficult to apply in understanding the evolution of the human mind. First, the human mind does not fossilize, so the tools of paleontology and archaeology are of minimal value. Second, in spite of the great advances that have taken place in the mapping of the human genome, we still do not have a good understanding of which specific genes (or gene interactions) code for particular adaptations of the human mind. All is not lost, however; there are ample remnants that can be used to elucidate the evolutionary forces that have shaped the human mind. They are everywhere around us. The songs that we listen to while stuck in traffic; the billboards that we whiz by on the highway; the television shows and movies that tickle our emotional fancy; the great literary works that engross us; the self-help books and advice columns that we turn to for comfort; the religious narratives that provide us with answers to our existential angst; and the art that titillates our visual system, to name but a few examples.

Countless cultural products are fossils of the human mind or "cultural remains," as they function as an archival repository of the invariant forces that shape our humanity. Specifically, our cultural products contain certain recurring themes irrespective of cultural setting and historical period because they serve as windows to our shared biological heritage and universal human nature. Such content analyses can be applied to other cultural products including comic books, toy figures, reality-based television shows, soap operas, video games (e.g., avatars; *World of Warcraft* versus *Sims*), music videos, romance novels, hardcore pornography, news headlines, personal ads, proverbs, urban legends, rumors, and so forth. By studying the universal contents found in these cultural products, we are able to understand human nature at its most fundamental level.

Prior to delving into an analysis of specific "cultural remains," let us look at other evolutionary-based approaches for studying culture.[2] One can construe cultural products as adaptations. In the same way that various morphological traits and behavioral patterns can be selected, via natural or sexual selection—if they increase an organism's survival or reproductive outlook—some authors have argued that cultural products can also serve such purposes. The operative question under such an approach becomes: "What is the adaptive value for art, music, or literature?" Ellen Dissanayake applied this approach in arguing that the creation of art is a form of "making-special" that ultimately promotes group cohesiveness (i.e., an adaptive goal for a social species).[3] Geoffrey Miller asserts that cultural products are sexual signals typically used by men to augment their value on the mating market. Miller proposes that in the same way the peacock's tail is an honest signal of his fitness because it is wasteful (in that he can possess such a tail despite the fact that it hinders his ability to avoid predators), the mastery of many cultural forms are wasteful signals that ultimately speak to the reproductive value of those who produce them.[4] Undoubtedly, it is this mechanism that explains why the short-statured and hardly dashing Pablo Picasso could apparently command the attention of so many women. In his 2009 book *The Art Instinct: Beauty, Pleasure, and Human Evolution*, Dennis Dutton suggests that our innate appreciation for art is due both to natural as well as sexual selection; thus he agrees with both Dissanayake and Miller. Other evolutionists have proclaimed that many cultural products are exaptations (by-products) of particular adaptations, not unlike how the color of our skeletal system (white) is a by-product of other evolutionary forces. This position has been generally argued by Steven Pinker,[5] the famed popularizer of evolutionary psychology, as well as by Pascal Boyer in his evolutionary account of the origins of religion. Specifically, Boyer proposes that cognitive processes that originally evolved for other purposes drive our capacity for religiosity.[6]

What might explain the evolution (in the non-Darwinian sense of the term) of particular cultural forms? For example, what (if any) are the predictable forces that have generated art movements such as impressionism, cubism, art deco, surrealism, and neo-expressionism? Colin Martindale argued that in the same way that random genetic mutations constitute the driving engine for Darwinian selection to operate, a sufficient level of novelty from an existing art form is the means by which new movements are founded[7] (or "speciated," if one were to use the biological analogy to its fullest). The evolution of genres within a particular culture form is shaped by Darwinian selection, albeit the substrate for selection is novelty from the status quo.

Whereas all of the latter approaches contribute toward a Darwinian understanding of culture, I adopt a different approach. Specifically, I examine five cultural products—namely, song lyrics, music videos, television shows, movie themes, and literary narratives—and observe how their contents speak to the indelible marks of our common biological-based human nature and consumer instinct.

SONG LYRICS AND MUSIC VIDEOS

Song lyrics constitute some of the most powerful cultural fossils for those wishing to understand the evolution of the human mind.[8] The majority of songs—be they sung by troubadours in the Middle Ages; by contemporary Arabic, French, or Hindi singers; or by contemporary American and British pop singers—share one thing: they deal with love and sex, and as such they constitute a powerful repository of universal mating preferences. To be more precise, roughly 90 percent of songs have mating as their central theme, and this holds true regardless of cultural setting or historical period.[9] In a way, this is not surprising. We are a highly intelligent sexually reproducing species. As such, it would only make sense that songs, which are ultimately about expressing raw emotions, should deal with mating, one of our most basic Darwinian concerns. If Abraham Maslow were correct that the apex of human needs is self-actualization, we should find more songs about reaching one's potential as a human being and fewer about sex!

Songs contain invaluable information regarding the attributes that men and women seek in their romantic partners. Numerous studies have revealed that men and women display universal mating preferences irrespective of economic, social, cultural, ethnic, religious, or political factors.[10] These immutable preferences are also impervious to temporal settings. Men and women in ancient Greece possessed the same mating preferences as those living today in New York City. On a few attributes, men and women see eye to eye, whereas on others there are clear sex differences. Specifically, both sexes value intelligence and kindness in their prospective partners. However, given that men place a much greater importance on a woman's physical beauty (as these serve as important indicators of youth and fertility), they are overwhelmingly more likely than female singers to sing about such matters. One does not find song titles such as "You Are So Intelligent" or "You Have Such a Nice Personality" but endless songs lauding women's beauty: Joe Cocker's classic "You Are So Beautiful," James Blunt's "You're Beautiful" (which received the all-important Oprah seal of approval), Jarvis Church's "So Beautiful," and more recently, "Beautiful" by Akon. At times, the language is not quite as romantic, as in the iconic hip-hop song "Baby Got Back" by Sir Mix-A-Lot. In the song, the rapper goes so far as to express specific bodily measurements (36-24-36) that he perceives as insufficiently curvaceous. Of interest, the represented waist-to-hip ratio is 0.667, which is indeed slightly below the near-universal male preference of 0.68 to 0.72.[11]

What do female singers sing about? They definitely do not spend much time serenading men regarding their beautiful abs, tight buns, and muscular torsos. This does not imply that women do not care about male beauty, for they certainly do. However, it is unequivocally clear that this is not the main attribute that drives women's mating preferences. Several studies have repeatedly found that no matter what the context, women have a preference for high-status males (or at least men who have the potential to attain high status). Few women are turned on by the thought of a lazy, socially submissive, and talentless man. This is why we do not have songs with titles such as "Ravage Me, Unemployed Man" or "Your Apathy and Lack of Ambition Are Turning Me On." However, we have endless examples of songs that either describe a woman's desire for a high-status man (or a man who possesses resources) or that denigrate men for being of low status. For example, Destiny's Child's "Bills, Bills,

Bills" and TLC's "No Scrubs" both refer to men who fail to invest in, and provide resources to, their women and who are of low status (e.g., do not own a car, are living at their parents' home). Gwen Guthrie's "Ain't Nothin' Goin' On but the Rent" explicitly warns that there will be no loving if the man does not have the necessary job and corresponding resources. Marlena Shaw's "Go Away Little Boy" refers to the rebuffing of her man's advances given his repeated inability to secure resources (the song's title could not be any clearer). Sister Sledge's "The Greatest Dancer" describes a highly desirable man at a nightclub by enumerating the high-status clothes he is wearing. Apparently, the suit does make the man. Missy Elliott's "Hot Boyz" makes it clear that attractive men drive expensive cars and own premium credit cards. Beyoncé's "Upgrade U" featuring her husband, Jay-Z, equates an "upgrade" of a man with the possession of high-status items (classic Rolls Royce, fancy suits, expensive jewelry, large diamond). The song's video consists of a continuous flow of aesthetically pleasing images of luxury items.

Even though women singers are most likely to sing about men's social status, they regularly express their attraction to physically dominant men (as captured by their athleticism, heroic jobs, or thuggish "bad boy" nature). This is well exemplified in Bonnie Tyler's "Holding Out for a Hero" and Destiny's Child's "Soldier," as the ladies make it clear that alpha dominant males are desirable. Note that this is radically different from what some refer to as "benevolent sexism." The general idea is that women face two forms of sexism: the "traditional" hostile sexism and a more benign form of sexism that construes women as delicate creatures in need of male help. Accordingly, various forms of chivalry, gallantry, courtship gift giving, and protective behaviors (e.g., intervening to help a woman who is being aggressively accosted by a man) are all supposed representations of benevolent sexism. Another example is a man stating that he places his wife on a pedestal, and that his life would be incomplete without her love.[12] The reality is that most of women are highly desirous of such "benevolent sexist" traits in their prospective suitors. This is captured not only in surveys meant to elucidate women's mating preferences but also in the cultural products that are created by women for other women (e.g., in song lyrics or romance novels).

Not surprisingly, the issues that men boast about in their songs are meant to appeal to women's mating preferences. Most hip-hop songs contain roughly the same theme: "I have the money and the status, you have the nice body. Let's hook up." For example, the contemporary rapper T. I. has a song titled "You Can Have Whatever You Like," in which he makes the point that he can provide all the material benefits to his love interest. *Making bank* is a recent urban idiom that refers to making a lot of money quickly, which is a highly sought-after route for many male rappers. At least three hip-hop songs are titled "Money in the (da) Bank," including the songs by Lil Scrappy (featuring Young Buck), Lil Wayne, and Swizz Beatz (featuring Young Jeezy, Eve, and Elephant Man). One of Lloyd Banks's albums shares that song title as well (at times *Banks* is written as *Bank$* to cue that he is rich, I suppose). While boasting about one's resources is a frequent theme covered by male singers, another mating-related topic is the ever-looming threat of paternity uncertainty as captured memorably in such songs as Michael Jackson's "Billie Jean" and Kanye West's "Gold Digger."

Music videos are an equally powerful medium from which to study evolved mating preferences. This is especially the case with R&B videos in that they do not adhere to the political correctness that is so prevalent in contemporary society. There is a raw honesty about this discourse, at least when it comes to some of the attributes that men and women find attractive in one another. Generally speaking, the same universal theme is displayed; namely, male rappers exhibit their ostentatious newly found wealth against the backdrop of an endless parade of scantily clad beautiful women. One particular behavior repeatedly displayed by male rappers might at first appear peculiar. Why are these young men repeatedly shown throwing away large amounts of cold hard cash? I am not referring here to wasteful spending; the behavior in question involves the artist (and at times his male entourage) literally throwing away thick wads of bills. At first glance, the behavior appears to demonstrate a wanton disregard for money and an obscene penchant for waste. It's one thing to talk about wasteful consumption and another to throw away money in nightclubs, from balconies, and from moving vehicles. Examples of this action can be found in music videos such as "Money Ain't a Thang" by Jermaine Dupri and featuring Jay-Z,[13] "I Am So Fly" by Lloyd Banks, "Balla Baby" by Chingy, and "Make It Rain" by Fat Joe featuring Lil Wayne. I propose that this posturing is a form of costly signaling akin to the peacock's ostentatious tail. In throwing away large sums of money, the male artist is effectively saying, "I am so wealthy that such extravagant waste carries little consequences to me. I am the real deal. Otherwise, I could not afford to engage in this behavior." The street credentials of Darwinian theory are now assured!

Whereas one typically associates product placements with television shows and movies, a more recent form of product placements is the incorporation of brand mentions within song lyrics.[14] Agenda Inc., a consulting firm located in San Francisco and Paris, conducted a project a few years ago coined *American Brandstand* in which they kept track, for three consecutive years (2003–2005), of brand mentions in songs on Billboard charts. In almost all instances, the products mentioned were luxury items meant to signal one's abundant resources. As expected, male singers uttered most of such mentions. Of the forty-five top mentions (over the three years), twenty-three were of cars, all but one of which were luxury cars (Mercedes, Lexus, Cadillac, Lamborghini, Chevrolet, Range Rover, Bentley, Rolls Royce, Jaguar, Maybach, and Porsche); eleven were of clothing items and related accessories, most of which were luxury brands (Gucci, Burberry, Prada, Payless Shoe Source, Dolce & Gabbana, Manolo Blahnik, Nike, Rolex, and Louis Vuitton); seven were of alcoholic beverages (Cristal, Hennessy, Dom Perignon); three of guns (AK-47 and Beretta)—undoubtedly as a means of signaling one's capacity to engage in male-based intrasexual rivalry; and one toiletry (Calgon). To the extent that song lyrics speak to our basal Darwinian drives, it makes perfect sense that the advertised products within this art form are consistent with these biological concerns.

In 1975, the country singer Mickey Gilley recorded a song titled "Don't the Girls All Get Prettier at Closin' Time" that subsequently spawned a scientific study to test this exact premise.[15] In the song, Gilley notes with remarkable poignancy how men's opinions regarding prospective female suitors change as the likelihood of leaving the bar alone increases. In other words, men have the capacity to alter their minimal acceptable thresholds when looking for partners for short-term dalliances. Such a process is much less likely for women, as their cost-benefit calculus for short-term versus long-term mating is much different than that of men.[16] Men's mating preferences can be radically different, depending on the temporal context of the relationship (e.g., promiscuity is desired in short-term mates but detested in long-term ones), but women's preferences are more consistent across the two temporal settings, as their cost for making a suboptimal mating choice is the same without regard to whether they are impregnated by a short-term or long-term mate. This is precisely why we are unlikely to ever have a song titled "Don't the Men All Get More Handsome at Closin' Time." On a related note, YouTube has a highly popular post of a television advertisement attributed to the Danish brewery Tuborg, which has apparently been banned for its supposed sexist undertones. A man is shown drinking a beer as he watches an average-looking woman sitting facing him at another table. The more he drinks, the more beautiful the woman appears to him. That men's mating perceptions might be particularly malleable when "liquid courage" is consumed again speaks to the differential costs and benefits associated with making a poor mate choice for each of the two sexes. This "alcohol effect" has been validated in two separate studies: in one instance the effect only applied in ratings of opposite-sex individuals,[17] while in the other study, it was operative when rating both same-sex as well as opposite-sex individuals.[18] It is surprising that the effect was found for both sexes, when one might otherwise expect it to be largely operative for men.

TELEVISION STORYLINES

According to a recent quarterly report released by the Nielson Company, in the first quarter of 2009, Americans watched on average 153 hours and 27 minutes of television per month. This amounts to roughly five hours per day of television viewing. If you live for seventy-five years and start watching television only at the age of five (i.e., seventy operative years of television viewing), five hours a day translates into roughly 14.5 years of your life spent watching television! Here is another way to look at the same number: If you assume that the average person sleeps eight hours a day, this leaves sixteen waking hours. At five hours per day of television viewing, this means that most people spend more than 30 percent of their waking hours in front of the television. I share these numbers as a means of establishing the importance of analyzing the contents of television shows. What is it about television that can serve as such an alluring pull that we are willing to forego other choices vying for our valuable time? At its most basic level, television entertains us. If you enjoy bowling, then watching a professional bowler on television might be an enriching experience. Similarly, if cooking is your hobby, you might appreciate a show that highlights the culinary talents of famous chefs. In this sense, television simply recognizes the fact that we have large brains that need constant nourishment.

Television does more than merely entertain us. It provides us with content that caters to our evolutionary hot buttons by virtue of the central storylines found in a given sitcom or prime-time drama. We become emotionally attached to television characters because we relate to the issues that they face within their fictional worlds. In other words, successful screenwriters generate transportable storylines to innumerable cultural settings precisely because they are universally shared (e.g., the global success of *Seinfeld*). In this sense, television shows constitute a rich "cultural fossil" from which one can glean deep insights regarding the evolution of the human mind. I demonstrate this point via a content analysis of storylines from *The King of Queens*, *Seinfeld*, and *Curb Your Enthusiasm*.

The King of Queens was a highly successful CBS sitcom that ran for nine years (1998–2007). It chronicled the lives of a blue-collar married couple (Doug and Carrie Heffernan, played by Kevin James and Leah Remini), their entourage of friends, and Carrie's wacky father, Arthur Spooner (played by Jerry Stiller, who also played George Costanza's father on *Seinfeld*). There are a multitude of episode themes that are indicative of evolutionary-based phenomena. In a 2002 episode titled "Food Fight" (season 4, episode 13), Carrie becomes excessively jealous that Doug is appreciating his friend Spence's girlfriend's cooking. Because of this, Doug and Becky (the girlfriend) develop an emotional bond rooted in their respective love of good food (she is a chef and he is a glutton). This pushes Carrie over the edge, as she construes this as tantamount to emotional infidelity. Why would women care about such platonic relationships? The answer lies in universal sex differences in the triggers of romantic jealousy.

The two sexes are equally prone to experience romantic jealousy. However, if one were to explore the triggers of romantic jealousy, clear sex differences do indeed emerge. David Buss, one of the leading evolutionary psychologists of the past two decades, conducted a study with several colleagues wherein they had participants envisage their romantic partners engaging either in emotional or sexual infidelity.[19] In the former instance, an emotional bond is forged, but the relationship is strictly platonic. Buss and his coauthors measured respondents' physiological responses to such scenarios (heart rate, skin conductance, and facial electromyography), as people might otherwise lie on paper-and-pencil surveys when it comes to such sensitive issues. Although both forms of infidelity displease both sexes, men experienced the greater stress when exposed to the sexual infidelity scenario, whereas emotional infidelity triggered the greater stress in women. The evolutionary reasons behind this pervasive sex difference are quite simple. Only men experience the threats of parental uncertainty (recall that paternity uncertainty is a real concern—there is no such thing as maternal uncertainty). Hence, men would have evolved the emotional system that seeks to thwart such a threat. On the other hand, one of the greatest threats to women's reproductive interests in our evolutionary history would have been to be abandoned by their long-term male partners, given the extent of biparental investment required in the human context (e.g., resources, protection). Accordingly, when a man forms an emotional yet platonic bond with another woman, this is actually more predictive of his likelihood of withdrawing or diminishing his investment from his current partner (and children) than if he were to have a "meaningless" one-night stand with a woman he would never see again. This is precisely the reason that when men cheat, they will often use the justification "She meant nothing to me. It was just sex." As deplorable as this might sound, it is at times true. Men are able to fully disassociate love and sex in ways that are consistent with their reproductive interests. I wish to reiterate that providing an explanation for adultery does not in any way condone or justify it. In another episode of King of Queens titled "Deacon Blues" (season 3, episode 15), Doug catches his best friend, Deacon, having dinner with another woman. He shares the incident with his wife, Carrie, which subsequently leads to an argument, as they cannot agree about whether this constitutes cheating. Carrie thinks it is cheating, while Doug argues that void of sex, it is not cheating. Note again that the storyline accords with universal sex differences regarding infidelity.

In the 2004 episode titled "Damned Yanky" (season 6, episode 16), Carrie catches Doug fantasizing about several women while he is sedated at the hospital (his appendix had burst). Later, Carrie decides to take a moment to engage in some of her own fantasies, at which point she fantasizes about a single high-status man (the physician who was treating Doug at the hospital, who happens to be Leah Remini's husband in real life). Why didn't the screenwriters write the pattern of fantasies in the opposite manner (i.e., Carrie fantasizing about many male partners and Doug about one high-status woman)? Scientific research that has explored sex differences in the frequency and content of sexual fantasies are exactly congruent with the latter episode.[20] Men fantasize much more frequently and do so about a much greater number of sexual partners (and with a much greater likelihood of the fantasy being devoid of emotional attachment). Therefore, screenwriters are not being sexist in depicting a given difference between the two sexes. Rather, they are simply recognizing evolved sex differences that are universally valid. On a related note, "The Contest" (season 4, episode 11) was one of the most infamous *Seinfeld* episodes and spawned the iconic phrase "master of my domain." The four leading characters—Jerry, George, Kramer, and Elaine—take up a bet with one another to see who can last the longest without masturbating (or, more colorfully, remain "master of their domain"). The episode is particularly poignant in terms of highlighting universal sex differences in sexuality. First, Elaine has to contribute a larger amount of money into the pool (as compared with the three male characters) in recognition of the physiological fact that men have a much more difficult time resisting masturbatory urges. Second, the stimuli that drive the various characters over the masturbatory edge are quite revealing. For example, Kramer "loses" as a result of repeatedly seeing through the window a beautiful female neighbor exercising in provocative attire; a visual image served as his downfall. Elaine, too, succumbs to her urges. However, in her case, it is the thought of becoming the wife of John F. Kennedy Jr. (whom she had met earlier in the episode) that serves as her masturbatory catalyst. Sexual imagery is more intoxicating to men, and long-term coupling with a high-status partner is a stronger driver of women's mating preferences. Contrary to the

social constructivist argument that television serves as a sexist socialization agent of gender roles, the screenwriters of *Seinfeld* have created storylines that are consistent with our evolved biological-based human
nature (along with the associated sex differences).

The universal import of social status is another theme that is accurately captured in fictional storylines. In the *King of Queens* episode
"Pour Judgment" (season 7, episode 11), on the behest of Carrie, who
wishes for Doug to be more professionally ambitious, Doug decides to
pursue his dream of becoming a bartender. This displeases Carrie
greatly, as she is not particularly proud of being the wife of a bartender
(a low-status profession). She eventually alters her unfavorable view of
the profession when she sees the amount of tips that Doug is able to
garner, and accordingly pushes him to take a bartending job at a swanky
Manhattan nightclub. This storyline is perfectly consistent with the fact
that women are desirous of high-status and ambitious mates, who are
otherwise capable of generating sufficient resources to invest in their
families. No culture has yet been found in which men value the social
status of their respective mates more so than women do. Accordingly,
the "transportability" of this story, via syndication, to several other cultures is natural. This is what allows individuals stemming from various
cultural settings to appreciate storylines from ancient Greek mythology
thousands of years after they were created.

In another episode titled "Patrons Ain't" (season 4, episode 22),
Doug and Carrie are confronted with the fact that they are not charitable people. As a means of remedying the situation, they decide to
donate $500 to an elementary school library. They become upset upon
realizing that they have been wrongly recognized on the plaque of
donors. They should have been placed in the "patrons" section (given
the size of their donation) whereas they are incorrectly listed in the
"friends" section. They end up engaging in several machinations in the
hope of remedying the situation. On a related note, in the *Curb Your
Enthusiasm* episode titled "The Anonymous Donor" (season 6, episode

2), Larry David and Ted Danson each donate money to a museum. Although Larry's donation is publicly recognized, Ted's is attributed to "anonymous." However, Larry quickly finds out that the supposed anonymity of Ted's generosity is hardly that, since everyone seems aware that the donation in question is Ted's. This angers Larry, as he argues that Ted is garnering too much gratitude and goodwill, both for his charitable donation as well as for having "refused" to identify himself.

These two episodes are a powerful demonstration of the fact that philanthropy is often used as a public signal of social status. As a business school professor, I am only too aware of the lengths that universities and other institutions go to in order to attract wealthy benefactors via the allure of having the school named after them. I work at the John Molson School of Business, not at the Anonymous Benefactor School of Business. In a sense, these named philanthropic acts cater to individuals' narcissistic needs. But from a biological perspective, they often serve as costly and hence honest signals. Pretenders might be able to match the purchase of a $200,000 car but not a $40 million donation. In this sense, philanthropy is at times tantamount to the peacock's tail. The inherent benefits of signaling (e.g., increased social prestige) associated with philanthropy were recognized by Maimonides, one of the greatest Jewish theologians, who was also a physician and philosopher. He argued that one of the purest forms of *Tzedakah* (charity) was when neither the benefactor nor the recipient was aware of the other's identity. Despite his religious pedigree, Maimonides was ultimately a Darwinian being and able to espouse religious and moral tenets that are perfectly consistent with evolutionary principles.

Other than tickling universal affective triggers, television also caters to the human need to gossip. Several genres of television programming, be they talk shows, celebrity gossip shows, or soap operas, ultimately serve a key function—they provide us with social information to share at the proverbial office watercooler.

HUNGRY FOR GOSSIP: *TMZ* VERSUS *GENERAL HOSPITAL*

Social species have evolved elaborate communication systems in part to share ecologically relevant information with their group members. The information can be relayed by several sensorial systems, including pheromones (e.g., social ants), vocalization (e.g., wolf howling), non-verbal cues (e.g., gelada baboons flipping their lips to show off their large canines), and bubbling (e.g., vibrations that male crocodiles emit as part of their courtship ritual). My wife and I often joke that when we take our two dogs out for a walk, their incessant sniffing is akin to our reading the gossip section of a newspaper. In their case, they are "reading" the latest canine gossip news from the neighborhood via the urine markings. This is one of the reasons that walking one's dog is important beyond the exercise benefits reaped by both humans and their canine partners.

The human ability to communicate via language is what differentiates us from all other species. This allows us to share social information congruent with the complexity of our social world. Of the endless functions that our language faculties serve, gossip is a universally important one. Robin Dunbar's book *Grooming, Gossip, and the Evolution of Language* provides a thorough analysis of the adaptive value of this form of social exchange. Not only do the great majority of conversations revolve around gossip but also the contents of gossip deal with issues of evolutionary import. We do not gossip about our neighbor's quest for self-actualization by his having purchased season tickets to the opera. Rather, we are more than happy to gossip that his wife is cheating on him, that he has an impotence problem, that he just lost his job, or how his wife's breast augmentation surgery went. In the end, humans are particularly interested in gossiping about sexual matters (e.g., promiscuity, closeted homosexuality), as poignantly captured in the 1986 hip-hop song "Rumors" by the Timex Social Club. I spent quite a bit of time writing my first book (*The Evolutionary Bases of Consumption*) as well as this current one at one of several cafés. As might be expected in such public settings, I have been privy to endless conversations from surrounding tables. Ambient noises travel even when one is trying to avoid eavesdropping! I can assure you that I have seldom heard people engaging in deep intellectual conversations. Most chats are either about mundane life decisions ("we need to purchase a new dinner table") or juicy gossip.

Evolutionary psychologists have actually studied what people gossip about and whom they gossip about. Of ten possible sets of people (e.g., relatives, friends, acquaintances), individuals preferred most to gossip about friends for eight of the ten listed gossip topics. These were substance-related problems (drug abuse and drunken behavior), gambling problems, sexual misconduct (promiscuity and sexual infidelity), sexual dysfunction, and ethical and criminal lapses (academic cheating and computer theft). Receipt of a sizable inheritance and contracting leukemia were the two topics that people preferred to gossip about with relatives. This is not surprising, since wills are distributed according to genetic relatedness, and life-threatening diseases are typically most anxiety-provoking when they strike our family members. Of note, individuals preferred to gossip about same-sex individuals and about issues that are particularly important to each of the two sexes. For example, men and women preferred to gossip about same-sex individuals who had gambling problems and were promiscuous respectively.[21] The bottom line is that we enjoy sharing social information about the vices and problems faced by same-sex others. Incidentally, teenage girls are particularly amenable to using false gossip as a bullying tactic against intrasexual rivals as a means of damaging their reputation. As the brilliant British philosopher Bertrand Russell quipped: "No one gossips about other people's secret virtues, but only about their secret vices."[22]

Numerous commercial offerings cater to consumers' insatiable appetite for celebrity gossip. These include television shows such as *TMZ, Entertainment Tonight, Access Hollywood,* and *Extra,* as well as long-lasting tabloid magazines such as *Star, National Enquirer,* and

People. Think of the most memorable celebrity gossip you've heard over the past five years. In most instances, the gossip is probably an example of one of the topics listed in the previous paragraph: drug abuse (Amy Winehouse), drunken behavior (Lindsay Lohan), sexual infidelity (John Edwards), promiscuity and infidelity (Tiger Woods), gambling problems (Michael Jordan), life-threatening diseases (Patrick Swayze), and moral lapses (Mel Gibson's threats to his young girlfriend and drunken anti-Semitic diatribe). Why do we care to exchange gossip about celebrities, all of whom are otherwise total strangers to us? If we prefer to gossip about friends as discussed earlier, why care about celebrities?

Satoshi Kanazawa, an evolutionary psychologist from the London School of Economics, has proposed a compelling explanation for this conundrum. He argues that in the same way that pornography usurps men's evolved physiological reaction at the sight of seeing a naked woman (i.e., having an erection), even though it carries no reproductive benefit, celebrities cause our affective system, which was originally meant to be activated in our interactions with real friends, to misfire. In other words, adaptations meant to solve problems in our evolutionary environments can be artificially triggered in contemporary settings. After all, many of these celebrities are invited into our homes on a weekly (if not daily) basis. We develop a sense of intimacy with the celebrities if not the characters they play, and in so doing our brains are tricked into viewing them as part of our Dunbar circle.[23] Kanazawa demonstrated empirically a positive correlation between the extent to which people viewed particular television shows and their satisfaction with their real-life friends. For example, a woman who watches several shows dealing with friendship (e.g., sitcoms) is more likely than others to transfer that illusory reality into her real-life friendships.[24]

Moving beyond celebrity news, one can also explore the contents of sensational news (e.g., headlines) as a means of gauging the stories that capture our attention and tug at our emotions. How do news outlets decide which stories are newsworthy? I propose that stories that cater to one of the key Darwinian pursuits (survival, mating, kin, and reciprocity) are likely to be heavily represented. Headlines about predator attacks, natural disasters, and violent criminality speak to our interest in stories of survival (or death). Captions about sexual misconduct are obviously catering to our obsession with all matters related to mating. Gruesome stories about infanticide or uplifting ones about long-lost siblings who are reunited speak to the kin meta-drive. Finally, headlines about heroic acts of physical bravery (jumping into a river to save a random stranger) or of bewildering generosity (a company owner bequeaths his firm to his employees upon his retirement) represent the reciprocity meta-drive (acts of altruism toward nonkin typically rooted in the desire to establish bonds of reciprocity). In a content analysis of gripping stories, as reported on the front page of newspapers and spanning more than three hundred years and five continents (North America, Europe, Oceania, Asia, and Africa), many themes were manifestations of one of the four Darwinian meta-drives, including stories about courtships (mating), family dynamics (kin selection), human attacks (survival), and heroic acts of bravery (reciprocal altruism).[25] The frequency rankings of the various types of headlined stories were invariant to cultural settings and to particular epochs. This suggests that the stories we most want to read are universally defined, as they are precisely those that had great import in our evolutionary past. When watching news broadcasts or reading newspapers, we are catering to our innate desire to gossip, especially about information that was valuable to share in our evolutionary past.[26]

I conclude this section with a brief discussion of soap operas. This is a universal genre that is found across highly heterogeneous cultural settings. *Wikipedia* lists soap operas originating from fifty-five different countries.[27] Several content analyses of soap operas have uncovered recurring universal themes in this television genre including sexual infidelity (with the requisite paternity uncertainty), power struggles, sibling rivalries, parenting challenges, love and romance, bonds of friendships, and a wide range of interpersonal betrayals and deceptions, to name a few.[28] All of these map quite clearly onto the Darwinian meta-pursuits discussed earlier. Whether you are watching an Indian, Egyptian, American, or Mexican (telenovela) soap, you can be assured that roughly the same set of issues drive the open-ended storylines.

Gossip is a central facet of soap operas.[29] The storylines within soap operas move forward in large part via the gossiping that takes place within the shows. Soap opera characters are gossip maestros! Then viewers of soap operas engage in extensive gossiping about the events that transpire within their favorite soaps. As a matter of fact, there are several forums—magazines (e.g., *Soap Opera Digest* and *Soap Opera Weekly*), newspaper columns, websites, blogs, and other online communities—that exist for the sole purpose of gossiping about the events that transpire within the fictional worlds of soaps. No matter the cultural setting, the majority of soap opera viewers are women. Accordingly, the contents of soaps are illustrative of the evolutionary forces that have shaped women's sex-specific psychology. For example, male protagonists fall under a very predictable universal archetype; they are typically tall, powerful, socially dominant men, who hold prestigious occupations (e.g., physician, CEO). At times, they can also be high-risk-taking "bad boys." Feeble, effeminate, submissive, unemployed, short-statured men are seldom (if ever) depicted as soap opera heroes. The bottom line is that successful products, whether pornography, soap operas, or romance novels, recognize the innate preferences of the target audience in question.

MOVIES

In a report released by the Motion Picture Association of America in 2008 titled *Theatrical Market Statistics*,[30] domestic (United States and Canada) and international box office sales for 2008 were $9.8 billion US and $18.3 billion US. The report adds that in 2008 alone, 610 films were released domestically. If we were to include DVD movie rentals, movies watched on television via broadcast (e.g., ABC), regular cable (e.g., AMC) or pay stations (e.g., HBO), and those viewed on commercial flights, this amounts to a large chunk of a consumer's discretionary leisure time and income. At times, movies entertain us because they provide escapism from any semblance of reality (e.g., superheroes who fly). However, in most instances, they offer us gripping fictional depictions of our innate human nature. The central plots are nearly always about issues of evolutionary import, including survival (*Cast Away, Panic Room,* horror movies), romantic love (*Love Story, An Affair to Remember, The Notebook*), infidelity (*Fatal Attraction, Unfaithful, Moonstruck, The Graduate*), cuckoldry (*Chaos Theory*), parental love (*Sophie's Choice, Lorenzo's Oil, Kramer vs. Kramer*), sibling rivalry (*The Other Boleyn Girl, Hannah and Her Sisters*), sibling support (*Rain Man*), family businesses (*The Godfather*), altruism (*Schindler's List*), and friendships (see the long list of examples in chapter 5).

Movie plotlines are emotionally gripping and cognitively engaging because they push the right evolutionary buttons.[31] This is why movies are so easily transportable across cultural settings, let alone time periods. The pull of most movies is not rooted in postmodernist, feminist, deconstructionist, Marxist, or Freudian realities, which constitute some of the more common frameworks used in film analysis. Rather, movies are spellbinding because they engage us at the most fundamental of our Darwinian selves. A heart-wrenching sad scene that makes an American viewer cry is likely as poignant when viewed by individuals from Bermuda, Japan, Mexico, or Papua New Guinea. I suspect that were it possible to show the scene to a Bronze Age audience, they would have reacted in the same manner.

Let's look at a few film plotlines that are indicative of an underlying evolutionary principle. I begin with a recent movie that captures our innate drive to engage in positional conspicuous consumption, usually referred to as "keeping up with the Joneses," memorably captured by advertising slogans such as "Neighbour's envy, owner's pride" (Onida TV), and "If you've got it, flaunt it" (Braniff Airlines). What matters most to consumers is not some absolute level of achieved wealth (or accumulated products) but having more than others who are relevant to us. This is precisely the idea behind social comparison theory. Women might not feel insecure about their looks when compared with supermodels, as these are literally genetic mutants who are unlikely to navigate within most women's social circles. However, a beautiful girl next door can be quite threatening. The 2006 movie *Keeping Up with the Steins* captures the competitive nature of conspicuous consumption by using the backdrop of showy bar mitzvah ceremonies as the means by which families display their social status.[32] After discussing several extravagant and ostentatious themes, the parents (played by Jeremy Piven, best known for his portrayal as a sleazy Hollywood agent on HBO's *Entourage*, and Jami Gertz) decide to hold an understated no-frills bar mitzvah ceremony at their home. A rival couple is astonished by their friends' decision to forgo the opportunity to show off. The male rival eventually provides an explanation that is a near-perfect definition of honest signaling. He argues that by forgoing the ostentatious ceremony, the family is sending the signal that they are so rich that they do not need to engage in this form of competition (i.e., they can bear the social costs of not organizing a lavish ceremony). Recall that this is the exact logic behind the handicap principle, which is used to explain the evolution of the peacock's tail. To reiterate, the insight regarding the Steins's refusal to engage in showy ceremonies is rooted in costly signaling, a phenomenon found across a wide range of species. In this case, spending little money on the ceremony is the costly signal.

Chaos Theory, released in 2007 and starring Ryan Reynolds, Emily Mortimer, and Stuart Townsend, chronicles the story of a happily married couple (Reynolds and Mortimer) about to receive some problematic news regarding the conception of their daughter. During a visit to a physician, Reynolds's character finds out that he suffers from Klinefelter syndrome, a condition that causes male infertility. As such, he realizes that he could not have fathered his daughter, and is therefore assured of having been cuckolded (Townsend being the "cuckolderer"). The next few scenes of the movie are heart-wrenching, as one sees the extraordinary emotional pain that Reynolds's character experiences at having received such devastating news. The audience need not be primed for such emotional drama. Everyone, but particularly the male viewing audience, can immediately empathize with the cuckold, as cuckoldry triggers one of the most primal and visceral of all Darwinian-rooted rages.

On a related note, the *Maury Povich Show* (now simply known as *Maury*) is a low-brow talk show that seems to repeatedly deal with one topic: paternity uncertainty. Couples are brought on the show, and the male partners are subjected to DNA paternity tests, at which time they often find out that they have been cuckolded. The emotional drama that ensues is gripping, which makes for good television ratings. Based on the general tone of the colorful invectives shouted by the cuckolds upon hearing the DNA results, and the frequency that this topic is addressed on the show, one might think it better to change the show's title to *Bitch, That Ain't My Kid!*

Indecent Proposal (1993) depicts the story of a young, financially strapped married couple in love (played by Demi Moore and Woody Harrelson) who meet a rich and dashing industrialist (played by Robert Redford) during a gambling trip to Las Vegas. During their chat, the young couple and the industrialist disagree about whether money can buy everything. The young couple posit that people cannot be bought, at which point Redford's character puts their strongly held belief to the test by offering an "indecent proposal": the chance to spend one night with Demi Moore's character for $1 million. At first, the couple is horrified by the offer and categorically rejects it. However, the insidious seed begins to grow in their minds. After mulling it over, they eventually decide to accept the offer, and accordingly go through with the deal (resulting in a severe strain on their marriage). This storyline works well precisely because a man is asked to share sexual access to his wife. This is a terribly difficult decision to make precisely because it triggers primal emotions linked to paternity uncertainty. Had the storyline been reversed such that a rich female industrialist had asked a young couple if she could spend the night with the husband, the wife might reply, "Don't let the door hit his butt on the way out!"

There are other movie-related phenomena separate from plotlines that can be explored from an evolutionary perspective. For example, the popularity of particular American actresses is linked to the prevailing macroeconomic and social environments. Specifically, actresses who possess neonate facial features are favored during good times (e.g., Ann Sheridan, Bette Davis, and Judy Garland), whereas those with more mature features are preferred during more difficult periods (e.g., Marie Dressler and Janet Gaynor).[33] Sandra Bullock and Amanda Seyfried are contemporary actresses (not included in the aforementioned study) who possess mature versus neonate traits, respectively.[34] In a manner similar to how fashion trends follow macro-indicators in ways consistent with evolutionary theory, our preferences for actresses' facial features appear equally malleable to the prevailing macro-conditions. I next turn to another form of fiction, literature, and demonstrate how it, too, can be analyzed via a Darwinian lens.

LITERATURE

Similarly to film studies, literary criticism has historically been tackled from particular political, philosophical, or epistemological ideologies. If you are a Marxist, the literary narrative is analyzed through the lens of class struggles. A feminist might dissect the same narrative and identify instances of sexual conflict as manifestations of patriarchal oppression. A Freudian analyst will generate hallucinatory psychoanalytic explanations for every imaginable literary situation notwithstanding the famous warning attributed to Freud that "sometimes a cigar is just a cigar." Postmodernists propose that all knowledge is relative, while deconstructionists posit that language creates reality, so under these worldviews, a literary text can be analyzed in endless possible idiosyncratic ways to extract meaning. On the other hand, evolutionary psychology purports that human universals exist. It recognizes that reality exists outside of linguistic conventions (as do all scientific disciplines), and it espouses the existence of innate sex differences. Accordingly, it is expected that some might construe literary Darwinism as heretical.

How would literature be tackled from a Darwinian perspective? Generally speaking, the approach taken by Darwinian literary critics has been to demonstrate that literary narratives contain universal themes that are manifestations of our common biological heritage. In other words, literature moves us and engrosses us because it contains storylines of great evolutionary import (similar to my earlier argument regarding television and movie themes). Some of the leading proponents of literary Darwinian criticism include Joseph Carroll, Brian Boyd, and Jonathan Gottschall.[35] Typically, literary Darwinists conduct content analyses of a particular literary piece (e.g., the ancient Japanese novel *The Tale of Genji*[36] or Gustave Flaubert's *Madame Bovary*[37]), multiple pieces from a single author (e.g., Homer's ancient Greek epics,[38] Shakespearean plays[39]), samples of a literary genre from multiple authors (e.g., romance novels[40]), or cross-cultural samples of a given genre (e.g., folktales from around the world). The goal is to show that universally recurring elements happen in all the latter literary genres regardless of time and place. For example, folktales from an extraordinarily varied cross-cultural sample have yielded the exact same mating preferences (e.g., women prefer men of high social status, and men favor youth and beauty).[41] On a related note, in describing a literary character, it is nearly always the case that attractiveness is associated with female characters, and this holds true across varied cultural settings and time periods.

Of all forms of fiction, romance novels garner large yearly sales.[42] Understanding the factors that propel the success of this literary genre carries both scientific as well as commercial implications. Romance novels, which are almost exclusively written by women for the reading pleasure of women, describe the male protagonist in nearly identical fashion. Male heroes are bold, tall, socially dominant, confident, and muscular (among other female-preferred traits).[43] Anthony Cox and Maryanne Fisher recently conducted a content analysis of the titles of several thousand *Harlequin* romance novels spanning more than six decades.[44] They gauged whether particular words along with associated themes occurred frequently, and if so, whether these conformed to evolutionary predictions about women's mating preferences. Some of the most common themes dealt with long-term commitment (e.g., marriage, bride), reproduction (e.g., paternity, maternity), and high-status positions of the male characters (e.g., doctor, surgeon, king, CEO). Another common theme was the description of male occupations that involve heroism and physical bravery (e.g., cowboy, rancher, sheriff, bodyguard, knight). If you'd like to know what women fantasize about, read the titles of romance novels! Literature provides us with the opportunity to escape into fictional worlds that are ultimately rooted in human universals shaped by common biological forces.

The Oxford evolutionary biologist and staunch atheist Richard Dawkins has famously stated that religion should be taught as part of a liberal education, albeit as a form of literature (fiction). With that spirit in mind, I provide herewith a discussion of a recent content analysis that was conducted on the Old Testament, the most famous of all "novels." The contents of religious narratives betray that these stories were created by Darwinian beings rather than by divine sources. Take the universal finding that there is a positive correlation between a man's status and the number of mating opportunities that are afforded to him. It turns out that this exact reality is found in the Old Testament. Specifically, Laura Betzig, who in 1986 wrote a book about the reproductive benefits that accrue to despotic rulers, turned her attention to the Old Testament to explore the link between men's social status and their sexual conquests.[45] Not surprisingly, Betzig found that the men who possessed the highest social status—such as patriarchs, kings, and judges—had the most sexual access to a wide range of women, including wives, concubines, servants, and slaves; they also took the greatest liberty in poaching other men's wives (e.g., King David and Bathsheba). Of course, all these unadulterated sexual conquests led to greater reproductive fitness (i.e., more children) for the most powerful men of the Old Testament.

Along these lines, a rabbi once explained to me that there is a Talmudic edict that requires of Torah scholars to marry the most beautiful women. In the context of highly religious Orthodox communities, the term *scholar* is reserved for students of the Torah and the Talmud. Physicists, chemists, mathematicians, psychologists, historians, and other academics, intellectuals, and scientists are not covered by the orthodox appellation of what it means to be a scholar. This is why the rabbi in question had once "explained" to me that my scientific career should be considered a "daytime hobby," and that I should attend religious classes at night for "real studies." Viewed from this perspective, since experts of the Torah and the Talmud—namely, rabbis—are the men with the greatest social status, it only makes logical sense that they be afforded the most beautiful women!

CONCLUSION

Since the human mind does not fossilize, evolutionary scientists must utilize alternative means for studying the evolutionary forces that have forged the human mind. Cultural products, spanning countless cultural settings and epochs, can be construed as fossils of the human mind. A wide range of cultural products—including song lyrics, music videos, television and movie themes, and literary narratives—contain universally recurring themes that are indicative of our common biological heritage. Accordingly, the detailed study of these ubiquitous cultural remains sheds light on the Darwinian realities that have shaped the evolution of our human nature.

CHAPTER 7
LOCAL VERSUS GLOBAL ADVERTISING

The greetings are different, the need to feel
welcome is the same. You don't just stay
here—you belong.
> —*SLOGAN FOR SHERATON HOTELS
> & RESORTS*

It is insight into human nature that is the key
to the communicator's skill.
> —*WILLIAM BERNBACH,
> ADVERTISING PROFESSIONAL*[1]

We have seen that a wide range of cultural products could be construed as fossils of the human mind. The contents of advertising could also be viewed as cultural remains that inherently project both the importance of human universals and culture-specific traditions. One of the most heated and still unresolved debates in international marketing is the so-called local versus global issue (also known as adaptation versus standardization). Should Coca-Cola design one advertising campaign from its Atlanta headquarters and transport it to all its global markets? Alternatively, should it tweak its advertising copy in recognition of local cross-cultural differences? Is the use of sex in advertising equally effective in all countries? Can the same beautiful endorsers be used in different cultures? Do humorous ads require culture-specific adjusting? Does the use of the color green result in the same connotations around the world? These questions have substantial financial implications, given that the estimated global spending on advertising for 2010 was $456 billion.[2]

Academics and practitioners have yet to propose a framework that can identify when the global or local approach is optimal, as evidenced by these two quotes stemming from recent reviews of the relevant literature:

> After 40-plus years of academic research activity, and over almost 80 years of practitioner debate, the standardization/adaptation issue has remained a viable topic, as measured by academic/practitioner interest and the leading journals in the field. Surprisingly, it has done so without the development of solid theory to support it and with the methodological flaws indicated.[3]

> Advertising standardisation versus adaptation has been discussed in some detail in the marketing literature. Despite previous attempts, there is still no widely used decision-making model available that has been accepted by marketing practitioners and academics.[4]

Generally speaking, practitioners have been stronger proponents of the standardization (i.e., global) approach. Specifically, numerous advertising executives have correctly noted that many human motives and needs are universal, and hence advertising messages that target such drives can be exported across cultural settings. Their position does not stem from an appreciation of evolutionary theory. Rather, their insights are rooted in the fact that, as Darwinian beings, they recognize the obvious reality that consumers from around the world share a common human nature. On the other hand, marketing scholars have strongly supported the local approach. Their position stems in part from the singular academic focus on identifying statistically significant effects, which in this case results in an epistemological bias for identifying cross-cultural differences. If a phenomenon is universal (i.e., yielding no differences between groups), marketing academics construe this as a null effect (i.e., as a statistically insignificant finding).

There are innumerable cultural traits (e.g., individualism versus collectivism) as well as limitless advertising copy variables (e.g., use of fear, humor, sexual imagery, or celebrity endorsements) that can be utilized to generate comparisons across countries.[5] This creates a research opportunity for the marketing academic who wishes to conduct cross-cultural studies likely to yield statistically significant differences between groups. Are comparative ads (e.g., Toyota versus Mazda) as effective in Korea as in the United States? Do Swedish ads contain more humor than their British counterparts? How often are celebrity endorsers used in Japanese and Brazilian ads? Do sexually explicit ads appear more often in countries that have greater gender equality? Are emotional or rational appeals better suited for different countries? The combinations and permutations are nearly endless. The reality is that in many instances, such studies are nothing short of fishing expeditions for statistically significant findings. The obtained results are seldom if ever replicated (a hallmark of science), and as such marketing practitioners are rarely able to rely on such findings in designing their advertising copy.

Nevertheless, evolutionary psychology can be used to resolve this practical matter. Explicitly, evolutionary psychology is helpful in determining which advertising copy elements are culture-specific and outside the purview of evolutionary theory (e.g., why yellow flowers have become associated with infidelity in France); which are universally similar and thus within the purview of evolutionary theory (e.g., facially symmetric endorsers are perceived as beautiful regardless of cultural setting); and which are culture-specific but arise as adaptations to local environments and therefore are also within the purview of evolutionary theory (e.g., as discussed in chapter 2, the extent to which a country uses hot spices is determined by its latitude).[6] When marketers speak of global consumers, they are typically referring to the homogenization of cultures that arises as a result of globalization. Generally, globalization has been viewed as the amalgamation of forces that contribute to the eradication of cultural barriers. These might include the hegemony and diffusion rate of American culture around the world, the global inter-connectivity afforded by the Internet, and the accessibility of air travel to a growing number of people across the globe. However, at its most fundamental level, members of the global village are connected by their common biological heritage. The global consumer possesses certain consumption needs, wants, preferences, and motives that are invariant to cultural or temporal contexts. In this sense, the global consumer is defined by a universal human nature.

I would compare the local versus global debate to the universal versus culture-specific elements that shape a child's language acquisition. Languages are extraordinarily varied in terms of their lexicon, grammar (morphology and syntax), and phonology. There are concepts that are captured in one language that are not present in others (e.g., *schaden-freude* in German, which means to rejoice at the misfortune of another; *Tarbih Jmilé* in Arabic, which means "to remind someone that they are indebted to you"). Some languages have gender accord (e.g., Arabic and French). Others do not (Armenian and English). Arabic has guttural sounds that are next to impossible for non-Arabic speakers to replicate. The letter *p* does not exist in Arabic, so native speakers of Arabic will often pronounce English words that start with *p* as though it were a *b* (*paradise* becomes *baradise*). Despite the countless ways by which languages vary from one another, all humans use an underlying universal cognitive computational system in learning their particular languages. This idea was first espoused by linguist Noam Chomsky via his Universal Grammar[7] but has since been popularized by the evolutionary linguist Steven Pinker.[8] As such, in spite of the untold linguistic varieties, there is a fundamental innate biological instinct for learning languages. Consequently, both cross-cultural differences and cross-cultural similarities exist in the arena of linguistic phenomena.

The same principle applies to the local versus global advertising debate. It is unquestionable that there are innumerable phenomena that are culture-specific when it comes to advertising copy. However, it is equally true that many of the ways in which people respond to advertising messages, as well as the contents of particular advertising messages, are invariant to cultural settings. Evolutionary psychology allows us to know with reasonable certitude whether a phenomenon is locally specified or globally invariant.

DARWINIAN ROOTS OF ADVERTISING EFFECTIVENESS

Whenever consumers watch an advertisement, several cognitive processes operate. The perceptual system kicks in as soon as we notice an ad. Perhaps it was the beautiful woman who caught our attention, or the mellifluous voice of the endorser. Maybe it was the use of vivid colors. Understanding these perceptual processes is of great practical importance, as the advertising clutter is extraordinarily high, with the typical North American consumer being exposed to well over six hundred advertising messages in a given day. To advertisers, it is quite disheartening to know that as few as three or four of these ads will be remembered, which leads us to the related cognitive processes of learning. One objective of advertising is to have us learn new product information, which will then become part of our long-term memory. A second objective is to serve as a reminder, such that the next time that you feel hungry, remember to eat a Big Mac (top-of-mind awareness). A third objective is to enhance consumers' attitudes toward the advertised brand, possibly via a liking of a given advertisement. Not surprisingly, then, advertising practitioners and scholars alike have come up with a broad range of variables to measure the effectiveness of an ad. These include attitudes toward the ad (A_{ad}) and toward the brand (A_{br}), brand recognition, brand recall, and purchase intention. Sponsors hope that a good advertisement yields an increase in each of these intermediate variables, thus ultimately resulting in a corresponding increase in sales: $A_{ad} \uparrow \rightarrow A_{br} \uparrow \rightarrow$ Brand recognition $\uparrow \rightarrow$ Brand recall $\uparrow \rightarrow$ Purchase intention $\uparrow \rightarrow$ Sales $\uparrow$. Of course, this linear progression of effects does not always hold true. For example, a highly charged sexual ad might result in an increase in A_{ad} but a corresponding decrease in brand recall. This might occur if the sexual imagery is so overpowering that all attention is devoted to it to the detriment of the advertised brand, which falls to the background.

Brand recall is one of the variables in the latter linear progression. Clearly, to understand recall, one needs to have a good understanding of human memory. Interestingly, marketers and advertisers alike have rarely bothered to explore the adaptive role of memory. This is in stark contrast to animal behaviorists, who typically explore the memory system of a given species via an evolutionary lens (i.e., why would this species have evolved the particular characteristics of its memory system?). A few concrete examples might clarify this point. I have often noticed the squirrels around my house busily stashing food in several spots, undoubtedly in preparation for the long and harsh Montreal winters. Somehow they are able to accurately recall the exact locations where they have buried their stashes without necessarily being able to smell them. Numerous animals display similar feats of memory that are typically linked to food foraging. In addition to having to recall cache sites, they have to remember migratory routes, locations of water holes, and distribution of food patches within their territories. They have to remember which plants are poisonous and which are edible. The folk belief regarding the astounding memory of elephants is rooted in scientific facts. Of course, social species also make use of their memory to keep track of the status of shifting social alliances. If I have invited you to dinner on five different occasions and you have yet to reciprocate, it is worthwhile for me to remember this information. As a matter of fact, when shown the faces of several individuals, people are better able to recall those who were labeled as cheaters.[9] Furthermore, both sexes are better capable of

Male red-capped manakins and human males both use dancing as a strategy to attract prospective female mates. *Lynn E. Barber (top). "Chaoss"/Veer (bottom).*

Architectural constructions, be it a bower created by the male Satin bowerbird or an opulent mansion, serve as sexual signals meant to display desirable mating traits: aesthetic and architectural abilities (bower) or social status (mansion). *Steve Bowman/Corbis (top). Yuriy Davats/Veer (bottom).*

Both the peacock's tail and the luxury sports car serve as honest mating signals. Both communicate the message "I can pull off this extravagant tail [or afford this expensive car] precisely because I am the real deal. Choose me instead of the fakers and poseurs." *"Creatista"/ Veer (top). "Fckncg"/Veer (bottom).*

Females in innumerable species signal their receptivity to sexual advances as a function of their menstrual status. Whereas a female chimpanzee might advertise her engorged genitalia when in estrus, women dress more provocatively during the fertile phase of their menses. *Irven DeVore/Anthro-Photo (top). "Chaoss"/Veer (left).*

Whether it is the hummingbird's need to consistently amass caloric intake given its extraordinarily high metabolism or our innate penchant for all-you-can-eat buffets, food gorging as an adaptation to the threat of caloric scarcity is found in numerous species. *Susan McKenzie/ Veer (top). "Picsfive"/Veer (bottom).*

An inborn gustatory preference for fatty foods is an adaptation to caloric scarcity and caloric uncertainty. Grizzly bears gorge on fatty salmon in preparation for the looming harsh winters, and humans display an irresistible pull to equally fatty foods such as a juicy burger. *Ocean Photography/Veer (top). Nuno Garuti/Veer (bottom).*

Kin selection explains the deep bonds of affiliation that are found in numerous species, including in baboon society or in human families *(my family in December 2009, below)*. Such kin bonds explain a wide range of consumer-related behaviors, including gift exchanges between family members. *Barbara Smuts/Anthro-Photo (top). Saad family (bottom).*

Reciprocal altruism is found in numerous social species. It serves as a social lubricant for interactions between nonkin. In chimpanzee society, this might manifest itself via reciprocal grooming ("I'll groom you now, and you'll reciprocate later."). In the human context, gift giving between friends is a similar phenomenon ("I'll buy you a birthday gift now, and you'll give me a present later when it's my birthday."). *Richard Wrangham/Anthro-Photo (top). "OJO Images Photography"/Veer (bottom).*

Biomimicry utilizes solutions that have evolved in nature in the service of developing better human-made products. Spiral designs *(as shown in the Nautilus shell, above left)* can optimize the flow of energy (relevant when designing green buildings or efficient impellers); in other instances they augment the strength and buoyancy of the material. A gecko's feet contain adhesive properties that material scientists are seeking to synthetically replicate in their laboratories. Many spiral designs found in nature are generated by fractals, which are self-replicating algorithms that generate symmetric patterns of great aesthetic beauty. Ultimately, nature is the most innovative and prolific product designer. *"Corbis Photography"/Veer (top left and right). Germán Ariel Berra/Veer (bottom).*

The red patch on the chest of the male Gelada baboon, which is correlated to his status and hence testosterone levels, is a potential warning signal to ward off rival males. Women use the color red to attract prospective male suitors. Hence, the same color can have different biological-based connotations depending on whether it is used for intrasexual rivalry or intersexual wooing. *Chadden Hunter (top). "Corbis Photography"/Veer (bottom).*

The N'Gol ritual, practiced by the indigenous people of the island of Pentecost (part of the archipelago of Vanuatu), is an honest signal of male courage. Pretenders would be incapable of "faking" their way through such a rite of passage. Bungee jumping is a commercial off-shoot of this tribal practice. During the Geerewol festival, Wodaabe men (Western Africa) beautify themselves for prospective mates, even though female beauty remains of primary importance within this society. *John Nicholls/http://www.vanuatu-hotels.vu. (top). Dan Lundberg/flickr (bottom).*

Many forms of beautification such as those shown in the above photographs are culture specific, namely, lip and ear plating *(Mursi woman from southern Ethiopia, left)* and neck elongation *(Kayan woman from Thailand, right)*. However, some components of beauty are universally defined, such as a preference for symmetric faces, as shown in the photographs below. *Ariadne Van Zandbergen/Afripics.com (top left). Wojciech Samotij (top right).*

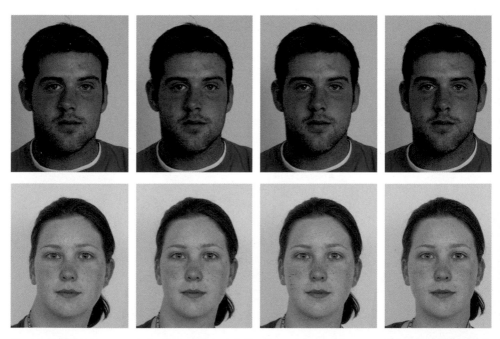

For each of the two panels (male and female), the faces increase in symmetry from left to right. The two leftmost faces had their symmetry decreased via a morphing program; the right-most face had its symmetry artificially increased; the third photo from the left is the original. Most individuals would likely evaluate the rightmost faces as being the most attractive. *Lisa M. DeBruine and Benedict C. Jones/Face Research Lab, University of Aberdeen.*

recalling beautiful female faces.[10] This puts a new twist to Nat King Cole's classic song "Unforgettable."

There are several ways to study the adaptive nature of human memory. James Nairne and his colleagues have shown that human memory is enhanced when information processing is linked to a survival scenario.[11] Suppose you were shown a list of thirty words and then asked to gauge how important each would be to your survival if you were stranded somewhere. Alternatively, you might be asked to evaluate the importance of the same set of thirty words in completing your move to a new home (e.g., how valuable would a car be in both scenarios). Subsequently, a surprise memory test is administered to gauge how many of the words are recalled. The survival scenario consistently outperforms all other forms of information-encoding scenarios. In other words, the provision of a "survival prime" results in improved memory. This might explain why some advertisements based on evoking fear can lead to greater recall. In a sense, the fear appeal is tantamount to a survival prime.

A second way to explore human memory from a Darwinian vantage point is to gauge the semiotics that make an ad memorable. We have evolved a memory bias that allows us to better recall stimuli that carry great evolutionary import (e.g., particular words, faces, or smells). In the same way that Pavlovian conditioning is best achieved via different senses depending on the organism in question (e.g., taste for rats, vision for humans, olfaction for dogs), the memorability of a stimulus is species-specific. In the human context, advertisements that contain evolutionarily memorable content will be universally more likely to be recalled, irrespective of the cultural setting. All other things equal, advertisements containing cute babies, sexy endorsers, and fear-inducing stimuli are typically attention grabbing and will likely yield greater recall.

Frequently, advertisers use various forms of conditioning to associate their products with desired images, attributes, lifestyles, or outcomes. By repeatedly associating a rugged, virile, masculine cowboy to Marlboro cigarettes, it is hoped that there will be a transfer of these attributes to the advertised product. Or advertisers will suggest that by using a particular product, important rewards will befall the consumer (e.g., recall the Axe effect, wherein the use of the deodorant will make a man irresistible to hoards of women). The reality is that many unconditioned Pavlovian responses and rewards in Skinnerian conditioning are universally valid because they appeal to our common biological heritage. As discussed earlier, an example of a universal unconditioned response is our innate positive reaction to animals, especially those possessing neotenous features (as occurs with babies, puppies, and kittens). Two of Canada's leading telecommunications companies, Fido and Telus, use animals as an integral part of their branding and advertising. Recently, Telus revived the classic 1953 song "I Want a Hippopotamus for Christmas" by Gayla Peevey, which generated considerable buzz. The insurance company Geico uses a talking gecko as its endorser. Other famous animal endorsers have included the Aflac duck, Charlie the Tuna, Budweiser's Clydesdale horses, the Energizer Bunny, Esso Tiger, Joe Camel, the Meow Mix cat, Morris the Cat, Smokey the Bear, the Taco Bell dog, Tony the Tiger, the Cottonelle kittens, and Bud Light's Spuds MacKenzie. Again, the assumption here is that for most individuals, consumers' positive feelings toward animals constitute an unconditioned response. That is, advertisers need not worry about having to condition this favorable affection toward animals, as it already exists in us. As such, by associating their products with particular animals, marketers are hoping for a transfer of the positive feeling from the animals to their products.

There are numerous other universal unconditioned responses, along with the associated advertising effects and cues, that hold true across cultural settings, which include innate responses to deep voices, sexual imagery, and fear appeals.

ADVERTISING EFFECTS AND CUES
AMENABLE TO A GLOBAL APPROACH

The Barry White Effect

Here is a thought experiment. Suppose that during the last US presidential campaign, we had magically substituted Barack Obama's voice for that of Ross Perot, who, you might recall, ran for the presidency as a third-party candidate both in 1992 and 1996. Imagine that every single syllable that Obama uttered publicly during his campaign would remain the same; however, his voice would be altered to that of Perot. Do you think that Obama still would have won the election? The reality is that the populace uses several such peripheral cues in judging political candidates, none of which have anything to do with substantive issues. These include voice pitch, oratory skills, personal charisma, facial features, and height.[12] Whereas political candidates are selling themselves, advertisers will often use endorsers to sell their products. At times, a celebrity's voice pitch is instrumental in deciding whether he is appropriate for a particular advertising campaign. As a means of demonstrating the power of voice quality, I provide first a few classic examples of famous narrators, all of whom possess hypnotic and deep voices. The actor Dennis Haysbert endorses Allstate Insurance Company. James Earl Jones—the voice of Darth Vader in *Star Wars*—intones the iconic "This is CNN." Will Lyman narrates PBS's *Frontline* as well as numerous movie trailers. The late Paul Winfield was the first narrator of A&E's *City Confidential* and was eventually replaced by the actor Keith David. Finally, the Oscar-winning actor F. Murray Abraham, whose voice has been described as well modulated and mellifluous, has lent his talents to a *Nova* episode on Sir Isaac Newton as well as to numerous *Nature* episodes.

Deep voices in men are linked to greater exposure to pubertal testosterone, and as such are preferred by women. Incidentally, women's preferences for men with deep voices is greatest during the maximally fertile stage of their menstrual cycles,[13] which suggests that voice quality is a measure of phenotypic quality. Interestingly, a recent study found that men's voice pitch was correlated to their reproductive fitness.[14] This reminds me of a personal story from the annals of my single days. I had been put in touch with a beautiful Eastern European model via a mutual friend. He thought that we might hit it off as prospective romantic partners. The woman and I chatted on the phone on several occasions prior to finally meeting face-to-face. One of the first things that she uttered when we finally met was her surprise at the incongruity between my voice and my height (I am shorter than she is). She had thought that someone with my "phone voice" should have been much taller. We recently reconnected, at which time I teasingly reminded her of this story (to her dismay at having been so direct in sharing this particular thought). It is worth noting that in some instances, having a beautiful voice would have resulted in a reproductive Darwinian cul-de-sac, as was the case with the eighteenth-century Italian castrato Carlo Maria Broschi (see the 1994 movie *Farinelli*, which chronicles his life). More generally, young boys who possessed beautiful voices were castrated as a means of preserving their prepubescent vocal ranges.

Returning to the spokesmen, we see that they all share one attribute: deep voices that exude an air of trustworthiness, authority, and expertise. When peddling insurance, serving as the voice of a news service, or narrating political or scientific shows, deep voices immediately confer a sense of credibility. This fact is likely true in all cultural settings. In other words, there is no reason to expect that men who possess high-pitched nasal voices render women weak in the knees in Bolivia. The link between testosterone and voice pitch is a universally valid one, as is women's preferences for dominant high-status men. Accordingly, advertisers can rest assured that the use of male endorsers who possess deep voices will yield the same effect in all cultural settings. And although James Earl Jones might be the appropriate voice for CNN, a British accent might be required for the BBC. The local-global issue arises here as well; the evolutionary framework permits us to identify the attribute that is universally valid (voice pitch), as well as the one that is locally specified (local accent).

Universal Response to Ad Repetition

One of the most important issues when designing an advertising campaign is to identify the optimal number of times that an advertisement should be repeated, a topic known among advertising scholars as repetition effects. One might think that this is largely determined by a firm's advertising budget, but this is not always the case. Even if a firm had unlimited financial resources at its disposal, more ad exposures do not necessarily translate into better outcomes (in terms of the various metrics of advertising success). Rather, repetition effects follow an inverted-U shape; repeating a message is beneficial up to a point, subsequent to which if one exceeds the optimal number of exposures, one enters the diminishing returns section of the curve.

Psychologist Daniel E. Berlyne proposed that the inverted-U repetition curve is an amalgamation of two separate forces, which he coined the two-factor theory.[15] When we are first exposed to a message, a great amount of incremental learning takes place. With each additional exposure, there are fewer nuggets of information to take away from the message. Thus, incremental learning increases at a decreasing rate and ultimately reaches a plateau (i.e., no new learning can occur after a certain number of exposures). An opposing factor, tedium (or boredom), is also operative. Imagine the first time you watch a surprisingly humorous ad. Perhaps you broke out into boisterous laughter. The second time, the humor is markedly diminished. Maybe the tenth time you see the ad, you now hate it! Tedium increases at an increasing rate. The joint effect of the two opposing forces (i.e., incremental learning and tedium) results in the inverted-U shape that captures repetition effects.

Doug Stayman, one of my former doctoral committee members, and

I conducted several studies to explore how the sequence in which various advertisements are shown might affect their subsequent evaluation. Presume that a firm has a budget to show an advertisement nine times over a given time period. Furthermore, suppose that the advertising campaign consists of three executions of the ad, each of which is to be shown three times (i.e., three ad executions are to be shown three times each for a total of nine showings). For example, the Energizer Bunny "Keep Going" campaign contains numerous ad executions of the same central message. In this instance, the various ads consist of cosmetic changes in the execution of the same advertising message. In other cases, the executional changes are more substantive (e.g., providing novel information with each new execution). If the three executions are denoted by E1, E2, and E3, the advertiser still has to decide how to sequence these within the nine exposures. For example, two sequences might be:

E1 E2 E3 E1 E2 E3 E1 E2 E3 (string length = 1)
E1 E1 E1 E2 E2 E2 E3 E3 E3 (string length = 3)

Stayman and I coined a new term, *string length*, to refer to the number of times that one execution is shown prior to switching to another. As shown, the first sequence above has a string length of 1, and the second one has a string length of 3. Which of the two sequences is best to use? According to classical economics, since both sequences contain the same total information, their ultimate efficacy should be identical irrespective of the order in which the information is presented. This viewpoint proposes that humans are hyperrational decision makers (*Homo economicus*) who should not be swayed by such "irrelevant" factors. Since this mythical species exists solely in the fertile imagination of economists, it is no shock that members of *Homo sapiens* do indeed care about the order in which information is presented.

More than forty years ago, Norman H. Anderson—one of the founding members of the psychology department at the University of

California at San Diego—developed information integration theory to explain precisely how information is processed when presented serially. His extensive research shows that order affects matter greatly. Suppose that you were shown a list of adjectives about a prospective coworker and then asked to judge her upon seeing the full list of adjectives (e.g., how likely would you be willing to work with this person on a 1–10 scale, with 1 meaning "not at all" to 10 meaning "fully willing"). Of course, in describing any individual, some of the adjectives are positive (+) ones (e.g., hardworking, honest, respectful) while others are negative (-) (e.g., manipulative, domineering, dogmatic). If the list consists of six adjectives, then one could generate many sequences in which to present the information including: [+ + + − − −], [− − − + + +], [+ − + − + −], [− + − + − +], among others. Not surprisingly, order matters greatly. For example, when early information carries more weight than the ending information, it is known as the primacy effect. When the ending information is weighed more heavily than early information, it is referred to as the recency effect. Generally speaking, for evaluative tasks such as the one described above, primacy is more likely to be operative, as the early information serves as the anchor (or prism) against which later information is processed. So if you were to see three positive adjectives first, you would start developing a "glowing hue" in support of this prospective coworker. As the negative information starts to filter in, you might discount some of its impact in light of the affirmative anchor that you've already established.[16] The recency effect is more likely to matter for memory tasks (e.g., if you were asked to list as many of the adjectives that were used to describe the prospective coworker after having seen the full list). It makes intuitive sense that the most recently viewed information would be more readily accessible in our memory.

In our sequencing study, Stayman and I predicted and found that the optimal string length depends on the complexity of the advertising message. If an advertisement is complex (e.g., it contains a lot of substantive information), then a longer string length is preferred. Conversely, if the ad is simple, then a shorter string length is a superior choice. We used Berlyne's two-factor theory to make these predictions. When a message is complex, it takes a greater number of exposures to the same message before one reaches the plateau of incremental learning. As such, tedium will be forestalled until little or no new information can be gleaned from an additional exposure. But when presented with a simple message, a consumer might learn all the information contained therein very quickly (i.e., the incremental learning plateau is reached after one exposure), in which case tedium sets in much earlier. Accordingly, switching to another execution of the ad will likely maintain the interest of the consumer, and as such will delay the eventual boredom that is sure to set in.

The manner in which humans habituate to novel stimuli is a psychological universal and hence should be impervious to cultural setting or historical specificity. The cognitive mechanisms that drive these sequencing and repetition effects are likely universal ones. As a result, an advertiser can rest assured that these findings are transportable across cultural boundaries.

Universal Response to Fear Appeals

Fear appeals are one of the most frequently used tools in public service announcements, especially ones dealing with public safety (e.g., drinking and driving) or personal safety (e.g., the risks of suntanning, the dangers of engaging in unprotected anal sex, the health consequences of living a sedentary lifestyle, and having poor eating habits). A practical question gauges the amount of "optimal" fear that an advertiser should elicit in a given advertisement; the relationship between the efficacy of a fear appeal and the amount of fear that is elicited follows an inverted-U shape. Specifically, too little fear will fail in drawing one's attention to the ad, as well as perhaps signaling that the issue is not of paramount importance. However, triggering too much fear can yield a fatalistic outlook or possibly a freezing mechanism akin to that experienced by deer when facing the lights of an oncoming car.[17] Too much fear can also cause an individual to avoid the message. Sarah McLachlan's song "Angel," which plays as a background to an animal abuse public service announcement, generates a feeling of horror in me. Upon hearing the first few notes, my sole concern is to find a way to change the channel as quickly as possible as a means of avoiding the unbearable images of suffering animals (my empathy for animals makes me fearful of such horrifying images). A recent *Saturday Night Live* skit played on this exact issue; there is now such a conditioned relationship between McLachlan's song and the animal abuse ad that it causes many animal lovers to recoil in horror upon hearing one or two notes of the song.

An intermediate level of fear is typically vivid enough to cause individuals to dedicate cognitive resources to the message while at the same time empowering them with strategies to address and hopefully resolve the fear-inducing issue. There is no reason to think that the manner in which humans respond to varying levels of fear appeals is a culture-specific phenomenon. Rather, the fear response is a universal emotion that originally evolved as an adaptation to environmental threats. Advertisers can accordingly rest assured that the inverted-U shape described above is operative across all cultural settings and hence is definitely within the purview of a global advertising approach. Incidentally, not only is the fear response curve a likely human universal, but also certain images trigger universally innate fears. For example, snakes and spiders cause many people to recoil in horror. It is not difficult to imagine how such fears, which at times can manifest themselves as clinical phobias, might have evolved.

Universal Use of Sexual Imagery and Beauty Metrics

Though some may believe otherwise, advertisers do not have hidden agendas associated with sex-based identity politics. They are in the business of creating advertisements that are maximally effective in reaching targeted audiences. It is their business to get the message right. To the extent that visual imagery associated with young and beautiful women is alluring to men, advertisers will use such tactics to sell any product under the sun.[18] There is no logical connection between beer and beautiful women, and yet the two are habitually linked when selling beer to men. One might argue that such tactics are demeaning to women. If so, then advertisements that highlight high-status tall men are demeaning to short-statured men who happen to be unemployed janitors.

Sexual imagery in advertising is used in similar ways around the world,[19] and the advertising of actual sexual services contains recurring universal themes as well. As a means of testing this premise, I conducted a study to determine whether the waist-to-hip ratios (WHR) of female escorts as advertised on the Internet would conform to the near-universal male WHR preference of 0.68 to 0.72. This preferred hourglass figure serves as a reliable marker of health and likely fertility.[20] From an evolutionary perspective, it is clear how men would have evolved a visual preference for this particular WHR. My data was collected from forty-eight countries in Europe, Latin America, North America, Asia, and Oceania. In total, the WHRs of 1,068 advertised escorts were recorded. Congruent with the evolutionary prediction, the mean WHR around the globe was 0.72, although some regions yielded slightly higher WHRs (e.g., WHRs of North American escorts = 0.763, and that of escorts from the Oceania region was 0.75).[21]

It is important to note that this WHR preference is not learned via exposure to advertising images; it has been found in cultural settings where the men are unlikely to have been exposed to supposed Western ideals of feminine beauty. Barnaby J. Dixson and colleagues explored the WHR preferences of men in remote regions of Papua New Guinea.[22] Their preferences were perfectly consistent with the hourglass figure (mean WHR of 0.72). Note, though, that men's WHR preferences are coined a near-universal (and not a universal) precisely because evolutionists recognize the importance of local environments in tweaking the evolutionarily established set point. For instance, researchers have shown that in some environments where caloric scarcity is an endemic challenge, men display a preference for slightly higher WHRs.[23] Hence, an innate biological-based preference interacts with idiosyncratic niches in establishing the culture-specific WHR norm.

Many WHR studies have typically elicited preferences via a paper-and-pencil methodology. Recently, researchers have applied novel approaches to confirm men's preference for a WHR of 0.70. Using an eye-tracking methodology, Dixson—along with several colleagues—confirmed that of six anatomical areas of a naked woman, men very quickly evaluated the breasts and the midriff area. Furthermore, a WHR of 0.70 was judged to be more attractive than a corresponding image with a WHR of 0.90.[24] Steven Platek and Devendra Singh showed men preoperative and postoperative photos of women who had had surgery meant to yield a WHR close to the preferred near-universal of 0.70. As the men viewed the photos, their brains were scanned using an fMRI (functional Magnetic Resonance Imaging) machine. Amazingly, when viewing the postoperative photos, there was greater activation in regions of the brain associated with the processing of rewards. In other words, there is evidence at the neuronal level for men's evolved preferences for the hourglass figure.[25] Finally, a recent study has found that even congenitally blind men display similar WHR preferences, as gauged via touch![26] The totality of these findings makes it rather fatuous to argue for the social and arbitrary construction of beauty.

Given that many beauty metrics are universally defined (e.g., WHR and facial symmetry), advertisers are assured of the universal response to such cues. For example, an endorser for a beauty product is overwhelmingly likely to possess facial symmetry (as this is a universal marker of beauty), and this reality holds true whether peddling cosmetics to women in Peru, Saudi Arabia, or Japan. Along those lines, Patrick Vyncke manipulated fitness cues in print ads (e.g., endorsers' waist-to-hip ratios and facial symmetry) to establish how these might affect viewers' ad preferences. Predictably, the favorite ads contained endorsers exhibiting the evolutionarily preferred fitness cues.[27] This fact would hold true regardless of time or place.

Need to Belong versus Need for Uniqueness: A Universal Struggle

Earlier I discussed how the need to belong is a human universal, and how the fashion industry relies on this exact instinct. That said, our need to belong waxes and wanes throughout our lifetime. A young couple who just had their first child is less likely to be absorbed with the need to belong as compared with an average teenager. As a matter of fact, the desperate need to belong is perhaps never as great as during adolescence. Advertisers seek to communicate with teenagers by frequently using that powerful appeal. Pepsi-Cola has been particularly adept at employing this desire throughout more than four decades of advertising campaigns. Typically, the message revolves around belonging to the hip and youthful "Pepsi generation." Classic slogans include "Come Alive, You're in the Pepsi Generation," "Join the Pepsi People Feelin' Free," and "Pepsi. The Choice of a New Generation." This form of advertising appeals to the herd,[28] which in this case corresponds to groups of impressionable teenagers, most of whom possess a desperate need to belong and to con-form to group expectations. Of note, consumers' innate proclivities to engage in, and respond to, herding behavior extend beyond fashion trends (see chapter 5) and advertising appeals. Herd mentality is an ever-present threat within the financial industry, as evidenced with the run on the banks during the recent financial crisis. It is this herding threat that ultimately forced the Obama administration to raise the amount of an individual's savings that the FDIC will insure.[29]

Though all humans have an innate need to belong—and teenagers around the world constitute the group with the greatest penchant for that need—this universal phenomenon is tempered by cultural settings.

For example, a country's score on the individualism-collectivism (I-C) continuum will determine the strength of an individual's desire to conform to group norms. All other things equal, both American and Japanese teenagers have a strong desire to conform to fashion trends, though these pressures to conform might be greater for those hailing from a collectivist society (Japan) as compared to their individualist counterparts (United States). This demonstrates the interaction between our biology and our environment in shaping our behaviors as consumers. Incidentally, a driving factor for a country's score on the I-C continuum is the extent to which pathogens have historically been present within its geographical niche. Collectivism ensures lesser intergroup mixing (in-group and out-group boundaries are more clearly and rigidly defined), as well as a greater likelihood for conformity (e.g., in establishing norms of hygiene). Researchers found that the greater the amount of pathogens within a particular environment, the greater the country's score on collectivism.[30] In other words, collectivism is a cultural adaptation to a greater likelihood of being exposed to pathogens. Note how culture and biology intermingle in a seamless manner in arriving at a complete understanding of the phenomenon in question.

As we discussed, for a social species such as ours, conforming to group norms is a central feature of our universal human nature, as is our equally strong drive to express our individuality.[31] It follows that advertisers have devised messages that cater to each of these two psychological needs, namely, social proofing (proposing that if many individuals take a course of action, it must be appropriate, as in McDonald's "Billions and Billions Served"), and scarcity appeals (proposing that if an item is rare, it must be valuable, as in "limited-edition" wines or car models). In the first instance, the advertiser states that the sheer number of consumers who have used this product serves as a badge of quality; in the second instance, the appeal is for uniqueness and distinctiveness. Vlad Griskevicius and his colleagues recently demonstrated that depending on whether survival or mating concerns were primed (by watching one of two movies—*The Shining* or *Before Sunrise*) had an effect on which of the two appeals was most effective. Specifically, social proofing worked best when survival was primed (i.e., safety in numbers) whereas scarcity was more effective when mating was primed (i.e., one should appear unique within the mating domain).[32] It is difficult to imagine why this phenomenon would be culture-specific. One might expect that the reactions to such appeals would be universally valid.

ADVERTISING EFFECTS AND CUES AMENABLE TO A LOCAL APPROACH

French-Canadians are fiercely protective over their unique North American heritage. Growing up in Lebanon within a minority Jewish community, I understand the feeling of being a small cog in a big wheel. French-Canadians have always felt that the English-speaking Canadian and American tsunami would swallow them if they did not take drastic measures to protect their linguistic and cultural heritage (as evidenced by the Draconian measures of the Quebec Language police). Pepsi was able to brilliantly seize upon the existential insecurity of French-Canadians. In the perennial global battle of the two cola giants, Quebec is one of the few places in the world where Pepsi has maintained a larger market share than Coca-Cola. One of the key reasons driving this reality is Pepsi's recognition of the unique character of the French-Canadian consumer. Accordingly, Pepsi has utilized a local advertising strategy in targeting the French-speaking market of Quebec (e.g., the use of the Quebecker comedian Claude Meunier). A standardized message originating from Atlanta (headquarters of Coca-Cola) that does not recognize the distinctiveness of the French-Canadian consumer is likely doomed for failure. As a side note, French-Canadians are at times referred to as "Pepsi" (by anglophone Canadians) as a means of denigrating them, perhaps in part due to this rare market share reality.

Having provided an example of the power of local advertising from my own backyard, I turn next to a discussion of two advertising copy elements that are culturally determined: color connotations and language use.

Color Connotations

Colors are used extensively in marketing, be it in packaging, branding, or advertising. Most people easily recognize that Coca-Cola and Pepsi are associated with red and blue, respectively. Colors can be used to tug at our feelings (as in creating a mood via the use of colors) or to elicit cognitive associations (gold and red might be associated with prestige and passion correspondingly). Colors are associated with culture-specific holidays and occasions such as Christmas (red and green), Valentine's Day (red), and Halloween (orange and black), all of which are replete with gift-giving implications. We typically assume that blue and pink are universal depictions of masculinity and femininity particularly. These color connotations are so ubiquitous in North America that they have become emblematic of gender socialization (blue is for boys and pink is for girls). That said, in the Netherlands, blue represents femininity.[33] The professional soccer team of Palermo, which plays in the top Italian division, is famous for its pink jerseys. Clearly, then, in international advertising, a key objective is to identify which color connotations or color preferences are universal (if any) and which ones are culture-specific.[34]

The importance of colors is well captured in the number of idioms that utilize specific colors to convey meaning. In the English language, a partial list includes: seeing red, green with envy, tickled pink, feeling blue, clear as black and white, black sheep of the family, the company is in the red (or black), calling someone out of the blue, painting the town red, telling a white lie, being yellow-bellied, having a heart of gold, black comedies, once in a blue moon, having a green thumb, being red in the face, red tape, red carpet treatment, pink slip, and white flag. Needless to say, these color idioms are language-specific and do not necessarily translate well into other languages. For example, "black sheep" in English is equivalent to "white crow" in Russian. In addition, whereas "black sheep" is typically defined as being an outcast, it symbolizes independence in Italy.[35] In Quebec French, *"ma blonde"* (literally translated as "my blonde") means "my girlfriend," even if the girlfriend is a brunette. In this case, a standard hair color is used to describe girlfriends of all races and hair colors.

Colors often become emblematic of one's national identify via the colors of a country's flag. Most people can probably state the colors of the Canadian and Japanese flags (both red and white) or those of the United States and France (red, white, and blue). Companies can also at times become strongly associated with specific colors; the generic term "blue chip companies" refers to financially stable and reputable firms. Owens Corning has a trademark on the color PINK (capitalized), which it uses for its insulation products (using the Pink Panther as the mascot). IBM is known as Big Blue, and UPS is associated with the color brown, which it used in its recent advertising slogan "What can Brown do for you?" NBC's logo, the multicolored peacock, is a historic television icon. T-Mobile took out a trademark on the color magenta, using the logic that within the telecommunications industry, consumers will immediately associate this color with the company. Two of the most famous examples of color use as part of a company's branding are the United Colors of Benetton advertising campaign and Life Savers (multicolored candies). Today, the rainbow flag is a ubiquitous symbol that identifies gay-friendly establishments.

Whereas many color connotations are culture-specific, there is evidence that some responses to colors are universal. For example, blue is the universally preferred color, although it is unclear whether this preference is rooted in our biology.[36] Recall the "red effect," namely, the innate penchant displayed by men when evaluating the attractiveness of women associated with red.[37] In the latter case, red serves as a form of intersexual wooing; it triggers a separate innate response in the context of intrasexual rivalry. In the Olympics, athletes partaking in combat sports are randomly assigned to wear blue or red. Theoretically speaking, this should not have any effect on the likelihood of either athlete winning the match. However, an analysis from the 2004 Olympics found that those wearing red had a substantially higher likelihood of winning, especially so if the two combatants were of roughly equal talent.[38] The authors in question argued that the color red is commonly linked to higher levels of testosterone across numerous species and serves as an honest indicator of dominance and likely aggression. Gelada male baboons (found in the Ethiopian highlands) advertise their fitness via the intensity of a red patch on their chests. Those who possess redder patches reap multiple social and reproductive benefits.[39] Hence, it is important to distinguish the evaluative contexts—intersexual wooing versus intrasexual rivalry—in establishing how the color red affects people.

On a related note, red is frequently the color of luxury sports cars (e.g., the classic red Ferrari). The vividness of the color is what matters most, as a means of ensuring that it is eye-catching and attention grabbing. This is why Ferraris in otherwise "bizarre" colors, such as a bright yellow, exist. It's as though the owner is saying that if you did not notice the roaring motor or the sleek design of his car, at least he'll get your attention with his otherwise nauseating car color! The use of bright and vivid colors as part of a conspicuous consumption act, such as driving a luxury sports car, is likely a human universal.

Language Mishaps

Language mishaps are a common pitfall in international advertising. Most textbooks on the topic provide lots of humorous if not tragic examples of mistranslated slogans as well as unfortunate brand names (viewed through the prism of another language). For example, in the context of the bilingual society in which I reside in Montreal, the shampoo *Pert* is potentially problematic, as *perte* in French means "loss." In a francophone environment, one could conceivably associate the use of this particular shampoo with hair loss. Few Americans would understand the phrase "to bottle out," which is the British equivalent to the more familiar "to chicken out." The prescribed remedy against such mishaps is to engage in back-translation, or to have one individual translate from language A to B, and another individual translate back from B to A. If the translation is accurate, one should end up with roughly the same starting slogan. The problem is that in most instances, perhaps due to expediency and cost considerations, translations are unidirectional, which at times yields embarrassing outcomes.

Language mishaps can take place in other marketing-related contexts, such as when eliciting satisfaction surveys from consumers. Suppose that you are a hotel chain that operates in countries covering twenty-five different languages. It might be difficult to generate twenty-five properly translated surveys with all the idiosyncratic idioms of a particular language. As a means of overcoming some of these linguistic traps, Holiday Inn at one point utilized a "pictorial" satisfaction survey in which respondents would choose from a happy, neutral, or sad face when providing their satisfaction scores (see figure 2 for examples of universally understood emoticons). In the images used by Holiday Inn, the corrugator muscle (presence or absence of frowning) was also drawn to further accentuate the three emotionally valenced faces. The company was able to use these images across cultural settings precisely because there exists a set of six basic emotions—anger, disgust, fear, sadness, happiness, and surprise—that manifest themselves on individuals' faces in universally similar manners (as originally documented by psychologist Paul Ekman). This is in stark contrast to the position espoused by some cultural relativists who have doggedly (and incorrectly) argued against the mapping of particular emotions to universally recurring facial grimaces. On a related note, many retail employees who are otherwise mandated to provide happy and effusive greetings to entering customers betray their artificiality via their non-Duchenne (i.e., fake) smiles. The ability of consumers to identify genuine versus fake smiles is an evolved universal capacity. Although our linguistic traditions might be culture-specific, our ability to detect nonverbal cues is part of our common biological heritage.

Figure 2. These happy, neutral, and sad faces are universally understood.

CONCLUSION

The local versus global debate has raged in advertising for well over eight decades without any clear solution. Is it best to create a singular ad that is transportable across cultural settings, or must one always tailor advertisements to fit individual cultures? Evolutionary psychology can help resolve the debate, as it offers the requisite framework for identifying culture-specific versus universally shared elements. For example, although color connotations and linguistic idioms are culturally bound, innate unconditioned responses to specific advertising sights and sounds including sexual stimuli, facially symmetric endorsers, and male endorsers with deep voices are universally similar. Furthermore, whereas some advertising executions might be differentially efficacious across cultural settings (e.g., whether one should use comparative ads), other advertising effects are universally similar (e.g., response to fear appeals).

CHAPTER 8
MARKETING HOPE BY SELLING LIES

Hope deceives more men than cunning does.
— *MARQUIS DE VAUVENARGUES,*
FRENCH ESSAYIST [1]

Hope in a jar.
— *KATHY PEISS, AMERICAN HISTORIAN* [2]

There are numerous similarities between marketing and religion, and the line between the two has become increasingly blurred.
— *MARA EINSTEIN* [3]

There are many biological-based realities that are difficult to accept, including aging, mortality, the sexual boredom that can occur in a monogamous relationship, and the fact that children are born with innate differences in abilities. Many of the most successful products ever devised, and ideologies ever espoused, seek to convince us that these realities do not exist. Religion promises us immortality. Cosmetics sell us the fleeting allure of eternal youth and beauty. Social constructivism convinces us that we are all born with equal potentiality and it is only the environment that subsequently hinders our progress (and pollutes our otherwise "clean" tabula rasa minds). Self-help books guarantee us hot monogamy forever, eternal virility, unlimited female orgasms, seamless parenting, thin bodies, popularity, and the ability to generate endless money streams. It is not unusual that many of the books on any bestseller list are self-help books. In a sense, humans have an evolved capacity to engage in self-deception in order to navigate through life in a delusional state of blissful ignorance. Interestingly, clinically depressed individuals are the sole people who do not suffer from such a delusional glow. The bottom line is that peddlers of promise (e.g., cosmetic companies, preachers, self-help authors) seek to assuage our most basic Darwinian fears linked to survival, mating, family relationships, and friendships.

Hope is an elixir of life. It is the engine that propels us forward in our pursuit of countless goals, all of which might otherwise be impossible to undertake if we were bereft of hope. Individuals who lose hope (or who have less optimistic outlooks), be it in penitentiaries, hospitals, or in everyday life, are more likely to suffer adverse health consequences.[4] Generally speaking, optimistic and hopeful people are better able to deal with life's trials and tribulations. Therefore, hope is a valuable commodity that is "sold" to the populace by a wide range of peddlers. The great majority of individuals are susceptible to hopeful messages, be it those originating from religious narratives, advertisements, or self-help books. At the same time, a smaller percentage of the populace is well aware of the inherent duplicity of such messages. Accordingly, they set up mechanisms to counteract the claims of the hope peddlers. The four horsemen of atheism—Richard Dawkins, Daniel Dennett, Sam Harris, and Christopher Hitchens—bring to light the lunacy of religious narratives. Culture-jamming organizations[5] attempt to highlight the lies behind corporate advertising along with firms' unabated greed. Evolutionary scientists repeatedly demonstrate the fallacy of the otherwise hopeful view that we are all born with blank-slate minds, and that only the environment shapes our individual outcomes in life. Despite such laudable attempts to infuse rationality into the various arenas ripe for hope peddling, most people remain easy prey to the messages of hope.

THE GREATEST PRODUCT EVER DEVISED: RELIGION

The commercial might of religious products is undeniable. Mel Gibson's *The Passion of the Christ* generated $1 billion from box office receipts and DVD sales. Religious and spiritual books constitute the fourth largest category of books, with fourteen thousand books published in 2004. There are more than ten faith-based television channels (e.g., TBN, God TV). In 2002, Christian and gospel music garnered $845 million in sales. Rick Warren's *The Purpose Driven Life* has sold a mind-boggling twenty-five million copies.[6] Joel Osteen's pastoral messages are broadcast to a global audience totaling in the millions. The all-time best-selling book is the Bible. If American presidential candidates wish to successfully sell themselves to the electorate, they must demonstrate religiosity. Religion sells. Atheists need not apply.

Religion possesses unique attributes that render it a marketer's dream product. First, its key selling point is maximally powerful. It's one thing for a skin cream to proclaim that it can reverse skin damage due to sun exposure or aging. Religion provides the granddaddy of key selling points—it guarantees immortality. Now that's an invention I am willing to buy! Second, religion engenders intergenerational brand loyalty. Imagine a product wherein your parents' product preferences (e.g., they are Mac users, Pepsi drinkers, and Mazda owners) are nearly perfect predictors of your eventual preferences. There is no manufactured good that comes remotely close to the intergenerational brand loyalty garnered by religion. One's religion is almost always the same as that of one's parents. The reality is that children are not "born" Christian, Jewish, or Muslim. They are culturally indoctrinated into their parents' religion. Third, religion promotes lifelong brand loyalty, as it dissuades variety seeking by imposing a death sentence or condemnation to hell on apostates (in the worst-case scenario), and extraordinary social scorn on others. That should keep you brand loyal.

That religion is the sole product permitted to target children straight out of the womb is its fourth uniquely defining attribute. In many Western countries, it is illegal for companies to advertise directly to children below a certain age. Even though the legal age varies across cultural settings, it is clear that most people agree that there is something particularly pernicious in seeking to manipulate or persuade children via advertising. The psychological argument is that young children do not have the cognitive ability to erect defenses against such persuasive intent, so the regulatory and legal system steps in to protect them. Think about it for a minute. Companies cannot peddle cereals, toys, and chewing gum to children in certain Western countries, but it is perfectly legal, ethical, and moral for parents to religiously indoctrinate their children immediately upon birth. Having children develop a preference for McDonald's (via advertising) is "evil," but teaching them Bronze Age superstitions that are antithetical to every rational and scientific tenet is not. I concur with Dawkins when he proposed that targeting religious messages to children is tantamount to child abuse.

These four points are sufficient to anoint religion as the most "perfect" product ever devised (from a marketer's perspective).[7] However, religion has a lot more going for it in terms of its ability to parasitize human minds. As I write these words, Toyota is facing an unprecedented crisis. Several of its recent models have been deemed unsafe to drive, and as a result the company has had to recall hundreds of thousands of its cars. Short of religion, all products, even those from reputable and venerable firms, are potentially fallible. Religion maintains its hold on people irrespective of the massive evidence that suggests that it is the most "defective" of all invented products. Why did God allow a four-year-old child to die of leukemia? Because He is calling those He loves most to be with Him in heaven. Why did the leukemia go into remission in the case of a different four-year-old child? Because God protects the pure and the innocent. Why did God allow the Holocaust to happen? He was angry with His chosen people, so He turned away from them. Why was Hitler unsuccessful in implementing the Final Solution?

Because God loves His chosen people. The tautologies are endless. Unlike other products that can be recalled from the market if they fail, the religion hawkers have a foolproof product.

The earthquake that struck in Haiti in 2010 was devastating, with well over one hundred thousand deaths and countless people injured and left homeless. One might think that such a calamity might shake the Haitians' faith in an all-loving, benevolent, and protector God. It turns out that their faith in God *increased* subsequent to the disaster. I vividly remember the images of a woman who was rescued from the rubble after being buried alive for several days. As she was being freed, she broke out into a rapturous religious hymn, as Jesus had apparently intervened to save her. Too bad He was too busy to save the other hundreds of thousands of people who perished. Human narcissism is truly limitless.

One of the strongest allures of religion is that it plays on our deep-seated Darwinian need to view the world through the us-versus-them prism. As discussed in chapter 5, coalitional thinking is part of our innate psychology. There are Jews and gentiles; Muslims (believers) and infidels (kafirs); Christians and the unsaved; Believers (Jews, Christians, Muslims) and atheists. Needless to say, this "dichotomonia" can be applied at a more granular level. Muslims can be divided into the Shi`ia and the Sunni. Jews can be divided into the priestly castes (Cohen and Levi) and the Israel tribe (the commoners); Sephardic and Ashkenazi; Orthodox and others (reconstructionist, reform, and conservative); Hasidim versus Mitnagdim (these were originally forbidden to intermarry); within the Sephardic community, there is a distinction between Middle Eastern Jews (oriental or Mizrahi Jews) and North African Jews; Zionists versus non-Zionists; Orthodox converts versus those who converted in a non-Orthodox process (unacceptable, according to strict rabbinical codes); birth Jews versus converts; and Black Jews (Falasha/Yemeni/Indian) versus white Jews. Such tribalism is also rampant in Arab cultures. It causes some Arabs to prefer to be squashed by their "own" dictators (e.g., "at least we had peace under Saddam Hussein") rather than be freed from the throes of autocracy by the American "infi-dels." It is that simple. Being tortured by your own is better than living "under the occupation" of those who freed you. Such is tribalism in its purest form (I should know; I hail from the Middle East). This is well captured by Leon Uris, in his book *The Haj*:

> So before I was nine I had learned the basic canon of Arab life. It was me against my brother; me and my brother against our father; my family against my cousins and the clan; the clan against the tribe; and the tribe against the world. And all of us against the infidel.[8]

THE ALLURE OF RELIGIOUS BELIEF

The 2009 movie *The Invention of Lying* starring Ricky Gervais and Jennifer Garner tells the story of the first man who discovers the power of lying, in a world that had heretofore existed without any lies. Picture a world where people share all their thoughts without any filtering. Everyone is an open book. All conversations are rooted in full truths: no posturing, no filtering, no fibbing, no exaggerating. In such a truthful world, the sole liar (Gervais's character) would quickly rule the world. You need money. Tell the bank teller that you have more money in your bank account than what is currently shown on the system. Since the teller is unaware of the concept of lying, she obliges and forks over the requested amount of money. Feel like having sex. You tell a beautiful woman that you immediately need to have sex together to save the world. She will oblige, as lies do not exist in her world. Your mother is terrified on her deathbed by the prospect of eternal nothing-ness. Create a story about a forever afterlife where she will have a huge mansion and be reunited with all her loved ones. Since your mother is unaware of the existence of lies, she dies fully comforted by the thought of such a place.

Having provided the original lie—in contrast with the Original Sin in the Bible—Gervais's character is now well placed to establish the foundational tenets of religion. As news spreads about his afterlife narrative (as told to his dying mother), crowds gather to obtain additional details about his unique knowledge. He surfaces to face the crowd armed with two pizza boxes containing written rules that people should follow if they wish to enter the afterlife (an obvious comedic analogy to the Mosaic tablets on which the Ten Commandments were inscribed). As audience members grill him with detailed questions, he provides on-the-spot deceptive responses (e.g., there is a man in the sky who keeps track of all your actions). Again, it is important to note that he is the sole person in the world capable of lying. Hence, everyone fully and unconditionally accepts his made-up narrative. There you have it, folks. A comedic but insightful interpretation of how religion began.

As far as we know, humans are the only species who experience existential angst due to the recognition of their mortality. In his book *Why Zebras Don't Get Ulcers*, Robert Sapolsky discusses the immediacy of the stress response that is typically experienced by animals.[9] The zebra does not ponder the existential complexities of being surrounded by many dangerous predators in the African savanna. It goes about its daily routine and only activates its flight response when threatened. Unfortunately for us humans, a downside of our large brains is the ability to think of ugly truths that lie in our not-too-distant futures. Of course, no future outcome is as troubling as the recognition of one's eventual passing. If you suffer from high cholesterol, your physician can prescribe one of several statins to manage your lipid profile. There are no pills, though, that one can take to be immortal or to be reunited with loved ones who have died. We may not have a physical pill to address our mortality, but an existential/spiritual pill already exists. It is called religion.

In his 2002 bestselling book *Why People Believe Weird Things*, Michael Shermer proposes that humans are pattern seekers.[10] In other words, we have an innate need, perhaps as a by-product of our evolved intelligence, to identify patterns as a means of ascribing meaning to the world. In many instances, the patterns are illusory but nonetheless comforting in that the world is more comprehensible when it appears less random. A good friend of mine recently shared with me an anecdote, which is quite telling of the innate need to seek meaning through patterns. He had recently dreamed of an old friend whom he had not seen in many years. A day or two later, he ran into him in a location that struck him as highly unlikely for such a serendipitous encounter. He seemed to suggest that some cosmic forces were at play, for how else could such a reality come about? He failed to calculate the number of times that he had dreamed of someone he knew and not run into shortly thereafter.

My friend's decisional error is precisely the mechanism by which individuals believe that their prayers are answered. For argument's sake, let's assume that in any given year, a woman prays for one thousand different outcomes, one of which comes to fruition. Hallelujah! Apparently, God has answered her prayers even though He apparently ignored the other 999. This is similar to thinking that "it always rains when I forget to take my umbrella with me." Let us suppose that this event has happened on five occasions. The brain codes each of these instances as an instantiation of that event. However, there are three other relevant events that are ignored: (1) the times it rained and I had an umbrella; (2) the times it did not rain and I had an umbrella; (3) the times it did not rain and I did not have an umbrella. Once all four possible events are accounted for, the frequency of the original event is placed in its proper perspective.

Prognosticators, including those who offer religious prophecies, take advantage of the infinite capacity of the human mind to identify patterns in otherwise random events. One of my paternal aunts is known for her ability to "see" the future by reading coffee stains left in your cup, a practice known as tasseography. Her readings are listened to with alacrity, in a manner similar to how the Catholic faithful might hinge on the pope's last syllable. She utters extraordinarily inane and general statements such as "I see a joyous event in your future." If one is constipated, a good bowel movement might constitute a joyous event. If one's favorite football team wins its next match, this might constitute a joyous event. If a couple were to have sex in the next day or two after having gone weeks without any physical intimacy, this might constitute a joyous event. There is an infinite number of ways by which her "predictions" can come true. She never predicted that you would receive a job promotion with a 15 percent salary increase that would require relocating to Atlanta. Specificity is indeed the enemy of psychics. On the chance that readers might be tempted to think that belief in such fairytales is a harmless exercise, I might remind you that Nancy Reagan consulted an astrologer prior to some of her husband's (President Ronald Reagan) decisions, as did military rulers in the past.

Existential angst about our mortality coupled with our desire to seek cosmological meaning through the identification of grand patterns ensures that religion will always remain part of the human condition.[11] Intelligence and education are the only effective inoculations against religious indoctrination. Over the past eight decades, research has repeatedly uncovered a negative correlation between individuals' intelligence and their religiosity. This negative relationship holds at the level of nations as well; that is, there exists a negative correlation between the religiosity of nations and their national intelligence scores. Academics constitute perhaps the least religious occupational group, which again captures the intelligence-religiosity negative correlation (by virtue of the high IQ scores of academics). Finally, the more eminent a group of scientists, the less likely they are to be religious.[12] Even within academia, one can differentiate between levels of religiosity as a function of scientific renown. All told, God will continue to play an important role in human affairs, not because He truly exists but rather because He will continue to exist in the minds of countless individuals.

PEDDLING RELIGION USING DARWINIAN TOOLS

I recently watched a television episode (infomercial?) of the televangelist Apostle Don Stewart. He promises viewers that his Green Prosperity Handkerchief (GPH; the slogan on his website is "Gift of Hope") can be used as a vehicle to have your prayers answered. I am not exactly sure how the process works, but Apostle Stewart will send you a GPH that he has personally blessed and anointed. This token serves as a divine vehicle by which your prayers will come true. He even has several testimonials to prove that the GPH works. This ruse is part of a spiritual movement known as *prosperity theology*. The general idea is that God wishes to reward those who believe in Him; pray to God, and He will reward your belief by answering your prayers. Having always wanted to move to Southern California, I truly wonder if the GPH can serve as my ticket to my "promised land." None other than Reverend Pat Robertson (700 Club) has proclaimed that this principle is known as the Law of Reciprocity. Give to God, and He will reward you, the most divine instantiation of the tit-for-tat rule. Of course, such deals are not restricted to Christian televangelists. The scam mutates into several other variants, all of which are equally virulent in tricking the naive and gullible out of their money.

Religious-based affinity scams such as those perpetrated by the Greater Ministries International Church and the Baptist Foundation of Arizona, each of which resulted in accumulated thefts of more than $500 million, are extremely alluring Ponzi schemes.[13] The fraudsters rely on several Darwinian mechanisms to entrap the credulous parishioners. First, the context of the fraud takes place among in-group members, which triggers people's innate coalitional thinking (us versus them). Outsiders might be dishonest and untrustworthy, but our church congregation is made up of honorable people we can trust. The bottom line is that individuals are more trusting of in-group members and more suspicious of their out-group counterparts. The ultimate purveyor of trust is the leader of the in-group—not the priest, but God Himself:

"Blessed are all they that put their trust in him" (Psalm 2:12). Many religious-based affinity scams piggyback on the parishioners' proclivity to grant trust within this religious context. In other words, all cognitive and affective guards are weakened if not altogether dropped, allowing the charlatan to pounce on the defenseless individuals. A second way by which swindlers usurp a Darwinian principle is via the narrative of reciprocity, as mentioned in the previous paragraph. The Greater Ministries International Church Ponzi scheme made frequent allusions to a sentence in Luke 6:38: "Give, and it shall be given unto you." The evolutionarily stable strategy of tit-for-tat is repackaged as a religious edict, and subsequently used to fleece the believers.

SHOPPING FOR THE TRUE RELIGION: AN EXTRATERRESTRIAL'S QUEST

There are roughly ten thousand documented religions.[14] On some matters, religious doctrines share many similarities; however, on others they are utterly contradictory with one another. Clearly, if all ten thousand religions proclaim to be the Truth, and yet they contradict one another on endless topics, someone must be wrong or maybe even lying. When I press religious believers to resolve this conundrum, they typically look at me with disgust and incredulity and respond as follows: "My religion is the revealed truth. That's how I know that my religion is the correct one!" I see. The logic of the "I am right because I am right" is unassailable. Bravo. I am assuming that those who offer such a response missed the philosophy class that discussed tautologies and circular reasoning.

Let's assume for a moment that Mr. Jupiter, an extraterrestrial, has decided to relocate to Earth. Very quickly, he realizes that religion is a very powerful element of the human experience. Wishing to integrate within the human melting pot, he decides to shop around in the hope of identifying the one true religion among the ten thousand available ones.

Being a highly rational being (think Mr. Spock on *Star Trek*), he decides as a first step to seek answers to some fundamental questions. He begins with some basic dietary concerns; namely, whether he can drink alcohol (he loves red wine), eat crabmeat, have a shrimp cocktail, or enjoy some thinly sliced prosciutto? He is surprised to find out that each query has a different response depending on who the true God might be. He proceeds to ask some questions about sexuality and romantic relationships, including whether it is acceptable to masturbate, whether premarital sex is allowed, the number of wives that he may marry, the ease with which he can divorce (if at all), and the punishment (if any) for homosexuality (e.g., assuming that his son turns out to be gay). Mr. Jupiter is growing exceedingly confused because, again, each question yields a different response depending on who the true God is. He then proceeds to ask about the religious edicts regarding particular daily activities. Can he listen to music? Is he allowed to turn on his television, computer, or DVD player on Saturday? If he develops bacterial pneumonia, is he allowed to take prescription drugs? Once he finds a nice female Earthling to marry, are there divine rules regarding how she must dress? If they end up having children, is it divinely ordained that their children be circumcised? Since coming to Earth, Mr. Jupiter has developed an affinity for Italian leather shoes. Is he allowed to always wear them, or are there days when he is prohibited from doing so? When about to pray, does he have to be cognizant of his position in relation to the cardinal coordinates? He recently caught an episode of *Miami Ink* and has decided that it would be fun to get a tattoo. Is this allowed? Since starting his new job at NASA, he discovered that some of his colleagues are trying to sabotage his career advancement. Should he seek revenge in equal measure or turn the other cheek? Again, the answer to each query depends on who the true God is.

Having addressed some worldly issues and come away utterly befuddled, Mr. Jupiter decides to focus instead on theological matters. Surely, this is where the religious precepts might yield some convergence across belief systems. He begins with perhaps the most fundamental theological question: Is there only one true God or multiple Gods? Are the sun, the moon, particular rivers, or specific animals considered divine? Are we awaiting the first coming of the Messiah, or has he already revealed himself? Does God have a personal vicar on Earth who represents His interests? Are other planets inhabited by souls? Are pilgrimages a divinely ordained duty? Should people of other faiths be converted to the one true faith? Is evolution a scientific fact, or is it a concerted plot (probably by atheists) to reject the existence of the one true God, the creator of the universe? The answer to each question wholly rests on who the one true God is.

In a last-ditch effort, Mr. Jupiter decides to tackle the most fundamental existential issue of all, the one that I argued is the key Darwinian driver of people's belief in religion: our fear of mortality. Mr. Jupiter decides to ask a series of questions dealing with death to gauge whether the various religious narratives can at the very least agree on this life-and-death matter (literally). May he commit suicide should his life become unbearable? Will he go to hell for doing so? More generally, does hell actually exist? Is reincarnation a distinct possibility? Mr. Jupiter detests the idea of his beloved dead ancestors rotting in purgatory. Can he buy some indulgences that might expedite their entry into heaven? Should he put money away for his retirement or is armageddon close at hand? The year 2012, you say? Were he to decide that all religions are utter nonsense and become an atheist, has he guaranteed himself entry into hell (assuming that the one true God exists, of course)? As he prepares to make his final decision, he wonders how easy or difficult it will be to join his religion of choice, and what the repercussions will be (if any) were he to one day decide to leave the chosen religion (apostasy). Mr. Jupiter is dismayed to find out that yet again the answer to any of these queries is completely contingent on who the bona fide God is. It seems that both the devil and God are in the details!

On January 11, 2010, I published an article on my *Psychology Today* blog titled "It Can Be Confusing to Find the One True Religion." In the post, I mentioned many of the examples discussed above. Of the more than 2,400 readers who have thus far read this particular piece of writing, none has provided a rebuttal to the glaring contradictions that I have enumerated. One highly religious person wrote me a private e-mail in which he admitted that upon seeing the outlandish randomness and contradictory nature of the religious edicts, he could see how one might question the existence of God. But this did not cause him to question his own belief system. The nonfalsifiability of religion rears its ugly head yet again.

MARKETER'S DREAM, BUT HUMANITY'S NIGHTMARE

To the extent that religion possesses attributes that render it the most "perfect" product ever devised, it is indeed a marketer's dream. This should not be taken as an implicit endorsement of the religion memeplex (i.e., a set of related memes). It is impossible to provide an accurate historical estimate, but the number of deaths caused by religious strife is certainly greater than several hundred million. That said, the misery inflicted by religion is not simply measured by death totals. Religion parasitizes the human mind in the most insidious of ways. It teaches people that the suspension of reason, logic, and evidence is laudable. It infantilizes the human spirit by holding people captive to superstitions and fairy-tales. It holds humans in eternal bondage to *celestial dictators* (to use Hitchens's poignant term). It turns close neighbors into enemies (witness the Lebanese civil war, the recent conflict in the Balkans, and the sectarian violence in Iraq). The misery-inducing capacity of religion is genuinely limitless. Of course, religion can also cause people to behave in moral, altruistic, and kind ways; however, as Hitchens repeatedly pointed out, each such act is equally accessible to the atheist. As a matter of fact, I would go much further than Hitchens in positing that an atheist who commits an act of great purity is immeasurably more pious than the religious person who commits the same act because her religious narrative mandates her to do so.

I began this section by arguing that religion "solves" the mortality problem that looms in some distant future. Occasionally though, individuals are forced to deal with their mortality earlier than expected. Imagine the young child who is stricken with leukemia or the young mother who contracts breast cancer. Desperation can set in as all sources of hope are eviscerated. This creates an incredibly fertile ground for peddlers of medical quackery, a topic to which I turn next.

MEDICAL QUACKERY AS RELIGIOUS BELIEFS

Jehovah's Witnesses have a strict religious edict against blood transfusions. Accordingly, children of that faith who contract leukemia are assured of a death sentence. Some adherents of the Christian Science faith refuse medical treatments for their children, as they believe that such matters should be left in God's hands. They seek healing through prayers. Note the power of the religious memeplex. It can genuinely override some of our most basic Darwinian drives, namely, to survive and protect our kin. Medical quackery is not rooted necessarily in any particular religious tradition, although the central tenets usually take the form of inerrant fervent belief (e.g., "aromatherapy works—period"). As is true of many religious folks, adherents of a given quackery are not amenable to having their belief systems put to the test. The efficacy of the quackery is presumed true akin to the veracity of religious doctrine. No need to bother with scientific testing. Have faith. It works!

In 2007, Americans spent \$33.9 billion on products and services rooted in various complementary and alternative medicine (CAM) movements.[15] The survey in question took into account solely the more "reputable" variants of CAM; the actual dollar figure is substantially higher than the latter estimate. I'll briefly discuss two examples of such quackery, the Q-Ray bracelet and Therapeutic Touch, although there are innumerable other forms of medical charlatanism. The Q-Ray bracelet is sold as a form of alternative medical therapy based on ions and energy flows. It is sold as a cure for all sorts of ailments, one of which is that it reduces body aches via the balancing of one's energy flows (yin and yang). A group of scientists tested the claim by conducting the requisite scientific experiment to gauge whether the reduction of pain (if any) due to the Q-Ray bracelet would be greater than the placebo effect (measured by having participants wear a "placebo" bracelet). Not surprisingly, the Q-Ray bracelet yielded a decrease in pain equivalent to that of the placebo effect (i.e., it does not work).[16] This should suffice in demonstrating that this product is utter quackery, as would be concluded if one were testing the efficacy of an FDA-tested drug. However, the Q-Ray's adherents have come up with a multitude of nonsensical babble to explain away the scientific findings. My favorites include that the bracelet can only work on those who believe in energy flows, and that the scientific testing of its efficacy alters the energy flows. Apparently, incredulous scientists and participants alike are sending "bad vibes" to the bracelet, and this negates its otherwise miraculous effects.

In 1998, Emily Rosa, a precocious eleven-year-old, became the youngest person to ever publish a paper in the *Journal of the American Medical Association*. She had heard of Therapeutic Touch (TT), a practice in which touch healers could administer soothing energy fields by simply hovering their hands over afflicted or painful areas of patients' bodies. As part of her grade four science project, Rosa devised a simple yet clever experiment to test one of TT's central claims. Healers slid their hands through a partition subsequent to which Emily placed her hand either above a healer's right or left hand and asked them to determine the location of her energy field (i.e., state whether her hand was above their right or left hands). By randomly guessing, one could obtain a base score of 50 percent correct responses. Twenty-one TT healers participated in the experiment, with TT experience varying from one to twenty-seven years. Of 280 trials, the healers obtained a hit rate of 44 percent, even lower than what might be expected by chance! As mentioned in this discussion, the typical uproar when such nonsense is refuted was levied, including that such alternative procedures only work on those who believe and that the experimental conditions inherently interfere with the procedure. Logically, one could never falsify such quackery, which is a fundamental tenet of science (Karl Popper's Falsification Principle).

An important lesson to take away from Rosa's experiment is that it demonstrates quite vividly the inherent democratic tenets of the scientific method. Anyone, including an eleven-year-old child, can conceivably participate in the scientific enterprise. In contrast to religious "truths," there are no arguments from authority ("I am the rabbi, priest, or imam and hence I know God's mind"). Regrettably, these "alternative" medical therapies, be it TT or endless other medical quackeries, are alluring because they play on people's most basic Darwinian instinct—the desperate need to survive. Some of you might remember the comedian Andy Kaufman's travels to the Philippines to have a "psychic surgery" performed on him as a last-ditch effort to have cancerous tumors removed from his body. Shortly upon returning from his trip, Kaufman succumbed to his illness. (Interested readers should visit http://quackwatch.org/, as it is an incredibly rich source of information on fraudulent medical practices.)[17]

Recall that adaptations arise either via natural selection (survival) or sexual selection (mating). Whereas religion and medical quackery largely cater to our deep-rooted desire to survive (possibly as immortal beings), I next tackle a form of hope peddling that caters to our relative standing on the mating market. It assures us that we are all equally beautiful and desirable in our own unique ways.

BEAUTY IS A SOCIAL CONSTRUCTION

The Dove Campaign for Real Beauty has been a highly successful campaign over the past five years or so. The main theme is that beauty is a social construction, and therefore no universal metrics of beauty exist. The uplifting message works something as follows: You may not have a perfect face or body. No need to worry; metrics of beauty are arbitrary, hence you are beautiful in your unique way. This is a wonderful message in terms of protecting prospective customers' fragile self-esteem. Clearly, hopeful messages work across endless settings. After all, Barack Obama won both the US presidency and the Nobel Peace Prize to some degree because of his message of hope (one of his books is aptly titled *The Audacity of Hope*). The French emperor Napoleon Bonaparte stated it perfectly: "A leader is a dealer in hope." However, such messages are seldom rooted in any objective reality. Universal metrics of desirability do exist, and as such they are not arbitrary social constructions. All other things equal, men of high status are preferred to unemployed janitors. Young women are typically preferred to their postmenopausal counterparts. Tall and athletic men with strong facial features are viewed as more attractive than short, overweight, pear-shaped men. Women with large eyes, symmetrical faces, and clear skin are judged as more beautiful than those who have asymmetric faces, beady eyes, and acne scars. Men who possess deep and raspy voices are judged as sexier than those who have high-pitched nasal ones. Women with fat deposits in all the right places (e.g., Scarlett Johansson) are judged as sexier than the Eastern German female swimmers of the Soviet era (who had exceptionally masculinized body types). It might make you feel uncomfortable to read these words, but it is the banal truth. Of course advertisers are selling us hope. They are not in the business of providing us with ugly truths. They cajole us into thinking that we are all equally beautiful in our own unique and distinct ways. This duplicity is well captured by Charles H. Revson, the founder of Revlon, who is reputed to have said in 1975: "In the factory, we make cosmetics; in the store, we sell hope."[18]

The Beauty Myth by Naomi Wolf, published in 1991, was a hugely successful book. In it, Wolf argues that there is no such thing as a universal standard of beauty. Rather, the beauty myth is apparently a last-ditch effort by the patriarchy to maintain its control over women by "forcing" them to obsess about their appearance and having them abide to arbitrary standards of beauty. This creates insecurities in women who must engage in a never-ending cycle of intrasexual competition, all of which permits the patriarchy to maintain control over the female populace. This conspiratorial message is certainly a hopeful one to many women who might not otherwise adhere to the so-called patriarchal universal metrics of beauty. Alas, it is a delusional position fully removed from reality.

To reiterate, the banal truth is that universal markers of beauty do exist.[19] Though people fall in love with men and women of all shapes and sizes, scientists have yet to discover a single culture in which asymmetric people are judged as more attractive than their symmetric counterparts. When individuals are shown photos of people of different races, one obtains a near-perfect agreement as to who is considered beautiful. People—e.g., the Yanomamö, who reside deep in the Amazon—who might not have been exposed to Western media images will fully agree with New Yorkers as to who is considered beautiful. Infants, who are at a presocialization developmental stage, will stare the longest at the most beautiful face among a greater set of facial photos.[20] It is difficult to argue that infants are socialized into this preference when it is unequivocally known that they do not yet have the cognitive abilities to be socialized. Cultural artifacts spanning thousands of years and originating from widely different cultural settings provide similar descriptions of female beauty (clear skin, large eyes, lustrous hair, symmetric face). It is not by chance that the same universal standards of beauty exist across varied cultures and different epochs or that the pleasure center in men's brains (the nucleus accumbens) is activated when shown images of beautiful female faces.[21]

Does this imply that culture is irrelevant when it comes to definitions of beauty? Beautification rituals are extraordinarily different around the world. Surma and Mursi women of Ethiopia wear large lip plates; Kareni and Padaung women of Myanmar engage in neck elongation; Niv and Yoruba women of Nigeria scar their bodies; Chinese women have historically engaged in foot binding. That many facets of beauty are socially constructed says nothing about the fact that many others are indeed universally defined. Lip plates might be a culture-specific beauty marker. The beauty associated with facial symmetry is not.

Some argue that the greater premium on women's looks is a culture-specific sexist practice, as in other cultures men engage in extensive rites of beautification. The Wodaabe men (from West Africa) provide perhaps the most colorful and vivid instance of such a rite, as an integral element of the Geerewol festival.[22] Maori men have historically tattooed their faces, and Papua New Guinea men engage in body scarification (as an initiation rite). That men beautify themselves is hardly surprising (e.g., the rise of metrosexuals in contemporary Western societies); yet it detracts in no way from the fact that in all known societies, a greater premium is placed on female beauty. Incidentally, in many instances, male "beautification" rituals are actually not linked to aesthetic beauty but instead might signal one's warrior status, rite of passage into manhood, and so forth. In this sense, the ritual is signaling traits valued by women, such as higher social status more so than merely serving as a metric of aesthetic beauty.

The beauty-is-a-social-construction mantra provides a hopeful message to assuage our aesthetic insecurities. However, individuals succumb to endless other forms of self-doubts. Will I find my soul mate? Am I a competent parent? Am I a good lover? Is there a recipe for having more friends, better sex, higher-paying jobs, and succeeding as a financial trader? With an assuredness tantamount to religious zealotry, self-help gurus promise the believing consumers that all their life challenges will be solved if only they were to buy their books.

PRAYING AT THE ALTAR OF THE SELF-HELP GURU

Stuart Smalley, played by the recently elected senator of Minnesota, Al Franken, was a recurring character on *Saturday Night Live* who was infamous for being addicted to twelve-step programs and related self-affirmation mantras. The 2008 comedy *The Promotion*, starring Seann William Scott and John C. Reilly, chronicled the struggles of two men vying for the same promotion as managers of a soon-to-open supermarket. Throughout the movie, Reilly's character is shown listening to a self-help tape espousing inane banalities. These two examples are quite telling in that they demonstrate the extent to which self-help mantras have seeped into the American conscience.

Self-help books constitute one of the most successful book genres. Close to four thousand self-help books were newly published in 2003 alone.[23] More generally, consumers possess an insatiable appetite for seeking self-improvement (estimated at $12 billion for 2008)[24] and achieving wellness (estimated at $1 trillion for 2010.)[25] These varied products of "hope" all promise concrete solutions to universal concerns of evolutionary import (as do advice columns, hence their popularity). Contrary to Abraham Maslow's edict that the epitome of all human needs is self-actualization, most self-help books do not seem to be selling solutions for becoming more self-actualized beings. Rather, they seem to overwhelmingly focus on the four key Darwinian meta-drives that I have mentioned repeatedly; namely, survival, mating, kin, and reciprocity. Examples of such books include:

- *Forever Feminine*
- *Male Menopause*
- *Red-Hot Monogamy: Making Your Marriage Sizzle*
- *How to Make Love to the Same Person for the Rest of Your Life and Still . . . Love It*

- *Orgasm Every Day Every Way Every Time: A Woman's Guide to Sexual Pleasure*
- *Become Your Own Matchmaker: 8 Easy Steps for Attracting Your Perfect Mate*
- *Fat! So? Because You Don't Have to Apologize for Your Size*
- *The Beck Diet Solution: Train Your Brain to Think Like a Thin Person*
- *Eat Right 4 Your Type: The Individualized Diet Solution to Staying Healthy, Living Longer & Achieving Your Ideal Weight*
- *New Parent Power!*
- *1-2-3 Magic: Effective Discipline for Children 2–12*
- *How to Win Friends and Influence People*
- *Think & Grow Rich*
- *The Secret*
- *Law of Attraction*

The first two books promise eternal femininity and virility, respectively. Needless to say, this selling point is impossible to realize; but since it caters to our desperate need to remain vital and youthful, we are willing to suspend reality. Eternal femininity/masculinity is tantamount to the promise of immortality as offered by endless religious narratives. The next two books deal with the secrets for maintaining sexual excitement in a long-term monogamous relationship. The Coolidge Effect refers to the pronounced penchant that males of various species (including humans) possess for sexual variety. This does not mean that women do not also desire some sexual variety, nor does it imply that men are incapable of having the moral restraint to stay true to their monogamous unions. However it does imply that the titillations implicit to the start of a sexual relationship cannot be maintained forever. When asked about his sexual exploits, Wilt Chamberlain—who is purported to have slept with twenty thousand women (I did the math, and it seems highly improbable that he could have reached such a number)—apparently retorted that it took much more of a man to sleep with the same woman twenty thousand times than to sleep with twenty thousand women. I suppose that he meant it as a moral indictment of his sexual conquests, and hence he was condoning the virtues of monogamy. However, my sense is that he was conveying a deeper subconscious meaning. Specifically, to be able to be sexually aroused by the same woman on twenty thousand occasions suggests that you are a true stud, as the Coolidge Effect would have predicted satiety at a much earlier stage (and hence a quest for novel partners). Incidentally, Ashley Madison is an online dating service that caters to married people desirous of short-term sexual dalliances outside their marriages. One of their signature slogans is "When Monogamy Becomes Monotony."

The next two books deal with two equally impossible mating-related promises. All scientific surveys that have documented women's sexuality recognize that it is extraordinarily rare for women to experience an orgasm in every single intimate encounter. As a matter of fact, a substantial number of women are inorgasmic (5 to 10 percent of all women), while a third of women are incapable (or rarely able) of having orgasms strictly via intercourse (manual and/or oral stimulation of the clitoris is needed to achieve an orgasm.)[26] Therefore, any book that promises endless daily orgasms is suspect. Given the number of lonely single people in search of love, or those who toil in unhappy unions, a book that provides an eight-step program for finding one's perfect mate sounds like a real lifesaver. That said, it is a questionable proposition, as there are likely no general prescriptions (let alone eight of them) for finding one's so-called perfect mate. For an unemployed male janitor who last held a job in 2002 and who also happens to be physically unattractive and possesses a dull personality, a perfect mate might be any woman who enjoys his company. However, a tall neurosurgeon who has the eloquence of Martin Luther King Jr. and the looks of Brad Pitt has a much broader playing field from which to choose. Still, while it is indeed true that there are universal mating preferences, our idiosyncratic realities (e.g., our own mating value) make it such that a "perfect mate" can be defined in an endless number of ways. Furthermore, mate choice (and love) is generally a compensatory process. In other words, a man might be short, but he can compensate for it by possessing other valued attributes (e.g., high status and a sense of humor). Similarly, there are many elements that men use when evaluating women as prospective mates. A woman can compensate for her ordinary looks by having other valued qualities (e.g., kindness and magnetic charm). Ultimately, falling in love will always possess an element of mystery, as we do not always choose the prettiest woman or the man at the top of the social hierarchy.

Nevertheless, I watched a documentary not too long ago on "fat acceptance" in which a woman who was morbidly obese (probably over four hundred pounds) was proclaiming that it was discriminatory of men to reject her at the numerous dating events that she attended. Apparently, she felt that the men had been "socialized" into preferring a "thin ideal," and as a rule they were incapable of seeing her inner beauty. In a moment of defiance, she reiterated that she had the right to be loved. Such "pro-fat" self-affirmation epitomizes the central message of the next book on the list, *Fat! So? Because You Don't Have to Apologize for Your Size*, as well as of organizations such as the National Association to Advance Fat Acceptance.[27] Incredibly, some overweight women take exception to men who are so-called fat admirers as they find it offensive that such men appreciate them strictly because of their large size. If a man is not attracted to an overweight woman, he is discriminatorily shallow. If he is particularly fond of overweight women, he is objectifying their fat! In the famous words of the Scottish poet Sir Walter Scott, "Oh, what a tangled web we weave, when first we practise to deceive." Lest I be accused of "weightism," the reader should know that I have struggled with my weight for the past two decades (at times being more than fifty pounds overweight).

Close to 95 percent of people fail in their long-term attempts at dieting. Dieting is difficult because it requires us to resist a Darwinian drive that is next to impossible to temper: our love for food. When faced with such a daunting challenge, diet self-help books provide the necessary hopeful messages that are akin to religion's "solution" to mortality. Given the obesity epidemic that has afflicted American society, people are desperate to find a panacea for their ever-expanding waistlines. This creates a fertile environment for the diet self-help niche. The reality is that an individual will lose weight if the amount of exerted energy is greater than ingested energy. The homeostatic equation is that simple. Of course, individual differences affect where the breakeven caloric point is set. For example, people have different basal metabolic rates, in part determined by how the hormone leptin operates within their bodies. That said, diet books are not the solution.

The next two books address parental angst, which is obviously linked to kin selection. It is rather easy to convince insecure parents that an optimal parental recipe exists, as all caring parents worry about their abilities to provide their children with the appropriate types and amounts of nurturance, love, and discipline. The underlying faulty assumption here is one that the pediatrician Benjamin Spock helped to promulgate; namely, that even banal parental decisions can have a profound and lasting effect on a child's life. Generally speaking, the import of this source of influence is grossly overestimated, as eloquently explained by Judith R. Harris in her book *The Nurture Assumption: Why Children Turn Out the Way They Do*. Furthermore, whereas there are a few steadfast rules of good parenting (e.g., consistent forms of discipline coupled with nurturance and love, open lines of communication), there are no magic recipes. In the same way that professors must attune their supervisory styles to the idiosyncratic personalities and needs of their graduate students, good parents recognize that children are unique individuals with distinct parental needs. If anything, the recipe for good parenting is to avoid applying a singular formula across the board!

The last four books promise more friends, more money, and the ability to will anything that you desire! Such prescriptions are nonexistent. Take the bestselling book *The Secret* by Rhonda Byrne, rooted in the principles of New Thought Theology. The "secret" is based on the so-called law of attraction. Basically, by sending out (consciously or subconsciously) positive energy ("I believe that I deserve the red Ferrari"), the cosmos/universe will grant you your wish. Somehow, the "gurus" of this movement seek to dress this "concept" in the cloak of scientific respectability by arguing that the process is based on sound principles of quantum physics. The late Nobel laureate (in physics) Richard Feynman famously quipped: "I think I can safely say that nobody understands quantum mechanics."[28] One of the scientific giants of the twentieth century proclaims that quantum physics is so complex as to baffle even the most sophisticated of physicists, but somehow new age gurus have understood its ability to grant us our wishes!

Steve Salerno's book *Sham: How the Self-Help Movement Made America Helpless* provides a trenchant indictment of the unregulated and largely fraudulent self-help industry. He astutely notes that there are two foundational, and at times contradictory, fulcrums of self-help: victimhood and empowerment. In one instance, the message is that some environmental factor has stopped you from reaching your full potential. Accordingly, members of the self-help populace are encouraged to view themselves as victims of their circumstances. In the empowerment movement, self-help gurus promise that there is nothing stopping anyone from achieving all their dreams and aspirations (as per life coach Anthony Robbins's motto "Awakening the Giant Within"). All our personal goals are apparently within our reach; the only requirement is finding the inner force to go for it. The brilliance of this two-pronged approach is that it is sufficiently fuzzy that failure to achieve one's goals, subsequent to having paid the necessary exorbitant fees for the self-help books, DVDs, and seminars, can always be blamed on the individual and never on the guru. Perhaps individuals did not work hard enough to break free of their victimhood, or they did not sufficiently strive to unleash their potential. Similar to how God is never at fault for human misery and personal failings, the self-help sage is equally immunized from any reproach. It is not surprising that many self-help gurus are considered demigods by their adoring fans and disciples.

Prior to their market release, new pharmaceutical drugs go through a very rigorous FDA-approved process. Consumers must be assured that the drug they'll be ingesting will accomplish what it promised to do, and they also must be informed of any possible side effects. Self-help proclamations are not bound by any such oversight despite the fact that in many instances, such advice is substantially more toxic to one's life than typical over-the-counter medicine. What allows this dreadful reality to persist is the desperate need of consumers to hang on to the quasi-religious belief that self-help leaders possess the all-encompassing life secrets to assuage their Darwinian fears and insecurities. The human need for hope ultimately serves as the means by which the phonies perpetuate their self-help scams.

CONCLUSION

Humans suffer from numerous insecurities, the most potent of which deal with matters of evolutionary import, including concerns with mortality, romantic relationships, sexuality, parenting, dieting, wellness, status, and social influence. Accordingly, it is not surprising that numerous peddlers of hope have historically pounced on these Darwinian insecurities and have accordingly sold the desperate-to-believe populace various "foolproof" solutions. Religion guarantees us eternal life. Cosmetic companies promise eternally youthful skin. The beauty-is-a-social-construction mantra assures us that we are all equally beautiful in our own unique ways. New age medical healers assure us that they possess the definitive cures. Self-help books provide solutions for every ailment, desire, want, and need. All these promissory vehicles constitute forms of quasi-religious belief systems, and as such are easy to take over the human mind and terribly difficult to eradicate.

CHAPTER 9

DARWINIAN RATIONALE
FOR CONSUMER IRRATIONALITY

Nothing defines humans better than their willingness to do irrational things in the pursuit of phenomenally unlikely payoffs. This is the principle behind lotteries, dating, and religion.
— SCOTT ADAMS,
CREATOR OF THE DILBERT COMIC STRIP[1]

There's no evidence whatsoever that men are more rational than women. Both sexes seem to be equally irrational.
— ALBERT ELLIS, AMERICAN PSYCHOLOGIST[2]

The rationality of irrationality.
— HERMAN KAHN,
AMERICAN NUCLEAR STRATEGIST, AND
THOMAS C. SCHELLING,
AMERICAN ECONOMIST AND
2005 NOBEL LAUREATE[3]

I f humans are adaptive creatures shaped by a long evolutionary process, why do they engage in numerous acts that yield deleterious consequences for themselves and, at times, those around them? Why

does maladaptive consumption exist, or—more generally—why do individuals take part in apparently irrational behaviors? Examples include
unsafe sex practices, excessive suntanning, eating disorders, excessive
overeating that result in morbid obesity, drug and substance abuse,
pornographic addiction, compulsive buying, pathological gambling,
and "nongreen" lifestyles. As I briefly mentioned at the end of chapter 1,
most public policy interventions operate on the premise that either poor
socialization (e.g., the media causes eating disorders or the contradictory
premise that the media also causes childhood obesity)[4] or incomplete
information explains such negative activities. Teach consumers to
behave "properly," and seemingly the maladaptive behaviors will be eradicated. Here, I demonstrate the fallacy of this position. For instance,
despite the fact that women are more knowledgeable than men about
the negative consequences of suntanning, they engage in it much more
frequently.[5] This choice is not due to lack of information. I will show
that in most cases, many maladaptive behaviors possess a strong
sex-specificity, irrespective of cultural setting or time period. Men are
overwhelmingly more likely to suffer from pathological gambling,
pornographic addiction, and other forms of excessive risk taking (e.g.,
reckless driving), while women comprise most of the patients who suffer
from eating disorders, compulsive buying, and excessive suntanning.
These dysfunctional actions are rooted in adaptive processes that have
become misaligned or poorly tuned. Thus, contrary to the social constructivist mantra that poor socialization and incomplete information
lead to such bad choices, I propose that these are rooted in our biology.

Several years ago, one of my students shared a memorable personal
anecdote. He was an avid smoker and clearly aware of the ill consequences of prolonged smoking. However, he claimed to have uncovered
a "foolproof" method for avoiding worrisome and intrusive thoughts
about such negative repercussions. Whenever he purchased a new pack
of cigarettes, he would only purchase a pack that had a warning message
that could not apply to him. For example, my student could discount the

US Surgeon General's warning message "Smoking by pregnant women may result in fetal injury, premature birth, and low birth weight[,]" as it did not apply to him! The links between smoking and heart disease, lung cancer, and erectile dysfunction hit too close to home. But the ill effects of smoking on pregnant women and their babies were irrelevant to his reality. I was astonished not only by the student's candor in sharing this tale but also by his blatant irrationality. Yet he insisted that his dissonance was greatly reduced. I share this account because it serves as a clear demonstration that lack of information is seldom the mechanism that drives consumers to engage in ill-conceived behaviors.

In the 1995 movie thriller *Se7en*, Brad Pitt and Morgan Freeman play detectives tracking down a somewhat unique serial killer (played by Kevin Spacey). The killer begins by murdering five individuals, each of whom represents one of the seven deadly sins (gluttony, greed, lust, sloth, and pride). He then succumbs to a sixth deadly sin by envying the life that Brad Pitt's character has built for himself (e.g., being married to a beautiful wife, played by Gwyneth Paltrow). Because of his sadistic envy, the killer decapitates her and sends a box containing the severed head to Pitt's character. The climax of the movie occurs when Pitt receives the box when the serial killer is in his custody. The detective's natural reaction is to seek revenge, and he succumbs to the seventh and last of the deadly sins—wrath—by shooting the serial killer. Moral philosophers and theologians alike have written extensively about the allure of the seven deadly sins. Not surprisingly, scores of consummatory excesses that we engage in can ultimately be traced back to these sins, as they cater to many of our most basic Darwinian instincts.[6] In other words, it is precisely the enticing pull of these sins that has forced us to come up with a codified moral system to try to avoid them. Pathological gambling can in the end be traced to greed, excessive plastic surgeries to vanity, unrestrained eating to gluttony, and pornographic addiction to lust. Rather than construing these consumer-related behaviors as "irrational," a more illuminating approach is to inquire: What in human biology makes us so susceptible to these temptations? If we ask the right questions, we can then have a better chance of identifying the appropriate public policy and intervention strategies.

Let's look at various seemingly irrational behaviors and demonstrate their Darwinian roots, beginning with compulsive buying.

COMPULSIVE BUYING

A&E and TLC recently premiered new series titled *Hoarders* and *Hoarding: Buried Alive*, respectively. They chronicle the lives of individuals who suffer from a particular form of obsessive-compulsive disorder (OCD) known as hoarding. A hoarder's house is typically so cluttered with endless collected items that the home eventually becomes unsafe to occupy (e.g., physical dangers associated with the collapse of stacks of collected items or the airborne pollutants). When asked by a therapist, typically as part of cognitive-behavioral therapy, to discuss why a particular item cannot be thrown away (e.g., empty milk cartons more than a decade old), the hoarder is able to "rationally" see the failed logic in his thinking. However, on an affective level, the item takes on a monumental importance in terms of its association to a past event or its potential for future use ("I might need this exact carton someday"). For that reason, decluttering becomes a nearly impossible endeavor, as each item within the endless collected ones is attributed a distinctively important status.

I have argued elsewhere that many OCD manifestations occur in largely sex-specific manners because they map onto issues of sex-specific evolutionary import.[7] For instance, intrusive and obsessive thoughts (a form of OCD) about one's social status—"Did I say something moronic at yesterday's meeting causing everyone to think that I am an idiot?"— should be more likely to occur in men, as this concern is, evolutionarily speaking, of greater importance to men. A similar logic can be applied to intrusive thoughts about the harming of one's baby: "I am worried that

I might throw my baby from the balcony"; in this case, women are more likely to experience such thoughts. Generally speaking, evolutionary-minded researchers have argued that OCD is the overactivation of an otherwise adaptive scanning of environmental or social threats. Whereas most individuals can move on from an intrusive thought (e.g., "I'll check once to make sure that the oven is off"), the OCD sufferer is stuck in an infinite loop of checks, irrespective of the OCD manifestation that the individual is afflicted with. For example, someone with contamination fears will repeatedly wash her hands; one obsessed with a need for symmetry will spend hours ensuring that a set of objects is perfectly aligned in a symmetric manner. And a person suffering from the intrusive thought "I am sure that I ran over someone while driving home from work" will incessantly repeat the drive to make certain that no such occurrence has taken place.

Compulsive buying can be construed as a form of hoarding (albeit, technically speaking, they are distinct disorders). Rather than collecting a litany of items—each of which possesses no functional value, as is the case with "classic" hoarding—compulsive buyers often hoard beautification products (e.g., shoes, clothes, cosmetics). Thus it is perhaps not unexpected that the great majority of compulsive buyers, roughly 90 percent, are women. The environmental threat is the concern over one's attractiveness even if such a threat is not consciously available to the sufferer. If compulsive buying were a domain-general psychiatric disorder, we should be able to document a never-ending variety of products as part of the purchasing binges (e.g., widgets and kitchen accessories). Instead, compulsive buying is triggered by a warning flag in the compulsive buyer linked to mating-related insecurities, which are subsequently assuaged by purchasing beautification products. Support for this view stems from findings that show that compulsive buyers may have lower levels of dopamine and serotonin, possess lower self-esteem, have a stronger interest in appearance-related issues, have greater fashion interest, and utilize purchases as a means of regulating their moods.[8] A woman who has low self-esteem and is looking for a dopaminergic and affective boost will purchase products that are intimately connected to her self-concept. In light of the differential import that men place on women's physical attractiveness in the mating arena, it makes perfect sense that beautification-related products constitute the bulk of purchases during a compulsive buying binge.

EATING DISORDERS

Karen Carpenter, the iconic lead singer of the Carpenters with a hauntingly angelic voice, died in 1983 at the age of thirty-two from complications due to anorexia nervosa. Tracey Gold, who starred in the highly successful 1980s sitcom *Growing Pains*, spent several years combating the disease. The list of famous actresses who have either admitted to suffering from an eating disorder or who were suspected of suffering from one is indeed substantial. What can make highly successful women who are otherwise in the prime of their lives succumb to such a cruel and devastating disease? Note that while the disorder is hardly restricted to celebrities, it is largely confined to women, who constitute 90 to 95 percent of eating disorder sufferers. When men do suffer from such disorders, the circumstances are typically associated with concerns with musculature, a condition known as muscle dysmorphia (or bigorexia). In other words, the desired aesthetics sought by male and female sufferers are radically different. Research shows that gay men are more likely than their heterosexual counterparts to suffer from eating disorders. Given the premium that is placed on physical attractiveness by both heterosexual and gay men in their prospective partners, it follows that heterosexual women and gay men are the most likely groups to suffer from eating disorders.[9]

According to a good number of experts, one key cause of eating disorders is the frequent exposure to media images that promote the supposed thin ideal. There are numerous studies that repeat the mantra that being bombarded with images of unrealistic physical ideals (be it thin and beautiful women or athletic and muscular guys) gnaws away at the self-esteem of the message recipients. In their quest to reach these impossible standards, individuals evidently get caught up in disordered eating patterns that ultimately result in the onset of a full-blown eating disorder. This sounds like a plausible explanation, but it is largely incorrect. Hippocrates, the ancient Greek physician and founder of modern medicine, reported more than two millennia ago that eating disorders tend to occur predominantly in women. This puts into doubt the notion that media images are to blame. Furthermore, in all cultures in which eating disorders have been studied, women are always the overwhelming majority of sufferers (i.e., even in cultures in which the exposure to the Western media's thin ideal is not nearly as prevalent).[10] Very few of the women who are exposed to the supposed culprit pictures will develop an eating disorder. Hence, if media images cause eating disorders, one would have to explain why they seem to have no effect on the great majority of women who are otherwise exposed to these images.

To comprehend this cruel disease, one must understand certain aspects of a woman's menstrual cycle. The onset of a girl's menses is known as menarche. If menarche does not occur by age fourteen (if secondary sexual characteristics, such as breast growth, are absent) or sixteen (if secondary sexual characteristics are present), the girl has a condition known as primary amenorrhea. Secondary amenorrhea is when a woman who has had regular menstrual cycles ceases to menstruate for three or more months. Of relevance to the current discussion, women who suffer from eating disorders are much more likely to be amenorrheic, which is tantamount to shutting down a woman's reproductive potential. Accordingly, several evolutionists have argued that eating disorders are an instantiation of the reproductive suppression model.[11] The general idea is that across numerous mammalian species, females have evolved the capability to shut off their reproductive system if the species-relevant environmental conditions are not conducive to the successful rearing of an offspring; the lack of food sources might constitute one such environmental challenge. In the human context, the environmental threats are regularly social in nature and may include lack of familial or mate support, poor attachment styles, and perceived onslaught of intrasexual rivalry[12] (which might be driven in part by media images of beautiful women). Numerous evolutionary psychologists have found that women who suffer from eating disorders are more likely to be facing environmental threats, thus causing them to subconsciously shut down their reproductive system. Therefore, even though reproductive suppression is an adaptive mechanism meant to serve as a temporary "off" switch, it "misfires" when applied to extreme levels well beyond that for which it was originally designed (as occurs with eating disorders).[13]

PATHOLOGICAL GAMBLING AND FINANCIAL TRADING

Across sexually reproducing species, the sex that provides less requisite parental investment is typically the one that engages in greater risk taking (men, in the human context), in part because it is a required trait when competing for mating opportunities. As such, via the process of sexual selection, women have repeatedly chosen men who can negotiate risk taking successfully; one of the traits of the standard male hero is an ability to take risks and come out on top. James Bond epitomizes such an archetype. Several common themes and related scenes are prevalent in many of the Bond series' installments, regardless of the era in question. There is always a sinister and maniacal villain; there are always beautiful women (Bond girls); and James Bond always engages in extreme forms of risk taking while coming out unscathed. Perhaps this is best captured in the requisite casino scenes. Mr. Bond is shown gambling some exorbitant sum of money while remaining cool, calm, and collected. He always seems to emerge victorious (think of 2006's *Casino Royale*, wherein he participated in a high-stake poker competition hosted by the film's villain). The gaming sites also always contain one or more beautiful girls seated at, or in proximity to, the gambling table. Comedian Mike Myers brilliantly spoofed this ubiquitous Bond theme in the first installment of his *Austin Powers* trilogy.

The availability of gorgeous women is good business practice from the perspective of the casino operators, as it increases men's risk-taking proclivities. Men engage in greater physical risk taking when in the presence of women, especially if the women are attractive, with the effect in part mediated by men's increased levels of testosterone.[14] Even in instances when men are merely primed with photos of women prior to being asked to complete a financial-related task, males display greater risk taking[15] and greater impulsivity.[16] It would thus appear that men use various forms of risk taking as a sexual signal. This serves a first indication as to why gaming might be more alluring to men and would augment men's chances of succumbing to pathological gambling. A second related reason for men's greater representation within the pathological gambling population deals with the acquisition of resources. At the end of the day, men who possess (or can obtain) resources are attractive to women. For that reason, men are willing to take any and all risks to obtain what women desire. Women might constitute 91 percent of plastic surgery patients in the United States[17] (to be appealing to men), but men kindly reciprocate the madness by gambling away their lives (often to be appealing to women).

Studies on pathological gamblers from around the world—including the United States (several states), Canada, Norway, Spain, Sweden, Switzerland, and Hong Kong—have arrived at one incontrovertible fact: men are the predominant sufferers of this behavioral disorder.[18] This does not mean that women do not enjoy gambling or that they might not become pathological gamblers themselves. However, it is clear that irrespective of cultural setting, this form of risk taking caters largely to men's psyches.[19] I recently reviewed the list of the 250 top poker players as ranked in the *Bluff Magazine*/ESPN Poker Power Rankings.[20] I verified the players' first names to determine their sex. When I was unsure about the player's gender, I clicked on the player's link to view a photo. In a few cases, photos were not available, in which case I Googled the full name of the players in question to establish their biological sex. Of the 250 players listed, four were women: Kathy Liebert, Vanessa Rousso, Vanessa Selbst, and Joanne (J. J.) Liu, ranked 39, 43, 71, and 189, respectively. In other words, 98.4 percent of the top 250 ranked professional poker players are men, all of whom hail from a broad range of countries and cultures. On a related note, Eric T. Steiner and his colleagues at the University of Nevada at Las Vegas investigated the effects of playing poker on men's testosterone levels. Thirty-two participants took part in head-to-head matches. The researchers made sure to pair players of roughly equal experience with each other. The mere act of playing poker caused men's testosterone levels to rise, and this held true regardless of the eventual outcome of the game (i.e., whether a man won or lost his match).[21]

The great majority of participants in the financial industry, whether those working for particular firms (e.g., floor traders and investment bankers) or those who are self-employed (e.g., online day traders), share one common feature: They are almost always male.[22] Men constitute more than 90 percent of the employees and members at the American Commodities Exchange trading floor, and more than 95 percent of the workforce in the higher echelon of traders and clerks.[23] Men comprised 82 percent of 16,831 Swedish investors who made transactions at an Internet discount brokerage outfit,[24] and 85.7 percent of 1,607 investors who switched from phone to online trading were men.[25] Men made up 89.5 percent and 87.9 percent of managers of domestic and international equity funds, respectively,[26] as well as 95.6 percent of the speculators on the commodities futures market.[27] Finally, not only are men the majority of participants in various financial trading domains, but they are also substantially greater risk takers across countless financial instruments.[28] Although women have not had equal access to these positions historically, this cannot explain the extent of the sex difference that currently exists, nor can it explain the lack of female participation in financial activities that do not possess any institutional barriers to entry (e.g., day trading).

In a memorable scene in the iconic 1983 movie *Scarface*, Tony Montana (played by Al Pacino) explains to his protégé, Manny Ribera (played by Steven Bauer), the relationship between money, power, and women. Specifically, Montana pontificates correctly that money leads to power, and power leads to getting more women. Having discussed the great lengths that men go to in order to obtain money, it is only befitting that the next section be devoted to men's unabated pursuits of sexual conquests.

SEXUAL COMPULSIONS AND MISCONDUCT

If one were to compile an exhaustive list of sex scandals involving public figures, one demographic reality would stand out, although politically correct social constructivists might not want to admit it. Men constitute the great majority of sexual transgressors. This does not imply that a famous woman has never succumbed to a sexual indiscretion, but it is an extraordinarily rare phenomenon (Cleopatra was perhaps the ultimate beguiling femme fatale). Today's American political pundits will have us believe that lechery is reserved for one political party or the other. However, the banal truth is that neither Republicans nor Democrats hold a monopoly over sexual improprieties. On the Democratic side, some of the most infamous transgressors include President John F. Kennedy (philanderer par excellence), Gary Hart (former Colorado senator who was caught in the throes of an affair during his presidential run in 1984), President Bill Clinton (the Monica Lewinsky affair), Eliot Spitzer (former governor of New York who sought the services of a young female prostitute), James McGreevy (former governor of New Jersey who had an affair with another man), and John Edwards (former North Carolina senator and presidential candidate who admitted to an affair). The Republicans have produced their own all-star lineup, including Mark Foley (former Floridian congressman who made repeated advances to male pages), Larry Craig (former senator from Idaho who was caught trying to have sex with a man in an airport public bathroom), David Vitter (senator from Louisiana who was a client of a Washington, DC, madam), and Mark Sanford (governor of South Carolina) and John Ensign (senator from Nevada), both of whom have admitted to having extramarital affairs.

Of course, politicians are not the sole ones to engage in sexual activities that can shatter their professional careers if not their families. Perhaps the greatest hypocrites are the supposed men of God who preach a holier-than-thou message. The uncontested champion of hypocrites is undoubtedly Ted Haggard—the former leader of the National Association of Evangelicals—who preached against the sins of homosexuality while hiring male prostitutes for sessions of sex and drugs. Who could forget the crocodile tears of the televangelist Jimmy Swaggart as he apologized to his flock for having hired a prostitute? Actors, too, have been caught in highly compromising situations. The dashing actor Hugh Grant, who at the time was involved with one of the most beautiful women in the world (Elizabeth Hurley), sought the services of a street prostitute. Actor and comedian Eddie Murphy, who was married to a striking woman, was caught with a transvestite prostitute. Other men who have cheated on their stunningly gorgeous partners (albeit not with prostitutes) include the R&B singer Eric Benét (who cheated on actress Halle Berry), actor Jude Law (who cheated on the lovely Sienna Miller with his children's nanny), and businessman Peter Cook (who cheated on his supermodel wife Christie Brinkley). Not to be outdone by Hugh Grant and Eddie Murphy, the world-class Brazilian footballer—soccer player, to Americans—Ronaldo was apprehended with three transvestite prostitutes, although he claimed that he was unaware they were men. Finally, talk show host David Letterman admitted to having sexual liaisons with several of his female employees. Are all these men engaging in "irrational" behaviors?

The Tiger Woods sexual scandal in 2009 generated a mass amount of media coverage. That a high-status man was caught having extramarital affairs with numerous women is hardly shocking. Of greater interest was the endless psychobabble that filled the airways and the blogosphere's dissection of his dalliances. Some thought that the attention that Woods's father bestowed on him was at the root of his behaviors. Another supposed culprit was the emotional void present in his marriage (though one wonders how such pundits knew about the intimate details of Woods's marriage). Nonstop silly, irrelevant, and nonsensical causes were identified, all of which shared one commonality: each is fully removed from an accurate understanding of human nature in general and male sexuality in particular.

Why would men engage in sexual behaviors that could ruin their careers and destroy their families? Why would they cheat on extraordinarily attractive and sensual women? I suppose that the best way to answer the latter question is via a colloquialism that has now entered the pantheon of aphorisms: "Show me a beautiful woman, and I'll show you a man who's tired of sleeping with her." A variant of this adage is uttered in the 2007 movie *Perfect Stranger* starring Halle Berry, Bruce Willis, and Giovanni Ribisi. The saying serves as the central theme of the 2001 movie *Someone Like You*—starring Hugh Jackman, Ashley Judd, Greg Kinnear, and Marisa Tomei—which was based on Laura Zigman's novel *Animal Husbandry* (this keen observation of male sexuality is central to the storyline).

As I mentioned earlier, universally successful movies typically contain plot lines that are congruent with our innate human nature. It is perhaps not surprising then that the central premise behind *Someone Like You* is rooted in an established scientific fact known as the Coolidge

Effect (briefly mentioned in chapter 8). The effect owes its name to an anecdote that allegedly took place between President Calvin Coolidge (thirtieth US president), his wife, and a farmer. Mrs. Coolidge was impressed that a few roosters were able to service a large number of hens on a nightly basis, and directed the farmer to make President Coolidge aware of the roosters' sexual potency. President Coolidge then asked the farmer whether the same roosters were paired with the same hens, to which the farmer replied that to the contrary, the pairings were rotated. President Coolidge then advised the farmer that he should inform Mrs. Coolidge of that fact![29]

The Coolidge Effect has been documented across numerous species ranging from mammals, birds, fish, reptiles, and even invertebrates. Although there are instances in which the Coolidge Effect has been documented in females, the phenomenon is largely restricted to males. If traditional mores are to blame for the sexual double standard, they must be equally responsible for the "sexist" sexual behaviors of rats, livestock, burying beetles, and hermaphrodite snails. The plain reality is that parental investment theory dictates that the sex who has the lesser obligatory investment is more likely to be sexually indiscriminate (men), an element of which is a greater proclivity for sexual variety seeking.

It is important to reemphasize that providing a biological explanation for men's sexual transgressions does not in any way condone or justify their behaviors. If anything, humans are also equipped with the evolved capacity to engage in moral acts. We all have multiple Darwinian instincts tugging at us in different directions. Ultimately, it is up to each individual to decide which particular Darwinian pull will win. Hence, there is nothing biologically deterministic in anything I have discussed. I next turn to a sex-related industry that possesses perhaps the most pronounced sex specificity in terms of the individuals who purchase and consume its product offerings.

PORNOGRAPHY

In his 2010 paper aptly published in the *Journal of Happiness Studies*, Fabio D'Orlando cited several sources regarding the import of the global pornography market; its revenues totaled $97 billion in 2006 (apparently this constitutes larger revenues than those arising from the top three American professional sports leagues, as well as double those of the three major television networks). He further mentions that 12 percent of global web pages that existed in 2006 were pornographic.[30] In Julie M. Albright's 2008 study on Internet sexual behaviors, she provided some powerful opening statistics about the importance of sex in the online world, including that 50 percent of Internet traffic is associated with sex websites, and that 30 percent of trading conducted in *Second Life*, a popular virtual world where people interact with one another via personal avatars, dealt with sex.[31] Not only is the commercial might of pornography a universal reality but also the industry is an early adopter of many of the latest technologies in the ever-pressing quest to offer sexual material to the insatiable appetites of the consuming masses.[32] Despite the near-universal ubiquity of pornography, some view it as a patriarchal tool of oppression that serves no purpose other than to degrade women. Those who hold such a view are largely unaware of the evolutionary forces that have shaped male sexuality.

Detractors of pornography have repeatedly argued that pornography has adverse effects both on individuals and the society at large. Two of the most common accusations levied against pornography are that they generate hostile feelings toward women, which in turn leads to an increased likelihood of committing sex crimes against women. Milton Diamond, director of the Pacific Center for Sex and Society, recently conducted an extensive review of the research that has sought to establish whether pornography actually yields the deleterious effects that it has been accused of. He concluded that the scientific evidence did not support the premise (at the population level), and he went so far as to call it a myth.[33] The reality is that the more tolerant a society is toward pornography, the better the plight of its women (contrast Sweden, Canada, and the United States to strict Islamic societies). Incidentally, when users of pornography are directly asked about the effects of consuming hard-core pornography on their lives, the net effects were overwhelmingly positive; this held true for both sexes. As a matter of fact, for both sexes a positive correlation was found between the amount of hard-core pornography that was consumed and the extent of the beneficial effects (e.g., sex life, attitudes toward sex, perceptions and attitudes toward individuals of the opposite sex, life in general, and overall).[34]

Many antiporn crusaders believe that pornography should be banned in light of its supposed social ills. Can the individuals in question explain who will determine what should be banned? For example, fatty foods are extraordinarily more harmful to society than pornography (e.g., hundreds of thousands of people die of heart attacks linked to poor diet). Should we ban cheeses? What about fried foods? Let's outlaw them. What about lascivious music or dancing (think back to the 1984 movie *Footloose*)? The Taliban believe that music is *haram* (religiously forbidden). Islamic regimes prohibit alcohol consumption. More people die per year in car accidents than any social ill that might be supposedly linked to pornography. Should we ban cars? What about homosexuality? Should we reintroduce sodomy laws, an idea supported by many religious fundamentalists? Tipper Gore petitioned to have raunchy and violent song lyrics prohibited. Should she decide which songs we can listen to? Some believe that first-person shooter video games cause young men to be violent in the real world (a tenuous premise). Should we forbid video games? Where do we draw the line, and who draws it? In a free society, there is no external agent who serves as the absolute arbiter of morality, especially not when it comes to innate Darwinian drives that involve consenting adults.

By puritanical American standards, my hometown of Montreal is a very liberal city. Sexual services, sex stores, and strip bars are quite easy to find. But although there are innumerable strip clubs where female dancers strut their stuff for male patrons, I am aware of only one club of male dancers targeted at heterosexual women. Of course, in Montreal's vibrant gay village, there are many such clubs targeting a male homosexual clientele, but yet again there are many fewer (if any) clubs of female dancers for a lesbian audience. It would seem that regardless of whether a man is gay or straight, he is interested in the visual stimulation associated with strip clubs. Along the same lines, irrespective of whether a woman is straight or gay, she appears largely uninterested in this visual ritual. These realities cast doubt on the notion that strip clubs are yet another vehicle for the patriarchy to exploit women, as this premise would have to also clarify why gay men seem to be "exploiting" male dancers—unless the patriarchy has straight and gay divisions with the explicit mandate to exploit different segments of the population. If it were the case that sexuality is learned, shrewd entrepreneurs should find a way to cater to the untapped niches (heterosexual and gay women alike).

The same logic applies to the consumption of hard-core pornographic movies. The overwhelming majority of consumers of such products are men, whether straight or gay. Again, heterosexual women and lesbians lag far behind in their interest in this form of pornography. On the other hand, women constitute the main viewers of "positive pornography," a euphemism for soft porn or erotica, with this genre being minimally appealing to straight or gay men. On a related note, so-called sexual addiction is much more prevalent among both heterosexual as well as homosexual men, as compared with women in general. If sexuality were part of an elaborate socialization of gendered roles and gendered dynamics, we should not find that homosexual men—whose sexual appetite is obviously for other men—display the same penchant for unrestrained sexuality as do heterosexual men. The bottom line is that homosexual preferences can serve as a window for understanding sex differences in heterosexual mating.

The global consumption of pornography has everything to do with innate sex differences in sexual fantasies and far less to do with patriarchal oppression. It is certainly the case that both men and women engage in sexual fantasies; it is part of what makes us human. However, the frequency with which we engage in such carnal daydreaming and the content of such fantasies are very telling about crucial differences between the two sexes when it comes to human mating. In a now-classic study published over two decades ago, evolutionary behavioral scientists Bruce Ellis and Donald Symons explored this exact topic. Men were much more likely to fantasize than women, more likely to fantasize about a greater number of sexual partners, and more likely to fantasize about strangers; emotional matters were of lesser concern, visual imagery was much more important, touching was less crucial, and the pace at which one arrived at the sexual acts was much quicker in men's fantasies.[35] Now let's contextualize these sex differences within the prototypical hard-core porn movie targeting heterosexual males. The plot line tends to be skeletal, with a quick denouement into the sex acts, with minimal foreplay (e.g., caressing, touching, and so forth). The cinematography is such that it is visually centric on various body parts. Little is left to the imagination. There are multiple women in any given movie, most of whom are typically young, physically attractive, and highly willing to engage in short-term mating. Briefly put, the findings of Ellis and Symons are a near-perfect blueprint of the typical pornographic movie that is targeted to men. In the same manner that women comprise the majority of consumers of both romance novels and erotica, hard-core pornography is a largely male fascination because it caters to their evolutionary-based sexuality.[36]

Pornographic movies are rife with clues regarding the evolutionary origins of male sexuality. Take, for example, the so-called money shot, the climax (pun intended) of any scene in an adult movie. Specifically, it refers to the external ejaculation of the male actor on one or more body parts of the female actress. Interestingly, even though men will often state that one of their most frequent fantasies is to have sex with multiple women simultaneously, many pornographic movies are just as likely (if not more so) to show multiple men sharing one woman, with the requisite multiple money shots. There are even subgenres of pornographic movies that take this "polyandrous" depiction to bewildering levels in the extreme gangbangs and bukkake films (multiple men ejaculate on the face of one woman).

Evolutionary psychologist Nicholas Pound provided a compelling explanation for this otherwise recurrent image in pornographic movies. He argued that males in numerous species become sexually aroused at the sight of another male mating with a female. In other words, the presence of other males serves as an excitatory visual cue. It would appear that the possibility of sperm competition between rival males gets men to rise—literally—to the occasion. Pound investigated the prevalence of polyandrous (many men with one woman) versus polygynous (many women with one man) images in pornographic movies.[37] In his first study, he found that there were 1.79 times more polyandrous than polygynous images, as posted on adult websites. Of the 359 images containing multiple males with one woman, 304 were of two men with one woman and the other 55 were of three or more males with one woman (the largest number of men in a given scene was thirteen). In the case of polygynous scenes, none contained more than two females (with a given male). Hence, the polyandrous situations were more "pronounced" than their polygynous counterparts. In his second study, using a content analysis of 169 movies, Pound observed that polyandrous scenes were 2.41 times more frequent than polygynous ones. In the third study, he asked respondents which types of scenes they would be most interested in viewing (in still images, videos, or sexual stories). Respondents were 1.96, 2.03, and 1.58 times respectively more likely to prefer polyandrous as opposed to polygynous scenes. Lastly, in his fourth and final study, Pound kept track of which images people chose to view from an Internet sex site. They were 1.48 times more likely to choose polyandrous scenes than polygynous ones. Lest some readers might construe the money shot as a pernicious means of degrading women, it is important to note that male gay porn is equally laden with such depictions. In other words, the money shot is a visual stimulant for men regardless of their sexual orientation.

It seems unequivocal that men find sexual images laden with implications of sperm competition to be visually arousing. That said, if one were to discover that such images actually have an effect on men's sperm motility . . . now that would be something to get excited about! This is exactly what Sarah J. Kilgallon and Leigh W. Simmons found. They provided men with sexual images that cue sperm competition (two men with one woman) or alternate images that did not (three women). The men masturbated while watching the images, and subsequently provided the researchers with the fruits of their manual labor. Two key semen metrics were analyzed: sperm motility and sperm density. Amazingly, Kilgallon and Simmons found that the sexual image that cued sperm competition yielded sperm samples that possessed greater motility (though sperm density was lesser in those samples).[38] The mechanism by which men might generate sperm of differential motility—as a function of environmental contingencies such as sperm competition—is not known. Nonetheless, this is a truly astonishing finding.

The scientific study of pornography should not be marred in ideological debates. In the same way that a juicy burger caters to our evolved penchant for fatty foods, the visual imagery inherent to hard-core pornography ultimately appeals to men's sexuality. This scientific fact holds true irrespective of the moral position that one might hold toward the pornographic industry.

We now turn to another largely male-dominated pursuit; namely, the endless ways by which men engage in various forms of physical bravery—including a wide range of death-defying extreme sports. Are these calculated risks, or do men suffer from an irrational death wish?

EXTREME SPORTS AND OTHER FORMS OF PHYSICAL RISK TAKING

Men will go to great lengths to demonstrate their physical bravery, athletic prowess, and risk-taking propensities,[39] as these are traits desired by women. Via the process of sexual selection (which, recall, is driven by female mate choice), men have evolved a greater penchant for physical activities that permit them to showcase the desired qualities.[40] As such, many sports serve as means for men to engage in courtship signaling,[41] perhaps none more so than extreme sports. Examples of death-defying activities include bouldering (rock climbing without a rope or harness), buildering (or urban climbing), elevator surfing, free diving, caving, parachuting, skydiving, skysurfing, mountain climbing, and big wave surfing. No matter what the activity, the cultural setting, or the epoch, men constitute the founders of each of these activities along with being the great majority of participants.

The Spartathlon is an ultramarathon that has been held annually since 1983. It is 246 kilometers (152.86 miles) in length—from Athens to Sparta—making it just shy of six full marathons (42.2 kilometers, or 26.2 miles). The International Spartathlon Association provides on its website key statistics of this grueling race for the years covering 1997 through 2008, including the sex breakdown of the finishers for each listed year.[42] Of the 1,102 participants who have completed the race, 90.2 percent were men (yearly range: 85.6 percent to 96.1 percent). This demographic reality manifests itself for innumerable endeavors that test the limits of human endurance. For example, as of 2003, more than 95 percent of those who reached the summit of Mount Everest were men;[43] and of the 19 climbers who have thus far reached the summits of all fourteen 8,000-meter peaks (26,247 feet), 100 percent are men.[44]

Of all extreme sports, BASE jumping is one of the most dangerous. BASE jumpers leap from lower heights than do skydivers, and so they have little time to deploy their parachutes. The acronym represents the four types of fixed platforms from which individuals jump: buildings, antennas, spans (i.e., bridges), and earth (i.e., cliffs). BASE jumpers keep track of the number of successful jumps in part as a badge of status. Using a world fatality list available on the Internet,[45] Anton Westman reported in his doctoral dissertation—defended in 2009 at Umeå University (Sweden)—that of 106 fatalities between 1981 and 2006, 92 were men (another four were unclear). In other words, 90.2 percent of BASE jumping fatalities involve men. The US Bureau of Labor Statistics keeps tracks of fatal occupational injuries, broken down by a wide range of variables including the sex of the deceased.[46] I calculated the percentage of men of the total number of deceased workers for each year between 1992 and 2008 (the data of 2008 is considered preliminary). Men constitute the overwhelming number of occupational victims (range: 91.4 percent to 92.9 percent). Men perform almost exclusively many of the most dangerous jobs including Alaskan crab fishermen (see the Discovery Channel's hit series *Deadliest Catch*), oil shore rig men, high-rise steel workers, coal miners, pearl divers, and deep-sea divers.

BASE jumpers are perhaps fearless, but their extreme sport might be considered child's play compared to the N'Gol ritual (also known as land diving) practiced in the South Pacific on the island of Pentecost, which is part of the archipelago of Vanuatu. Young men hurl themselves headfirst off a platform that varies in height from roughly 20 to 30 meters (65 to 100 feet). The jumpers' feet are tied to vine ropes that are long enough to stop the free fall a few inches from the ground. In addition to having to calculate the exact length of the ropes, one must take into account the weight of the individual who is jumping as well as the humidity present within the ropes (as this affects their elasticity). Any miscalculation along any of these metrics, and the jumper suffers horrifying injuries if not certain death (as was reported during Queen Elizabeth II's visit to Vanuatu in 1974). This ritual was eventually commercialized into bungee jumping, with the first such site established in Queenstown, New Zealand. The town has since positioned itself as a leading destination for tourists (mainly male) wishing to actively seek death-defying experiences.

Similar types of jumping, leaping, or diving rites are found in otherwise disparate cultures. The La Quebrada cliff divers in Acapulco perform acts of bravery that are truly difficult to fathom. Taking off from dangerously jagged cliffs that are roughly 45 meters (150 feet) high, they must time their dives with the incoming tides to ensure that the water is deep enough when they hit it. Needless to say, most such divers are male, with very few women only recently braving the dizzying cliffs. On a related note, in the eighteenth century, the Maui king Kahekili instituted the practice of *lele kawa*, that is, jumping off cliffs (feet first while minimizing the splash) to demonstrate that male warriors had the necessary loyalty and courage.

Myriad cultures have sex-specific rites of passage required for entry into adulthood, possibly none as painful as that of the Satere-Mawe people, who reside in the Brazilian Amazon. In order for a young male to become a certified warrior, he must subject himself to the repeated stings of a *Paraponera clavata* ant, more colloquially known as a bullet ant. Its name stems from the fact that its sting is reputed to be more painful than if one were to be shot. In preparation for the initiation, tribe members collect several hundred ants, place them in a sedating liquid, and subsequently interweave them (while the ants are sedated) into gloves made of leaves. The stingers are positioned such that they point toward the inside of the gloves. The initiate then places his hands into the gloves, experiencing hundreds of stings as the bullet ants seek to disentangle themselves. The initiate must wear the gloves for ten minutes while he refrains from vocalizing his agonizing pain. For a man to be accepted into the temple of warriors, this rite of passage must be performed on twenty separate occasions.[47]

The Jaful Fulani people of Nigeria practice the Shadi (or Sharo) rite. It involves young, unmarried men flogging each other; when flogged, they should hardly flinch as a result of the inflicted pain. Naturally, the whole rite takes place in full view of young and beautiful women who watch the proceedings with discriminating eyes.[48] An equally bloody ritual of flagellation, albeit in this case self-inflicted, is the Ashura ritual practiced by Shi`ia men. In this case, the men flog themselves as part of a religious ceremony; however, it is instructive to note that the women do not engage in such a bloody ritual.[49] Rites of passage of street gangs, most of which are composed of young males, include the severe beating of initiates and/or the killing of random strangers (it takes guts to slay someone). Turkish oil wrestling, known as Kirkpinar, is a grueling competition dating back to the fourteenth century that pits powerful men against one another until a single male is left standing.[50] The purpose of such a long-standing ritual is to identify the courageous, heroic, and powerful men from the pretenders. Contemporary human blood sports such as extreme and ultimate fighting are less lethal examples of the combats held between male gladiators during the Roman era. The worldwide commercial success of MMA (mixed martial arts) speaks not only to the innate penchant of men to engage in intrasexual violent combats but also to the ravenous appetite of audiences to watch such brutal events. Ultimately, throughout all recorded history and across extraordinarily varied cultural settings, men are more than willing to engage in violent intrasexual combats. In some instances, men demonstrate their courage by pitting themselves against dangerous animals. For example, most participants who partake in the annual run with the bulls in Pamplona (Spain) are men. Similarly, men constitute the great majority of matadors and equestrian bullfighters in countries that engage in these cruel and torturous practices (e.g., Mexico, Spain, and Portugal). The romantic notion of the "noble savage" exists only in the wishful imagination of so-called anthropologists of peace.[51] Human history is paved with the blood of male-based violence, much of which is driven by the evolutionary forces implicit to sexual selection.

The bottom line is that men will challenge nature, their physical limits, other men, and dangerous animals, all in the hope of demonstrating that they possess specific traits highly sought out by women. This reality is not due to the arbitrary and sexist socialization of so-called patriarchal gender roles. Rather, it is part of the elaborate universal sexual signals that both sexes partake in to demonstrate their value in the mating market. Of course, men's greater appetite for physical risk-taking manifests itself in numerous consumer settings, including in their greater interest in bungee jumping, violent video games, and violent sports (e.g., fistfighting in the NHL has never been eradicated by the league because it helps fill seats).

CONCLUSION

Consumers succumb to numerous self-harming phenomena including compulsive buying, eating disorders, excessive suntanning, sexual misconduct, pornographic addiction, pathological gambling, and death-defying physical risk-taking. The standard and largely erroneous explanation espoused by social constructivists has been that consumer irrationality is rooted either in the lack of knowledge ("Consumers must be educated about the dangers of sun exposure") or in the availability of harmful information (e.g., "Media images cause eating disorders"). Each discussed maladaptive behavior possesses a strong sex-specificity in terms of its sufferers, and this holds true across cultural settings and time periods. This suggests that these universal realities are rooted in a shared biological heritage. The irrational behaviors in question are driven by mechanisms that evolved as adaptations, which at times misfire (or are subverted), yielding the associated deleterious outcomes. In the end, these phenomena cannot be decoupled from our biology. Consequently, any public policy intervention meant to curb these behaviors, that otherwise restricts the analysis to purely environmental causes, is bound to fail.

CHAPTER 10
DARWIN IN THE HALLS OF THE BUSINESS SCHOOL

> If I have a plea on which to end, it is that
> social scientists refrain from the kinds of knee-
> jerk abhorrence of the evolutionary approach,
> and ask instead how this approach might ben-
> efit what they do.
> —ROBIN I. M. DUNBAR,
> BRITISH ANTHROPOLOGIST[1]

Whereas I have thus far largely focused on consumer behavior, the relevance of evolutionary psychology—and more generally evolutionary theory—extends to business in countless other contexts. Evolutionists have recently demonstrated the link between men's basal testosterone levels and their entrepreneurial activities. Other scholars have explored the relationship between testosterone levels and the daily gains or losses of male financial traders. The manner by which highly attractive job candidates are evaluated has also been investigated via an evolutionary lens. Additionally, economists have calculated the salary benefits that accrue to tall employees (an evolutionarily relevant cue). Other business areas that have recently been explored via an evolutionary lens include family businesses, executive decision making, human resource management, organizational citizenship behavior, leadership, sexual harassment in organizations, technological change, total quality management, accounting, finance, economics, management information systems, and business ethics.[2] Notwithstanding these recent infusions of biology into business thinking, the nexus of evolutionary psychology and business remains largely unexplored territory.

BRIEF HISTORY OF THE BUSINESS SCHOOL

Business schools have existed for slightly more than one century. The earliest undergraduate, master's, and doctoral American business degree programs were founded between 1881 and 1920. In its early days, the business school focused on finding better ways to optimize the manufacturing process. This was in part due to the fact that business practice was driven by an ethos of production, as poignantly captured by Henry Ford's infamous edict: "Any customer can have a car painted any color that he wants so long as it is black." In other words, consumers' wants were largely unimportant. Viewed from this perspective, the key challenge facing a firm was to optimize its production runs along several possible metrics (e.g., minimize the waste of raw materials and/or maximize employee output). In the same way that customers' needs were not central to a firm's core mission statement, employees' needs were met only minimally (e.g., the requisite bathroom breaks). Employees' personal growth and self-actualization were not at the forefront of business managers' concerns at the turn of the twentieth century.

The next major philosophical shift in business practice took place when the customer was moved to the center of a business's core mission. Therefore, it was now important to consider consumers' needs and wants, and fields such as marketing gained prominence not only in the practice of business but also in the business school curricula, as well as in academic research in the business sciences. These new realities effectively meant that the behavioral sciences had now gained greater prominence within the business sciences. In the 1950s, marketers imported many psychoanalytic ideas in their attempts to uncover consumers' latent motives. Subsequently, social and cognitive psychology, as well as cultural anthropology and sociology, made inroads in the study of marketing.

The third important shift in the social contract between firms and their various constituents purported that businesses had to produce quality products in line with consumers' preferences; they also had to provide work environments that allowed their employees to have fulfilling professional lives (think of Google's nurturing organizational culture); and they had to pursue these objectives while ensuring that no third parties were injured (e.g., harming the environment in the pursuit of the first two objectives would violate this new business ethos). These new developments led to an increase in the teaching of the so-called soft sciences in addition to maintaining a focus on traditional areas such as microeconomics and business statistics.

Irrespective of the era-specific business practices, biology and evolutionary theory have been almost completely ignored in understanding business phenomena. Generations of students, managers, and future academics have been educated in a wide range of business disciplines while fully disregarding the biological underpinnings that drive the behaviors of consumers, employees, and employers alike. Ultimately, our biology permeates every aspect of our daily reality, including our actions in the marketplace, and it is high time for the biological sciences to take their rightful place at the business round table. Of note, a small but growing number of scholars have begun exploring ways by which the neurosciences might inform the business sciences.

NEUROBUSINESS

With the advent of several brain-imaging technologies (e.g., functional Magnetic Resonance Imaging, or fMRI), scientists are now using these tools across a wide range of business disciplines, perhaps none more so than in the field of neuroeconomics. This cottage industry has recently spawned an endless variety of neuro-[fill in the blank] disciplines including neuroaccounting, neuroentrepreneurship, neuroethology, neurotheology, neuro-information systems, neuroarchitecture, and neurolaw. There is little that differentiates each of the latter fields other than the types of stimuli that are used. If brain imaging is conducted while the participant is evaluating a political speech, making a moral decision, viewing a product advertisement, watching a movie, or judging a prospective employee to hire, then the field will be referred to as neuropolitics, neuroethics, neuromarketing, neurocinematics, or organizational cognitive neuroscience, respectively. Generally speaking, the paradigm involves having participants complete a given task while their brains are imaged in vivo. The idea is to demonstrate differential neuronal activation in various parts of the brain as a function of the cognitive task that is being performed. This then allows the researcher to make inferences about the regions of the brain that are supposedly involved in specific forms of computational processing. In neuroeconomics, the tasks typically involve the processing of risky financial decisions with their associated gains and losses. If the prefrontal cortex displays intense activity when an individual faces a risky financial choice, this would imply that these decisions involve substantial cognitive effort (as opposed to affective-based processing, which elicits neural activity linked to emotions and feelings). If the amygdala is differentially activated when viewing a fear-inducing ad (as opposed to, say, an ad containing a lot of technical information), this provides further evidence that this region of the brain is involved in the processing of emotional content.

In a recent review of the applicability of neuroimaging across several applied settings, Dan Ariely and Gregory S. Berns were guardedly optimistic about the potential usefulness of this paradigm.[3] They argued that neuronal-level data could potentially be used for predictive purposes. By correlating paper-and-pencil measures of consumer preferences with corresponding neuronal data, marketers might be able to better predict consumer wants, needs, and future purchases. This is based on the premise that brain-imaging data contain information that is otherwise unobtainable via standard marketing metrics. The reality though, as Ariely and Berns correctly point out, is that the existing research does not support this viewpoint. If anything, the additional predictive power of neuronal data is minimal at best. In a paper coauthored with Justin Garcia, I argued that the neuroimaging paradigm will largely remain a fishing expedition for pretty brain images as long as no organizing theoretical framework exists to guide the research and provide coherence to the otherwise disjointed findings.[4] Unlike the great majority of research that seeks to empirically test a priori hypotheses, much of the fMRI research typically provides fanciful posthoc explanations for the particular neuronal activation patterns that were captured. The allure of the paradigm lies in the complexity of the tool in question, along with the rigor of the associated analyses. This can at times lead to a phenomenon called the *illusion of explanatory depth*,[5] whereby in this case researchers overestimate the extent to which they comprehend the inner workings of the brain, in part due to the apparent sophistication of the brain-imaging technologies.

While brain imaging might eventually prove to be a powerful tool for better understanding our consuming instinct, currently there are too many unknowns when it comes to our accumulated knowledge of the human brain to allow us to make maximal use of neuronal data. I also worry about the very real concern of scientific reductionism, seeking in this case to study higher-order consumer phenomena via an exploration of neuronal firings. Although all human phenomena are ultimately rooted in specific neural activation patterns, this does not necessarily imply that one can bridge the immense gap between higher-order cognitions and lower-order neural processes in a manner that provides us with greater explanatory power. In 2010, the FIFA soccer World Cup took place in South Africa. Prognosticating the eventual winner—Spain—might have involved an endless number of possible variables.

However, let's assume that we had access to all the neuronal firings of all players during all the matches; these data would have added little if any additional explanatory or predictive information as to who the eventual winning country might be. Accordingly, individuals who are appalled by what could become apparent sinister applications of these technologies if placed in the "evil" hands of marketers need not worry. Lest you think that I am being melodramatic, a 2004 neuromarketing conference scheduled at Emory University was canceled after strong concerns were levied about the supposed ethical dangers if companies were to learn about consumers' "buy buttons." No such buttons exist, as the consumer's brain is infinitely more complex than that. Consequently, I fully agree with Ariely and Berns in their characterization of the brain-imaging paradigm as a mélange of hope and hype.

DARWINIAN RATIONALITY VERSUS ECONOMIC RATIONALITY

Earlier we explored the Darwinian rationales for various "irrational" consummatory behaviors. That said, behavioral scientists and economists have been engaged in a protracted debate regarding the inherent meaning and definition of human rationality. What does it mean to be a rational decision maker? Behavioral decision theorists have established unequivocally that humans do not adhere to the strict definition of rationality that is expected of *Homo economicus*.[6] This has been achieved via a never-ending array of clever experimental demonstrations of violations of rational choice.[7] For example, the transitivity axiom posits that if a consumer prefers car A to car B, and car B to car C, this automatically implies that car A is preferred to car C. However, Amos Tversky— who passed away in 1996 and regrettably did not share in the Nobel Prize that was awarded to his long-term colleague Daniel Kahneman in 2002 for their collaborative works—showed that humans display intransitive preferences (i.e., a violation of rational choice).[8] The reality is that one simply needs to watch *The Price Is Right* or *Deal or No Deal* to see individuals repeatedly violating chief tenets of economic rationality.[9]

The behavioral decision theory field has been so singularly focused on identifying such violations that many started to sarcastically refer to this research stream as the "violation-of-the-month club." The one-sentence conclusion of more than four decades of research is that humans do not adhere to the tenets of *Homo economicus*. Without wishing to sound too dismissive, this is similar in spirit to physiologists, anatomists, and psychologists spending forty years conducting research to finally conclude that humans have bodies and minds that are different from those of the unicorn. Rather than spending so much time and effort demonstrating that which we are not (*Homo economicus*), behavioral decision theorists should have spent greater effort trying to uncover *why* we are the way that we are (i.e., the evolutionary foundations of our decision-making processes). This reminds me of two excellent posts that Satoshi Kanazawa, a fellow evolutionary psychologist and *Psychology Today* blogger, published on his blog on October 11, 2009, and October 18, 2009, titled "Predictably Irrational, Yes; Explainably Irrational, No" (Parts I and II). The opening paragraph of his October 11 post reads as follows:

> My fellow *PT* blogger Dan Ariely is one of the most creative behavioral economists in the world today, one of the hotshots in currently the hottest academic field. Ariely is to behavioral economics what Steven Levitt (coauthor of *Freakonomics*) is to standard economics, simultaneously a superb and mind-bogglingly creative scientist and excellent communicator of their science to the general audience. As great as Dan Ariely is, however, he has one major flaw: He is not an evolutionary psychologist.[10]

I agree with Kanazawa's assessment of Ariely's brilliance, but more importantly Kanazawa hits the nail on the head regarding the lack of evolutionary insights in the work of behavioral decision theorists. For example, in his bestselling book *Predictably Irrational: The Hidden Forces That Shape Our Decisions*, Ariely does not mention the words *Darwin* or *evolution* once. The "hidden forces" that Ariely alludes to in his subtitle should be referring to the evolutionary forces that have shaped the human mind; however, they do not.

Recall that in chapter 5 I discussed the Ultimatum and Dictator Games in which an individual (player A) is given a sum of money (say $10) and is asked to split it with another (player B). Both of these games have had important roles in demonstrating that the axioms of rational choice inherent to *Homo economicus* are often blatantly incorrect. Specifically, the "rational" split for the Ultimatum Game should be the smallest possible denomination of the available sum of money to be split. For example, if $10 is to be split and it is available as forty quarters, then the "rational" split should be to offer player B nothing more than $0.25. This is based on the tenet that the utility of receiving something is greater than that of receiving nothing (from player B's perspective). Of course, there is a disutility in receiving an unfair offer, and accordingly individuals do not adhere to the axiom of income maximization and instead tend to offer roughly even and hence equitable splits. In the case of the Dictator Game, the "rational" behavior from player A's perspective would be to offer nothing (since player B has no veto power). However, given humans' innate desire to establish reciprocal arrangements and in light of the reputational concerns that are inherent in appearing greedy (even when the game is played anonymously), individuals do end up offering amounts greater than zero.

Tripat Gill and I conducted two studies wherein we applied an evolutionary lens to understand behaviors in these two games.[11] We argued that the sex of the two players would determine how much money player A offers to player B. There are four possible dyads: male-male, male-female, female-male, and female-female. We hypothesized that men would offer larger splits to women than they would to men. Specifically, when facing women, men seek to signal their resource-based generosity, whereas when interacting with other men, their intrasexual rivalry is particularly operative (given that the metric to be split is money). In addition, we argued that women should not display any differential behaviors as a function of whom they are playing against. In both games, the findings supported our hypothesis; that is, men offered more money to women than to other men. Women were equally generous regardless of the sex of player B. Of course, this does not imply that women are any less competitive with their same-sex rivals. However, their competitive juices are less driven by resource-based metrics. The important takeaway here is that our two studies moved beyond a mere demonstration that humans do not conform to axioms of rational choice. In identifying relevant evolutionary-based processes that drive social interactions, we provided a more complete understanding of behaviors in such economic contexts.

The framing effect constitutes another example of a violation of rational choice. If an advertisement were to state that three out of five dentists recommend a brand of toothpaste, this is logically equivalent to stating that two out of five do not. Similarly, describing a hamburger's content as 90 percent fat-free is identical to stating that it contains 10 percent fat. If one were to solicit consumers' attitudes toward the toothpaste or hamburger in question, they should arrive at the same evaluations irrespective of which frame is used to describe the product in question. However, as was originally shown by psychologists Daniel Kahneman and Amos Tversky and since replicated in innumerable settings, individuals succumb to the framing effect. In so doing, they violate the axiom of descriptive invariance; namely, that alternate but equivalent ways of describing data should always yield the same judgments and/or choices. Gill and I have been investigating the framing effect using an evolutionary lens. In one of our projects, we sought to determine whether the frame used to describe a prospective suitor might have an effect on how he is evaluated. For instance, how would an individual respond if she found out that 8 out of 10 friends thought that the suitor was intelligent (versus 2 out of 10 who did not)? Remember, the two statements are identical in their informational content, yet the framing effect posits that one's evaluation would be dramatically different across the two frames (higher in the positive frame). We argued that in the specific context of choosing mates, a suboptimal choice looms larger for women in light of the differential parental investment inherent to the two sexes. Hence, negatively framed information would serve as a more vivid warning flag to women, and in this sense we hypothesized that women would be more likely than men to succumb to the framing effect. This is exactly what we found.

In a subsequent study, we manipulated the quality of the prospective mates to determine how this would affect the likelihood of men and women succumbing to the framing effect. In the previous (8/10 versus 2/10) scenario, the overall quality of the prospective suitor was high, as most people viewed him as intelligent. One could just as easily test for the framing effect while changing the quality of the mates in question. For example, stating that 2 out of 10 people thought that the suitor was intelligent (versus the equivalent statement that 8 out of 10 did not think him as intelligent) also tests for the framing effect, albeit in this case, the overall quality of the described suitor is low since the majority of people view him as unintelligent. Having to choose between low-quality suitors serves as the key warning flag in this case, especially for women. That's why the manner in which information is framed when dealing with losers in the mating market has less of an impact. Accordingly, we predicted that the framing effect would be weaker when facing low-quality mates (as compared with high-quality mates), and this lessened propensity to succumb to the framing effect would be greater for women. Again, this is exactly what we found. This project would not have been possible had we not tackled it using an evolutionary lens. The bottom line is that when testing for the framing effect using the "90 percent fat-free versus 10 percent fat" hamburger, both sexes should be equally likely to succumb to the framing effect (as ancestrally speaking, both sexes have faced similar food-related challenges). However, when it comes to mating, the framing effect should yield sex differences in line with the distinct challenges that each sex has historically had to face within this particular domain.

Think back to your most recent major consumer purchase, say, your current car. You probably did not visit all relevant car dealerships or acquire all available car information prior to committing to a final choice. Rather, at some point, you decided that you had seen sufficient information to buy the Mazda SUV. Classical economists have historically argued that to ensure that an optimal choice is made, consumers should process all relevant and available information. Of course, since no one adheres to such an outlandish standard, subsequent generations of economists proposed that the search for new information should continue as long as the marginal benefits of additional searching (e.g., finding the same product at a lower price) are greater than the corresponding marginal costs (e.g., time wasted conducting the search). Such a stylized model is elegant in theory but tells us little to nothing about how consumers actually decide when to stop acquiring additional information.[12] Along with two of my former graduate students, I recently published a paper wherein we investigated how much information men and women acquire on prospective mates prior to making a final choice.[13] Given that the costs of making a suboptimal mate choice loom larger for women, we theorized that their information search strategies would reflect such a biological reality. As expected, women were more likely to reject prospective suitors (especially so for short-term mating opportunities) and sampled information on a greater number of suitors prior to making a choice. These findings and many others reported in the paper would have been impossible to predict had we not tackled the problem by using an evolutionary lens. In other words, contrary to the cost-benefit framework used by economists to explain information search across countless domains, individuals' search patterns are at times driven by biological realities specific to a particular domain (e.g., mate search).

Herbert Simon, the 1978 Nobel Laureate in Economics, famously introduced the notion of bounded rationality as a counterpoint to the classic normative rationality of *Homo economicus*. Simon proposed that humans do not have the computational ability to engage in the extensive calculations and information acquisition that is required of "rational" decision makers as postulated by economic rationality. Simon argued that because of time constraints (e.g., we cannot evaluate every possible car model prior to making a purchase) and cognitive limitations (e.g., it is difficult for most consumers to apply the mathematical models implicit to utility maximization), human rationality is bounded. In this sense, Simon relaxed the stringent (and irrational) definition of rationality as espoused by classical economists. More recently, several scientists have proposed definitions of rationality that are rooted in an understanding of the evolutionary forces that have forged the human mind. For example, ecological rationality recognizes that humans have evolved quickly deployable decision rules (or heuristics) that otherwise provide highly accurate outcomes (in most instances) while requiring a manageable level of mental effort.[14]

The recognition heuristic is an example of such a decisional process. It posits that when deciding between which of two options scores higher on a given measure (e.g., does Philadelphia or Hamburg have a greater number of museums?), choose the one that is recognizable. It is a cognitive adaptation that originally evolved to solve several problems of evolutionary import such as recognizing one's friends and foes, edible food sources, or dangerous predators. That said, its application in contemporary settings could be met with resounding success. For example, individuals who chose stocks simply on the basis of whether they recognized company names performed as well as those who utilized extremely complicated mathematical models.[15] In this sense, this strategy is ecologically rational in ways that are far removed from *Homo economicus* (which assumes that a more thorough and complete analysis of the available data should yield superior decisions).

Related to the notion of ecological rationality is deep rationality, as espoused by Doug Kenrick and his colleagues. Contrary to the classical economic tenet, humans do not seek to maximize utility in some vague sense. Particularly, to state that individuals choose cars, jobs, mates, or toothpastes that maximize their utility (a measure of relative fulfillment) is to say very little. Instead, deep rationality proposes that individuals apply decision rules that would have maximized their fitness (capacity to propagate one's genes) when tackling adaptive challenges in specific domains (e.g., mate search, kin protection, predator avoidance, maintenance of status).[16] In this sense, the metric of rationality should be defined according to an understanding of our ancestors' "deep evolutionary time" (i.e., our evolutionary history). Put concretely, it is evolutionarily rational to be attracted to people who possess facial symmetry because this visual signal confers information of evolutionary import. On the other hand, to propose that facial symmetry is preferred "because it maximizes one's utility" basically explains nothing.

Note that economists have spent well over one hundred years studying (and teaching) decision making and consumer behavior while seldom exploring how seemingly obvious factors such as lust, hunger, anger, and other visceral forces might affect our choices. *Homo economicus* and *Homo consumericus* are clearly two different species! Let's now turn to behavioral finance, an area that was historically dominated by classical economic thinking until the more recent infusion of psychological principles in the study of financial trading. Of late, a growing number of scholars have recognized that actions in the financial marketplace are driven by our biology. Financial traders do not exist in a universe where human physiology somehow ceases to matter. If we are to avoid future financial debacles, it might be worthwhile to have a complete understanding of the full set of forces—biological and others— that drive behaviors in the financial marketplace.

HORMONES FUEL THE FINANCIAL MARKETS

The Wall Street financial crisis of the late 2000s is a reminder of the human propensity to succumb to the "deadly" sin of greed. In this particular context, greed manifests itself by a lustful appetite for risk taking (with other people's money, nonetheless). Ultimately, Wall Street is a testosterone arena. Not unlike male elephants in musk or male elks during the rut season, financial traders and bankers, most of whom are men, utilize their endocrinological systems to oil the financial market. The classic 1987 movie *Wall Street* starring Michael Douglas and Charlie Sheen and the lesser known *Boiler Room*—released in 2000, with an ensemble cast that included Giovanni Ribisi, Vin Diesel, Nia Long, and Ben Affleck—provide good depictions of the testosterone-induced bravado that takes place in financial trading.

To reiterate, whereas it seems self-evident that hormones should have a profound effect on economic decision making, most economists have until very recently largely ignored how our biology affects our preferences and choices. Instead, they have construed humans as cold, calculating machines that follow invariant algorithms such as utility maximization (e.g., choose the product that provides the greatest fulfillment relative to all others in light of budgetary constraints); the effects of situational variables such as hunger, mood, or hormones are seldom investigated. Anyone who has attended meetings, either prior to or after lunch, knows better! John Coates and Joe Herbert, two Cambridge University scientists, recently investigated the relationship between men's financial trading and their testosterone and cortisol levels.[17] Not surprisingly, higher performance (profits) was linked to higher levels of testosterone. In contrast, cortisol levels fluctuated as a function of financial uncertainty (as captured by market volatility). Hence, in this case, cortisol, which is also known as the stress hormone, was triggered more so when facing uncertain environments than by a trader's actual trading performance. Incredibly, male traders' digit ratios (relative length of index to ring finger; recall that this is a proxy measure of an individual's exposure to androgens in utero) are predictive of how many years they spend in this occupation, as well as their long-term trading success. Specifically, the more masculinized their digit ratios, the longer they last in the business and the better they perform.[18] Furthermore, masculinized digit ratios are predictive of the likelihood of choosing a career in finance,[19] as well as for one's appetite for various forms of risk taking.[20]

Testosterone is both an antecedent and an outcome of particular behaviors. In the current context, not only are men who have higher basal levels of testosterone more likely to become traders (antecedent), but also their endocrinological responses to successful trades (outcome) affect their subsequent behaviors (e.g., greater risk taking), thus yielding a feedback loop of ever-growing hormonally driven trading bravado. That said, financial trading is not the only area where hormones play a key role. A recent study found that male MBA students who had entrepreneurial experience possessed higher basal levels of testosterone than their counterparts without any such experience.[21] Testosterone can serve as a driving engine for innovation while also providing the endocrinological impetus for financial debacles.

The succession of business scandals over the past twenty years include those involving Michael Milken, Ivan Boesky, Martha Stewart, and Joe Nacchio (Qwest Communications International) for insider trading; rogue financial traders Nick Leeson (Barings Bank) and Jérôme Kerviel (Société Générale); and senior executives Kenneth Lay and Jeffrey Skilling (Enron), John Rigas and his son Timothy Rigas (Adelphia), Dennis Kozlowski (Tyco International), Bernard Ebbers (WorldCom), and Gregory Reyes (Brocade Communications Systems). More recently was the AIG debacle, which was outshined only by the unadulterated malevolence of Bernard Madoff and his multibillion-dollar Ponzi scheme. Notwithstanding the presence of Martha Stewart, a clear demographic reality is apparent: men nearly always commit such financial-based ethical breaches. To the extent that such moral and legal violations are a form of risk taking, and in light of the links between testosterone and risk taking, it is unsurprising that men commit the most egregious forms of financial frauds.[22] The growing number of ethical lapses by a wide range of businesspeople has led to the call for a greater infusion of teaching ethics within the business school curricula. This is rooted in the optimistic view that by filling students' minds with ethical precepts in graduate schools, the likelihood of committing fraud in future careers will hopefully be reduced. Innate psychopathic tendencies (as exhibited by Madoff) coupled with the androgenic highs associated with testosterone—especially when siphoning billions of dollars to one's private bank account—make for an ugly mix.

In addition to serving as an endocrinological lubricant for greater risk taking, testosterone is also linked to a more pronounced penchant for impulsivity. What causes some people to be more impulsive than others? Are there situational factors that might alter individuals' proclivity to be impetuous? Many consumer decisions involve trade-offs between immediate versus future rewards and costs (e.g., spending now or saving for a rainy day). For that reason, a full understanding of the biological and psychological forces that shape consumers' differential levels of impulsivity is of primary importance, be it to individual consumers or to the whole economy.

I WANT IT NOW!

Think back to your high school days. I am sure that when you see (or saw) formerly popular and cool kids at your twentieth high school reunion, many of them appeared to have peaked in high school. In the highly popular sitcom *Married . . . with Children*, which originally aired between 1987 and 1997, Al Bundy personifies the man whose zenith occurred in high school when he was a football star. The path taken by many of these "early peakers" is quite familiar and is rooted in the tension between immediate versus postponed gratification. The "early peaker" might quit school because he wants to generate the necessary money to customize his muscle car (e.g., Ford Torino) with expensive wheel rims and tainted windows. Rather than delaying his gratification by staying in school (and remaining for several more years without any substantial income), his need for immediate gratification drives his career path in ways that are likely suboptimal over the long run. This tug-of-war between immediate versus future rewards has been studied by decision theorists; it is typically referred to as the discounting rate.

Suppose that you were asked to choose between receiving $100 today or $120 in one week. The trade-off is between obtaining an immediate but smaller amount of money now or a larger sum at some future date. By having you make several of these types of intertemporal choices, one can calculate your individual discount rate, which captures your impulsivity or impatience. Many important decisions that individuals make require trade-offs between immediate versus delayed costs and benefits, including how much one saves for retirement, whether to start a diet, or whether to enroll in graduate school or enter the job market. Generally speaking, men have higher discount rates than women, meaning that they have a greater penchant for immediate benefits.[23] This universally pervasive sex difference is driven by sexual selection. Specifically, given that men's reproductive fitness is more variable than that of women—because of men's lesser obligatory parental investment and in light of their shorter lives—men have evolved greater impatience.[24] Hence, one motive that propels men's greater proclivity to engage in extreme forms of financial risk taking is rooted in their greater penchant (as compared with women) to value immediate rewards more so than larger future ones (or to worry less about the future consequences of their immediate actions).

Although an individual's discounting rate is in part shaped by his personality (some people are inherently more present-oriented than others), situational variables come into play as well. For example, men's discounting rates increase subsequent to being shown photos of beautiful women or women in bikinis.[25] In other words, when a man is exposed to a mating-related stimulus, present rewards increase in value. As mentioned in the previous chapter, casino operators have long been aware of this phenomenon, as it is common practice to hire extremely attractive, often scantily clad waitresses to serve the largely male clientele. Not surprisingly from an evolutionary perspective, visual primes of attractive men do not have the same effect on women's discounting rates. Discounting rates are also affected by contextual cues linked to our survival. Exposure to greater amounts of sugar decreases the amount of future discounting (i.e., future rewards were valued to a greater extent). Less sugar consumed (i.e., lower glucose levels) led to greater discounting (I want it now!).[26] Again, from an evolutionary perspective, this makes perfect sense. Our fluctuating blood sugar levels serve as a signal of situational hunger or of satiety. When hungry (lower blood sugar levels), we seek immediate approach behaviors (eat now), whereas when satiated (higher blood sugar levels), we are willing to display greater temperance. If you are a casino operator, keep your players hungry! Perhaps this is why conspicuous clocks are seldom seen in casinos; knowing the time might alert gamblers that it is time to eat.

MORPHOLOGICAL TRAITS IN THE MARKETPLACE

In chapter 7, I briefly discussed the universal efficacy of using attractive endorsers in advertising. However, the power of one's looks and related morphological features (e.g., height, square jaw, bust size) is evident across other business settings as well. We have evolved the ability to read such cues, as they carry reliable and valuable information of evolutionary import. Take the proverbial job interview. We'd like to believe that interviewers are unbiased in their evaluations. Labor laws exist precisely to curb the likelihood that employers might discriminate against several variables including one's religion, race, age, or sexual orientation. But several bias-inducing variables (outside legal reach) have been shown to have a profound effect on both the likelihood of landing a job and of subsequently being promoted. Men are more likely to hire attractive women than women are to hire attractive men. Moreover, given the greater import of physical attractiveness to women's self-concepts, women are much less likely to hire other attractive women than men are to hire other attractive men (i.e., intrasexual rivalry based on looks is of greater concern to women). Finally, these biases are operative only when there is likely to be repeat interactions between the individual doing the hiring and the job applicant.[27]

Generally speaking, the processes by which personnel decisions are made are hardly consistent with axioms of rational choice as postulated by classical economists. For example, the primacy effect is highly operative in hiring decisions. The interviewer forms a very rapid opinion within the first thirty seconds of meeting a candidate, with the rest of the interview often being used to support the initial judgment. Incoming information that is incongruent with the rapidly formed first impression is discounted or ignored. Suppose that a man were to appear for an interview at a stuffy investment bank wearing a diamond-studded earring. The interviewer might very rapidly decide that this guy is a "rebel" who does not fit the firm's image. All subsequent information might suggest that this is the absolute top candidate; nonetheless, the interviewer has steadfastly anchored her position in the reject camp. This reminds me of the brilliant quip by the Harvard economist John Kenneth Galbraith, who reportedly stated, "Faced with the choice between changing one's mind and proving that there is no need to do so, almost everyone gets busy on the proof."[28]

Returning to how physical attributes might impact one's career, numerous studies have uncovered a "beauty effect" in the labor market.[29] Good-looking MBA graduates earn higher starting salaries and command larger future salaries,[30] as do good-looking lawyers.[31] Better-looking NFL quarterbacks earn higher salaries to the tune of an 8 percent higher salary for each standard deviation increase on facial symmetry.[32] Attractive professors receive higher teaching evaluations.[33] It truly pays to be beautiful. In the *Seinfeld* episode "The Pilot (1)" (season 4, episode 23), Elaine is angered by the fact that all the newly hired waitresses at the group's favorite restaurant seem to possess one common feature: large breasts. Of note, Michael Lynn, one of the preeminent experts on tipping behavior, found that a waitress's breast size was positively correlated to the size of her tips.[34] Finally, one's height, especially that of men, is positively correlated to career success.[35] For example, in US presidential elections, the taller candidate nearly always wins.[36]

If the eyes are the windows to the soul, then one's face is laden with endless "earthly" informational content. By simply looking at political candidates' faces, children are able to identify election winners.[37] Nicholas O. Rule and Nalini Ambady found that the facial features of male as well as female CEOs of Fortune 1000 companies were highly correlated to company profits. Specifically, independent raters provided evaluations of the CEOs' faces along several attributes (e.g., competence, dominance, facial maturity, likeability, trustworthiness, and global leadership ability). In the case of male CEOs, an aggregate power index made up of competence, dominance, and facial symmetry was correlated to profits, as was global leadership to profits.[38] For female CEOs, competence and leadership (as gauged from their faces) were each correlated to company profits.[39] Ulrich Mueller and Allan Mazur investigated the facial features of West Point cadets as displayed in their graduating photos. The idea was to explore whether cues of facial dominance—as exhibited via a square jaw or a more accentuated supraorbital ridge (also known as a heavy brow ridge)—predict a man's promotion later in his military career. The mechanism by which faces are either masculinized or feminized is shaped by exposure to sex-typing hormones such as estrogen and testosterone. Hence, cadets possessing facially dominant features are effectively signaling their greater pubertal exposure to testosterone. Mueller and Mazur indeed found that senior-level promotions were well predicted by the extent to which the cadets' faces were judged as dominant or submissive.[40] The bottom line is that we all want our military leaders to adhere to our collectively agreed-upon archetype of the dominant warrior.

Recall that the digit ratio is a morphological trait that captures the extent to which an individual has been exposed to androgens in utero. It turns out that this ratio is linked to male athletic ability. Professional soccer players who possess more masculinized digit ratios tend to be better players.[41] Testosterone-linked facial features have also been found to be predictive of male hockey players' aggressive behaviors on the ice;[42] the folk belief that tough hockey fighters have a goon's face has now been supported by scientific research. In a perhaps more ominous connection between morphology and aggressive behaviors, violent male criminals are more likely to possess a mesomorphic body type (as opposed to ecto-morphic or endomorphic), which is defined by greater musculature and as such is likely indicative of greater levels of testosterone.[43]

Some scholars have expressed incredulity if not disdain at research that seeks to link morphological traits to particular behaviors. In the minds of such detractors, the digit ratio is nothing but a newly packaged version of palmistry (reading the lines on individuals' palms to foretell their life paths) or perhaps of phrenology (gauging individuals' person-alities by studying their cranial shapes). Both of these practices are con-sidered quackery, so the implicit assumption is that the digit ratio must follow suit. This is a grossly misinformed position, as there have now been hundreds of studies on the digit ratio in highly reputable peer-reviewed journals across a very broad range of disciplines including but not limited to biology, psychology, anthropology, physiology, evolu-tionary theory, forensic science, and medicine. Over the past decade or so, there has been a proliferation of studies linking the digit ratio to phe-nomena as varied as sexual and gender orientation, transsexualism, semen quality, menarche (onset of the menses), offspring sex ratio (i.e., the number of sons versus daughters that one has), facial symmetry, cooperation, jealousy, dominance, aggression, reproductive success, various abilities (e.g., spatial, dancing, and musical), susceptibility to particular diseases (e.g., heart disease), occupational interests, academic performance, and psychological disorders (e.g., autism). Are the detractors of the digit ratio suggesting that all the latter works are quackery?

Some proponents of the victimology ethos propose that any advantage accrued because of one's physical features is a pernicious manifestation of discrimination (e.g., lookism and heightism). The reality is that it is naive to think that cues of evolutionary import (e.g., physical attractiveness, height, female nubile markers) should suddenly become irrelevant in contemporary environments. Our minds are vestiges of a long evolutionary process. Even though in today's world, we'd like to believe that career outcomes are solely judged on "appropriate and unbiased metrics," we carry penchants that were adaptive in our ancestral past.

Our instinctual need to focus on facial features, among other morphological cues, is such a central element of our human sociality that we create products that cater to these human expectations. In so doing, we engage in animism and anthropomorphism.

DOES THAT CAR LOOK ANGRY? DOES IT "LOOK" LIKE ME?

There is growing evidence that we are able to gauge important features about individuals (e.g., their personalities) by seeing the products they purchase,[44] the product preferences they hold (e.g., musical tastes), the manner in which they organize their home and work environments, and the ways in which they present themselves online, be it via their Facebook profiles or personal websites. In other words, many of our consumer choices are public signals of our personhood.[45] Recall that in chapter 4, I discussed several studies that found that dogs tend to resemble their owners. Might we be able to match products to their owners in a similar fashion? One might think that the bodybuilder is more likely to drive the proverbial muscle car (such as a Ford Mustang), while a young woman might favor the more delicate Mini Cooper or VW Beetle. If shown two sets of photos, one of individuals and another of their cars, do you think that you'd be able to match the cars to their rightful owners? German psychologists conducted such a study and found that people were able to do so at an accuracy rate above chance level.[46] Some of the visual metrics used to match cars with their owners might involve basic demographics (e.g., one's sex and age), such that an elderly man is indeed more likely to drive a Cadillac Sedan than a young woman is. However, there is evidence that the matching of products to their owners might implicate less obvious cues.

Sonja Windhager and her colleagues explored whether consumers attribute facial features to cars, and if so whether these attributions are consistent across individuals. If ten individuals were to look at a given car front, would they largely agree that it is associated with a particular type of human or animal face? Would they agree whether the car front looks angry, dominant, or feminine? Not only did many consumers identify eyes, mouths, noses, and ears on car fronts but also there was great agreement on the identified traits associated with car fronts (e.g., child-adult, submissive-dominant, arrogant, friendly-hostile, angry, male-female, afraid, happy, surprised).[47] Generally speaking, humans have an innate penchant to engage in both animism (ascribing agency to inanimate objects) and anthropomorphism (attributing human qualities to nonhuman animals and inanimate objects). These innate capacities permit us to enjoy television cartoons (in which animals are ascribed human qualities, including the capacity for language), animated movies such as *Toy Story* and *Cars*, and films like *Christine*—the 1983 cult classic by famed horror movie director John Carpenter—in which a car owned by a teenager possesses demonic powers. The movie's teaser is quite telling of our ability to suspend reality through animism: "How do you kill something that can't possibly be alive?"

Why would individuals have such a proclivity to see animate faces on inanimate products? As explained by Windhager and her colleagues, the evolutionary argument is rooted in error management theory, which posits in this case that the costs of attributing animate agency to an inanimate object are lesser than not attributing such agency to animate entities (some of which might be very dangerous predators). Accordingly, we have evolved this hyperactive mechanism for ascribing human agency to innumerable stimuli.[48] As noted earlier, toy marketers are particularly adept at developing products that cater to universal human needs (as manifested by children). Ultimately, many toys are successful precisely because they cater to children's inborn ability to anthropomorphize, as well as the ease with which they ascribe human agency to inanimate objects. Toy manufacturers might be highly innovative and astute in terms of their product designs, but they pale in comparison to the greatest of all product developers whose identity I reveal in the next section.

NEW PRODUCT DEVELOPMENT, BIOMIMICRY, AND ECOLOGICAL FOOTPRINTS

Irrespective of the metric used (e.g., total shareholder returns or profits), innovative companies typically perform better than their "static" counterparts.[49] Whereas not all successful firms rely on innovation to drive their profits (e.g., Coca-Cola's commercial triumph is largely due to marketing savvy and customer brand loyalty), generally speaking, successful companies are in part defined by their ability to innovate, a component of which is to develop new products that cater to consumers' needs. Several magazines such as *Fast Company* and *BusinessWeek* produce annual rankings of the most innovative companies, which have recently included revolutionary firms such as Amazon, Facebook, Apple, Google, Disney, and GE. Not surprisingly, many companies on these lists are in the computing sector, as the research envelope moves very quickly in such an industry. After all, it is unclear how many innovations a milk or egg company can be expected to produce.

Switching from companies to individuals, who are some of the greatest inventors of all time? Most people would likely agree that when it comes to practical inventions, the following individuals should certainly be listed: Johannes Gutenberg (printing press), Thomas Edison (lightbulb), the Wright Brothers (first flight), Henry Ford (car assembly line), Benjamin Franklin (bifocal glasses), Charles Babbage (mechanical computer), and Alexander Bell (telephone). I am sure that the readers could come up with other individuals and companies that epitomize innovative thinking. However, I would venture that the greatest innovator of all time is one that few readers will likely think of. I'll give you a hint via a classic Latin saying: *Mater artium necessitas* (Necessity is the mother of invention).

It is estimated that scientists have identified roughly 2 million currently existing species, although the actual number could be between 5 million to 100 million species (as estimated by the National Science Foundation's "Tree of Life" project). Of course, the great majority of species that ever existed are now extinct (up to 97 percent of them). If we assume that the actual figure for the number of existing species is 30 million, this would imply that roughly 1 billion species have ever existed. Each of these species has had to "come up" with an innovative set of adaptive solutions to survive and reproduce within its environment. These "innovations" are not consciously arrived at; they are due to the dual forces of natural and sexual selection.[50] So, to answer my original question, nature is the most innovative force that the world has ever seen. Human invention pales in comparison with the extraordinary solutions that nature has devised. Of course, nature has had several billion years to tinker with its optimal designs, a time period much greater than the mere 100,000 or so years that our species has existed!

In many instances, the best human-made machine cannot match the efficacy of its natural counterpart. Take a dog's nose, for example. Canine olfaction is an evolutionary marvel, so much so that we rely on it to sniff out drugs and bombs, as well as to locate lost people. This is the central premise behind the field of biomimicry; namely, the mandate to study nature's designs and solutions and subsequently mimic these in the development of human-made solutions. In her fascinating book *Biomimicry: Innovation Inspired by Nature*, Janine B. Benyus provides numerous examples of such endeavors. But first I share the definition of biomimicry as stated in the opening page of her book (italics in original):

1. *Nature as model.* Biomimicry is a new science that studies nature's models and then imitates or takes inspiration from these designs and processes to solve human problems, e.g., a solar cell inspired by a leaf.
2. *Nature as measure.* Biomimicry uses an ecological standard to judge the "rightness" of our innovations. After 3.8 billion years of evolution, nature has learned: What works. What is appropriate. What lasts.
3. *Nature as mentor.* Biomimicry is a new way of viewing and valuing nature. It introduces an era based not on what we can *extract* from the natural world, but on what we can *learn* from it.[51]

Some of the key examples provided by Benyus include the development of agricultural practices akin to a prairie's synergistic and homeostatic ecosystem;[52] harnessing energy in a manner similar to that achieved by a leaf via photosynthesis; creating durable, light, and water-resistant materials akin to a mollusk's shell or the silk produced by a spider; and maintaining good health by studying how animals use natural resources to heal themselves (or avoid illnesses), a field known as zoopharmacognosy. Other examples are the development of a flexible surgical catheter inspired by an octopus's tentacles; robots that move over uneven surfaces (e.g., for interplanetary exploration), inspired by movements of crabs; the improved understanding of animal motion, which has yielded toys that move more realistically and movie animations that are more authentic (think of Godzilla in the 1950s as compared to the realism of contemporary science-fiction creatures); and the development of superior prosthetics via a better understanding of the mechanics of actual limbs.[53]

Given humans' biophilic proclivity (as described in chapter 2), and in light of the benefits that can be reaped via biomimicry, how can one explain the uncountable ways by which our species has harmed the environment?[54] The sheer number of species that have either recently become extinct or are on the brink of extinction is staggering. I venture that there are several reasons for this incongruity between our love and appreciation of nature and our poor ecological footprint. First, most individuals succumb to the Tragedy of the Commons bias when it comes to their ecological behaviors (or lack thereof). Imagine that there are ten farmers who share a communal grazing area for their cows. They collectively decide that the land requires a period of recovery, and accordingly they each agree to restrict their cows from grazing the land. From the perspective of each individual farmer, it would be "optimal" if he were to cheat on the social contract while all other nine farmers were to abide by it. In this manner, he could still have his cows grazing on the land, and the ecological benefits would still largely accrue (assuming that all other nine farmers are honest and hence the land can recover). Needless to say, the Tragedy of the Commons refers to the fact that many if not all of the farmers have the same concurrent thought, and in so doing, many (if not all) end up violating the social contract.[55]

If individuals were able to stick to an agreed collusion, many issues could be quickly resolved. Take the outrageous salaries and endorsement figures that some professional athletes now command. To some, it seems obscene that Tiger Woods generated endorsements totaling $1 billion when millions of people around the world survive on roughly $1 per day. We could collectively "solve" this global inequity by refusing to consume, for a given time period, all items associated with the sport in question. No sport merchandising. No television viewing. No stadium attendance. It would not be long before the market would very rapidly "adjust" the obscene salaries and endorsement deals. However, when Sunday comes around and there is an exciting NFL game on TV, a spectator may say, "Does it really matter if I break the collusion? After all, I am sure that millions of others won't be turning on their TVs. But I need to watch the game because my team is close to making the play-offs." The tenuous nature of collusions is the engine by which social injustices are in part maintained.

A second reason for our poor ecological record stems from our evolved penchant to discount future costs for more immediate benefits (as discussed earlier in this chapter). In the same manner that female sunbathers are particularly prone to discount the future risks of melanoma for an immediate aesthetic glow,[56] most people are minimally moved by appeals of how their immediate actions might impact future generations. There are adaptive reasons why we would have evolved a need to cater to our immediate needs and desires. Regrettably, many of these adaptive processes are maladaptively usurped, yielding suboptimal ecological outcomes. Finally, a third reason for our poor green record is rooted in the fact that most people find it difficult to care about issues or people that are not within their Dunbar circle. Recall that Robin Dunbar proposed that for much of our evolutionary history, we are likely to have held close intimate relationships with no more than 150 individuals within a locally centric geographical area. Hence, the depletion of the Amazonian forest seems removed from the daily existence of billions of people. The Rwandan genocide is somewhere far from our local neighborhood. The plight of the orangutan and numerous other sentient beings is someone else's problem. In the end, people are much more willing to offer aid to a specific foster child with whom they have established a relationship (even if merely as pen pals) than to write a check for a general child welfare cause. This reality is entrenched in our instinctual penchant to invest in those within our Dunbar circle.

Our consuming instinct is a double-edge sword. Unabated consummatory desires are at the core of our heavy ecological footprint. At the same time, we have the inherent capacity to serve as respectful stewards of the natural world. Ultimately, the future of our planet rests in our ability to strike the right balance between these two opposing instinctual forces.[57]

CONCLUSION

A growing number of scholars are applying biological-based frameworks and tools (e.g., neuroimaging) and first principles from evolutionary psychology across a wide range of business settings. Among many other breakthroughs, the infusion of biology within the business sciences has (1) yielded novel definitions of human rationality rooted in an understanding of our evolutionary history; (2) established the effects of hormones on financial trading; (3) offered a better understanding of the inherent trade-offs in intertemporal choice (now versus later); (4) recognized the power of one's morphology in various business settings (e.g., the beauty effect when interviewing prospective employees); (5) identified the crucial role that nature plays in helping us design superior products (biomimicry). Most business phenomena, be it those relevant to consumers, employees, or employers, are manifestations of the indelible forces of evolution in shaping our minds and bodies.

CHAPTER 11
CONCLUDING REMARKS

I suppose the process of acceptance will pass
through the usual four stages:
1. This is worthless nonsense,
2. This is an interesting, but perverse,
   point of view,
3. This is true, but quite unimportant,
4. I always said so.
   —*J. B. S. HALDANE,*
      EVOLUTIONARY GENETICIST[1]

In chapter 1, I discussed several recurring misconceptions regarding
evolutionary theory, which have served to hinder its diffusion within
the public consciousness. Can anything be done to accelerate its acceptance? Foremost, the intellectual landscape has to change such that
nonacceptance of evolutionary theory becomes akin to the rejection of
gravity.[2] The challenge is to educate hostile academics, and more generally the lay populace, about the extraordinary amount of evidence in
support of the role that evolution has had in shaping our humanity.
Unfortunately, academics and laypeople alike often irrationally hold
onto their deeply entrenched positions. This chapter's epigraph refers to
the stages that a scientific theory goes through prior to its eventual
acceptance by otherwise skeptical scholars. As you might imagine, the

more revolutionary the theory (as is the case with evolutionary theory), the greater the resistance to it, and hence the longer it takes for the theory to waddle its way through stages 1 through 4. I find the quote personally poignant because my academic career has been in large part representative of Haldane's truism, at least in my attempts to Darwinize the marketing and consumer behavior disciplines. Many of my marketing colleagues have been quite hostile to the notion that biology in general, and evolutionary theory in particular, are important in understanding consumption. I include below paraphrased examples that I have experienced within each of the four Haldane stages.

> Stage 1 (nonsense): Are you suggesting that we are animals? Consumers are not driven by instincts. This is silly. [During my talk at one of the leading business schools in the world.]

> Stage 2 (perverse): Why waste time promulgating "sexist" sex differences in consumer behavior (as interesting as these might be) when you could study phenomena that transcend sex? [Reviewer's comments to a paper I submitted to one of the elite consumer behavior journals in which I was reporting on sex differences in mating behavior.]

> Stage 3 (unimportant): Of course, there are human universals when it comes to consumption. But of greater interest is the study of differences between consumers. It's all about the heterogeneity of behaviors. [During my talk at one of the leading business schools in the world.]

> Stage 4 (agreement): I love your work. I always thought highly of it. [Phone conversation with a leading contemporary consumer scholar.]

The power of the scientific method lies in its ability to serve as a sieve in the marketplace of ideas. Unlike religious narratives, which proclaim their truth as an a priori condition, scientific ideas are put through the wringer in an attempt to falsify them. If they remain standing despite the repeated attempts to test their veracity, they are tentatively accepted within the pantheon of accumulated knowledge. At times, a previously accepted theory is eventually rejected in light of new evidence, or staunchly resisted ideas are eventually accepted once the old paradigmatic walls crumble. Ultimately, science is an autocorrective process, inching its way ever closer to a more complete and accurate knowledge base. Of note, the field of evolutionary epistemology proposes that the creation of new knowledge, along with its eventual rejection or acceptance, is akin to the Darwinian process of mutation and selection. Hence, even when it comes to the consumption of new knowledge, one cannot stray far from Darwinian processes. This book's central premise—namely that evolutionary psychology is central to the study of consumer behavior (and the business sciences more generally)—is undergoing a form of Darwinian selection.

THE FUTURE OF SCIENCE: CONSILIENCE AND INTERDISCIPLINARITY

I have argued elsewhere[3] that the most prestigious fields share one thing in common. They all possess a great deal of consilience (unified and well-integrated knowledge). This term had fallen into disuse but was revitalized by E. O. Wilson—Harvard evolutionist and two-time Pulitzer Prize–winner—in his 1998 book *Consilience: The Unity of Knowledge*. The natural sciences possess core knowledge bases that are, at any given point, accepted by all members within a given discipline. No chemists "disbelieve" the periodic table. All biologists accept the central tenets of evolution, although they might disagree about specific evolutionary mechanisms. All physicists recognize the four universal forces: gravitational, electromagnetic, weak, and strong forces (weak and strong forces are collectively known as the nuclear forces). Having a common and agreed-upon core knowledge permits natural scientists to develop integrative theories that are consistent with one another.

On the other hand, the social sciences are defined by their lack of consilience. Some academics reject the notion that biological-based differences exist, short of one's genitalia. All sex differences are apparently socially constructed. Postmodernists disavow the premise that science provides an objective approach for the exploration of universal truths. Some purport that science is one of many ways of knowing. Cultural relativists renounce the existence of human universals. Therefore, they are scornful of the notion that humans have a common universal nature, let alone that consumers have a biological-based instinct that drives their consumption habits. Accordingly, some social scientists erect paradigmatic walls that are consistent with their worldviews, these often being shaped by ideological concerns that have little to nothing to do with science, let alone with any semblance of reality. Since these paradigms exist in their own separate little universes, this creates fragmented if not contradictory knowledge bases resulting in little universally accepted core knowledge. As poignantly remarked by Robin Dunbar,[4] "The evolutionary approach is not an alternative to the various social science disciplines, but rather a complement. And, importantly, it is a complement that offers the opportunity of integrating the disparate social sciences into a single intellectual framework."

Fragmented and insular knowledge, both within and across disciplines, is a suboptimal reality, as most important scientific projects require interdisciplinary input. Karl Popper, a giant among twentieth-century philosophers of science, famously stated: "We are not students of some subject matter, but students of problems. And problems may cut right across the borders of any subject matter or discipline."[5] Several distinguished American scientific bodies have founded dedicated programs meant to promote and encourage interdisciplinary research.[6] Examples of important interdisciplinary scientific research abound, perhaps none more famous than the human genome project, which has involved the input of biologists, chemists, computer scientists, and biostatisticians. Another case example of the power of interdisciplinary research is magnetic resonance imaging. The Elsevier journal of that name states on its website: "*MRI* is dedicated to both basic research and medical applications, providing a single forum for communication among radiologists, physicists, chemists, biochemists, biologists, engineers, internists, pathologists, physiologists, computer scientists, and mathematicians."[7] *The Human Behavior and Evolution Society*—which is the premier scientific society for scholars interested in an evolutionary-informed analysis of human phenomena—has members stemming from well over thirty disciplines including anthropology, art, biology, child care, criminology, ecology, economics, education, family studies, feminism, forensics, genetics, history, law, literature, medicine, music, neurosciences, nutrition, ornithology, philosophy, political science, primatology, psychiatry, psychology, public health, religion, technology, and zoology. The number of disciplines that have applied evolutionary psychology or related evolutionary principles is actually substantially greater than the disciplines just listed.[8]

On the other hand, if one were to analyze the departmental affiliations of members of the *Association for Consumer Research* or of the *Society for Consumer Psychology*, the two premier scientific associations of consumer scholars, one pattern emerges. Almost all members stem from marketing departments. Since our consummatory nature pervades across so many areas of human import, why are the great majority of scholars who study consumer behavior housed mainly in marketing departments? Psychiatrists, neuroscientists, and clinical psychologists should be collaborating with consumer psychologists to study pathological gambling, eating disorders, pornographic addictions, excessive suntanning, and compulsive buying. Geneticists and marketing scholars should be working together to explore how particular gene polymorphisms might affect consumption choices. Design engineers, industrial designers, perceptual psychologists, and biomimeticists should team up with marketing scholars to study optimal product designs. The list of overlapping interdisciplinary interests should be endless for something as fundamental and pervasive as consumer behavior. The reality is that marketing scholars and practitioners alike can only benefit from acknowledging the relevance of our long evolutionary history in shaping our consumer instincts.

The evolutionary biologist David Sloan Wilson[9] recently instituted EvoS (short for Evolutionary Studies), a revolutionary interdisciplinary program at Binghamton University (State University of New York). The curriculum is now part of a larger consortium of schools, all of which are implementing the EvoS program at their respective universities. It is structured in a manner such that students from across the university can enroll in a cluster of evolutionary-based courses that permit them to appreciate the grand explanatory power of evolutionary theory. In 2005, Wilson invited me to give a lecture on my first book as part of the EvoS speaker series. It was incredibly enriching to interact with a broad range of scholars and students alike, all of whom shared a common interest in applying evolutionary theory in their respective areas of interest, an experience that I have been able to replicate at several other evolutionary centers (e.g., the University of New Mexico in 2006). My hope is that a greater number of consumer scholars in particular and business scholars more generally will eventually come to realize that human minds are the product of sexual and natural selection. In doing so, they will view evolutionary theory as a theoretical framework that can help them augment the explanatory power of their research, be it in economics, organizational behavior, advertising, or consumer behavior. Of note, three of the mandates of my Concordia University Research Chair in Evolutionary Behavioral Sciences and Darwinian Consumption, is to develop an EvoS program at my university, to expand it into an interuniversity center for evolutionary studies across the four Montreal universities, and to found a research center that promotes work at the nexus of biology and business.

Evolutionary psychologists have done a wonderful job in identifying many of the basic Darwinian mechanisms that define our human nature. The future belongs to those who can demonstrate the applicability of the evolutionary sciences in general, and evolutionary psychology in particular, across countless applied settings (e.g., in medicine, law, business, architecture, and advertising). In this book, I have sought to pinpoint the relevance of evolutionary theory in understanding our consummatory nature. The reader should walk away with a deep appreciation of the power of evolutionary theory in helping us navigate through our daily lives. Whether we crave a juicy hamburger, dream of owning a red Ferrari, enjoy a pornographic movie, or rejoice at the pleasure of offering gifts to our family members and friends, our consuming instinct is always guided by our ever-present biological heritage.

NOTES

CHAPTER 1. CONSUMERS: BORN AND MADE

1. Matt Ridley, *Nature Via Nurture: Genes, Experience, & What Makes Us Human* (New York: HarperCollins, 2003), p. 280.

2. Marcia L. Colish, transl., *The Stoic Tradition from Antiquity to the Early Middle Ages* (Leiden, Netherlands: E. J. Brill, 1985), p. 176.

3. For an evolutionary-based account of human motivation, see Larry C. Bernard et al., "An Evolutionary Theory of Human Motivation," *Genetic, Social, and General Psychology Monographs* 131, no. 2 (2005): 129–84.

4. See relevant references in Michel Laroche et al., "A Cross-Cultural Study of In-Store Information Search Strategies for a Christmas Gift," *Journal of Business Research* 49 (2000): 113.

5. See relevant references in Hyun-Hwa Lee and Jihyun Kim, "Gift Shopping Behavior in a Multichannel Retail Environment: The Role of Personal Purchase Experiences," *International Journal of Retail & Distribution Management* 37, no. 5 (2009): 420.

6. This is a rewording of the famous truism of Theodosius Dobzhansky: "Nothing in biology makes sense except in the light of evolution."

7. Jerome H. Barkow, Leda Cosmides, and John Tooby, eds., *The Adapted Mind: Evolutionary Psychology and the Generation of Culture* (New York: Oxford University Press, 1992); David M. Buss, ed., *The Handbook of Evolutionary Psychology* (New York: John Wiley, 2005); Charles Crawford and Dennis Krebs, eds., *Foundations of Evolutionary Psychology* (Mahwah, NJ: Lawrence Erlbaum, 2008).

8. Martin Daly and Margo Wilson, *Homicide* (New York: Aldine de Gruyter, 1988).

9. Kevin N. Laland and Gillian R. Brown, *Sense and Nonsense: Evolutionary Perspectives on Human Behaviour* (Oxford: Oxford University Press, 2002).

10. Peter J. Richerson and Robert Boyd, *Not By Genes Alone: How Culture Transformed Human Evolution* (Chicago: University of Chicago Press, 2005); Robert Aunger, *The Electric Meme: A New Theory of How We Think* (New York: Free Press, 2002); Susan Blackmore, *The Meme Machine* (Oxford: Oxford University Press, 1999).

11. Ernst Mayr, "Cause and Effect in Biology: Kinds of Causes, Predictability, and Teleology Are Viewed by a Practicing Biologist," *Science* 134, no. 3489 (1961): 1501–1506; Nikolaas Tinbergen, "On Aims and Methods of Ethology," *Zeitschrift für Tierpsychologie* 20 (1963): 410–33.

12. Margie Profet, "Pregnancy Sickness as Adaptation: A Deterrent to Maternal Ingestion of Teratogens," in Barkow et al., *The Adapted Mind*, pp. 327–65; Samuel M. Flaxman and Paul W. Sherman, "Morning Sickness: A Mechanism for Protecting Mother and Embryo," *Quarterly Review of Biology* 75, no. 2 (2000): 113–48; Gillian V. Pepper and S. Craig Roberts, "Rates of Nausea and Vomiting in Pregnancy and Dietary Characteristics Across Populations," *Proceedings of the Royal Society B: Biological Sciences* 273, no. 1601 (2006): 2675–79.

13. Gene Wallenstein, *The Pleasure Instinct: Why We Crave Adventure, Chocolate, Pheromones, and Music* (New York: Wiley, 2008).

14. Charlotte Perkins Gilman, *Women and Economics* (New York: Cosimo Classics, 2007 [1898]), p. 74.

15. For a broad overview of movements and issues raised against evolutionary psychology and related biological formalisms, see Daniel W. Leger, Alan C. Kamil, and Jeffrey A. French, "Fear and Loathing of Evolutionary Psychology in the Social Sciences," in *Evolutionary Psychology and Motivation*, ed. Jeffrey A. French, Alan C. Kamil, and Daniel W. Leger (Lincoln: University of Nebraska Press, 2001), pp. xi–xxiii; Ullica Segerstråle, *Defenders of the Truth: The Sociobiology Debate* (New York: Oxford University Press, 2001); Edward H. Hagen, "Controversial Issues in Evolutionary Psychology," in *The Hand-*

book of Evolutionary Psychology, ed. David M. Buss (New York: Wiley, 2005), pp. 145–73; Gad Saad, "The Collective Amnesia of Marketing Scholars Regarding Consumers' Biological and Evolutionary Roots," *Marketing Theory* 8 (2008): 425–48; George Perry and Ruth Mace, "The Lack of Acceptance of Evolutionary Approaches to Human Behaviour," *Journal of Evolutionary Psychology* 8, no. 2 (2010): 105–125.

16. Joshua M. Tybur, Geoffrey F. Miller, and Steven W. Gangestad, "Testing the Controversy: An Empirical Examination of Adaptationists' Attitudes toward Politics and Science," *Human Nature* 18 (2007): 313–28.

17. Eva Jablonka and Gal Raz, "Transgenerational Epigenetic Inheritance: Prevalence, Mechanisms, and Implications for the Study of Heredity and Evolution," *Quarterly Review of Biology*, 84, no. 2 (2009): 131–76.

18. John Tooby and Leda Cosmides, "Psychological Foundations of Culture," in Barkow et al., *The Adapted Mind*, pp. 19–136.

19. Steven Pinker, *The Blank Slate: The Modern Denial of Human Nature* (New York: Viking, 2002).

20. Donald E. Brown, *Human Universals* (New York: McGraw Hill, 1991); Ara Norenzayan and Steven J. Heine, "Psychological Universals: What Are They and How Can We Know?" *Psychological Bulletin* 131, no. 5 (2005): 763–84.

21. Gad Saad, "*Homo consumericus*: Consumption Phenomena as Universals, as Cross-Cultural Adaptations, or as Emic Cultural Instantiations" (submitted for publication, 2007).

22. Timothy Ketelaar and Bruce J. Ellis, "Are Evolutionary Explanations Unfalsifiable? Evolutionary Psychology and the Lakatosian Philosophy of Science," *Psychological Inquiry* 11 (2000): 1–21; Lucian Gideon Conway III and Mark Schaller, "On the Verifiability of Evolutionary Psychological Theories: An Analysis of the Psychology of Scientific Persuasion," *Personality and Social Psychology Review* 6, no. 2 (2002): 152–66.

23. Robert L. Trivers, "Parental Investment and Sexual Selection," in *Sexual Selection and Descent of Man: 1871–1971*, ed. B. Campbell (Chicago: Aldine, 1972), pp. 136–79.

24. Marcel Eens and Rianne Pinxten, "Sex-Role Reversal in Vertebrates: Behavioural and Endocrinological Accounts," *Behavioural Processes* 51 (2000): 135–47.

25. See Victor J. Stenger, *The New Atheism: Taking a Stand for Science and Reason* (Amherst, NY: Prometheus Books, 2009).

26. Stephen Jay Gould, *Rocks of Ages: Science and Religion in the Fullness of Life* (New York: Ballantine Books, 1999).

27. Sam Harris, *The Moral Landscape: How Science Can Determine Human Values* (New York: Free Press, 2010).

28. From his 1850 poem titled *In Memoriam A. H. H.*

29. Jean Halliday, "For $2 Million, You Get to Pick the Sheets," *Automotive News* 80, no. 6192 (2006): 22F.

30. Victor Nell, "Why Young Men Drive Dangerously: Implications for Injury Prevention," *Current Directions in Psychological Science* 11 (2002): 75–79.

CHAPTER 2. I WILL SURVIVE

1. http://www.goodreads.com/author/quotes/1408429.M_F_K _Fisher (accessed February 28, 2011); also quoted in Tom Hughes and Meredith Sayles Hughes, *Gastronomie!: Food Museums and Heritage Sites of France* (Piermont, NH: Bunker Hill, 2005), p. 9.

2. Andrew M. Prentice, "Early Influences on Human Energy Regulation: Thrifty Genotypes and Thrifty Phenotypes," *Physiology & Behavior* 86 (2005): 640–45; see also Michael L. Power and Jay Schulkin, *The Evolution of Obesity* (Baltimore, MD: Johns Hopkins University Press, 2009).

3. "Top 400 Restaurant Chains," *Restaurants & Institutions* 118, no. 10 (2008): 30; "Top 400 Restaurant Chains," *Restaurants & Institutions* 117, no. 10 (2007): 26.

4. Julie A. Mennella, Coren P. Jagnow, and Gary K. Beauchamp, "Prenatal and Postnatal Flavor Learning by Human Infants," *Pediatrics* 107, no. 6 (2001): e88; Gary K. Beauchamp and Julie A. Mennella, "Early Flavor Learning and Its Impact on Later Feeding Behavior," *Journal of Pediatric Gastroenterology and Nutrition* 48, suppl. 1 (2009): S25–S30.

5. For other evolutionary-informed analyses of cooking and cuisine, see Solomon H. Katz, "An Evolutionary Theory of Cuisine," *Human Nature* 1, no

3 (1990): 233–59; Richard Wrangham and NancyLou Conklin-Brittain, "Cooking as a Biological Trait," *Comparative Biochemistry and Physiology Part A* 136 (2003): 35–46; Richard Wrangham, *Catching Fire: How Cooking Made Us Human* (New York: Basic Books, 2009).

6. Paul W. Sherman and Jennifer Billing, "Darwinian Gastronomy: Why We Use Spices," *BioScience* 49 (1999): 453–63; Paul W. Sherman and Geoffrey A. Hash, "Why Vegetable Recipes Are Not Very Spicy," *Evolution and Human Behavior* 22 (2001): 147–63; see also Gary Paul Nabhan, *Why Some Like It Hot: Food, Genes and Cultural Diversity* (Washington, DC: Island Press, 2004).

7. Sherman and Billing, "Darwinian Gastronomy," p. 462.

8. Yohsuke Ohtsubo, "Adaptive Ingredients against Food Spoilage in Japanese Cuisine," *International Journal of Food Sciences and Nutrition* 60, no. 8 (2009): 677–87.

9. Catherine E. Woteki and Paul R. Thomas, eds., *Eat for Life: The Food and Nutrition Board's Guide to Reducing Your Risk of Chronic Disease* (Washington, DC: National Academies Press, 1992), p. 119; see also relevant references in David M. Roder, "The Epidemiology of Gastric Cancer," *Gastric Cancer* 5, suppl. 1 (2002): 5–11.

10. See Washington State Department of Health, "Biotoxins—Myths & Misconceptions," http://www.doh.wa.gov/ehp/sf/pubs/biotoxinmyths.htm (accessed January 13, 2010).

11. See the Office of Minority Health, US Department of Health & Human Services, "Stroke and African Americans," http://minorityhealth.hhs .gov/templates/content.aspx?ID=3022 (accessed January 14, 2010).

12. Emma E. Thompson et al., "CYP3A Variation and the Evolution of Salt-Sensitivity Variants," *American Journal of Human Genetics* 75 (2004): 1059–69.

13. Susan Parman, "Lot's Wife and the Old Salt: Cross-cultural Comparisons of Attitudes toward Salt in Relation to Diet," *Cross-Cultural Research* 36, no. 2 (2002): 123–50.

14. Daniel M. T. Fessler, "An Evolutionary Explanation of the Plasticity of Salt Preferences: Prophylaxis against Sudden Dehydration," *Medical Hypotheses* 61 (2003a): 412–15.

15. Sarah A. Tishkoff et al., "Convergent Adaptation of Human Lactase Persistence in Africa and Europe," *Nature Genetics* 39, no. 1 (2007): 31–40.

16. Albano Beja-Pereira et al., "Gene-Culture Coevolution between Cattle Milk Protein Genes and Human Lactase Genes," *Nature Genetics* 35, no. 4 (2003): 311–13.

17. Abigail K. Remick, Janet Polivy, and Patricia Pliner, "Internal and External Moderators of the Effect of Variety on Food Intake," *Psychological Bulletin* 135, no. 3 (2009): 434–51; Leonard H. Epstein et al., "What Constitutes Food Variety? Stimulus Specificity of Food," *Appetite* 54, no. 1 (2010): 23–29.

18. Barbara J. Rolls et al., "Variety in a Meal Enhances Food Intake in Man," *Physiology & Behavior* 26, no. 2 (1981): 215–21.

19. Barbara E. Kahn and Brian Wansink, "The Influence of Assortment Structure on Perceived Variety and Consumption Quantities," *Journal of Consumer Research* 30, no. 4 (2004): 519–33.

20. Barbara J. Rolls, Edward A. Rowe, and Edmund T. Rolls, "How Sensory Properties of Foods Affect Human Feeding Behavior," *Physiology & Behavior* 29, no. 3 (1982): 409–17.

21. Sheena S. Iyengar and Mark R. Lepper, "When Choice Is Demotivating: Can One Desire Too Much of a Good Thing?" *Journal of Personality and Social Psychology* 79, no. 6 (2000): 995–1006.

22. For additional details on this point, see the work of Paul Rozin.

23. Sheena Sethi-Iyengar, Gur Huberman, and Wei Jiang, "How Much Choice Is Too Much? Contributions to 401(k) Retirement Plans," in *Pension Design and Structure: New Lessons from Behavioral Finance*, ed. Olivia S. Mitchell and Stephen P. Utkus (New York: Oxford University Press, 2004), pp. 83–96.

24. Barry Schwartz, *The Paradox of Choice: Why More Is Less* (New York: HarperCollins, 2004), pp. 9–10.

25. Brian Wansink and Jeffery Sobal, "Mindless Eating: The 200 Daily Food Decisions We Overlook," *Environment and Behavior* 39, no. 1 (2007): 106–123.

26. Paul Rozin and Maureen Markwith, "Cross-Domain Variety Seeking in Human Food Choice," *Appetite* 16 (1991): 57–59.

27. Paul Rozin et al., "Attitudes towards Large Numbers of Choices in the Food Domain: A Cross-Cultural Study of Five Countries in Europe and the USA," *Appetite* 46 (2006): 304–308.

28. Brent McFerran and his colleagues have recently published several papers demonstrating that the presence of a thin or heavy person (e.g., a waitress) can alter both how much food is consumed and which foods consumers choose to eat. For example, dieters and nondieters ate more when in the presence of a heavy and thin waitress, respectively. Hence, the social context is yet another important determinant of our food-hoarding instinct.

29. Larry Christensen and Alisa Brooks, "Changing Food Preference as a Function of Mood," *Journal of Psychology* 140, no. 4 (2006): 293–306.

30. Nitika Garg, Brian Wansink, and J. Jeffrey Inman, "The Influence of Incidental Affect on Consumers' Food Intake," *Journal of Marketing* 71, no. 1 (2007): 194–206.

31. Brian Wansink and Cynthia Sangerman, "The Taste of Comfort: Food for Thought on How Americans Eat to Feel Better," *American Demographics* 22, no. 7 (2000): 66–67.

32. See the CDC report titled "Do Increased Portion Sizes Affect How Much We Eat?" for a review of the relevant literature at http://www.cdc.gov/nccdphp/dnpa/nutrition/pdf/portion_size_research.pdf (accessed January 8, 2010).

33. Richard E. Nisbett and David E. Kanouse, "Obesity, Food Deprivation, and Supermarket Shopping Behavior," *Journal of Personality and Social Psychology* 12, no. 4 (1969): 289–94.

34. Dora I. Lozano, Stephen L. Crites, and Shelley N. Aikman, "Changes in Food Attitudes as a Function of Hunger," *Appetite* 32 (1999): 207–218.

35. Viren Swami and Martin J. Tovée, "Does Hunger Influence Judgments of Female Physical Attractiveness?" *British Journal of Psychology* 97 (2006): 353–63; Leif D. Nelson and Evan L. Morrison, "The Symptoms of Resource Scarcity: Judgments of Food and Finances Influence Preferences for Potential Partners," *Psychological Science* 16, no. 2 (2005): 167–73; Terry F. Pettijohn II, Donald F. Sacco Jr., and Melissa J. Yerkes, "Hungry People Prefer More Mature Mates: A Field Fest of the Environmental Security Hypothesis," *Journal of Social, Evolutionary, and Cultural Psychology* 3, no. 3 (2009): 216–32.

36. Barbara Briers et al., "Hungry for Money. The Desire for Caloric Resources Increases the Desire for Financial Resources and Vice Versa," *Psychological Science* 17, no. 11 (2006): 939–43.

37. Daniel M. T. Fessler, "Luteal Phase Immunosuppression and Meat Eating," *Rivista di Biologia / Biology Forum* 94, no. 3 (2001): 403–426; Daniel M. T. Fessler, "No Time to Eat: An Adaptationist Account of Periovulatory Behavioral Changes," *Quarterly Review of Biology* 78, (2003b): 3–21.

38. Gad Saad and Eric Stenstrom, "Calories, Beauty, and Ovulation: The Effects of the Menstrual Cycle on Food and Appearance-Related Consumption," submitted for publication (2010).

39. Val Curtis, Robert Aunger, and Tamer Rabie, "Evidence That Disgust Evolved to Protect from Risk of Disease," *Proceedings of the Royal Society B: Biological Sciences* 271, suppl. 4 (2004): S131–33; Valerie Curtis and Adam Biran, "Dirt, Disgust, and Disease: Is Hygiene in Our Genes?" *Perspectives in Biology and Medicine* 44, no. 1 (2001): 17–31.

40. Mark Schaller et al., "Mere Visual Perception of Other People's Disease Symptoms Facilitates a More Aggressive Immune Response," *Psychological Science* 21, no. 5 (2010): 649–52.

41. Gordon H. Orians and Judith H. Heerwagen, "Evolved Responses to Landscapes," in *The Adapted Mind: Evolutionary Psychology and the Generation of Culture*, ed. Jerome H. Barkow, Leda Cosmides, and John Tooby (New York: Oxford University Press, 1992) pp. 555–80; John H. Falk and John D. Balling, "Evolutionary Influence on Human Landscape Preference," *Environment and Behavior* 42, no. 4 (2010): 479–93.

42. Brian Hudson, "The View from the Verandah: Prospect, Refuge and Leisure," *Australian Geographical Studies* 31, no. 1 (1993): 70–78.

43. Brian J. Hudson, "The Experience of Waterfalls," *Australian Geographical Studies* 38, no. 1 (2000): 71–84.

44. Mary Ann Fischer and Patrick E. Shrout, "Children's Liking of Landscape Paintings as a Function of Their Perceptions of Prospect, Refuge, and Hazard," *Environment and Behavior* 38, no. 3 (2006): 373–93.

45. Edward O. Wilson, *Biophilia* (Cambridge, MA: Harvard University Press, 1984).

46. Cecily Maller et al., "Healthy Nature Healthy People: 'Contact with

Nature' as an Upstream Health Promotion Intervention for Populations," *Health Promotion International* 21, no. 1 (2006): 45–54.

47. Roger S. Ulrich, "View through a Window May Influence Recovery from Surgery," *Science* 224, no. 4647 (1984): 420–21.

48. For example, see some of the research reports prepared by the Heschong Mahone Group at http://www.h-m-g.com/downloads/Daylighting/order_daylighting.htm (accessed March 21, 2010).

49. See, for example, Evergreen, http://www.evergreen.ca.

50. Nathan Petherick, "Environmental Design and Fear: The Prospect-Refuge Model and the University College of the Cariboo Campus," *Western Geography* 10/11 (2000): 89–112.

51. Richard W. Bohannon, "Number of Pedometer-Assessed Steps Taken Per Day by Adults: A Descriptive Meta-Analysis," *Physical Therapy* 87, no. 12 (2007): 1642–50.

52. Marlon G. Boarnet, "Planning's Role in Building Healthy Cities," *Journal of the American Planning Association* 72, no. 1 (2006): 5–9; Lawrence D. Frank et al., "Many Pathways from Land Use to Health: Associations between Neighborhood Walkability and Active Transportation, Body Mass Index, and Air Quality," *Journal of the American Planning Association* 72, no. 1 (2006): 75–87.

53. Eugene Tsui, *Evolutionary Architecture: Nature as a Basis for Design* (New York: John Wiley, 1999).

54. Richard Dawkins, *The Extended Phenotype: The Long Reach of the Gene* (Oxford: Oxford University Press, 1982).

55. For a discussion of biophilic architecture, see Yannick Joye, "Architectural Lessons from Environmental Psychology: The Case of Biophilic Architecture," *Review of General Psychology* 11 (2007): 305–328; Stephen R. Kellert, Judith Heerwagen, and Martin Mador, eds., *Biophilic Design: The Theory, Science and Practice of Bringing Buildings to Life* (New York: Wiley, 2008).

56. Suzanne C. Scott, "Visual Attributes Related to Preference in Interior Environments," *Journal of Interior Design* 18, no. 1/2 (1993): 7–16.

57. Yannick Joye et al., "The Effects of Urban Retail Greenery on Consumer Experience: Reviewing the Evidence from a Restorative Perspective," *Urban Forestry & Urban Greening* 9 (2010): 57–64. On a related note, the use

of particular scenes of nature in the design of green ads yields positive outcomes as shown by Patrick Hartmann and Vanessa Apaolaza-Ibáñez, "Beyond
Savanna: An Evolutionary and Environmental Psychology Approach to Behavioral Effects of Nature Scenery in Green Advertising," *Journal of Environmental Psychology* 30, no. 1 (2010): 119–28.

CHAPTER 3. LET'S GET IT ON

1. Henry Miller, *Tropic of Capricorn* (New York: Grove Press, 1961), p. 192.

2. Graham Swift, *Shuttlecock* (Toronto: Vintage Canada, 1997), p. 73.

3. Simran Khurana, "Marilyn Monroe Quote: Read a Marilyn Monroe
Quote to Understand Her True Nature," http://quotations.about.com/
od/morepeople/a/MarilynMonroe2.htm (accessed December 9, 2009).

4. For a thorough discussion of the evolution of human sex differences,
see David C. Geary, *Male, Female: The Evolution of Human Sex Differences*,
2nd ed. (Washington, DC: American Psychological Association, 2009).

5. William M. Brown et al., "Dance Reveals Symmetry Especially in
Young Men," *Nature* 438 (2005): 1148–50.

6. Amotz Zahavi and Avishag Zahavi, *The Handicap Principle: A
Missing Piece of Darwin's Puzzle* (New York: Oxford University Press, 1997).

7. Gad Saad and John G. Vongas, "The Effect of Conspicuous Consumption on Men's Testosterone Levels," *Organizational Behavior and Human
Decision Processes* 110, no. 2 (2009): 80–92.

8. Lawrence Dorfman, *The Snark Handbook: A Reference Guide to
Verbal Sparring* (New York: Skyhorse Publishing, 2009), p. 13.

9. Michael J. Dunn and Robert Searle, "Effect of Manipulated Prestige-
Car Ownership on Both Sex Attractiveness Ratings," *British Journal of Psychology* 101 (2010): 69–80.

10. Hot or Not, http://www.hotornot.com/.

11. Gregory A. Shuler and David M. McCord, "Determinants of Male
Attractiveness: 'Hotness' Ratings as a Function of Perceived Resources," *American Journal of Psychological Research* 6, no. 1 (2010): 10–23, http://www
.mcneese.edu/ajpr/issues.html (accessed February 2, 2010).

12. Anthony N. Doob and Alan E. Gross, "Status of Frustrator as an Inhibitor of Horn-Honking Responses," *Journal of Social Psychology* 76, no. 2 (1968): 213–18.

13. Andreas Diekmann et al., "Social Status and Aggression: A Field Study Analyzed by Survival Analysis," *Journal of Social Psychology* 136, no. 6 (1996): 761–68.

14. Cristina M. Gomes and Christophe Boesch, "Wild Chimpanzees Exchange Meat for Sex on a Long-Term Basis," *PLoS ONE* 4, no. 4 (2009): e5116, doi:10.1371/journal.pone.0005116.

15. Amy Stewart, *Flower Confidential: The Good, the Bad, and the Beautiful in the Business of Flowers* (Chapel Hill, NC: Algonquin Books, 2007).

16. Jeannette Haviland-Jones et al., "An Environmental Approach to Positive Emotion: Flowers," *Evolutionary Psychology* 3 (2005): 104–132.

17. Céline Jacob et al., "'Love Is in the Air': Congruence between Background Music and Goods in a Florist," *International Review of Retail, Distribution and Consumer Research* 19, no. 1 (2009): 75–79.

18. Lee Cronk and Bria Dunham, "Amounts Spent on Engagement Rings Reflect Aspects of Male and Female Mate Quality," *Human Nature* 18, no. 4 (2007): 329–33.

19. Francis J. Flynn and Gabrielle S. Adams, "Money Can't Buy Love: Asymmetric Beliefs about Gift Price and Feelings of Appreciation," *Journal of Experimental Social Psychology* 45 (2009): 404–409.

20. Steven W. Gangestad and Randy Thornhill, "Menstrual Cycle Variation in Women's Preferences for the Scent of Symmetrical Men," *Proceedings of the Royal Society of London: Series B, Biological Sciences* 265 (1998): 927–33.

21. For a review, see Jan Havlicek and S. Craig Roberts, "MHC-Correlated Mate Choice in Humans: A Review," *Psychoneuroendocrinology* 34 (2008): 497–512.

22. Chandler Burr, "Perfumers Breathe in Sales Data, and Strategize," *New York Times,* June 19, 2009, http://www.nytimes.com/2009/06/20/business/20perfume.html (accessed December 19, 2009); Diana Dodson, "Growth Upturn in the Global Fragrances Market," *Euromonitor International*, February 14, 2008, http://www.euromonitor.com/Growth_upturn_in_the_global_fragrances_market (accessed December 19, 2009).

23. Manfred Milinski and Claus Wedekind, "Evidence for MHC-Correlated Perfume Preferences in Humans," *Behavioral Ecology* 12, no 2. (2001): 140–49.

24. Claus Wedekind et al., "The Major Histocompatibility Complex and Perfumers' Descriptions of Human Body Odors," *Evolutionary Psychology* 5, no. 2 (2007): 330–43.

25. Mark J. T. Sergeant et al., "The Self-Reported Importance of Olfaction during Human Mate Choice," *Sexualities, Evolution, & Gender* 7, no. 3 (2005): 199–213.

26. S. Craig Roberts et al., "Manipulation of Body Odour Alters Men's Self-Confidence and Judgements of Their Visual Attractiveness by Women," *International Journal of Cosmetic Science* 31 (2009): 47–54.

27. Jan Havlicek and Pavlina Lenochova, "The Effect of Meat Consumption on Body Odor Attractiveness," *Chemical Senses* 31, no. 8 (2006): 747–52.

28. The three quotes are from Catherine M. Roach's *Stripping, Sex, and Popular Culture* (Oxford, UK: Berg Publishers, 2007), pp. 34, 35 (two quotes), respectively.

29. For an evolutionary account of high heels, see Euclid O. Smith, "High Heels and Evolution: Natural Selection, Sexual Selection and High Heels," *Psychology, Evolution, & Gender* 1 (1999): 245–77.

30. Piotr Sorokowski and Boguslaw Pawlowski, "Adaptive Preferences for Leg Length in a Potential Partner," *Evolution and Human Behavior* 29 (2008): 86–91.

31. Kikue Sakaguchi and Toshikazu Hasegawa, "Person Perception through Gait Information and Target Choice for Sexual Advances: Comparison of Likely Targets in Experiments and Real Life," *Journal of Nonverbal Behavior* 30 (2006): 63–85.

32. Geoffrey Miller, Joshua M. Tybur, and Brent D. Jordan, "Ovulatory Cycle Effects on Tip Earnings by Lap Dancers: Economic Evidence for Human Estrus?" *Evolution and Human Behavior* 28, no. 6 (2007): 375–81.

33. Smith, "High Heels and Evolution."

34. Maria Angela Cerruto, Ermes Vedovi, and William Mantovani, "Women Pay Attention to Shoe Heels: Besides Causing Schizophrenia They Might Affect Your Pelvic Floor Muscle Activity!!" *European Urology* 53, no. 5 (2008): 1094.

35. John Stuart Gillis and Walter E. Avis, "The Male-Taller Norm in Mate Selection," *Personality and Social Psychology Bulletin* 6, no. 3 (1980): 396–401.

36. John Marshall Townsend and Gary D. Levy, "Effects of Potential Partners' Costume and Physical Attractiveness on Sexuality and Partner Selection," *Journal of Psychology* 124, no. 4 (1990): 371–89.

37. Valerie Steele, *The Corset: A Cultural History* (New Haven, CT: Yale University Press, 2001).

38. For a discussion of the evolutionary roots of these preferences, see Devendra Singh, "Female Mate Value at a Glance: Relationship of Waist-to-Hip Ratio to Health, Fecundity and Attractiveness," *Neuroendocrinology Letters* 23 (2002): 81–91.

39. George Taylor was reputed to have been the first to propose this relationship in 1926; see "Dressing for the Downturn," *Economist*, February 15, 2001, http://www.economist.com/node/507380 (accessed October 6, 2010). Other works that have explored this relationship include Paul H. Nystrom, *Economics of Fashion* (New York: Ronald Press Company, 1928), and Helmut Gaus, *Why Yesterday Tells of Tomorrow* (Philadelphia: Coronet Books, 2001).

40. "Cosmetics in the Downturn: Lip Reading," *Economist*, January 22, 2009, http://www.economist.com/node/12995765 (accessed October 6, 2010).

41. Madison Park, "Women Risk Snapped Ligaments for Shoe Fashion," CNN, April 9, 2010, http://www.cnn.com/2010/HEALTH/04/09/fashion.shoes.heels/index.html (accessed April 9, 2010).

42. Russell A. Hill, Sophie Donovan, and Nicola F. Koyama, "Female Sexual Advertisement Reflects Resource Availability in Twentieth-Century UK Society," *Human Nature* 16 (2005): 266–77.

43. Nigel Barber, "Women's Dress Fashions as a Function of Reproductive Strategy," *Sex Roles* 40 (1999): 459–71.

44. Maria Perla Colombini et al., "An Etruscan Ointment from Chiusi (Tuscany, Italy): Its Chemical Characterization," *Journal of Archaeological Science* 36 (2009): 1488–95.

45. But see the men of the Wodaabe people for an exception: Mette Bovin, *Nomads Who Cultivate Beauty: Wodaabe Dances and Visual Arts in Niger* (Uppsala, Sweden: Nordiska Afrikainstitutet, 2001).

46. Fortune 500 2009: Women CEOs, CNN, http://money.cnn.com/magazines/fortune/fortune500/2009/womenceos/ (accessed February 4, 2010).

47. Rebecca Mulhern et al., "Do Cosmetics Enhance Female Caucasian Facial Attractiveness?" *International Journal of Cosmetic Science* 25 (2003): 199–205.

48. Jean Ann Graham and A. J. Jouhar, "The Effects of Cosmetics on Person Perception," *International Journal of Cosmetic Science* 3 (1981): 199–210.

49. Nicolas Guéguen, "The Effects of Women's Cosmetics on Men's Approach: An Evaluation in a Bar," *North American Journal of Psychology* 10, no. 1 (2008): 221–28.

50. Céline Jacob et al., "Waitresses' Facial Cosmetics and Tipping: A Field Experiment," *International Journal of Hospitality Management* 29, no. 1 (2010): 188–90.

51. Rodrigo Andrés Cárdenas and Lauren Julius Harris, "Symmetrical Decorations Enhance the Attractiveness of Faces and Abstract Designs," *Evolution and Human Behavior* 27 (2006): 1–18.

52. Richard Russell, "Sex, Beauty, and the Relative Luminance of Facial Features," *Perception* 32 (2003): 1093–1107; Richard Russell, "A Sex Difference in Facial Contrast and Its Exaggeration by Cosmetics," *Perception* 38 (2009): 1211–19.

53. See Nadine Samson, Bernhard Fink, and Paul J. Matts, "Visible Skin Condition and Perception of Human Facial Appearance," *International Journal of Cosmetic Science* 32, no. 3 (2010): 167–84, for the relevant references to the findings reported in the last two sentences; on a related note, see also Stephen Kellett and Paul Gilbert, "Acne: A Biopsychosocial and Evolutionary Perspective with a Focus on Shame," *British Journal of Health Psychology* 6 (2001): 1–24.

54. Andrew J. Elliot and Daniela Niesta, "Romantic Red: Red Enhances Men's Attraction to Women," *Journal of Personality and Social Psychology* 95, no. 5 (2008): 1150–64.

55. Verlin B. Hinsz, David C. Matz, and Rebecca A. Patience, "Does Women's Hair Signal Reproductive Potential?" *Journal of Experimental Social Psychology* 37 (2001): 166–72.

56. Norbert Mesko and Tamas Bereczkei, "Hairstyle as an Adaptive Means of Displaying Phenotypic Quality," *Human Nature* 15 (2004): 251–70.

57. See S. Craig Roberts et al., "Female Facial Attractiveness Increases during the Fertile Phase of the Menstrual Cycle," *Proceedings of the Royal Society of London B: Biological Sciences* 271, suppl. 5 (2004): S270–72, and references therein.

58. Gad Saad and Eric Stenstrom, "Calories, Beauty, and Ovulation: The Effects of the Menstrual Cycle on Food and Appearance-Related Consumption," submitted for publication (2010).

59. Kristina M. Durante, Norman P. Li, and Martie G. Haselton, "Changes in Women's Choice of Dress Across the Ovulatory Cycle: Naturalistic and Laboratory Task-Based Evidence," *Personality and Social Psychology Bulletin* 34, no. 11 (2008): 1451–60; Karl Grammer, LeeAnn Renninger, and Bettina Fischer, "Disco Clothing, Female Sexual Motivation, and Relationship Status: Is She Dressed to Impress?" *Journal of Sex Research* 41, no. 1 (2004): 66–74; Martie G. Haselton et al., "Ovulatory Shifts in Human Female Ornamentation: Near Ovulation, Women Dress to Impress," *Hormones and Behavior* 51 (2007): 40–45.

60. Tobias Uller and L. Christoffer Johansson, "Human Mate Choice and the Wedding Ring Effect: Are Married Men More Attractive?" *Human Nature* 14, no. 3 (2003): 267–76.

61. Organisation for Economic Co-operation and Development (OECD), "The Economic Impact of Counterfeiting and Piracy," http://www.oecd.org/dataoecd/13/12/38707619.pdf (accessed April 16, 2010).

62. International AntiCounterfeiting Coalition, http://www.iacc.org/about-counterfeiting/ (accessed April 16, 2010); International AntiCounterfeiting Coalition, http://www.iacc.org/about-counterfeiting/counterfeit-gallery/index.php (accessed April 16, 2010).

63. See, for example, Jeffrey A. Hall et al., "Strategic Misrepresentation in Online Dating: The Effects of Gender, Self-Monitoring, and Personality Traits," *Journal of Social and Personal Relationships* 27, no. 1 (2010): 117–35, and references therein.

64. As described in Luuk Van Kempen, "Fooling the Eye of the Beholder: Deceptive Status Signalling among the Poor in Developing Countries," *Journal of International Development* 15, no. 2 (2003): 157–77.

CHAPTER 4. WE ARE FAMILY

1. These were gathered from several Internet repositories of proverbs.

2. William D. Hamilton, "The Genetical Evolution of Social Behaviour, Parts I and II," *Journal of Theoretical Biology* 7 (1964): 1–52; the gene-centric perspective was popularized to the masses in Richard Dawkins's book *The Selfish Gene* (New York: Oxford University Press, 1976).

3. Richard G. Bribiescas, *Men: Evolutionary and Life History* (Cambridge, MA: Harvard Unviersity Press, 2008), p. 26.

4. For a broad overview of evolutionary approaches to the study of families, see Catherine A. Salmon and Todd K. Shackelford, eds., *Family Relationships: An Evolutionary Perspective* (New York: Oxford University Press, 2007).

5. Keith Zvoch, "Family Type and Investment in Education: A Comparison of Genetic and Stepparent Families," *Evolution and Human Behavior* 20 (1999): 453–64.

6. Anne Case, I-Fen Lin, and Sara McLanahan, "Educational Attainment of Siblings in Stepfamilies," *Evolution and Human Behavior* 22 (2001): 269–89.

7. Gregory D. Webster, "Prosocial Behavior in Families: Moderators of Resource Sharing," *Journal of Experimental Social Psychology* 39 (2003): 644–52.

8. Martin S. Smith, Bradley J. Kish, and Charles B. Crawford, "Inheritance of Wealth as Human Kin Investments," *Ethology and Sociobiology* 8, no. 3 (1987): 171–82.

9. Nancy L. Segal and Sarah L. Ream, "Decrease in Grief Intensity for Deceased Twin and Non-Twin Relatives: An Evolutionary Perspective," *Personality and Individual Differences* 25 (1998): 317–25.

10. Thomas V. Pollet and Daniel Nettle, "Dead or Alive? Knowledge about a Sibling's Death Varies by Genetic Relatedness in a Modern Society," *Evolutionary Psychology* 7, no. 1 (2009): 57–65.

11. Eugene Burnstein, Christian Crandall, and Shinobu Kitayama, "Some Neo-Darwinian Rules for Altruism: Weighing Cues for Inclusive Fitness as a Function of the Biological Importance of the Decision," *Journal of Personality and Social Psychology* 67, no. 5 (1994): 773–89.

12. William Jankowiak and Monique Diderich, "Sibling Solidarity in a

Polygamous Community in the USA: Unpacking Inclusive Fitness," *Evolution and Human Behavior* 21 (2000): 125–39.

13. Thomas V. Pollet, "Genetic Relatedness and Sibling Relationship Characteristics in a Modern Society," *Evolution and Human Behavior* 28 (2007): 176–85.

14. Elainie A. Madsen et al., "Kinship and Altruism: A Cross-Cultural Experimental Study," *British Journal of Psychology* 98 (2007): 339–59.

15. See references in Nigel Nicholson, "Evolutionary Psychology and Family Business: A New Synthesis for Theory, Research, and Practice," *Family Business Review* 21, no. 1 (2008): 112.

16. Gad Saad and Tripat Gill, "An Evolutionary Psychology Perspective on Gift-Giving among Young Adults," *Psychology & Marketing* 20 (2003): 765–84.

17. Antonia J. Z. Henderson et al., "The Living Anonymous Kidney Donor: Lunatic or Saint?" *American Journal of Transplantation* 3 (2003): 203–213.

18. James R. Rodrigue et al., "The Expectancies of Living Kidney Donors: Do They Differ as a Function of Relational Status and Gender?" *Nephrology Dialysis Transplantation* 21 (2006): 1682–88.

19. J. Michael Cecka, "Kidney Transplantation from Living Unrelated Donors," *Annual Review of Medicine* 51 (2000): 393–406.

20. "Average Wedding Costs," Chateau at Forest Park, http://www.chateauatforestpark.com/pricing-Averageweddingcosts.html (accessed February 8, 2010).

21. Robin I. M. Dunbar, "The Social Brain: Mind, Language, and Society in Evolutionary Perspective," *Annual Review of Anthropology* 32 (2003): 163–81; Russell A. Hill and Robin I. M. Dunbar, "Social Network Size in Humans," *Human Nature* 14 (2003): 53–72.

22. One of my former graduate students (Soumaya Cheikhrouhou) and I had planned several years ago on testing some of these ideas in the Tunisian patriarchal society.

23. Alexander Pashos and Donald H. McBurney, "Kin Relationships and the Caregiving Biases of Grandparents, Aunts, and Uncles: A Two-Generational Questionnaire Study," *Human Nature* 19 (2008): 311–30.

24. US Toy Industry Association, as cited by the US Department of Commerce Industry Outlook (2006), "Dolls, Toys, Games, and Children's Vehicles NAICS Code 33993," http://www.trade.gov/td/ocg/outlook06_toys.pdf (accessed July 13, 2008).

25. Sheri A. Berenbaum and Melissa Hines, "Early Androgens Are Related to Childhood Sex-Typed Toy Preferences," *Psychological Science* 3, no. 3 (1992): 203–206.

26. John T. Manning, *The Finger Book: Sex, Behaviour, and Disease Revealed in the Fingers* (London: Faber & Faber, 2008).

27. Johannes Hönekopp and Christine Thierfelder, "Relationships between Digit Ratio (2D:4D) and Sex-Typed Play Behavior in Pre-School Children," *Personality and Individual Differences* 47, no. 7 (2009): 706–710.

28. Gerianne M. Alexander and Melissa Hines, "Sex Differences in Response to Children's Toys in Nonhuman Primates (*Cercopithecus aethiops sabaeus*)," *Evolution and Human Behavior* 23 (2002): 467–79; Gerianne M. Alexander, "An Evolutionary Perspective of Sex-Typed Toy Preferences: Pink, Blue, and the Brain," *Archives of Sexual Behavior* 32, no. 1 (2003): 7–14; Janice M. Hassett, Erin R. Siebert, and Kim Wallen, "Sex Differences in Rhesus Monkey Toy Preferences Parallel Those of Children," *Hormones and Behavior* 54, no. 3 (2008): 359–64.

29. Marek Špinka, Ruth C. Newberry, and Marc Bekoff, "Mammalian Play: Training for the Unexpected," *Quarterly Review of Biology* 76, no. 2 (2001): 141–68; Anthony D. Pellegrini, Danielle Dupuis, and Peter K. Smith, "Play in Evolution and Development," *Developmental Review* 27 (2007): 261–76.

30. See, for example, Paul H. Morris, Vasudevi Reddy, and R. C. Bunting, "The Survival of the Cutest: Who's Responsible for the Evolution of the Teddy Bear?" *Animal Behaviour* 50 (1995): 1697–1700.

31. Stephen Jay Gould, *The Panda's Thumb: More Reflections in Natural History* (New York: W. W. Norton, 1980), pp. 95–107.

32. Frank J. Sulloway, *Born to Rebel: Birth Order, Family Dynamics, and Creative Lives* (New York: Pantheon, 1996).

33. Frank J. Sulloway and Richard L. Zweigenhaft, "Birth Order and Risk Taking in Athletics: A Meta-Analysis and Study of Major League Baseball,"

Personality and Social Psychology Review 14, no. 4 (2010): 402–416.

34. Gad Saad, Tripat Gill, and Rajan Nataraajan, "Are Laterborns More Innovative and Non-Conforming Consumers Than Firstborns? A Darwinian Perspective," *Journal of Business Research* 58 (2005): 902–909.

35. Martin Daly and Margo Wilson, *The Truth about Cinderella: A Darwinian View of Parental Love* (New Haven, CT: Yale University Press, 1999).

36. Harald A. Euler and Barbara Weitzel, "Discriminative Grandparental Solicitude as Reproductive Strategy," *Human Nature* 7 (1996): 39–59; Thomas V. Pollet, Daniel Nettle, and Mark Nelissen, "Maternal Grandmothers Do Go the Extra Mile: Factoring Distance and Lineage into Differential Contact with Grandchildren," *Evolutionary Psychology* 5, no. 4 (2007): 832–43; David I. Bishop et al., "Differential Investment Behavior between Grandparents and Grandchildren: The Role of Paternity Uncertainty," *Evolutionary Psychology* 7, no. 1 (2009): 66–77.

37. Rebecca Sear and Ruth Mace, "Who Keeps Children Alive? A Review of the Effects of Kin on Child Survival," *Evolution and Human Behavior* 29 (2008): 1–18.

38. Martin Daly and Margo I. Wilson, "Whom Are Newborn Babies Said to Resemble?" *Ethology and Sociobiology* 3 (1982): 69–78; Jeanne M. Regalski and Steven J. C. Gaulin, "Whom Are Mexican Infants Said to Resemble? Monitoring and Fostering Paternal Confidence in the Yucatan," *Ethology and Sociobiology* 14, no. 2 (1993): 97–113.

39. Coren L. Apicella and Frank W. Marlowe, "Perceived Mate Fidelity and Paternal Resemblance Predict Men's Investment in Children," *Evolution and Human Behavior* 25 (2004): 371–78.

40. Alexandra Alvergne, Charlotte Faurie, and Michel Raymond, "Father-Offspring Resemblance Predicts Paternal Investment in Humans," *Animal Behaviour* 78 (2009): 61–69.

41. Lisa S. Hayward and Sievert Rohwer, "Sex Differences in Attitudes toward Paternity Testing," *Evolution and Human Behavior* 25 (2004): 242–48.

42. Cheryl S. Rosenfeld and R. Michael Roberts, "Maternal Diet and Other Factors Affecting Offspring Sex Ratio: A Review," *Biology of Reproduction* 71 (2004): 1063–1070.

43. Fiona Mathews, Paul J. Johnson, and Andrew Neil, "You Are What Your Mother Eats: Evidence for Maternal Preconception Diet Influencing

Foetal Sex in Humans," *Proceedings of the Royal Society B: Biological Sciences* 275 (2008): 1661–68.

44. For a thorough review of the hypothesis, see Matthew C. Keller, Randolph M. Nesse, and Sandra Hofferth, "The Trivers-Willard Hypothesis of Parental Investment: No Effect in the Contemporary United States," *Evolution and Human Behavior* 22, no. 5 (2001): 343–60; see also Clare Janaki Holden, Rebecca Sear, and Ruth Mace, "Matriliny as Daughter-Biased Investment," *Evolution and Human Behavior* 24, no. 2 (2003): 99–112.

45. Elissa Z. Cameron and Fredrik Dalerum, "A Trivers-Willard Effect in Contemporary Humans: Male-Biased Sex Ratios among Billionaires," *PLoS ONE* 4, no. 1 (2009): e4195, doi:10.1371/journal.pone.0004195.

46. Lee Cronk, "Preferential Parental Investment in Daughters over Sons," *Human Nature* 2, no. 4 (1991): 387–417.

47. Glenn Weisfeld, *Evolutionary Principles of Human Adolescence* (New York: Basic Books, 1999).

48. Michele K. Surbey, "Family Composition, Stress, and the Timing of Human Menarche," in *Socioendocrinology of Primate Reproduction. Monographs in Primatology, Vol. 13*, ed. Toni E. Ziegler and Fred B. Bercovitch (New York: Wiley-Liss, 1990), pp. 11–32; for a review, see Bruce J. Ellis, "Timing of Pubertal Maturation in Girls: An Integrated Life History Approach," *Psychological Bulletin* 130 (2004): 920–58.

49. US Department of Commerce, "Projections of the Number of Households and Families in the United States: 1995 to 2010," April 1996, p. 11, http://www.census.gov/prod/1/pop/p25-1129.pdf (accessed January 21, 2010); American Pet Products Association, "Industry Statistics & Trends," http://www.americanpetproducts.org/press_industrytrends.asp (accessed January 21, 2010).

50. But see Elizabeth C. Hirschman, "Consumers and Their Animal Companions," *Journal of Consumer Research* 20 (1994): 616–32, and the recent 2008 special issue of the *Journal of Business Research* on animal companions.

51. See study 4 in Nicolas Guéguen and Serge Ciccotti, "Domestic Dogs as Facilitators in Social Interaction: An Evaluation of Helping and Courtship Behaviors," *Anthrozoös* 21 (2008): 339–49.

52. John Archer, "Why Do People Love Their Pets?" *Evolution and Human Behavior* 18 (1997): 237–59.

53. Richard Dawkins, *The Greatest Show on Earth: The Evidence for Evolution* (New York: Free Press, 2009), pp. 71–73.

54. Christina Payne and Klaus Jaffe, "Self Seeks Like: Many Humans Choose Their Dog Pets Following Rules Used for Assortative Mating," *Journal of Ethology* 23 (2005) 15–18; Michael M. Roy and Nicholas J. S. Christenfeld, "Do Dogs Resemble Their Owners?" *Psychological Science* 15, no. 5 (2004): 361–63.

CHAPTER 5. THAT'S WHAT FRIENDS ARE FOR

1. All three epigraphs were obtained from the Matti Kuusi International type system of proverbs.

2. Robert L. Trivers, "The Evolution of Reciprocal Altruism," *Quarterly Review of Biology* 46 (1971): 35–57.

3. Steve Stewart-Williams, "Human Beings as Evolved Nepotists: Exceptions to the Rule and Effects of Cost of Help," *Human Nature* 19, no. 4 (2008): 414–25; Steve Stewart-Williams, "Altruism among Kin vs. Nonkin: Effects of Cost of Help and Reciprocal Exchange," *Evolution and Human Behavior* 28, no. 3 (2007): 193–98.

4. See, for example, Howard Rachlin and Bryan A. Jones, "Altruism among Relatives and Non-Relatives," *Behavioural Processes* 79, no. 2 (2008): 120–23.

5. Joshua M. Ackerman, Douglas T. Kenrick, and Mark Schaller, "Is Friendship Akin to Kinship?" *Evolution and Human Behavior* 28 (2007): 365–74.

6. Peter DeScioli and Robert Kurzban, "The Alliance Hypothesis for Human Friendship," *PLoS ONE* 4, no. 6 (2009): e5802, doi:10.1371/journal.pone.0005802.

7. Jacob M. Vigil, "Asymmetries in the Friendship Preferences and Social Styles of Men and Women," *Human Nature* 18, no. 2 (2007): 143–61.

8. But see Adrian Palmer, "Co-Operation and Competition: A Dar-

winian Synthesis of Relationship Marketing," *European Journal of Marketing* 34, nos. 5/6 (2000): 687–704.

9. See, for example, Peter E. Digeser, "Friendship between States," *British Journal of Political Science* 39 (2009) 323–44.

10. For figures regarding the average number of times that adults older than twenty-five switch jobs and careers, please see Ann K. Jordan and Lynne T. Whaley, *Investigating Your Career* (Mason, OH: Thomson/South-Western, 2008), p. 5.

11. See, for example, Paul J. Zak, "The Neurobiology of Trust," *Scientific American* (June 2008): 88–95.

12. Alessio Avenanti, Angela Sirigu, and Salvatore M. Aglioti, "Racial Bias Reduces Empathic Sensorimotor Resonance with Other-Race Pain," *Current Biology* (2010), doi:10.1016/j.cub.2010.03.071.

13. Roy F. Baumeister and Mark R. Leary, "The Need to Belong: Desire for Interpersonal Attachments as a Fundamental Human Motivation," *Psychological Bulletin* 117, no. 3 (1995): 497–529.

14. Quentin Crisp, *The Naked Civil Servant* (New York: Penguin Classics, 1997), p. 126.

15. See relevant references in Cynthia Rodriguez Cano and Doreen Sams, "Body Modifications and Young Adults: Predictors of Intentions to Engage in Future Body Modification," *Journal of Retailing and Consumer Services* 17 (2010): 80.

16. Marilynn B. Brewer, "The Social Self: On Being the Same and Different at the Same Time," *Personality and Social Psychology Bulletin* 17, no. 5 (1991): 475–82.

17. Robert B. Cialdini et al., "Basking in Reflected Glory: Three (Football) Studies," *Journal of Personality and Social Psychology* 34 (1976): 366–75.

18. Filip Boen, Norbert Vanbeselaere, and Jos Feys, "Behavioral Consequences of Fluctuating Group Success: An Internet Study of Soccer-Team Fans," *Journal of Social Psychology* 142, no. 6 (2002): 769–81.

19. Nick Neave and Sandy Wolfson, "Testosterone, Territoriality, and the 'Home Advantage,'" *Physiology & Behavior* 78 (2003): 269–75.

20. Paul C. Bernhardt et al., "Testosterone Changes during Vicarious Experiences of Winning and Losing among Fans at Sporting Events," *Physiology & Behavior* 65, no. 1 (1998): 59–62.

21. Joshua Wolf Shenk, "What Makes Us Happy?" *Atlantic*, June 2009, http://www.theatlantic.com/magazine/archive/2009/06/what-makes-us-happy/7439/3/ (accessed March 1, 2010).

22. See, for example, Albert-László Barabási, *Linked: How Everything Is Connected to Everything Else and What It Means for Business, Science, and Everyday Life* (New York: Plume, 2002).

23. Kwang-II Goh et al., "The Human Disease Network," *Proceedings of the National Academy of Sciences of the United States of America* 104 (2007): 8685–90.

24. Seth Godin, *Tribes: We Need You to Lead Us* (New York: Portfolio, 2008).

25. Mark Earls, *Herd: How to Change Mass Behaviour by Harnessing Our True Nature* (West Sussex, England: Wiley, 2007).

26. Scott A. Golder, Dennis Wilkinson, and Bernardo A. Huberman, "Rhythms of Social Interaction: Messaging within a Massive Online Network," Third International Conference on Communities and Technologies (CT2007), East Lansing, Michigan, June 28–30, 2007; Laura E. Buffardi and W. Keith Campbell, "Narcissism and Social Networking Web Sites," *Personality and Social Psychology Bulletin* 34, no. 10 (2008): 1303–1314.

27. For a discussion of how evolutionary psychology informs our understanding of cyber-behavior, see Jared Piazza and Jesse M. Bering, "Evolutionary Cyber-Psychology: Applying an Evolutionary Framework to Internet Behavior," *Computers in Human Behavior* 25, no. 6 (2009): 1258–69.

28. For an example of such an analysis, albeit one that is not evolutionarily informed, see Melissa Joy Magnuson and Lauren Dundes, "Gender Differences in 'Social Portraits' Reflected in MySpace Profiles," *CyberPsychology & Behavior* 11, no. 2 (2008): 239–41.

CHAPTER 6. CULTURAL PRODUCTS: FOSSILS OF THE HUMAN MIND

1. Edward O. Wilson, *On Human Nature* (Cambridge, MA: Harvard University Press, 1978), p. 167.

2. Gene-culture coevolution modeling and memetic theory, both of which I briefly addressed in chapters 1 and 2, constitute two other paradigms for studying human culture from an evolutionary perspective, although they will not be discussed here.

3. Ellen Dissanayake, *Homo Aestheticus: Where Art Comes From and Why* (New York: Free Press, 1992).

4. Geoffrey F. Miller, *The Mating Mind: How Sexual Choice Shaped the Evolution of Human Nature* (New York: Doubleday, 2000).

5. Steven Pinker, *How the Mind Works* (New York: W. W. Norton, 1997).

6. Pascal Boyer, *Religion Explained: The Evolutionary Origins of Religious Thought* (New York: Basic Books, 2001).

7. Colin Martindale, *The Clockwork Muse: The Predictability of Artistic Change* (New York: Basic Books, 1990).

8. For several evolutionary-based approaches to the study of music, see the references in Gad Saad, "Song Lyrics as Windows to Our Evolved Human Nature," in *The Evolutionary Review: Art, Science, Culture (Volume 2)*, ed. Alice Andrews and Joseph Carroll (Albany, NY: SUNY Press, 2011), pp. 127–33.

9. See, for example, Richard L. Dukes et al., "Expressions of Love, Sex, and Hurt in Popular Songs: A Content Analysis of All-Time Greatest Hits," *Social Science Journal* 40 (2003): 643–50; Deborah R. Ostlund and Richard T. Kinnier, "Values of Youth: Messages from the Most Popular Songs of Four Decades," *Journal of Humanistic Education & Development* 36 (1997) 83–91; Donald Horton, "The Dialogue of Courtship in Popular Songs," *American Journal of Sociology* 62, no. 6 (1957): 569–78.

10. David M. Buss, *The Evolution of Desire: Strategies of Human Mating* (New York: Basic Books, 1994).

11. Devendra Singh, "Female Mate Value at a Glance: Relationship of Waist-to-Hip Ratio to Health, Fecundity and Attractiveness," *Neuroendocrinology Letters* 23 (2002): 81–91.

12. For additional details, see my two posts on the topic at my *Psychology Today* blog dated January 7 and 8, 2009. "The Acronym for Benevolent Sexism Is BS: The Linguistic Irony is Delicious," http://www.psychologytoday.com/blog/homo-consumericus/200901/the-acronym-benevolent-sexism-is-bs-the

-linguistic-irony-is-delicious; "Exploring the Items Used to Measure Benevolent Sexism," http://www.psychologytoday.com/blog/homo-consumericus/200901/exploring-the-items-used-measure-benevolent-sexism.

13. I thank Matt Hutson, the former news editor at *Psychology Today*, for having reminded me of this particular video.

14. See, for example, the Kluger Agency (http://klugeragency.com/), which specializes in this recent promotional tool.

15. James W. Pennebaker et al., "Don't the Girls Get Prettier at Closing Time: A Country and Western Application to Psychology," *Personality and Social Psychology Bulletin* 5, no. 1 (1979): 122–25.

16. David M. Buss and David P. Schmitt, "Sexual Strategies Theory: An Evolutionary Perspective on Human Mating," *Psychological Review* 100 (1993): 204–32.

17. Barry T. Jones et al., "Alcohol Consumption Increases Attractiveness Ratings of Opposite-Sex Faces: A Possible Third Route to Risky Sex," *Addiction* 98, no. 8 (2003): 1069–1075.

18. Lycia L. C. Parker et al., "Effects of Acute Alcohol Consumption on Ratings of Attractiveness of Facial Stimuli: Evidence of Long-Term Encoding," *Alcohol & Alcoholism* 43, no. 6 (2008): 636–40.

19. David M. Buss et al., "Sex Differences in Jealousy: Evolution, Physiology, and Psychology," *Psychological Science* 3, no. 4 (1992): 251–55.

20. Bruce J. Ellis and Donald Symons, "Sex Differences in Sexual Fantasy: An Evolutionary Psychological Approach," *Journal of Sex Research* 27, no. 4 (1990): 527–55.

21. The findings reported here are from Francis T. McAndrew and Megan A. Milenkovic, "Of Tabloids and Family Secrets: The Evolutionary Psychology of Gossip," *Journal of Applied Social Psychology* 32 (2002): 1–20. For other explorations of gossip from an evolutionary perspective, see Francis T. McAndrew, Emily K. Bell, and Contitta Maria Garcia, "Who Do We Tell and Whom Do We Tell On? Gossip as a Strategy for Status Enhancement," *Journal of Applied Social Psychology* 37, no. 7 (2007): 1562–77; Kevin M. Kniffin and David Sloan Wilson, "Evolutionary Perspectives on Workplace Gossip: Why and How Gossip Can Serve Groups," *Group & Organization Management* 35, no. 2 (2010): 150–76.

22. Bertrand Russell, *On Education, Especially in Early Childhood* (Routledge: London, 2006 [1926]), p. 50.

23. See also Charlotte J. S. De Backer et al., "Celebrities: From Teachers to Friends. A Test of Two Hypotheses on the Adaptiveness of Celebrity Gossip," *Human Nature* 18, no. 4 (2007): 334–54.

24. Satoshi Kanazawa, "Bowling with Our Imaginary Friends," *Evolution and Human Behavior* 23 (2002): 167–71.

25. Hank Davis and S. Lyndsay McLeod, "Why Humans Value Sensational News: An Evolutionary Perspective," *Evolution and Human Behavior* 24 (2003): 208–16.

26. Pamela J. Shoemaker, "Hardwired for News: Using Biological and Cultural Evolution to Explain the Surveillance Function," *Journal of Communication* 46, no. 3 (1996): 32–47.

27. *Wikipedia*, "List of Soap Operas," http://en.wikipedia.org/wiki/List_of_soap_operas (accessed August 4, 2010).

28. See, for example, Marilyn J. Matelski, *The Soap Opera Evolution: America's Enduring Romance with Daytime Drama* (Jefferson, NC: McFarland, 1988).

29. Henriette Riegel, "Soap Operas and Gossip," *Journal of Popular Culture* 29 (1996): 201–209.

30. Motion Picture Association of America, http://www.mpaa.org (accessed December 17, 2009).

31. For applications of evolutionary principles in the analysis of films, see Torben Grodal, "Love and Desire in the Cinema," *Cinema Journal* 43 (2004): 26–46; Mette Kramer, "The Mating Game in Hollywood Cinema," *New Review of Film and Television Studies* 2, no. 2 (2004): 137–59; Torben Grodal, "Pain, Sadness, Aggression, and Joy: An Evolutionary Approach to Film Emotions," *Projections* 1, no. 1 (2007): 91–107; Gad Saad, *The Evolutionary Bases of Consumption* (Mahwah, NJ: Lawrence Erlbaum Associates, 2007), pp. 183–88.

32. For additional examples of such forms of conspicuous consumption, see Francis Bloch, Vijayendra Rao, and Sonalde Desai, "Wedding Celebrations as Conspicuous Consumption: Signaling Social Status in Rural India," *Journal of Human Resources* 39 (2004): 675–95; and Aryeh Spero, "'Conspicuous Consumption' at Jewish Functions," *Judaism* 37 (1988): 103–110.

33. Terry F. Pettijohn II and Abraham Tesser, "Popularity in Environmental Context: Facial Feature Assessment of American Movie Actresses," *Media Psychology* 1 (1999): 229–47; the specific actresses mentioned in parentheses were offered by Terry F. Pettijohn II, e-mail message to author, October 10, 2010.

34. Terry F. Pettijohn II offered these two examples, e-mail messages to author, October 10, 2010, and October 23, 2010.

35. Brian Boyd, Joseph Carroll, and Jonathan Gottschall, eds., *Evolution, Literature, and Film: A Reader* (New York: Columbia University Press, 2010); Brian Boyd, *On the Origin of Stories: Evolution, Cognition, and Fiction* (Cambridge, MA: Harvard University Press, 2009); Jonathan Gottschall and David Sloan Wilson, eds., *The Literary Animal: Evolution and the Nature of Narrative* (Evanston, IL: Northwestern University Press, 2006); Joseph Carroll, *Literary Darwinism: Evolution, Human Nature, and Literature* (New York: Routledge, 2004).

36. Del Thiessen and Yoko Umezawa, "The Sociobiology of Everyday Life: A New Look at a Very Old Novel," *Human Nature* 9, no. 3 (1998): 293–320.

37. David P. Barash and Nanelle R. Barash, *Madame Bovary's Ovaries: A Darwinian Look at Literature* (New York: Delacorte, 2005), chap. 5.

38. Jonathan Gottschall, *The Rape of Troy: Evolution, Violence, and the World of Homer* (New York: Cambridge University Press, 2008).

39. James Stiller, Daniel Nettle, and Robin I. M. Dunbar, "The Small World of Shakespeare's Plays," *Human Nature* 14 (2003): 397–408.

40. Cynthia Whissell, "Mate Selection in Popular Women's Fiction," *Human Nature* 7 (1996): 427–47.

41. Jonathan Gottschall et al., "The 'Beauty Myth' Is No Myth: Emphasis on Male-Female Attractiveness in World Folktales," *Human Nature* 19, no. 2 (2008), 174–88; Jonathan Gottschall et al., "Sex Differences in Mate Choice Criteria Are Reflected in Folktales from around the World and in Historical European Literature," *Evolution and Human Behavior* 25 (2004): 102–112.

42. Romance Writers of America, "Romance Literature Statistics: Overview," http://www.rwanational.org/cs/the_romance_genre/romance_literature_statistics (accessed August 4, 2010).

43. See, for example, the content analysis in April Marie Gorry, "Leaving

Home for Romance: Tourist Women's Adventures Abroad" (doctoral diss., University of California at Santa Barbara, 1999).

44. Anthony Cox and Maryanne Fisher, "The Texas Billionaire's Pregnant Bride: An Evolutionary Interpretation of Romance Fiction Titles," *Journal of Social, Evolutionary, and Cultural Psychology* 3, no. 4 (2009): 386–401.

45. Laura Betzig, "Politics as Sex: The Old Testament Case," *Evolutionary Psychology* 3 (2005): 326–46.

CHAPTER 7. LOCAL VERSUS GLOBAL ADVERTISING

1. One of the leading figures of twentieth-century American advertising and cofounder of DDB Worldwide, the advertising firm with the highest revenues in 2008.

2. Steve McClellan, "Zenith Says Global Ad Spend Will Rise 2.2%," *Adweek*, April 7, 2010.

3. John K. Ryans Jr. and David A. Griffith, "International Advertising Research: Standardization/Adaptation and the Future," in *Handbook of Research in International Marketing*, ed. Subhash C. Jain (Northampton, MA: Edward Elgar, 2003), p. 305.

4. Ewa Krolikowska and Sven Kuenzel, "Models of Advertising Standardisation and Adaptation: It's Time to Move the Debate Forward," *Marketing Review* 8, no. 4 (2008): 383.

5. An analysis of cross-cultural advertising research published in top journals between 1995 and 2006 revealed that the two most common topics studied were cultural values and the local versus global issue: Shintaro Okazaki and Barbara Mueller, "Cross-Cultural Advertising Research: Where We Have Been and Where We Need to Go," *International Marketing Review* 24, no. 5 (2007): 499–518.

6. Gad Saad, "*Homo consumericus*: Consumption Phenomena as Universals, as Cross-Cultural Adaptations, or as Emic Cultural Instantiations," submitted for publication (2007).

7. Noam Chomsky, *Aspects of the Theory of Syntax* (Cambridge, MA: MIT Press, 1965).

8. Steven Pinker, *The Language Instinct: How the Mind Creates Language* (New York: William Morrow, 1994).

9. Linda Mealey, Christopher Daood, and Michael Krage, "Enhanced Memory for Faces of Cheaters," *Ethology and Sociobiology* 17 (1996): 119–28.

10. D. Vaughn Becker et al., "Concentrating on Beauty: Sexual Selection and Sociospatial Memory," *Personality and Social Psychology Bulletin* 31 (2005): 1643–52.

11. James S. Nairne, Sarah R. Thompson, and Josefa N. S. Pandeirada, "Adaptive Memory: Survival Processing Enhances Retention," *Journal of Experimental Psychology: Learning, Memory, and Cognition* 33, no. 2 (2007): 263–73; James S. Nairne, Josefa N. S. Pandeirada, and Sarah R. Thompson, "Adaptive Memory: The Comparative Value of Survival Processing," *Psychological Science* 19, no. 2 (2008): 176–80; Yana Weinstein, Julie M. Bugg, and Henry L. Roediger III, "Can the Survival Recall Advantage Be Explained by Basic Memory Processes?" *Memory and Cognition* 36, no. 5 (2008): 913–19.

12. Gad Saad, "Evolution and Political Marketing," in *Human Nature and Public Policy: An Evolutionary Approach*, ed. Steven A. Peterson and Albert Somit (New York: Palgrave Macmillan, 2003), pp. 121–38; John Antonakis and Olaf Dalgas, "Predicting Elections: Child's Play!" *Science* 323, no. 5918 (2009): 1183; see also the 2010 special issue of the *Journal of Nonverbal Behavior* on politics and nonverbal cues.

13. See, for example, David Andrew Puts, "Mating Context and Menstrual Phase Affect Women's Preferences for Male Voice Pitch," *Evolution and Human Behavior* 26 (2005) 388–97.

14. Coren L. Apicella, David R. Feinberg, and Frank W. Marlowe, "Voice Pitch Predicts Reproductive Success in Male Hunter-Gatherers," *Biology Letters* 3 (2007): 682–84.

15. Daniel E. Berlyne, "Novelty, Complexity, and Hedonic Value," *Perception & Psychophysics* 8 (1970): 279–86.

16. Along these lines, my former doctoral advisor J. Edward Russo has developed a research program that explores how individuals distort information as a means of supporting a "leading" alternative during the choice process. See, for example, Samuel D. Bond et al., "Information Distortion in the Evalu-

ation of a Single Option," *Organizational Behavior and Human Decision Processes* 102 (2007): 240–54, and relevant references therein.

17. See, for example, Tatiana M. Azevedo et al., "A Freezing-Like Posture to Pictures of Mutilation," *Psychophysiology* 42 (2005): 255–60.

18. For reviews of the efficacy of the use of sex in advertising, see Tom Reichert, "Sex in Advertising Research: A Review of Content, Effects, and Functions of Sexual Information in Consumer Advertising," *Archives of Sex Research* 13 (2002): 241–73; Aimee Stephanie Edison, "Does Sex Really Sell? Research on Sex in Advertising: A Meta-Analysis" (doctoral diss., University of Alabama, 2008).

19. For an evolutionary-informed analysis of advertising, see Gad Saad, *The Evolutionary Bases of Consumption* (Mahwah, NJ: Lawrence Erlbaum Associates, 2007), chap. 4, and Gad Saad, "Applying Evolutionary Psychology in Understanding the Representation of Women in Advertisements," *Psychology & Marketing* 21 (2004): 593–612.

20. Devendra Singh, "Female Mate Value at a Glance: Relationship of Waist-to-Hip Ratio to Health, Fecundity and Attractiveness," *Neuroendocrinology Letters* 23 (2002): 81–91.

21. Gad Saad, "Advertised Waist-to-Hip Ratios of Online Female Escorts: An Evolutionary Perspective," *International Journal of e-Collaboration* 4, no. 3 (2008): 40–50.

22. Barnaby J. Dixson et al., "Male Preferences for Female Waist-to-Hip Ratio and Body Mass Index in the Highlands of Papua New Guinea," *American Journal of Physical Anthropology* 141, no. 4 (2010): 620–25.

23. See, for example, Adam Westman and Frank Marlowe, "How Universal Are Preferences for Female Waist-to-Hip Ratios? Evidence from the Hadza of Tanzania," *Evolution and Human Behavior* 20 (1999): 219–28.

24. Barnaby J. Dixson et al., "Eye-Tracking of Men's Preferences for Waist-to-Hip Ratio and Breast Size of Women," *Archives of Sexual Behavior* 40, no. 1 (2011): 43–50.

25. Steven M. Platek and Devendra Singh, "Optimal Waist-to-Hip Ratios in Women Activate Neural Reward Centers in Men," *PLoS ONE* 5, no. 2 (2010): e9042, doi:10.1371/journal.pone.0009042.

26. Johan C. Karremans, Willem E. Frankenhuis, and Sander Arons,

"Blind Men Prefer a Low Waist-to-Hip Ratio," *Evolution and Human Behavior* 31, no. 3 (2010): 182–86.

27. Patrick Vyncke, "Cue Management: Using Fitness Cues to Enhance Advertising Effectiveness," in *Evolutionary Psychology in the Business Sciences*, ed. Gad Saad (Heidelberg, Germany: Springer, 2011).

28. Mark Earls, "Advertising to the Herd: How Understanding Our True Nature Challenges the Ways We Think about Advertising and Market Research," *International Journal of Market Research* 45, no. 3 (2003): 311–36.

29. For a discussion of human herding across many contexts, see the review paper by Ramsey M. Raafat, Nick Chater, and Chris Frith, "Herding in Humans," *Trends in Cognitive Sciences* 13, no. 10 (2009): 420–28.

30. Corey L. Fincher et al., "Pathogen Prevalence Predicts Human Cross-Cultural Variability in Individualism/Collectivism," *Proceedings of the Royal Society B: Biological Sciences* 275, no. 1640 (2008): 1279–85; on a related note, see Joan Y. Chiao and Katherine D. Blizinsky, "Culture-Gene Coevolution of Individualism-Collectivism and the Serotonin Transporter Gene," *Proceedings of the Royal Society B: Biological Sciences* 277, no. 1681 (2010): 529–37.

31. Marilynn B. Brewer, "The Social Self: On Being the Same and Different at the Same Time," *Personality and Social Psychology Bulletin* 17, no. 5 (1991): 475–82.

32. Vladas Griskevicius et al., "Fear and Loving in Las Vegas: Evolution, Emotion, and Persuasion," *Journal of Marketing Research* 46 (2009): 384–95.

33. Mubeen M. Aslam, "Are You Selling the Right Colour? A Cross-Cultural Review of Colour as a Marketing Cue," *Journal of Marketing Communications* 12, no. 1 (2006): 20.

34. See, for example, Thomas J. Madden, Kelly Hewett, and Martin S. Roth, "Managing Images in Different Cultures: A Cross-National Study of Color Meanings and Preferences," *Journal of International Marketing* 8, no. 4 (2000): 90–107.

35. Aslam, "Are You Selling the Right Colour?" p. 26.

36. W. Ray Crozier, "The Meanings of Colour: Preferences among Hues," *Pigment & Resin Technology* 28, no. 1 (1999): 6–14.

37. Andrew J. Elliot and Daniela Niesta, "Romantic Red: Red Enhances

Men's Attraction to Women," *Journal of Personality and Social Psychology* 95, no. 5 (2008): 1150–64.

38. Russell A. Hill and Robert A. Barton, "Red Enhances Human Performance in Contests," *Nature* 435 (May 19, 2005): 293.

39. Thore J. Bergman, Lucy Ho, and Jacinta C. Beehner, "Chest Color and Social Status in Male Geladas (Theropithecus gelada)," *International Journal of Primatology* 30, no. 6 (2009): 791–806.

CHAPTER 8. MARKETING HOPE BY SELLING LIES

1. http://www.quotegarden.com/hope.html (accessed April 10, 2010).

2. Kathy Peiss, *Hope in a Jar: The Making of America's Beauty Culture* (New York: Metropolitan Books, 1998).

3. Mara Einstein, *Brands of Faith: Marketing Religion in a Commercial Age* (New York: Routledge, 2008), p. 92.

4. Anthony Scioli et al., "A Prospective Study of Hope, Optimism, and Health," *Psychological Reports* 81 (1997): 723–33; Laura D. Kubzansky et al., "Is the Glass Half Empty or Half Full? A Prospective Study of Optimism and Coronary Heart Disease in the Normative Aging Study," *Psychosomatic Medicine* 63 (2001): 910–16; Martin E. P. Seligman, *Learned Optimism: How to Change Your Mind and Your Life* (New York: Pocket Books, 1998).

5. See, for example, Adbusters Media Foundation, http://www.adbusters.org; American Legacy Foundation, http://www.thetruth.com.

6. All the latter statistics are cited in Einstein, *Brands of Faith*, pp. 1, 41, 29–30, 53, and 40.

7. For recent books that have construed religion as a product that is branded, promoted, and ultimately consumed, see Mara Einstein, *Brands of Faith: Marketing Religion in a Commercial Age* (New York: Routledge, 2008); Phil Cooke, *Branding Faith: Why Some Churches and Nonprofits Impact Culture and Others Don't* (Ventura, CA: Regal Books, 2008); James B. Twitchell, *Shopping for God: How Christianity Went from In Your Heart to In Your Face* (New York: Simon & Schuster, 2007); Vincent J. Miller, *Consuming Religion: Religious Belief and Practice in a Consumer Culture* (New York: Continuum,

2003); and Tom Beaudoin, *Consuming Faith: Integrating Who We Are with What We Buy* (Lanham, MD: Sheed & Ward, 2007).

8. Leon Uris, *The Haj* (New York: Bantam Books, 1985), p. 14.

9. Robert M. Sapolsky, *Why Zebras Don't Get Ulcers* (New York: Henry Holt, 2004).

10. Michael Shermer, *Why People Believe Weird Things: Pseudoscience, Superstition, and Other Confusions of Our Time* (New York: Henry Holt, 2002).

11. For overviews of the evolutionary roots of religion, see Pascal Boyer and Brian Bergstrom, "Evolutionary Perspectives on Religion," *Annual Review of Anthropology* 37 (2008): 111–30; Ilkka Pyysiäinen and Marc Hauser, "The Origins of Religion: Evolved Adaptation or By-Product?" *Trends in Cognitive Sciences* 14, no. 3 (2010): 104–109.

12. See Richard Lynn, John Harvey, and Helmuth Nyborg, "Average Intelligence Predicts Atheism Rates Across 137 Nations," *Intelligence* 37 (2009): 11–15, and references therein.

13. Lisa M. Fairfax, "The Thin Line between Love and Hate: Why Affinity-Based Securities and Investment Fraud Constitutes a Hate Crime," *UC Davis Law Review* 36, no. 5 (2003): 1073–1143.

14. David B. Barrett, George T. Kurian, and Todd M. Johnson, eds., *World Christian Encyclopedia: A Comparative Survey of Churches and Religions in the Modern World (2 volumes)* (New York: Oxford University Press, 2001).

15. Richard L. Nahin et al., "Costs of Complementary and Alternative Medicine (CAM) and Frequency of Visits to CAM Practitioners: United States, 2007," *National Health Statistics Reports* 18 (July 30, 2009); available at http://nccam.nih.gov/news/camstats/costs/nhsrn18.pdf.

16. Robert L. Bratton et al., "Effect of 'Ionized' Wrist Bracelets on Musculoskeletal Pain: A Randomized, Double-Blind, Placebo-Controlled Trial," *Mayo Clinic Proceedings* 77, no. 11 (2002): 1164–68.

17. See also Stephen Barrett and William T. Jarvis, eds., *The Health Robbers: A Close Look at Quackery in America* (Amherst, NY: Prometheus Books, 1993).

18. Andrew Tobias, *Fire and Ice: The Story of Charles Revson, the Man Who Built the Revlon Empire* (New York: Quill, 1983), chap. 8 epigraph.

19. Judith H. Langlois et al., "Maxims or Myths of Beauty? A Meta-Analytic and Theoretical Review," *Psychological Bulletin* 126, no. 3 (2000):

390–423; Gillian Rhodes et al., "Attractiveness of Facial Averageness and Symmetry in Non-Western Cultures: In Search of Biologically Based Standards of Beauty," *Perception* 30 (2001): 611–25; Nancy Etcoff, *Survival of the Prettiest: The Science of Beauty* (New York: Doubleday, 1999).

20. Alan Slater et al., "Newborn Infants Prefer Attractive Faces," *Infant Behavior & Development* 21, no. 2 (1998): 345–54. Judith H. Langlois, Lori A. Roggman, and Loretta A. Reiser-Danner, "Infants' Differential Social Responses to Attractive and Unattractive Faces," *Developmental Psychology* 26, no. 1 (1990): 153–59.

21. Itzhak Aharon et al., "Beautiful Faces Have Variable Reward Value: fMRI and Behavioral Evidence," *Neuron* 32 (2001): 537–51.

22. Mette Bovin, *Nomads Who Cultivate Beauty: Wodaabe Dances and Visual Arts in Niger* (Uppsala, Sweden: Nordiska Afrikainstitutet, 2001).

23. Steve Salerno, *Sham: How the Self-Help Movement Made American Helpless* (New York: Crown Publishing Group, 2005), p. 8.

24. Ibid.

25. Ibid., p. 86.

26. Griet Vandermassen, "Women's Evolutionary Enigmas," book review of David P. Barash and Judith Eve Lipton, *How Women Got Their Curves and Other Just-So Stories, Evolutionary Psychology* 7, no. 4 (2009): 530.

27. See National Association to Advance Fat Acceptance (NAAFA), http://www.naafaonline.com.

28. Richard P. Feynman, *The Character of Physical Law* (New York: Random House, 1994 [1965]), p. 123.

CHAPTER 9. DARWINIAN RATIONALE FOR CONSUMER IRRATIONALITY

1. Scott Adams, *The Dilbert Principle: A Cubicle's-Eye View of Bosses, Meetings, Management Fads, & Other Workplace Afflictions* (London: Boxtree, 1996), p. 76.

2. Albert Ellis, http://www.great-quotes.com/quote/1410828 (accessed on April 18, 2010).

3. Numerous scholars and analysts have argued that the appearance of being irrational might at times prove to be a rational strategy to pursue, particularly in the context of military conflict. See, for example, Herman Kahn, *On Thermonuclear War* (Princeton, NJ: Princeton University Press, 1960), and Thomas C. Schelling, *Arms and Influence* (New Haven, CT: Yale University Press, 1966).

4. For a rebuttal of this premise, see Gad Saad, "Blame Our Evolved Gustatory Preferences," *Young Consumers* 7, no. 4 (2006): 72–75.

5. Gad Saad and Albert Peng, "Applying Darwinian Principles in Designing Effective Intervention Strategies: The Case of Sun Tanning," *Psychology & Marketing* 23 (2006): 617–38.

6. For additional details, see Gad Saad, *The Evolutionary Bases of Consumption* (Mahwah, NJ: Lawrence Erlbaum, 2007), chap. 6.

7. Gad Saad, "Sex Differences in OCD Symptomatology: An Evolutionary Perspective," *Medical Hypotheses* 67 (2006): 1455–59.

8. For relevant references, see Julianne Trautmann-Attmann and Tricia Widner Johnson, "Compulsive Consumption Behaviours: Investigating Relationships among Binge Eating, Compulsive Clothing Buying, and Fashion Orientation," *International Journal of Consumer Studies* 33, no. 3 (2009): 267–73; see also Tricia Johnson and Julianne Attmann, "Compulsive Buying in a Product Specific Context: Clothing," *Journal of Fashion Marketing and Management* 13, no. 3 (2009): 394–405.

9. Norman P. Li et al., "Intrasexual Competition and Eating Restriction in Heterosexual and Homosexual Individuals," *Evolution and Human Behavior* 31, no. 5 (2010): 365–72.

10. See, for example, Merry N. Miller and Andrés J. Pumariega, "Culture and Eating Disorders: A Historical and Cross-Cultural Review," *Psychiatry* 64, no. 2 (2001): 93–110.

11. Samuel K. Wasser and David P. Barash, "Reproductive Suppression among Female Mammals: Implications for Biomedicine and Sexual Selection Theory," *Quarterly Review of Biology* 58 (1983): 513–38.

12. Riadh T. Abed, "The Sexual Competition Hypothesis for Eating Disorders," *British Journal of Medical Psychology* 71 (1998): 525–47.

13. For additional evolutionary-based studies of eating disorders, see

Nicholas Gatward, "Anorexia Nervosa: An Evolutionary Puzzle," *European Eating Disorders Review* 15 (2007): 1–12; Catherine Salmon, Charles B. Crawford, and Sally Walters, "Anorexic Behavior, Female Competition and Stress: Developing the Female Competition Stress Test," *Evolutionary Psychology* 6, no. 1 (2008): 96–112; Catherine Salmon et al., "Ancestral Mechanisms in Modern Environments: Impact of Competition and Stressors on Body Image and Dieting Behavior," *Human Nature* 19 (2008): 103–17. For a survey of nonevolutionary factors purported to be linked to eating disorders, see Janet Polivy and C. Peter Herman, "Causes of Eating Disorders," *Annual Review of Psychology* 53 (2002): 187–213.

14. Richard Ronay and William von Hippel, "The Presence of an Attractive Woman Elevates Testosterone and Physical Risk Taking in Young Men," *Social Psychological and Personality Science* 1, no. 1 (2010): 57–64.

15. Patrick McAlvanah, "Are People More Risk-Taking in the Presence of the Opposite Sex?" *Journal of Economic Psychology* 30 (2009): 136–46.

16. Margo Wilson and Martin Daly, "Do Pretty Women Inspire Men to Discount the Future?" *Proceedings of the Royal Society of London: Series B (Suppl.)* 271 (2004): S177–79.

17. The American Society for Aesthetic Plastic Surgery, "Cosmetic Procedures in 2007," February 25, 2008, http://www.surgery.org/media/news -releases/117-cosmetic-procedures-in-2007- (accessed August 6, 2010).

18. See Saad, *The Evolutionary Bases of Consumption*, pp. 245–55, for relevant references.

19. For evolutionary accounts of gambling, see Peter B. Gray, "Evolutionary and Cross-Cultural Perspectives on Gambling," *Journal of Gambling Studies* 20, no. 4 (2004): 347–71; Marcello Spinella, "Evolutionary Mismatch, Neural Reward Circuits, and Pathological Gambling," *International Journal of Neuroscience* 113 (2003): 503–512.

20. *Bluff* Magazine/ESPN Power Poker Ratings, http://www.bluff magazine.com/players/ (accessed March 7, 2010).

21. Eric T. Steiner et al., "The Deal on Testosterone Responses to Poker Competition," *Current Psychology* 29 (2010): 45–51.

22. For a comparison of the personality traits of stock investors and gamblers, see Janice W. Jadlow and John C. Mowen, "Comparing the Traits of

Stock Market Investors and Gamblers," *Journal of Behavioral Finance* 11, no. 2 (2010): 67–81.

23. Peter Levin, "Gendering the Market: Temporality, Work, and Gender on a National Futures Exchange," *Work and Occupations* 28, no. 1 (2001): 112–30.

24. Anders Anderson, "All Guts, No Glory: Trading and Diversification among Online Investors," *European Financial Management* 13, no. 3 (2007): 448–71.

25. Brad M. Barber and Terrance Odean, "Online Investors: Do the Slow Die First?" *Review of Financial Studies* 15, no. 2 (2002): 455–87.

26. Richard T. Bliss and Mark E. Potter, "Mutual Fund Managers: Does Gender Matter?" *Journal of Business & Economic Studies* 8, no. 1 (2002): 1–15.

27. W. Bruce Canoles et al., "An Analysis of the Profiles and Motivations of Habitual Commodity Speculators," *Journal of Futures Markets* 18, no. 7 (1998): 765–801.

28. See Saad, *The Evolutionary Bases of Consumption*, p. 78, for relevant references.

29. John P. J. Pinel, *Biopsychology* (Boston: Allyn & Bacon, 2009), p. 6. For a slightly different version of the same story, see David M. Buss, *The Evolution of Desire: Strategies of Human Mating* (New York: Basic Books, 1994), pp. 79–80.

30. Fabio D'Orlando, "The Demand for Pornography," *Journal of Happiness Studies* (2010, in press), doi:10.1007/s10902-009-9175-0.

31. Julie M. Albright, "Sex in America Online: An Exploration of Sex, Marital Status, and Sexual Identity in Internet Sex Seeking and Its Impacts," *Journal of Sex Research* 45, no. 2 (2008): 175–86.

32. Steven E. Stern and Alysia D. Handel, "Sexuality and Mass Media: The Historical Context of Psychology's Reaction to Sexuality on the Internet," *Journal of Sex Research* 38, no. 4 (2001): 283–91.

33. Milton Diamond, "Pornography, Public Acceptance, and Sex Related Crime: A Review," *International Journal of Law and Psychiatry* 32, no. 5 (2009): 304–314.

34. Gert Martin Hald and Neil M. Malamuth, "Self-Perceived Effects of Pornography Consumption," *Archives of Sexual Behavior* 37, no. 4 (2008): 614–25.

35. Bruce J. Ellis and Donald Symons, "Sex Differences in Sexual Fantasy: An Evolutionary Psychological Approach," *Journal of Sex Research* 27, no. 4 (1990): 527–55.

36. Readers interested in reading more about pornography from an evolutionary perspective can refer to Donald Symons, *The Evolution of Human Sexuality* (New York: Oxford University Press, 1979); Joseph Shepher and Judith Reisman, "Pornography: A Sociobiological Attempt at Understanding," *Ethology and Sociobiology* 6 (1985): 103–114; Neil M. Malamuth, "Sexually Explicit Media, Gender Differences, and Evolutionary Theory," *Journal of Communication* 46 (1996): 8–31; and Saad, *The Evolutionary Bases of Consumption*, pp. 228–35.

37. Nicholas Pound, "Male Interest in Visual Cues of Sperm Competition Risk," *Evolution and Human Behavior* 23 (2002): 443–66.

38. Sarah J. Kilgallon and Leigh W. Simmons, "Image Content Influences Men's Semen Quality," *Biology Letters* 1 (2005): 253–55.

39. For a discussion of men's greater risk-taking proclivities across a wide range of contexts, see James P. Byrnes, David C. Miller, and William D. Schafer, "Gender Differences in Risk Taking: A Meta Analysis," *Psychological Bulletin* 125, no. 3 (1999): 367–83.

40. For an evolutionary account of male intrasexual competition, see Margo Wilson and Martin Daly, "Competitiveness, Risk Taking, and Violence: The Young Male Syndrome," *Ethology and Sociobiology* 6 (1985): 59–73.

41. Andreas De Block and Siegfried Dewitte, "Darwinism and the Cultural Evolution of Sports," *Perspectives in Biology and Medicine* 52, no. 1 (2009): 1–16.

42. International Spartathlon Association, http://www.spartathlon.gr/main.php (accessed November 14, 2009).

43. Hartmut Bielefeldt, "Mount Everest—Some Aspects of the Climbing Statistics," http://www.bielefeldt.de/everestse.htm (accessed April 25, 2010).

44. *Wikipedia,* "Eight-thousander," http://en.wikipedia.org/wiki/Eight-thousanders (accessed April 25, 2010).

45. Splatula Rigging, "BASE Fatality List," http://www.splatula.com/bfl/ (accessed November 14, 2009).

46. See US Bureau of Labor Statistics, "Census of Fatal Occupational

Injuries (CFOI)—Current and Revised Data," http://www.bls.gov/iif/ oshcfoi1.htm (accessed November 21, 2009).

47. Alex Robinson, *Bahia: The Heart of Brazil's Northeast* (Bucks, UK: Bradt Travel Guides, 2010), p. 13.

48. Mustafa B. Ibrahim, "Fulani—A Nomadic Tribe in Northern Nigeria," *African Affairs* 65, no. 259 (1966): 171–72; Pat I. Ndukwe, *The Fulani* (New York: Rosen, 1996), pp. 27–30.

49. Martin Riesebrodt, *Pious Passion: The Emergence of Modern Fundamentalism in the United States and Iran* (Berkeley: University of California Press, 1993), p. 161.

50. Stephen Kinzer, *Crescent and Star: Turkey between Two Worlds* (New York: Farrar, Straus and Giroux, 2002), pp. 180–81; Thomas A. Green and Joseph R. Svinth, eds., *Martial Arts of the World: An Encyclopedia of History and Innovation* (Santa Barbara, CA: ABC-CLIO, 2010), pp. 85–87.

51. Steven Pinker, *The Blank Slate: The Modern Denial of Human Nature* (New York: Viking, 2002).

CHAPTER 10. DARWIN IN THE HALLS OF THE BUSINESS SCHOOL

1. Robin I. M. Dunbar, "Evolution and the Social Sciences," *History of the Human Sciences* 20, no. 2 (2007): 46.

2. Nigel Nicholson, "Evolutionary Psychology and Family Business: A New Synthesis for Theory, Research, and Practice," *Family Business Review* 21, no. 1 (2008): 103–118; Nigel Nicholson, *Executive Instinct: Managing the Human Animal in the Information Age* (New York: Crown Business, 2000); Stephen M. Colarelli, *No Best Way: An Evolutionary Perspective on Human Resource Management* (Westport, CT: Praeger, 2003); Sabrina Deutsch Salamon and Yuval Deutsch, "OCB as a Handicap: An Evolutionary Psychological Perspective," *Journal of Organizational Behavior* 27 (2006): 185–99; Mark Van Vugt, "Evolutionary Origins of Leadership and Followership," *Personality and Social Psychology Review* 10, no. 4 (2006): 354–71; Kingsley R. Browne, "Sex, Power, and Dominance: The Evolutionary Psychology of Sexual Harassment," *Managerial and Decision Economics* 27, nos. 2–3 (2006):

145–58; Tessaleno C. Devezas, "Evolutionary Theory of Technological Change: State-of-the-Art and New Approaches," *Technological Forecasting & Social Change* 72, no. 9 (2005): 1137–52; Philip R. P. Coelho, James E. McClure, and Enar Tunc, "Managing *Homo Sapiens*," *Total Quality Management* 15, no. 2 (2004): 191–204; Sudipta Basu and Gregory B. Waymire, "Recordkeeping and Human Evolution," *Accounting Horizons* 20, no. 3 (2006): 201–229; Andrew W. Lo, "Reconciling Efficient Markets with Behavioral Finance: The Adaptive Markets Hypothesis," *Journal of Investment Consulting* 7, no. 2 (2005): 21–44; Arthur E. Gandolfi, Anna Sachko Gandolfi, and David P. Barash, *Economics as An Evolutionary Science: From Utility to Fitness* (Piscataway, NJ: Transaction Publishers, 2002); Ned Kock, "Information Systems Theorizing Based on Evolutionary Psychology: An Interdisciplinary Review and Theory Integration Framework," *MIS Quarterly* 33, no. 2 (2009): 395–418; David M. Wasieleski and Sefa Hayibor, "Evolutionary Psychology and Business Ethics Research," *Business Ethics Quarterly* 19, no. 4 (2009): 587–616. For many additional references at the intersection of evolutionary psychology and business-related settings, see also the introductory chapter of my forthcoming edited book titled *Evolutionary Psychology in the Business Sciences* (Heidelberg, Germany: Springer, 2011).

3. Dan Ariely and Gregory S. Berns, "Neuromarketing: The Hope and Hype of Neuroimaging in Business," *Nature Reviews Neuroscience* 11 (2010): 284–92.

4. Justin R. Garcia and Gad Saad, "Evolutionary Neuromarketing: Darwinizing the Neuroimaging Paradigm for Consumer Behavior," *Journal of Consumer Behaviour* 7 (2008): 397–414.

5. Leonid Rozenblit and Frank Keil, "The Misunderstood Limits of Folk Science: An Illusion of Explanatory Depth," *Cognitive Science* 26 (2002): 521–62.

6. This mythical species exists solely in the deep recesses of classical economists' minds. Specifically, it is a framework that imposes very rigid and unrealistic standards for what constitutes rational decision making.

7. For a broad overview of this research stream, see Thomas Gilovich, Dale Griffin, and Daniel Kahneman, eds., *Heuristics and Biases: The Psychology of Intuitive Judgment* (Cambridge: Cambridge University Press, 2002).

8. Amos Tversky, "Intransitivity of Preferences," *Psychological Review* 76 (1969): 31–48.

9. Jonathan B. Berk, Eric Hughson, and Kirk Vandezande, "The Price Is Right, but Are the Bids? An Investigation of Rational Decision Theory," *American Economic Review* 86, no. 4 (1996): 954–70; Thierry Post et al., "Deal or No Deal? Decision Making under Risk in a Large-Payoff Game Show," *American Economic Review* 98, no. 1 (2008): 38–71.

10. Satoshi Kanazawa, "Predictably Irrational, Yes; Explainably Irrational, No I," October 11, 2009, http://www.psychologytoday.com/blog/the-scientific -fundamentalist/200910/predictably-irrational-yes-explainably-irrational-no-i.

11. Gad Saad and Tripat Gill, "Sex Differences in the Ultimatum Game: An Evolutionary Psychology Perspective," *Journal of Bioeconomics* 3, nos. 2–3 (2001): 171–93; Gad Saad and Tripat Gill, "The Effects of a Recipient's Gender in the Modified Dictator Game," *Applied Economics Letters* 8, no. 7 (2001): 463–66.

12. This was the exact problem that I tackled in my doctoral dissertation, "The Adaptive Use of Stopping Policies in Sequential Consumer Choice" (doctoral diss., Cornell University, Ithaca, NY, 1994). See also Gad Saad and J. Edward Russo, "Stopping Criteria in Sequential Choice," *Organizational Behavior and Human Decision Processes* 67, no. 3 (1996): 258–70.

13. Gad Saad, Aliza Eba, and Richard Sejean, "Sex Differences When Searching for a Mate: A Process-Tracing Approach," *Journal of Behavioral Decision Making* 22, no. 2 (2009): 171–90.

14. Gerd Gigerenzer, *Adaptive Thinking: Rationality in the Real World* (New York: Oxford University Press, 2000).

15. Daniel G. Goldstein and Gerg Gigerenzer, "The Recognition Heuristic: How Ignorance Makes Us Smart," in *Simple Heuristics That Make Us Smart*, ed. Gerd Gigerenzer, Peter M. Todd, and the ABC Research Group (New York: Oxford University Press, 1999), pp. 37–58.

16. Douglas T. Kenrick et al., "Deep Rationality: The Evolutionary Economics of Decision Making," *Social Cognition* 27, no. 5 (2009): 764–85.

17. John M. Coates and Joe Herbert, "Endogenous Steroids and Financial Risk Taking on a London Trading Floor," *Proceedings of the National Academy of Sciences of the United States of America* 105, no. 16 (2008): 6167–72.

18. John M. Coates, Mark Gurnell, and Aldo Rustichini, "Second-to-Fourth Digit Ratio Predicts Success among High-Frequency Financial Traders," *Proceedings of the National Academy of Sciences of the United States of America* 106, no. 2 (2009): 623–28.

19. Paola Sapienza, Luigi Zingales, and Dario Maestripieri, "Gender Differences in Financial Risk Aversion and Career Choices Are Affected by Testosterone," *Proceedings of the National Academy of Sciences of the United States of America* 106, no. 36 (2009): 15268–73.

20. Eric Stenstrom et al., "Testosterone and Domain-Specific Risk: Digit Ratios (2D:4D and *rel*2) as Predictors of Recreational, Financial, and Social Risk-Taking Behaviors," *Personality and Individual Differences* (2010, in press), doi:10.1016/j.paid.2010.07.003.

21. Roderick E. White, Stewart Thornhill, and Elizabeth Hampson, "Entrepreneurs and Evolutionary Biology: The Relationship between Testosterone and New Venture Creation," *Organizational Behavior and Human Decision Processes* 100 (2006): 21–34.

22. For a review of studies on sex differences in the propensity to commit ethical breaches, see Denis Collins, "The Quest to Improve the Human Condition: The First 1500 Articles Published in *Journal of Business Ethics*," *Journal of Business Ethics* 26, no. 1 (2000): 1–73.

23. Irwin W. Silverman, "Gender Differences in Delay of Gratification: A Meta-Analysis," *Sex Roles* 49, nos. 9–10 (2003): 451–63.

24. For an evolutionary account of future discounting, see Martin Daly and Margo Wilson, "Carpe Diem: Adaptation and Devaluing the Future," *Quarterly Review of Biology* 80 (2005): 55–60.

25. Margo Wilson and Martin Daly, "Do Pretty Women Inspire Men to Discount the Future?" *Proceedings of the Royal Society of London: Series B (Suppl.)* 271 (2004): S177–79; Bram Van den Bergh, Siegfried Dewitte, and Luk Warlop, "Bikinis Instigate Generalized Impatience in Intertemporal Choice," *Journal of Consumer Research* 35 (2008): 85–97.

26. Xiao-Tian Wang and Robert D. Dvorak, "Sweet Future: Fluctuating Blood Glucose Levels Affect Future Discounting," *Psychological Science* 21, no. 2 (2010): 183–88.

27. Marc F. Luxen and Fons J. R. Van De Vijver, "Facial Attractiveness,

Sexual Selection, and Personnel Selection: When Evolved Preferences Matter," *Journal of Organizational Behavior* 27 (2006): 241–55.

28. John Kenneth Galbraith, *A Contemporary Guide to Economics, Peace, and Laughter* (Boston: Houghton Mifflin, 1971), p. 50.

29. Daniel S. Hamermesh and Jeff E. Biddle, "Beauty and the Labor Market," *American Economic Review* 84, no. 5 (1994): 1174–94.

30. Irene Hanson Frieze, Josephine E. Olson, and June Russell, "Attractiveness and Income for Men and Women in Management," *Journal of Applied Social Psychology* 21, no. 13 (1991): 1039–1057.

31. Jeff E. Biddle and Daniel S. Hamermesh, "Beauty, Productivity, and Discrimination: Lawyers' Looks and Lucre," *Journal of Labor Economics* 16, no. 1 (1998): 172–201.

32. David J. Berri, "Do Pretty-Boy Quarterbacks Make More Money?" *New York Times*, September 16, 2008, http://www.nytimes.com/2008/09/14/sports/playmagazine/0914play-FBALL-QBS.html (accessed February 27, 2010).

33. Todd C. Riniolo et al., "Hot or Not: Do Professors Perceived as Physically Attractive Receive Higher Student Evaluations?" *Journal of General Psychology* 133, no. 1 (2006): 19–35.

34. Michael Lynn, "Determinants and Consequences of Female Attractiveness and Sexiness: Realistic Tests with Restaurant Waitresses," *Archives of Sexual Behavior* 38, no. 5 (2009): 737–45.

35. See, for example, Timothy A. Judge and Daniel M. Cable, "The Effect of Physical Height on Workplace Success and Income: Preliminary Test of a Theoretical Model," *Journal of Applied Psychology* 89, no. 3 (2004): 428–41.

36. Steven Pinker, *How the Mind Works* (New York: Norton, 1997), pp. 495–96.

37. John Antonakis and Olaf Dalgas, "Predicting Elections: Child's Play!" *Science* 323, no. 5918 (2009): 1183.

38. Nicholas O. Rule and Nalini Ambady, "The Face of Success: Inferences from Chief Executive Officers' Appearance Predict Company Profits," *Psychological Science* 19, no. 2 (2008): 109–111.

39. Nicholas O. Rule and Nalini Ambady, "She's Got the Look: Inferences from Female Chief Executive Officers' Faces Predict Their Success," *Sex Roles* 61, nos. 9–10 (2009): 644–52.

40. Ulrich Mueller and Allan Mazur, "Facial Dominance of West Point Cadets as a Predictor of Later Military Rank," *Social Forces* 74, no. 3 (1996): 823–50.

41. John T. Manning and Rogan P. Taylor, "Second to Fourth Digit Ratio and Male Ability in Sport: Implications for Sexual Selection in Humans," *Evolution and Human Behavior* 22 (2001): 61–69.

42. Justin M. Carré and Cheryl M. McCormick, "In Your Face: Facial Metrics Predict Aggressive Behaviour in the Laboratory and in Varsity and Professional Hockey Players," *Proceedings of the Royal Society: Series B, Biological Sciences* 275 (2008): 2651–56.

43. See, for example, James Q. Wilson and Richard J. Herrnstein, *Crime & Human Nature: The Definitive Study of the Causes of Crime* (New York: Free Press, 1985), for relevant references.

45. Geoffrey Miller, *Spent: Sex, Evolution, and Consumer Behavior* (New York: Viking Adult, 2009).

46. See, for example, Sam Gosling, *Snoop: What Your Stuff Says about You* (New York: Basic Books, 2008).

47. Georg W. Alpers and Antje B. M. Gerdes, "Another Look at 'Look-Alikes': Can Judges Match Belongings with Their Owners?" *Journal of Individual Differences* 27, no. 1 (2006): 38–41.

48. Sonja Windhager et al., "Face to Face: The Perception of Automotive Designs," *Human Nature* 19, no. 4 (2008): 331–46; see table 2, p. 336.

49. For nonevolutionary reasons that might drive the human desire to anthropomorphize, see Stewart Elliott Guthrie, *Faces in the Clouds: A New Theory of Religion* (New York: Oxford University Press, 1993). For conditions that either help or hinder product evaluations when anthropomorphism is used by marketers, see Pankaj Aggarwal and Ann L. McGill, "Is That Car Smiling at Me? Schema Congruity as a Basis for Evaluating Anthropomorphized Products," *Journal of Consumer Research* 34, no. 4 (2007): 468–79.

40. Barry L. Bayus, Gary Erickson, and Robert Jacobson, "The Financial Rewards of New Product Introductions in the Personal Computer Industry," *Management Science* 49, no. 2 (2003): 197–210.

50. Genetic drift is another evolutionary mechanism even though it is not driven by selection, and therefore cannot be construed as an "innovation" in the context of the current discussion.

51. Janine B. Benyus, *Biomimicry: Innovation Inspired by Nature* (New York: HarperCollins, 1997).

52. See the related concept of Darwinian agriculture: R. Ford Denison, E. Toby Kiers, and Stuart A. West, "Darwinian Agriculture: When Can Humans Find Solutions Beyond the Reach of Natural Selection?" *Quarterly Review of Biology* 78, no. 2 (2003): 145–68.

53. Many of these examples are discussed in greater detail in Yoseph Bar-Cohen, "Biomimetics—Using Nature to Inspire Human Innovation," *Bioinspiration & Biomimetics* 1, no. 1 (2006), P1–P12.

54. For a compelling evolutionary-informed analysis of our poor ecological footprint, see Dustin J. Penn, "The Evolutionary Roots of Our Environmental Problems: Toward a Darwinian Ecology," *Quarterly Review of Biology* 78, no. 3 (2003): 275–301.

55. The original formulation of this phenomenon, which is expressed slightly differently than my description here, was proposed by Garrett Hardin in "The Tragedy of the Commons," *Science* 162, no. 3859 (1968): 1243–48.

56. Steven R. Feldman et al., "Implications of a Utility Model for Ultraviolet Exposure Behavior," *Journal of the American Academy of Dermatology* 45, no. 5 (2001): 718–22.

57. For a discussion of the nexus between sustainable consumption and evolutionary psychology, see Tim Jackson, "Live Better by Consuming Less? Is There a 'Double Dividend' in Sustainable Consumption?" *Journal of Industrial Ecology* 9, nos. 1–2 (2005): 19–36.

CHAPTER 11. CONCLUDING REMARKS

1. J. B. S. Haldane, "The Truth about Death," *Journal of Genetics* 58:464.

2. For sobering figures regarding the nonacceptance of evolutionary theory among members of the American populace, see Allan Mazur, "Believers and Disbelievers in Evolution," *Politics and the Life Sciences* 23 (2005): 55–61. For a global perspective, see Jon D. Miller, Eugenie C. Scott, and Shinji Okamoto, "Public Acceptance of Evolution," *Science* 313, no. 5788 (2006): 765–66.

3. Gad Saad, *The Evolutionary Bases of Consumption* (Mahwah, NJ: Lawrence Erlbaum, 2007), chap. 7; Gad Saad, "The Collective Amnesia of Marketing Scholars regarding Consumers' Biological and Evolutionary Roots," *Marketing Theory* 8 (2008): 425–48.

4. Robin I. M. Dunbar, "Evolution and the Social Sciences," *History of the Human Sciences* 20, no. 2 (2007): 46.

5. Karl R. Popper, *Conjectures and Refutations: The Growth of Scientific Knowledge* (New York: Routledge and Kegan Paul, 1963), p. 88.

6. See, for example, the National Academies Keck Futures Initiative; see also the report by the National Academies Committee on Science, Engineering, and Public Policy, "Facilitating Interdisciplinary Research" (Washington, DC: US National Academies, 2005).

7. *Magnetic Resonance Imaging*, journal description, http://www .elsevier.com/wps/find/journaldescription.cws_home/525478/description #description (accessed August 1, 2010).

8. Gad Saad, "The Future of Evolutionary Psychology Is Bright," *Futures* (2011, forthcoming), table 1.

9. For a discussion of the broad relevance of evolutionary theory, see David Sloan Wilson, *Evolution for Everyone: How Darwin's Theory Can Change the Way We Think about Our Lives* (New York: Delacorte Press, 2007).

SUBJECT INDEX

acceptance of a scientific theory,
     stages prior to the, 287–88
     nonacceptance of evolutionary
          theory, 287
     as relating to my career, 288
actors/actresses
     Abraham, F. Murray, 185
     Affleck, Ben, 270
     Bacon, Kevin, 145
     Bauer, Steven, 241
     Berry, Halle, 242, 243
     Bullock, Sandra, 172
     Cruise, Tom, 31, 84
     Cusack, John, 116
     Danson, Ted, 163
     David, Keith, 185
     David, Larry, 100, 163
     Davis, Bette, 172
     De Niro, Robert, 63, 101
     Diesel, Vin, 270
     Douglas, Michael, 270
     Dressler, Marie, 172
     Franken, Al, 223
     Freeman, Morgan, 233
     Garland, Judy, 172

Garlin, Jeff, 100
Garner, Jennifer, 208
Gaynor, Janet, 172
Gertz, Jami, 170
Gervais, Ricky, 208, 209
Gibson, Mel, 166, 205
Gold, Tracey, 236
Grant, Hugh, 242
Harrelson, Woody, 171
Haysbert, Dennis, 185
Holmes, Katie, 31, 84
Hurley, Elizabeth, 242
Jackman, Hugh, 243
James, Kevin, 159
Johansson, Scarlett, 88, 220
Jones, James Earl, 185, 186
Judd, Ashley, 243
Kaufman, Andy, 219
Kidman, Nicole, 31, 84
Kinnear, Greg, 243
Kutcher, Ashton, 32
Lane, Diane, 116
Law, Jude, 242
LeBrock, Kelly, 88
Lewis, Richard, 100

Lohan, Lindsay, 166

Long, Nia, 270

Lopez, Jennifer, 80

McCarthy, Jenny, 20

Meunier, Claude (French-
    Canadian), 196

Miller, Sienna, 242

Monroe, Marilyn, 67, 77, 81

Moore, Demi, 32, 171

Mortensen, Viggo, 139

Murphy, Eddie, 242

Myers, Mike, 239

Pacino, Al, 241

Paltrow, Gwyneth, 233

Pitt, Brad, 225, 233

Piven, Jeremy, 170

Radner, Gilda, 88

Redford, Robert, 171

Reilly, John C., 223

Remini, Leah, 159, 161

Ribisi, Giovanni, 243, 270

Ritter, John, 113

Rock, Chris, 32

Scott, Seann William, 223

Seyfried, Amanda, 172

Sheen, Charlie, 270

Sheridan, Ann, 172

Stiller, Ben, 101

Stiller, Jerry, 159

Swayze, Patrick, 166

Tomei, Marisa, 23

Wilder, Gene, 88

Willis, Bruce, 243

Winfield, Paul, 185

Adams, Scott, 231

adaptation versus exaptation (evolu-
    tionary by-product), 151

adaptation versus standardization. *See*
    advertising, local versus global debate

adolescence
    age of obnoxiousness (*Sin il
        ch'lout*), 113
    daughters' revealing clothes,
        113–14
    and need to belong, 194
    parent-child conflicts in, 113

advertising
    ad executions, 188
    language mishaps in, 199–201
    local versus global debate, 35,
        177–81, 186–87
        EP as the integrative frame-
            work for the local-global
            debate, 179, 181
        local approach in Quebec,
            196
        practitioners versus acade-
            mics, 178–79
    measuring its effectiveness,
        181–82
    message complexity, 189–90
    objectives of, 181
    repetition effects, 187
    scarcity appeal (mating) versus
        social proofing (survival),
        195–96
    string length, 188, 189–90
    use of animals, 184

use of facially symmetric
  endorsers, 179, 193
use of fear appeals, 183, 190,
  191, 260
use of need to belong appeals,
  194
use of sexual imagery, 35, 192
use of universal images of beauty,
  35
use of various fitness-related
  cues, 193–94
Advertising Age, 77
advertising slogans, 77, 87, 96–97,
  129–30, 170
Agenda, Inc., 156
AIG financial debacle, 271
Albright, Julie M., 245
alcohol effect, 157–58
alliance hypothesis, 123
  nonkin coalitions, 123
  reciprocal alliances, 144
all-you-can-eat buffets, 50–51
Ambady, Nalini, 276
amenorrhea, 237
American Brandstand, 156
American Commodities Exchange,
  240
amygdala, 260
Anderson, Norman H., 188
animal architects, 64
animal communication, 164
animal cruelty, 115, 191
animals
  African wild dogs, 95

alligator snapping turtle, 91
antelopes, 75
apes, 95
Atlantic salmon, 95
baboons (female), 90
black widow spider, 75
bowerbird, 76
  Great and Vogelkop Gar-
    dener, 70
camels, 61
cassowaries, 29
cheetahs, 118
chimpanzees, 75, 149
cleaner fish, 115
crabs, 282
crocodiles, 164
cuckoo bird, 116
dogs, 33, 35, 115, 116, 117–18,
  144
eagles, 26
elephants, 95, 182, 270
elks (male), 270
gecko, 35
gelada baboons, 164
  male, 199
grizzly bear, 41–42, 43
ground squirrels, 95
hummingbird, 41
hyenas, 95, 107
lions, 95, 109, 118
mollusk, 282
monitor lizards, 26
monkeys, 95
  rhesus and vervet, 104

mosquitoes, 62

octopus, 282

oxpecker bird, 115

peacock, 67

polar bears, 61

praying mantis, 75

rams, 68

red-capped manakin, 69

red-crowned crane, 69

roosters, 244

sand tiger sharks, 107

silver foxes, 106

sloth, 41

snakes, 191

social ants, 95, 164

spiders, 35, 191, 282

    tarantula, 26

squirrels, 182

vampire bats, 122

wild turkeys, 95

wolves, 117, 164

zebras, 26, 115, 209

animals and children's products, 117

animism, 278, 279

anthropomorphism, 117, 278, 279, 280

anthrozoology, 116

anti-biology movements, 19–22

antievolution concerns (and rebuttals), 22–32

antimicrobial hypothesis, 46, 47

aposematic warnings (colors), 91

Arabic culture, 126, 127, 134, 135, 207–208

Archer, John, 116

Ariely, Dan, 260–61, 262, 263–64

artificial selection, 105, 106

    of dog breeds, 106

    of silver foxes, 106

    of wolves, 117

Aryan Brotherhood, 140

Ashley Madison (company), 225

    short-term mating encounters, 225

Association for Consumer Research, 291

astrology, 211

atheism, 30, 126, 204, 216

    and the American presidency, 205

    and evolutionary theory, 29

    four horsemen of atheism, 204

Atkins diet, 42–43

autism, 20

Axe effect, 80–81, 184

Barber, Nigel, 86

Barrett-Jackson auctions (luxury cars), 72

bar's closing time (and mate preferences), 157

basking in reflected glory, 141

Bata Shoe Museum, 85

beautification, culture-specific forms of

    facial tattooing, 222

    foot binding, 222

    lip plating, 221–22

    neck elongation, 222

    scarification, 222

beautification ritual (males)
 signal high status, 222
beauty
 cultural products and female
  beauty, 221
 infants recognize it, 221
 men's brains and female beauty,
  221
 as a social construction, 219–20,
  222
 universal metrics of, 221
beauty effect (in the labor market),
 257, 274–75, 276
beauty myth, the, 220–21
behavioral decision theory, 263, 264
Beirut International Airport, 124
Belyaev, Dmitri K., 106
Benyus, Janine B., 282
Berlyne, Daniel E., 187, 190
Bernbach, William, 177
Berns, Gregory S., 260–61, 262
Betzig, Laura, 174–75
blank slate (the mind as a), 19, 27,
 36, 203, 204
Bible, the, 107, 205, 209, 213
Billing, Jennifer, 46
biological (genetic) determinism,
 23–24, 25, 114, 244
 and marketers, 25
biomimicry, 35, 291
 examples of, 282–83
biophilia, 38–39, 61, 62, 76, 283
 is advantageous
  in company settings, 63

 in hospitals, 63
 in retail stores, 63
 and commercial spaces, 65
 and interior design, 65
 and love of animals, 184
 and urban/architectural design,
  63–64
"birds of a feather flock together," 79,
 119
 eHarmony, 119
 "opposites attract," 119
birth order, 107
 and athletic risk taking, 108
 and career choices, 108
 and consumer conformity, 108
 and early adopters of product
  innovations, 36, 108
 and life paths, 108
 and personality, 107
 and radical scientific innovations, 107
body modifications, 139
body odors
 and the consumption of meat,
  81
 and the major histocompatibility complex, 80
Bonaparte, Napoleon, 78, 220
Bond, James (movie character), 77,
 238–39
Bostwick, Kimberley, 69
bower, 70
Boyd, Brian, 173
Boyer, Pascal, 151

brand communities, 145–46
    Harley-Davidson, 145
    Macintosh, 146
Bronze Age, 47, 48, 169, 206
Brown, William M., 69
bukkake films (porn), 249
business school, history of the, 258–59
    current business ethos (do no
        harm), 259
    customer-centric ethos, 258
    production ethos, 258
Buss, David, 159
Byrne, Rhonda, 227

Cacioppo, John T., 144–45
California, living in, 132–34
caloric foods, 36, 42, 59, 66
caloric scarcity/uncertainty, 42,
    50–51, 66, 122, 193
Cameron, Elissa Z., 113
Camp David Accords, 132
Canal Street (New York City),
    92–93
car brands
    Aston Martin, 70, 71
    Bentley Continental GT, 73
    Bugatti, 70
    Dodge Neon, 74
    Duesenberg, 70
    Ferrari, 33, 71, 93, 293
    Fort Fiesta ST, 73
    Maybach, 70
    Mercedes, 12, 72, 73
    Porsche, 33, 68, 71
    Rolls Royce, 154
    Toyota, 71
    Volkswagen Jetta, 74
car collectors, 72
    Astor, Art, 72
    Beckham, David, 72
    Kay, Jay, 72
    Lauren, Ralph, 72
    Leno, Jay, 72
    McMullen, John, 72
    Seinfeld, Jerry, 72
    Sultan of Brunei, 72
    Winfrey, Oprah, 72
car status
    and flashing of headlights, 74
    and honking, 74
    and perceived physical attrac-
        tiveness of men, 73–74
cars as peacocking (sexual signals),
    70–72
car-with-owner matching, 279
Carroll, Joseph, 173
cattle genes, 50
celebrities (non-actors and non-
    singers)
    Baryshnikov, Mikhail, 69
    Brinkley, Christie, 242
    Carpenter, John (director), 279
    Chamberlain, Wilt, 224–25
    Chyna (wrestler), 32
    Edwards, John, 166
    Gore, Tipper, 37, 246
    Hilton, Paris, 128
    Jordan, Michael, 166

Kennedy Jr., John F., 161
Lyman, Will, 185
Millan, Cesar (dog whisperer), 117
Ramsay, Gordon (chef), 54
Rivers, Joan, 137
Robbins, Anthony (life coach), 228
Warhol, Andy, 43
Winfrey, Oprah, 32, 72, 153
Woods, Tiger, 32, 166, 243, 283
celestial dictator, 216. *See also* God
Cerruto, Maria Angela, 84
cheating
    greater recall of faces of social cheaters, 182
    keeping tabs on social, 128
    on social contracts, 134
childhood vaccinations, 20
Chomsky, Noam, 180
Christakis, Nicholas A., 145
Christian Science faith, 217
Christianity, 123, 124, 126, 207
Cialdini, Bob, 141
Cinderella effect, 109
    stepfather and child abuse, 109
circumcision, 21
Cleopatra, 86, 241
clothes
    men's perceived attractiveness and, 85
    as sexual signals, 84
    women's willingness to initiate a relationship based on a man's, 85

coalitional psychology, 135–37
    in brand communities, 145–46
    in religion, 207–208
    in religious-based affinity scams, 212
    in sports competitions, 142
    in sports viewing, 141
Coates, John, 270
cognitive-behavior therapy, 234
cognitive dissonance, 232–33
collusions, 283–84
color connotations, 197–99
    color idioms, 197–98
    colors and gender socialization, 197
    colors and holidays, 197
    colors and luxury sports cars, 199, 293
    company colors, 197, 198
    local versus global elements of color, 197
    universal components of color, 198
comfort foods, 55, 56
company rumors (disgust-related), 59–60
complementary and alternative medicine, 217
compulsive buying, 81, 234–36
    beautification products are hoarded, 235–36
    domain-general, 235
    greater fashion interest (of sufferers), 235

Concordia University Research
   Chair in Evolutionary Behavioral
   Sciences and Darwinian Consumption, 292
congenital adrenal hyperplasia,
   103–104
consilience (unity of knowledge),
   289–90, 292, 293
      evolutionary theory as an orga-
         nizing framework of consumer
         behavior, 28
consuming instinct, 17, 25, 39, 261,
   284, 292, 293
consumption (definition), 12
content analysis of,
      gripping news stories, 167
      literary narratives, 173
      Old Testament, the, 174–75
      pornography, 249
      soap operas, 167–68
      titles of *Harlequin* romance
         novels, 174
conspicuous consumption, 33, 68,
   70, 71–72, 169–70
consumer decisions (everyday),
   11–12
Coolidge, Calvin, 244
Coolidge Effect, 224–25, 243–44
Cornell University, 16, 127, 131
corset, 85
cortisol
      and financial trading, 270
      and market volatility, 270
cosmetic companies, 34, 203, 220

advertised selling points and
   slogans, 87
cosmetics, 86–87
   and approaches at a bar, 87
   and attractiveness, 87
   and cues of sexual arousal, 87
   and facial luminance, 87
   and health, 87
   historical use of, 86
   and personality, 87
   and powerful women (used by),
      86
         Albright, Madeleine, 86
         Bhutto, Benazir, 86
         Cleopatra, 86
         Clinton, Hillary, 86
         Merkel, Angela, 86
         Queen Elizabeth II, 86
         Rice, Condoleezza, 86
   and symmetry, 87
   and waitresses' tips, 87
   and youthful appearance, 87
cost-benefit framework (for search),
   267
costly signaling, 70. *See also* handicap
   principle and honest signaling
      in movies, 170
      philanthropy as a form of,
         162–63
      in songs, 156
Cox, Anthony, 174
creationism, 29
Crisp, Quentin, 138
Cronk, Lee, 77–78, 113

cuckoldry, 16, 112, 116
    in movies, 171
    on a talk show, 171
cultural products
    as adaptations, 150–51
    content analysis of, 150, 152
    as cultural remains, 150, 177
    as exaptations (by-products), 151
    as fossils of the human mind,
        150, 177
    as sexual signals, 151
    as speciation, 151–52
    as wasteful signals, 151
cultural relativism, 27, 290
cultural transmission as an evolved
    capacity (of the human mind), 145
culture-jamming organizations, 204
cutting off reflected failure, 141

Dalerum, Fredrik, 113
Daly, Martin, 16, 109
dancing, 69, 83
    and body symmetry, 69
    and boy bands, 69
    moonwalk dance move, 69
    and strippers, 83
    on television shows, 69
    wedding dance, 69
Darwin, Charles, 97
Darwinian gastronomy, 44–48
    culture-specific culinary prefer-
        ences/traditions, 45
    meat versus vegetable dishes, 46
    use of spices, 28, 45–47, 179

Darwinian meta-drives, 12, 17
    and headlines in newspapers,
        167
    and movie plotlines, 169
    and peddlers of hope, 204
    and self-help books, 223
    and sensational news, 167
    and soap opera themes, 168
Darwinian Niche Partitioning
    Hypothesis, 107
Dawkins, Richard, 29, 30, 59, 64,
    117, 174, 204, 206
deadly sins, 233, 270
    greed, 125, 204, 233, 264, 270
death wish, 250
De Beers Consolidated Mines, 77
deceptive signals
    to fake higher social status, 93
    in personal ads and online chats,
        93
    as a survival strategy, 91
    universality of sex-specific forms
        of, 93
    as used by men, 92
        counterfeit Rolex watch, 92
        fake diplomas from "corre-
            spondence universities,"
            92
        fake wedding bands, 92
        sham luxury items, 92
    as used by women, 92
        booty-pop "butt bra," 92
        breast padding, 92
        high heels, 92

plastic surgery, 92
push-up bras, 92
deconstructionism, 169, 173
deep voices, 36, 220
in advertising, 185–86
democracies (and peace), 130–31
Dennett, Daniel, 204
Descartes, René, 11
dessert effect, 52
de Vauvenargues, Marquis, 203
Diamond, Milton, 21, 245
diamonds, 77, 154
Dictator Game, 136–37, 264–65
men display generosity to
women, 265
Diekmann, Andreas, 74
dieting, 226–27
differential grandparental solicitude,
33, 110
differential parental solicitude, 109
diffusion of fads, 145
digit ratio (2D:4D), 36, 104,
270–71, 277
and athletic ability, 277
and financial career, 271
numerous effects, 277–78
and play behavior, 104
and risk taking proclivity, 271
and trading, 270–71
direct versus indirect fitness, 98
discounting future costs for immediate benefits, 38, 284
discounting rate, 273
and mating, 274

men's discounting rates and
women's photos, 273–74
and survival (glucose levels), 274
Dissanayake, Ellen, 151
Dixson, Barnaby J., 192–93
DNA, 14, 149
DNA paternity testing, 33, 171
attitudes toward hospital paternity testing, 111–12
dog breeds, 118
dogs (benefits to humans), 116
dominance hierarchies, 74, 141
dopamine, 235–36
D'Orlando, Fabio, 245
double standard (sexual), 113, 244
Dove Campaign for Real Beauty,
219–20
Dunbar, Robin, 101, 164, 257, 284,
290
Dunbar's number, 101, 134, 166, 284
on Facebook (number of
friends), 146
Dunham, Bria, 77–78
Dunn, Michael J., 73
Dutton, Dennis, 151

eating disorders, 37, 236–38
actresses (as patients), 236
gay men (as patients), 236
media images (as the cause of),
236–37
universality of sex-specificity
(female effect), 237
ecological footprint, 283–84, 285

Einstein, Mara, 203
Ekman, Paul, 200
Elliot, Andrew J., 88
Ellis, Albert, 231
Ellis, Bruce, 248
engagement rings, 68, 77
    amount spent on (as a function
        of mate quality), 77–78
entomophagy, 45
entrepreneurs, 19
    Bezos, Jeff, 19
    Branson, Richard, 19
    Gates, Bill, 19
    Glazer, Brian, 19
    Schultz, Howard, 19
erotica, 68, 247, 248
error management theory, 280
Estée Lauder, 85
estrogen, 18, 88, 276
ethics (in the business school cur-
    riculum), 272
ethology, 16, 105, 260
evolutionary architecture, 64
evolutionary arms race between the
    sexes, 92
evolutionary epistemology, 289
evolutionary psychologists (leading
    female), 23
    Cosmides, Leda, 23
    Fisher, Helen, 23
    Haselton, Martie, 23
    Lace, Ruth, 23
evolutionary psychology
    does not offer moral justifica-

tions for reprehensible acts,
    16, 30, 160, 244
domain-specificity, 17
key doctrines of, 16–18
predecessor Darwinian fields,
    16–17
evolutionary tree of life, 26, 149, 281
EvoS (Evolutionary Studies) pro-
    gram, 292
existential angst, 209, 211
extended phenotype, 65, 70
extreme sports, examples of, 251

facial features, 36, 278
    of cars, 279
    of CEOs and company profits,
        276
    goon's face, 277
    of military cadets and subse-
        quent promotions, 276–77
    of politicians and electoral suc-
        cess, 276
facial grimaces (universal), 200–201
    of disgust, 59
    Duchenne smile, 76
    non-Duchenne smile, 201
facial symmetry, 220, 221, 222, 269
    in advertising, 179, 193
    of CEOs, 276
    and cosmetics, 87
    fluctuating asymmetry, 79
    and olfaction, 79
    and ovulation, 90
    of quarterbacks, 276

Falsification Principle (Popper's),
219, 289
    falsification of evolutionary
        principles, 29, 31
    unfalsifiable just-so stories, 28
families, depicted in
    advertising slogans, 96–97
    literary narratives, 96
    movies, 96
    sitcoms, 96
family linguistic terms
    in the Greek system (fraterni-
        ties/sororities), 97
    in the military, 97
    in religion, 97
    in street vernacular, 97
fashion
    and changing cues of belonging-
        ness, 138–39
    as a cue of ethnic or religious
        belongingness, 139
    as a cue of social class member-
        ship, 139
    Fashion TV (channel), 137
    and herd mentality/imitation, 139
    as an icon of a time period, 139
    and individuality, 138
    and macro indicators, 172
    magazines, 137
    miniskirts, 85
    movies (related to), 137–38
    and need to belong, 138
    styles, 33, 138
    and teenagers, 138

television shows (examples of),
    137
    Ugg boots, 139
fashion trends (women's)
    and economic conditions (from
        an evolutionary perspective),
        86, 172
    and number of educated women,
        86
fast-food commercials, 37
fast-food restaurants, 36, 42, 59
    Burger King, 25, 42
    Domino's Pizza, 42
    Dunkin' Donuts, 42
    KFC, 42
    McDonald's, 25, 42, 85
    Pizza Hut, 42
    Starbucks, 42
    Subway, 42
    Taco Bell, 42
    Wendy's, 25, 42
Fatah (Palestinian militia), 124–25
father absence and daughters' sexual-
    ized clothing, 114
fear
    as an adaptation, 191
    freezing mechanism, 191
    triggers of, 191
Federal Trade Commission, 36
feminism, 21, 169, 172
Fershtman, Chaim, 136
Feynman, Richard, 228
financial fraudsters (business
    scandals)

Boesky, Ivan, 271
Ebbers, Bernard, 271
Kerviel, Jérôme, 271
Kozlowski, Dennis, 271
Lay, Kenneth, 271
Leeson, Nick, 271
Madoff, Bernard, 271, 272
Milken, Michael, 271
Nacchio, Joe, 271
Reyes, Gregory, 271
Rigas, John, 271
Rigas, Timothy, 271
Skilling, Jeffrey, 271
Stewart, Martha, 271
financial trading, 269
    male effect, 240–41
Fisher, Mary Frances Kennedy (food
    critic), 41
Fisher, Maryanne, 174
Flaubert, Gustave, 173
Flehmen response, 90
flowers, 75–77, 179
    offering flowers, 76, 77
    music at a flower shop, 76–77
food
    idioms, 44
    and life events, 43
    in paintings, 43
    themes in movies, 43–44
    themes on television shows, 43
food availability and amount eaten,
    57
Food and Drug Administration, 36,
    218, 219

food decisions (number of daily), 53
food disgust, 59–60
    disgust and the immune system,
    60
    product contagion and disgust,
    60
    universal triggers of disgust, 59
food foraging, 17, 41, 52, 182
food-for-sex exchange, 75, 116
food gorging/hoarding, 42, 57, 56, 58
Food Network (television channel),
    43
food preferences transmitted via,
    amniotic fluid, 44–45
    breastfeeding, 44–45
food sharing, 75, 122
Ford, Henry, 258, 281
Fortune magazine, 86, 276
401(k) retirement plans, 52
Fowler, James H., 145
framing effect, 265–67
    evaluating prospective mates,
    265–66
    as a function of mate quality, 266
Freudianism, 169, 172–73
friendships, 122, 123, 124, 125
    are Americans more shallow
    friends?, 131
    generosity toward friends,
    127–28
    between nation-states, 130–31
friendships, as depicted
    in company slogans/names,
    129–30

in movies, 129
in songs, 128
on television shows, 128
Functional Magnetic Resonance
    Imaging (fMRI), 193, 259, 261

gambling, 165, 166, 233, 238–39
    casinos
        and players' hunger, 274
        and scantily clad waitresses,
            274
        pathological gambling (male
            effect), 239
Galbraith, John Kenneth, 275
gangbangs (porn), 249
Gangestad, Steve, 79
Garcia, Justin, 261
Geerewol festival, 222
gene-centric view of evolution (selec-
    tion), 97, 98
gene-culture coevolution, 49–50
gene-culture interactions, 114,
    192–93, 195
        interactionism, 25
            cake metaphor, 24
        epigenetic mechanisms, 25
        epigenome, 25
gene polymorphisms, 49, 291
genetic relatedness (coefficient of),
    99
gift giving, 13–14, 76, 99–100, 101,
    102–103, 126, 197, 293
        cost versus thoughtfulness of a
            romantic gift, 78

to friends, 122–23
nuptial gift, 75, 77
Gilded Age, The, 70
Gill, Tripat, 99, 108, 122, 135, 264,
    265
Gilman, Charlotte Perkins, 21
Gneezy, Uri, 136
God, 29, 48, 62, 109–110, 206–207,
    211, 212, 214, 215, 216, 217, 219,
    228, 242
        and answering prayers, 210
        and men's sexual desires, 109–10
        natural disasters and belief in,
            207
Google, 259, 280
gossiping
    celebrity gossip, 165–66
    about friends, 165
    need to gossip, 163, 164
    about matters of evolutionary
        import, 164–65
    news as gossip, 167
    with relatives about wills and
        diseases, 165
    with same-sex individuals about
        sex-specific issues of evolu-
        tionary import, 165
    on and about soaps, 168
    about the vices of same-sex
        others, 165
Gottschall, Jonathan, 173
Gould, Stephen Jay, 29, 105
green living, 65
    recycling, 37

Green Prosperity Handkerchief, 212

Griskevicius, Vlad, 195

gustatory preferences, 25, 42

Haag, Richard, 62

Hachnasat orchim (welcoming of strangers), 127

hair length (woman's)
    and age, 89
    and health, 89
    and marital status, 89
    and no children, 89
    as a signal of phenotypic quality, 89

Haiti earthquake, 207

Haldane, J. B. S., 98, 287, 288

Hamilton, Bill, 97–98

handicap principle, 170. *See also* costly signaling and honest signaling

Harlequin, 174

Harris, Judith R., 227

Harris, Sam, 204

Harvard Study of Adult Development, 144

headlines/sensational news, 166–67

height, 31
    dating a taller woman (model), 186
    female preference for taller men, 84, 220
    in the labor market, 257, career success, 276
    men lie about (their), 93
    of politicians, 185, 276

preference for longer legs (both sexes), 82

Hemline Index, 85, 86

Herbert, Joe, 270

herd marketing, 146

herd mentality, 139, 194

high heels, 33, 72, 92
    brands, 83
        Christian Louboutin, 83
        Jimmy Choo, 83
        Manolo Blahnik, 83
    and buttocks, 82
    and economic conditions, 85
    and gait, 82–83
    and good sex, 84
    and height, 84
    and pelvic floor muscle activity, 84
    and physical attractiveness/femininity, 83
    and podiatric injuries, 83
    and sexuality, 82
    and strippers, 81–82
    as a tool of oppression, 83
    and women's body shape, 82

Hinduism, 126

Hippocrates, 237

Hitchens, Christopher, 29, 204, 216

Holiday Inn, 200

Holocaust, 206

Homer, 173

Homo consumericus, 14, 34, 269

Homo economicus, 188, 262, 263, 264, 268, 269

humans as cold calculational
   decision makers, 270
homology versus analogy,
   14–15
homosexuality, 21–22, 198, 236,
   246, 247, 249
   affair, 242
honest signaling, 37–38, 70, 151,
   170, 199. *See also* handicap principle and costly signaling
hooligans (soccer), 142
hope
   "Gift of Hope," 212
   import of hope in our daily lives,
      204
   marketing of hope, 20, 34
   message of hope, 220, 222
   need for hope, 229
   products of hope, 223
Horace, 11
horticultural therapy, 62
hospitality, 126–28
   as an insurance policy against
      hunger or thirst, 127
Hot or Not (website), 73
hourglass figure, 85, 192, 193. *See
   also* waist-to-hip ratio
*Human Behavior and Evolution
   Society*, 291
human genome, 150, 290–91
human universals, 27, 34, 173, 180,
   191, 194
hypertension, 48

illusion of explanatory depth
   (regarding neuroimaging), 261
immediate versus delayed gratification, 272, 273
inclusive fitness, 98, 116
infanticide, 109, 167
in-group/out-group, 124, 127, 135
   in behavioral economic games,
      136–37
   and empathy, 136
   as expressed via fashion, 137
   and pain, 135–36
   in religious-based affinity scams,
      212
   and sports viewing, 140–41
   us-versus-them, 140
individual differences (behavioral
   heterogeneity), 27
   and sociality of species, 118
individualism-collectivism, 179, 195
   as an adaptation to pathogenic
      density, 195
individual versus population-level
   data, 31, 32
information integration theory, 189
innovative companies, 280–81
insularity of marketing and consumer
   scholars, 291
Intelligent Design, 29
interdisciplinarity, 290–92
International AntiCounterfeiting
   Coalition, 93
International Spartathlon Association, 251

intertemporal choice, 273
intrasexual rivalry
    female, 86, 221, 238
        gossip, 165
        on looks, 275
    male, 68, 83, 156–57, 199, 254
        resources, 265
inventors, 281
    Babbage, Charles, 281
    Bell, Alexander, 281
    Edison, Thomas, 281
    Franklin, Benjamin, 281
    Gutenberg, Johannes, 281
    Wright Brothers, 281
inverted-U curve of,
    fear appeals, 190
    repetition effects, 187
Islam, 89, 115, 123, 124, 125, 126,
    207, 246
    Ashura Shi`ia ritual (self-flagel-
        lation), 254
    haram, 246
    hijab (head cover), 89, 139
    Taliban, the, 246
Israeli, 124, 135, 136, 207
    spies, 125

Japanese cuisine, 47
Jehovah's Witnesses, 217
Jews Offering New Alternatives to
    Homosexuality, 22
John Molson School of Business, 163
    Naming of a business school as a
        social signal, 163

Judaism, 123, 124, 125, 126, 127,
    135, 140, 196, 206–207
    Ashkenazi Jews, 136, 207
    bar mitzvah as conspicuous con-
        sumption, 170
    kippah, 139
    kosher foods, 45, 47, 48
    Sephardic Jews, 136–37, 207
    Talmudic edict (rabbis and
        beautiful women), 175
    Torah, 175
        and animals, 48

Kahn, Barbara, 51
Kahn, Herman, 231
Kahneman, Daniel, 262, 265
Kanazawa, Satoshi, 166, 263–64
"keeping up with the Joneses," 68,
    169
Kenrick, Doug, 269
kidnapping, of my parents, 124–25
Kilgallon, Sarah J., 250
kin (greater investments toward
    closer), 98–99
    in allocating gift expenditures, 99
    in allocating hypothetical lottery
        earnings, 98
    in the amount of physical pain
        willing to incur, 99
    in bequeathing of wills, 99
    in feeling greater affiliation, 99
    in helpfulness, 99
    in knowing whether family
        members are dead or alive, 99

in patterns of bereavement
(twins), 99

kin-based altruism across many
animal taxa, 95

kin selection, 97–100, 121, 123
and allomaternal care, 95
and gift giving, 99–100
and grandparenting, 110
and organ donations, 100
and parenting, 112, 227

kin versus nonkin (differential
investments toward), 98–99, 123
in higher education, 98

King Jr., Martin Luther, 225

King Kahekili (Maui), 253

Klinefelter's syndrome, 170–71

lactose tolerance, 49–50

landscape and habitat preferences,
61–62
in children, 61
manifested across different cultural products and designs, 62
savannalike habitats, 61

Lauder, Leonard, 85

law of attraction (new age), 228

Lebanon, 196
civil war, 123, 124
political system, 123–24

legal contracts, 132–33

lek/lekking, 71–72

leptin, 227

Levitt, Steven, 263

Lipstick Index, 85

literature, 172–75
literary criticism, 172
literary Darwinian criticism, 173

lordosis, 82

Lorenz, Konrad, 105

Lost Boys of the FLDS (Fundamentalist Church of Jesus Christ of
Latter Day Saints), 109

Louv, Richard, 63

Lucy (partial skeleton), 149

Lynn, Michael, 276

Maimonides, 163

major histocompatibility complex
(MHC), 79–80
and disassortative mating
("opposites attract"), 79–80

making bank (urban idiom), 155

maladaptive consumption, 36, 38,
233, 291
examples of, 232
irrationality, 231, 233, 255
sex-specificity of, 232

Manet, Édouard, 43

Marcos, Imelda (as a shoe collector),
81

Markwith, Maureen, 53

Martindale, Colin, 151

Marxism, 169, 172

Maslow, Abraham, 152

mass customization, 54

masturbation, 161, 214, 250

maternal diet and offspring sex ratio,
112

mate search, 267
  women more likely to reject
    short-term suitors, 267
mating
  finding one's perfect mate, 225
  mating as a compensatory
    choice, 226
  mating value, 225
  short-term versus long-term
    mating, 157
mating preferences (universals),
  152–53, 220
  intelligence and kindness: cru-
    cially important for both
    sexes, 153
  men place greater premium on
    youth and beauty, 153, 173,
    192, 236
  women place greater premium
    on high social status, 153, 162,
    173
Matti Kuusi International–type
  system of proverbs, 126
Mazur, Allan, 276–77
MBA (degree), 132, 271, 275
medical quackery, 217–19
  unfalsifiability of, 218, 219
meme, 59, 145, 216, 217
memory
  brand recall, 182
  greater recall of beautiful faces,
    182–83
  greater recall of evolutionarily
    memorable content (in ads), 183

greater recall of faces of social
  cheaters, 182
greater recall with a survival
  prime, 183
recall of food burial site, 182
menarche, 114, 237
Mendelian genetics, 97
men's desire for sexual variety
  and hair colorant, 90
  and wigs, 90
menstrual cycle, 33, 79
  and beautification, 91
  and consumer behavior, 68
  and eating disorders, 237
  and food preferences, desires,
    consumption, 58–59
  and iPhone applications, 91
  luteal phase, 91
  onset of, 114
  and preference for men's deep
    voices, 185–86
  and skin quality, 88
  and strippers' tips, 83
mesomorphic body types (and criminality), 277
Middle East, 47–48, 123, 125, 127,
  133, 135
militia, 123, 124, 125
Miller, Geoffrey, 151
Miller, Henry, 67
misfiring of adaptive processes, 166,
  232, 235, 238, 284
molecular phylogenetics, 149
Money, John, 21

money shot (climactic scene in a
porn film), 248–49, 250
Montreal, 56, 63, 70–72, 124, 133,
139, 182, 200, 246–47
mood, definitions of, 55
and emotional eating, 55
and how much food is eaten,
55–56
and which foods are craved, 56
morality, 29–30, 31, 224, 225, 233,
244, 250, 271
arbiter of morality and proper
behaviors, 246
more-is-less effect, 52–53
mortality/immortality, 30, 205, 209,
211, 217, 219, 224
Motion Picture Association of
America, 168
Mount Everest, 251
movies
list
American Crime, An, 109
Awakenings, 63
Boiler Room, 270
Cars, 279
Casino Royale, 239
Christine, 279
Diamonds Are Forever, 77
Eastern Promises, 139
Farinelli, 186
Footloose, 246
Gentlemen Prefer Blondes,
77
Hangover, The, 13

Indecent Proposal, 171
Invention of Lying, The,
208–209
Keeping Up with the Steins,
170
Kinky Boots, 82
Meet the Parents, 101
Must Love Dogs, 116
Passion of the Christ, The,
205
Perfect Stranger, 243
Promotion, The, 223
Scarface, 241
Se7en, 233
Someone Like You, 243
Star Wars, 185
Super Size Me, 56
Toy Story, 279
Wall Street, 270
Woman in Red, The, 88
regulation of, 37
movie plotlines, 168–72, 243
MRI (journal), 291
Mueller, Ulrich, 276
muscle dysmorphia (bigorexia), 236
music videos, 155–56
mutualism, 115–16

Nairne, James, 183
Nataraajan, Rajan, 108
National Association to Advance Fat
Acceptance, 226
fat admirers, 226
obesity epidemic, 227

National Association of Evangelicals, 242

National Association for Research and Therapy on Homosexuality, 22

National Hockey League, 255

National Science Foundation, 281

natural vistas, 62–63

naturalistic fallacy, 30

natural selection, 14, 17, 25, 35, 38, 41, 48, 67, 97, 105, 106, 219, 281, 292

nature
    health benefits of, 63
    as the most innovative force, 281
    as the ultimate designer of "product" solutions, 35, 282–83

Nature Deficit Disorder, 63

nature versus nurture, 15, 19, 24, 25

need for connectedness, 143, 145
    in dogs, 144
    in humans, 144
    for prisoners, 144

neoteny, 105, 184
    and facial features of actresses (and macro and social conditions), 172
    and Mickey Mouse, 105
    and pets, 117, 118
    and the teddy bear, 105

networks (examples of), 144
    human brain, 144
    human diseases (their genetic roots), 144

Internet, 144
    scientometry, 144
    sociometry, 144

neurobusiness, 259–62
    brain imaging paradigm, 260
    "buy button," 262
    neuro-disciplines (listed fields), 260
    neuroeconomics, 260
    neuromarketing, 260–61, 262
        evils of, 262
        usefulness of the neuroimaging paradigm, 260–61

new atheism movement, 29

Newport (Rhode Island) cliff walk, 69

New Thought Theology (new age), 228

Nielsen Company, 158

Niesta, Daniela, 88

Nobel Prize, 231, 262, 268

"noble savage," 254

Non-Overlapping Magisteria (NOMA principle), 29–30

nucleus accumbens, 221

Obama, Barack, 185, 194, 220

obsessive-compulsive disorder (OCD), 234–35
    contamination fears, 235
    hoarding, 234, 235
    intrusive thoughts, 234–35
    need for symmetry, 235
    sex-specificity of OCD, 234

Occam's razor, 48

occupational injuries and fatalities (mainly men), 252

Ohtsubo, Yohsuke, 47

Old Testament, 174–75

olfaction (in mating), 78–79, 80

Olympics, 199

omnivores versus herbivores, 52

online trading, 240

optimal distinctiveness theory, 140
   individuality versus conformity, 140
   need to belong versus need for uniqueness, 194, 195

order effects, 188–89

organ donations/kidney transplants, 100

organogenesis, 18, 58

orgasm (female), 225

O'Rourke, P. J., 72

Osteen, Joel, 205

ovulation
   and body smell, 90
   cryptic ovulation, 90
   estrus, 90, 109
   and facial and breast symmetry, 90
   and skin quality, 90

oxytocin (cuddling hormone), 134–35

Pacific Center for Sex and Society, 245

paleontology, 149

palmistry, 277

parental investment hypothesis, 28–29, 75, 113, 238, 244, 266, 267, 273

parenting styles/abilities, 227

Parman, Susan, 49

pastoral living, 50

paternal resemblance
   and adoptions, 112
   and a child's health, 111
   and investment in children, 111
   once a baby is born (ascribed), 111
   in utero (ascribed), 111

paternity uncertainty, 16, 99, 101–102, 110–12, 160
   and gift giving/attendance at weddings, 101
   maternal grandmothers and the survival of children, 110
   maternal versus paternal aunts, 102
   as a movie plotline, 172
   and seating arrangements at weddings, 101
   on soap operas, 167
   in songs, 155
   on a talk show, 171
   and wet-nursing, 102

patriarchal oppression, 89, 172, 220–21, 245, 247–48

Patrick, William, 144–45

Pavlovian conditioning, 183

Peiss, Kathy, 203

peoples (tribes)
   Bedouin, 126, 127
   Jaful Fulani (Nigeria), 253–54

Kareni and Padaung women
(Myanmar), 222

Maori men, 222

Niv and Yoruba women
(Nigeria), 222

Papua New Guinean men, 192,
222

Satere-Mawe people (Brazilian
Amazon), 253

Surma and Mursi women
(Ethiopia), 221

Wodaabe men (West Africa),
222

Pepsi-Cola, 194, 196

perfumes, 78–81

self-preferences of perfumes and
the major histocompatibility
complex, 33, 80

periodic table (chemistry), 289

Perot, Ross, 185

personality (from an evolutionary
perspective), 27–28

pet-owner resemblance, 118, 119

pet parasitism, 116–17

pets, 114–15

phenotypic quality, 69, 79, 89, 186

philanthropy

as a costly signal, 162–63

as a social signal of status, 163

phobias, 62

arachnophobia, 62

biophobia, 62

entomophobia, 62

ophidiophobia, 62

phrenology, 277

physical risk taking, 255

BASE jumping, 251–52

bullet ant sting (ritual), 253

bungee jumping, 252

cliff diving (La Quebrada), 253

dangerous jobs, 252

Kirkpinar oil wrestling (Turkey),
254

lele kawa (cliff diving), 253

matadors and bullfighters, 254

mixed martial arts, 254

mountain climbing, 251

N'Gol ritual, 252

reckless driving, 37–38

running with the bulls (Pam-
plona), 254

Shadi (Sharo) rite, 253–54

street gangs, 254

Picasso, Pablo, 151

Pinker, Steven, 151, 180

plastic surgery, 92, 193, 233, 239

Platek, Steven, 193

play (adaptive value of), 104–105

pleasure instinct, 18

pleiotropy, 106

poker, 239, 240

Bluff Magazine/ESPN Poker
Power Rankings, 240

male effect in professional poker,
240

poker professional players (women),
240

Liebert, Kathy, 240

Liu, Joanne (J. J.), 240
Rousso, Vanessa, 240
Selbst, Vanessa, 240
political leanings (of evolutionary psychologists), 23
polyandry, 249
polycystic ovary syndrome, 88
polygyny, 109, 111, 249
Ponzi scheme, 213, 271
Popper, Karl, 219, 290
pornography, 34, 37, 68, 166, 233, 245–50, 293
benefits of pornography, 246
as an early adopter of new technologies, 245
homosexual versus heterosexual porn, 247, 249–50
ideological debates regarding porn, 250
ill effects of pornography (or lack thereof), 245–46
as patriarchal oppression, 245
plotline of hard-core porn movies, 248
polygynous versus polyandrous depictions in porn movies, 249
pornographic addiction, 232, 233
portion size (food), 56–57
supersizing, 56
postmodernism, 169, 173, 290
Pound, Nicholas, 249
predator avoidance, 41, 122, 269
pregnancy sickness, 17–18, 58
primacy effect, 189, 275

product design, 291–92
product placements (in song lyrics), 156–57
products as public signals of our personhood, 278
prospect-refuge theory
and home designs, 61
and interior design, cafés, and restaurants, 65
and safety, 64
prosperity theology, 211
prostitutes, 242, 243
online female escorts, 192
proverbs, about
families, 95
friends, 121
hospitality, 126
proximate versus ultimate explanations, 17
ultimate causation of decision making, 263–64
Psychology Today, 86, 215, 263

quantum physics/mechanics, 228
Quebec Language Police, 196
Queen Elizabeth II, 86, 252
Q-Ray bracelet, 217–18
quinceañera, 76

rappers
Chingy, 156
Elephant Man, 155
Eve, 155
Fat Joe, 156

Jay-Z, 154, 156
Jermaine Dupri, 156
Kanye West, 155
Lil Scrappy, 155
Lil Wayne, 155, 156
Lloyd Banks, 155, 156
Sir Mix-A-Lot, 153
Swizz Beatz, 155
T. I., 155
Young Buck, 155
Young Jeezy, 155
rationality
    axioms of rational choice, 262, 264, 265, 267, 275
    bounded rationality, 268
    deep rationality, 269
    descriptive invariance, 265
    ecological rationality, 268
    economic rationality, 263, 268
    transitivity, 262
    "violation-of-the-month club," 263
    violations of rational choice, 262
Reagan, Nancy, 211
Reagan, Ronald, 211
recency effect, 189
reciprocal altruism, 121–22
    as an insurance policy against starvation, 122
reciprocity, 126, 129, 264
    forms of, 122
        alarm calling (for predator avoidance), 122
        food sharing, 122

        predator mobbing, 122
        social grooming, 122
    hospitality, as a form of, 126–28
recognition heuristic, 268
recovered memory therapy, 20
red (color)
    and romance, 88
    as a signal of sexual arousal, 88
    in songs and movies, 88
red effect (intersexual wooing), 88–89
    intersexual wooing versus intrasexual rivalry, 198–99
Reimer, David, 21
relationship marketing, 36
    example of, 130
    as a means of forging a friendship with the customer, 130
    as reciprocity, 130
religion, 29, 30, 34, 47, 97, 107, 115, 123–25, 139, 140, 203, 204, 246
    affinity scams, 212–13
        Baptist Foundation of Arizona, 212
        Greater Ministries International Church, 212, 213
    allure of, 208–211
    brand loyalty of, 205
    and coalitional thinking, 207–208
    commercial might of, 205
    contradictory edits across religions, 213–15
    dietary edicts as biological-based cultural adaptations, 47–48

evolutionary origins of, 151

as fiction, 174

as a form of child abuse, 206

as humanity's nightmare, 216

indoctrination of children via, 205–206

inoculations against, 211

intergenerational loyalty of, 205

Law of Reciprocity, 212

as a memeplex, 216, 217

as pattern-seeking (by-product of our intelligence), 209–210

pattern-seeking (in random events), 210, 211

shopping for the true religion, 213–15

Ten Commandments, the, 209

and tribalism, 207–208

unfalsifiability of, 206–207, 213, 216, 288

unique attributes of, 205–207

Renoir, Pierre-Auguste, 43

replicability (as a hallmark of science), 179

reproductive fitness, 98, 175, 186, 273

and men's voices, 186

reproductive suppression model, 237–38

Republicans versus Democrats (sexual scandals), 241–42

Revson, Charles H., 220

Ridley, Matt, 11

risk taking, 37–38, 68, 83, 238, 251, 252–53, 254, 255, 271, 272

financial, 273

women's photos augment men's physical and financial risk taking, 239

Roach, Catherine M., 81

Robertson, Pat (Reverend), 211

role-playing, 89

romance novels, 26, 35, 68, 155, 173, 174, 248

high-status of male characters, 174

long-term commitment (as a theme), 174

male archetype caters to women's mating preferences, 174

Rosa, Emily, 218, 219

Rozin, Paul, 53

Rule, Nicholas O., 276

Russell, Bertrand, 165

Russell, Richard, 87

Russian mob, 139

Salerno, Steve, 228

salt

cultural attitudes toward, 49

and genes, 48–49

Sapolsky, Robert, 209

Schelling, Thomas C., 231

Schwartz, Barry, 52

scientific method, 30, 219, 288–89

ideology should not trump science, 290

science as an autocorrective process, 289

scientific reductionism, 261–62

Scott, Suzanne C., 65

Scott, Walter, 226

Searle, Robert, 73

Second Life (virtual world), 245

selective breeding, 106. *See also* artificial selection

self-actualization, 152, 258

self-deception, 204

self-help books, 203–204, 223–29
 commercial might of, 223
 list of, 223–24
 self-help advice as quasi-religious belief, 229
 self-help gurus, 34, 222, 229
 self-help industry, 228
 unfalsifiability of the self-help mantra, 228–29
 victimhood versus empowerment mantras, 228

self-presentation, 146, 278
 on Facebook, 146, 278
 on personal web pages, 146, 278

Semmelhack, Elizabeth, 85

serial killers, 115

serotonin, 235

sex differences, in
 discounting rate, the, 273
 friendship styles, 123
 height, 32
 masturbatory urges and triggers, 161
 mate preferences in folktales, 173
 reactions to one-night stands, 160

romantic jealousy, 159–60

sexual fantasies, 160–61, 247–48
 high-status men in women's fantasies, 161
 sexual variety in men's fantasies, 160–61
 succumbing to the framing effect, 266
 unrestrained sexuality, 25

sexism, 22
 benevolent sexism, 154–55
 hostile sexism, 154

sexual abuse, 20–21

sexual addiction, 247

sexual cannibalism, 75

sexual dimorphism, 29, 68. *See also* sex differences
 of the digit ratio, 104
 in size (of humans), 31
 in unrestrained sexuality, 32

sexual infidelity, 16, 165, 166, 167, 171–72
 and flowers, 179
 sexual versus emotional infidelity, 159–60
 why do men cheat?, 243

sexual scandals (offenders), 241–43
 Benét, Eric, 242
 Clinton, Bill, 241
 Cook, Peter, 242
 Craig, Larry, 242
 Edwards, John, 242
 Ensign, John, 242

Foley, Mark, 242
Grant, Hugh, 242
Haggard, Ted, 242
Hart, Gary, 241
Kennedy, John F., 241
Law, Jude, 242
McGreevy, James, 242
Monica Lewinsky affair, 241
Murphy, Eddie, 242
Ronaldo (Brazilian soccer
  player), 242–43
Sanford, Mark, 242
Spitzer, Eliot, 241–42
Swaggart, Jimmy, 242
Vitter, David, 242
Woods, Tiger, 243
sexual selection, 14, 17, 67–68, 70,
  219, 238, 251, 254, 273, 281, 292
sexual signals, 15, 255
  bower as a, 70
  cars as a, 12, 68, 70, 72
  clothes as, 84
  cultural products as, 151
  olfaction as a, 79
  peacock's tail, 70, 156, 163, 170
  products as, 68
  risk taking as a, 239, 251
  sex-specific forms of, 71, 83
Shakespeare, William, 173
Shanidar (Neanderthal burial site),
  76
Sheraton Hotels & Resorts, 177
Sherif, Muzafer, 135
Sherman, Paul W., 45–46

Shermer, Michael, 210
shopping for good genes, 68, 90–91
siblicide, 106–107
sibling rivalry, 106–107, 169
Silberstein, Chana, 127
Silberstein, Eli, 127
Simmons, Leigh W., 250
singers (and musical groups)
  Akon, 153
  Bassey, Shirley, 77
  Benét, Eric, 242
  Blunt, James, 153
  Broschi, Carlo Maria (castrato),
    186
  Carpenter, Karen, 236
  Carpenters, The, 236
  Church, Jarvis, 153
  Cocker, Joe, 153
  Cole, Nat King, 183
  de Burgh, Chris, 88
  Destiny's Child, 153, 154
  Gaye, Marvin, 12
  Gilley, Mickey, 157
  Guthrie, Gwen, 154
  Jackson, Michael, 69, 155
  Knowles, Beyoncé, 108, 154
  Knowles, Solange, 108
  Madonna, 77
  McLachlan, Sarah, 191
  Missy Elliott, 154
  Peevey, Gayla, 184
  Shaw, Marlena, 154
  Sister Sledge, 154
  Taylor, James, 128

Timex Social Club, 164
TLC, 154
Tyler, Bonnie, 154
Urban, Keith, 31, 84
White, Barry, 185
Winehouse, Amy, 166
Withers, Bill, 128
Singh, Devendra, 193
situational hunger, and
    food decisions, 57–58
    hunger for money, 58
    mate preferences, 58
six degrees of separation, 145
skin quality
    and androgens, 88
    and estrogen, 88
    import of clear and smooth skin,
      88
    as a universal marker of beauty,
      87, 220
Skinnerian conditioning, 183–84
Small World Phenomenon, 145
smoking, 38, 232–33
soap operas, 150, 163, 167–68
    male archetype caters to
      women's mating preferences,
      168
Sobal, Jeffery, 53
social comparison theory, 170
social constructivism, 19, 203
    in education, 20
    gender as a social construction,
      21
      patriarchal, 255

in medicine, 20
in mental health, 20
in penal system, 20
sex differences as a social con-
    struction, 290
sexual orientation as a social
    construction, 21
Social Darwinism, 22
socialization, 18
    of consumers (bad effects),
      36–37
    at the root of bad choices, 232
social networking websites, 143–44
    Facebook, 143, 146, 278, 280
    MySpace, 143
    Twitter, 143
    YouTube, 145, 157
social networks, 144–45
    and friendships and health, 145
    three degrees of influence, 145
social sciences versus natural sciences,
    289–90
social status (male)
    and sexual opportunities, 174
    and sexual conquests, 175
Society for Consumer Psychology, 291
Sociosexual Orientation Inventory, 53
song lyrics, 37, 152–57
    luxury cars in songs, 156
    luxury clothes in songs, 156
    male intrasexual rivalry in,
      156–57
    men boast about status and
      resources in songs, 155

men sing about physical attrib-
    utes, 153
men sing about status and
    resources, 156
most songs are about mating,
    152
women sing about athletic,
    "thuggish," hero, and domi-
    nant men, 154
women sing about status and
    resources, 153–54
songs
    "Ain't Nothin' Goin' On but the
        Rent," 154
    "Angel," 191
    "Baby Got Back," 153
    "Balla Baby," 156
    "Beautiful," 153
    "Billie Jean," 155
    "Bills, Bills, Bills," 153–54
    "Diamonds Are a Girl's Best
        Friend," 77
    "Diamonds Are Forever," 77
    "Don't the Girls All Get Prettier
        at Closin' Time," 157
    "Go Away Little Boy," 154
    "Gold Digger," 155
    "Greatest Dancer, The," 154
    "Holding Out for a Hero," 154
    "Hot Boyz," 154
    "I Am So Fly," 156
    "I Want a Hippopotamus for
        Christmas," 184
    "Lady in Red," 88

    "Lean on Me," 128
    "Make It Rain," 156
    "Material Girl," 77
    "Money Ain't a Thang," 156
    "Money in the (da) Bank," 155
    "No Scrubs," 154
    "Rumors," 164
    "So Beautiful," 153
    "Soldier," 154
    "Unforgettable," 183
    "Upgrade U," 154
    "You Are So Beautiful," 153
    "You're Beautiful," 153
    "You've Got a Friend," 128
species
    extinction of, 283
    number of existing and extinct,
        281
sperm competition (porn), 249, 250
Spock, Benjamin, 227
sports rivalries, 142–43
sports viewing and merchandising,
    140–43
    clothes worn by fans (following
        victory or defeat), 141
    language used by fans (following
        victory or defeat), 141
    most popular jerseys and shirts
        (of winners), 142
    website visits by fans (following
        victory or defeat), 142
Standard Social Science Model, 26–27
Stayman, Doug, 187–88, 189
Steiner, Eric T., 240

Stenstrom, Eric, 58, 91

Stewart, Don (Apostle), 212

stilettos, 81, 82. *See also* high heels

strip bars, 81–82, 83, 246–47

Sulloway, Frank, 107

sun tanning, 38, 232, 284

superbugs, evolution of, 38

survival of the fittest, 31

Swift, Graham, 67

symbiotic relationships (interspecies), 115, 116

symmetric
    artistic renditions, 87
    facial and body decorations, 87

Symons, Donald, 248

Tajfel, Henry, 135

takeaways (from the book) for,
    consumers, 33–34
    marketers, 34–36
    policy makers, 36–39

tasseography, 210–11

tattoos
    and criminality, 140
    as a form of belongingness, 140
    on television shows, 139

television shows
    Band of Brothers, 97
    Charlie Rose Show, 14
    City Confidential, 185
    Curb Your Enthusiasm, 100, 159,
      162–63
    Dancing with the Stars, 69
    Deadliest Catch, 252

Deal or No Deal, 263

Dog Whisperer, 117

*8 Simple Rules for Dating My
  Teenage Daughter*, 113

Entourage, 170

Frontline, 185

Growing Pains, 236

Hoarders, 234

Hoarding: Buried Alive, 234

King of Queens, The, 159,
  160–61, 162

Kitchen Nightmares, 54

Married . . . with Children, 272

Maury Povich Show, The, 171

Nature, 185

Nova, 185

Price Is Right, The, 263

*Real Football Factories Interna-
  tional, The*, 142

Restaurant Makeover, 65

Saturday Night Live, 191, 223

Seinfeld, 159, 161–62, 276

So You Think You Can Dance, 69

World's Greenest Homes, 65

television storylines, 158–63
    as cultural fossils, 159

television viewing
    amount watched per day, 158
    and satisfaction with one's real-
      life friends, 166

Tennyson, Alfred, 31

testosterone, 33, 68, 276
    and behaviors of hockey players,
      277

and cars, 71–72

and the color red, 199

and conspicuous consumption,
71–72

and deep voices, 185

and the digit ratio, 104

and entrepreneurship, 257, 271

and facial features, 277

in the financial arena, 257, 270

and impulsivity, 272

and musk and rut season, 270

and poker, 240

and risk taking, 239, 272

and soccer fans (victories/defeats
of favorite team), 142

and soccer players (home and
derby matches), 142

as an antecedent and as an outcome (in the financial arena),
271

Therapeutic Touch, 217, 218

thin ideal, 226, 237

Thornhill, Randy, 79

thrifty genotype, 42

tight social networks
lead to lesser mobility, 131–32
lead to tighter friendships,
131–32
reputational effects in, 134

tips
on *King of Queens* episode,
162
and menstrual cycle of exotic
dancers, 83

and waitresses' breast size, 276

and waitresses' wearing of cosmetics, 87

tit-for-tat strategy, 130, 213

toys, 34, 37
as an agent of gender socialization, 103, 104
and anthropomorphism, 280
and biomimicry, 282–83
and congenital adrenal hyperplasia, 103
as parental gift giving, 102–103
morphological features of toys, 105
retail sales, 102
universal preference for sex-
specific toys, 103
and vervet and rhesus monkeys,
104

Tragedy of the Commons, 283–84

transcranial magnetic stimulation,
136

tribal marketing, 146

tribalism, 135, 207–208

Trivers, Robert, 75, 121

Trivers-Willard hypothesis, 112–13

trust
in cohesive and nontransitory
social networks, 134
and economic vitality, 134
neurobiology of, 134
and oxytocin, 135
in religious-based affinity scams,
212–13

Tsui, Eugene, 64

Tversky, Amos, 262, 265
two-factor theory, 187, 190
Tzedakah (charity), 163

UK Vogue, 86
Ultimatum Game, 135, 136–37,
    264–65
    men display generosity to
        women, 265
universal forces (in physics), 289
Universal Grammar, 180
Uris, Leon, 208
US Bureau of Labor Statistics, 252
utility maximization, 268, 269, 270
    versus fitness maximization, 269

Vaillant, George, 144
Valentine's Day, 75, 76, 88, 197
variety effect (for foods), 51–52
    cross-cultural differences in food
        variety-seeking, 53–54
    evolutionary roots of the variety
        effect, 52
    individual differences in food
        variety-seeking, 53
victimology ethos, 228, 278
video games, 19, 37, 150, 246, 255
viral marketing, 145
Vongas, John, 71
Vyncke, Patrick, 193

waist-to-hip ratio, 85, 193. *See also*
    hourglass figure
    and blind men's preferences, 193

of online escorts, 192
    in songs, 153
walkability (of a city), 64
Wall Street financial crisis (late
    2000s), 270
Wansink, Brian, 51, 53
Warren, Rick, 205
wasteful (costly) signaling in R&B
    and rap videos, 155–56
Watson, James, 14
Watts, Duncan J., 144–45
weddings
    and genetic relatedness, 101
    marriage proposal, 78
    and number of guests at a wed-
        ding, 101
weight management, 57, 59
Westminster Kennel Club Dog
    Show, 118
West Point (military college),
    276–77
White, Tim D., 149
wigs, 89–90
Wikipedia, 167
Wilson, David Sloan, 292
Wilson, E. O., 14, 149, 289
Wilson, Margo, 16, 23, 109
Windhager, Sonja, 279, 280
Wolf, Naomi, 220
Women's National Basketball Associ-
    ation, 31
word of mouth, 145
World Cup (soccer), 140–41,
    261–62

Wright, Frank Lloyd, 62

xenophobia, 137

Yahya, Reem, 135

Zak, Paul, 134
Zigman, Laura, 243
zoopharmacognosy, 282